OFF THE BEATEN PATH® SERIES

British Columbia

FOURTH EDITION

Tricia T

The Globe Pequot Press

GUILFORD, CONNECTICUT

Text design by Laura Augustine
Maps created by Equator Graphics © The Globe Pequot Press
Text illustrations by Carole Drong from photographs by Tricia Timmermans

ISSN 1536–6154
ISBN 0-7627-2764-0

Manufactured in the United States of America
Fourth Edition/First Printing

Dedicated to the children in my life—
the "biggies" and the "littlies": Luke, Nikki, Evi,
Mary-Louise, Daniel, Jacob, Joey, and Tessa Timmermans.
May they be fortunate enough to see it all.

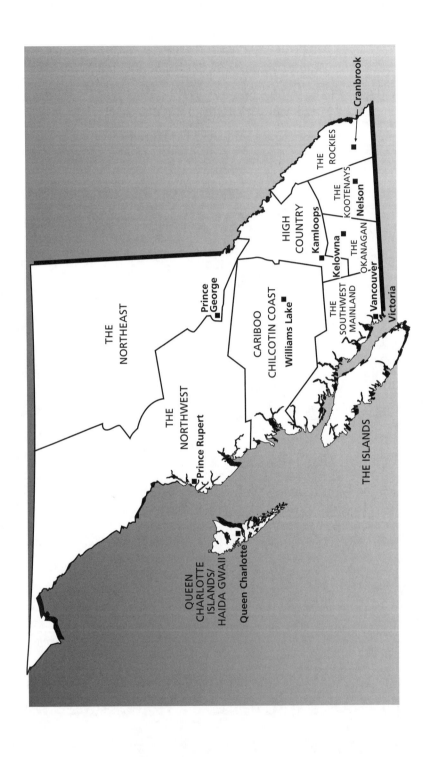

Contents

Acknowledgments vi

Introduction vii

The Islands. 1

The Southwestern Mainland 51

The Okanagan 87

The Kootenays. 113

The Rockies 143

High Country. 169

Cariboo Chilcotin Coast 195

The Northeast 221

The Northwest. 245

The Queen Charlotte Islands/Haida Gwaii. 279

Index. 299

About the Author. 320

Acknowledgments

As I worked through revisions for this, my fourth edition, I came to the realization that many of the people I reconnected with have become my *Off the Beaten Path* "family." I am indebted to them all for their helpful corrections and suggestions and their funny tales and trivia that have added color to their own special corner of beautiful British Columbia. Loving thanks to my supportive family and friends. Their encouragement (to hurry up and get finished) and other words of wisdom have helped me once again through this enlightening experience.

> I shall be telling this with a sigh
> Somewhere ages and ages hence:
> Two roads diverged in a wood, and I—
> I took the one less traveled by,
> And that has made all the difference.
>
> —Robert Frost (1874–1963), "The Road Not Taken"

Introduction

Canadian humorist Stephen Leacock once quipped about British Columbia: "If I had known what it was like, I wouldn't have been content with a mere visit—I'd have been born here." No doubt he was referring to the extraordinary beauty of BC's postcard-perfect, snow-covered mountains and blue lakes, the exciting history of this wild province, and the courage and friendliness of its people. This book is intended to help you discover what Leacock was enthusing about, while introducing you to some of the best of BC's lesser-known attractions—your fun will be in tripping over a few more on the way. I hope that as you continue to explore BC, my adopted province, with *British Columbia Off the Beaten Path®* in hand, you might soon be wishing you'd been "born here," too.

Contact Information

For general information and bookings write Tourism BC, Box 9830, Station Provincial Government, Victoria, V8W 9W5; or phone **Super, Natural BC** at (800) HELLOBC (435–5622) in North America including Mexico. Outside North America phone (250) 387–1642. In England visit Tourism British Columbia, Third Floor, 3 Regent Street, London, England, SW1Y 4NS. Visit www.hellobc.com for free reservations and information service.

Vancouver Island, Victoria, and the Gulf Islands

Tourism Vancouver Island, 203–335 Wesley Street, Nanaimo, V9R 2T5; (250) 754–3500; fax: (250) 754–3599; info@islands.bc.ca; www. islands.bc.ca

The Southwestern Mainland

Vancouver, Coast and Mountains Tourism Region, 250–1508 West Second Avenue, Vancouver, V7R 3C5; (800) 667–3306 or (604) 739–9011; fax: (604) 739–0153; info@coastandmountains.bc.ca; www. vcmbc.com

Thomson Okanagan and High Country

Thomson Okanagan Tourism Association, 1332 Water Street, Kelowna, V1Y 9P4; (800) 567–2275 or (250) 860–5999; fax: (250) 860–9993; info@thompsonokanagan.com; www.totabc.com

Cariboo Chilcotin Coast

Cariboo Chilcotin Coast Tourism Association, 118A North First Avenue, V2G 1Y8; (800) 663–5885 or (250) 392–2226; fax: (250) 392–2838; info@landwithoutlimits.com; www.landwithoutlimits.com

Kootenay Country and the Rockies

Tourism Rockies, P.O. Box 10, 1905 Warren Avenue, Kimberley, V1A 2Y5; (250) 427–4838; fax: (250) 427–3344; for brochure requests: (800) 661–6603; info@bcrockies.com; www.bcrockies.com

The Northeast, the Northwest, and Queen Charlotte Islands

Northern British Columbia Tourism Association, P.O. Box 2373, 850 River Road, Prince George, V2N 2S6; (800) 663–8843 or (250) 561–0432; fax: (250) 561–0450; info@NBCtourism.com; www.NBCtourism.com

BC Ferries, 1112 Fort Street, Victoria, V8V 4V2; (250) 386–3431 or (888) 223–3779 (in BC) for information and reservations. Call (604) 444–2980 or (888) 724–5223 (in BC) for automated vehicle reservations between Vancouver and Vancouver Island using Visa, American Express, or Mastercard or reserve on-line; fax: (250) 381–5452; www.bcferries.com

BC Museums Association, Suite 204-26 Bastion Square, Victoria, V8W 1H9; (250) 356–5700; fax: (250) 387–1251; BCMA@MuseumsAssn.bc.ca; www.MuseumsAssn.bc.ca

BC Parks, www.bcparks.ca. Information on *all* BC Parks can be accessed from this site.
(For camping reservations telephone the Discover Camping Campground Reservation Service at (800) 689–9025 or (604) 689–9025 in Vancouver between March 1 and September 15, or visit their Web site at www.discovercamping.ca.)

Fishing regulations and licenses: Available at most local fishing outlets and government agent offices. For information phone the Ministry of Fisheries and Oceans in Victoria at (250) 387–9589, or visit www.bcfisheries.gov.bc.

Forest Recreation (1,430 recreation sites with approximately 12,000 no-service campsites). Things are changing though, so check for information at www.for.gov.bc.ca/hfp/rec/rec.htm.

Hunting Regulations: Biodiversity and Wildlife, BC Ministry of Water, Land and Air Protection, Wildlife Branch, P.O. Box 9374, Station Provincial Government, Victoria, V8W 9M4; (250) 387–9739; wlapwww.gov.bc.ca/wld/hunting.htm

BC Highway Condition Information: Communications Branch, Ministry of Transportation and Highways, 5B 940 Blanshard Street, Victoria (P.O. Box 9850 Station Provincial Government) V8W 9T5; (250) 387–7787; fax: (250) 356–7706; www.th.gov.bc.ca/roadreports.htm

BC Hydro Recreation Areas: www.bchydro.com/recreation

The best on-line general information for travelers to BC can be found at www.BritishColumbia.com. Here you'll find extensive travel, sports and recreation, entertainment, tourism, and real estate information.

BC Facts

Where *is* BC?

BC lies between 114°03'12" and 139°03'40"W longitude and between 48°17'34" and 60°N latitude. Canada's most westerly province is bordered on the west by the Pacific Ocean and Alaska; Alberta is to the east, the Yukon and Northwest Territories to the north, and Washington, Idaho, and Montana to the south.

How many of us are there?

BC's population, as of July 1, 2002, was 4,141,272.

Capital stuff!

Victoria, located on Vancouver Island and named for Queen Victoria of England, is British Columbia's capital city.

Canadian dollar conversion to the U.S. dollar:

October 2003—$1.32 Canadian for one U.S. dollar (0.75 U.S. cents for one Canadian dollar)

BC is BIG!

Only thirty *countries* in the world are larger than British Columbia, which takes up a whopping 366,282 square miles (948,596 sq km). It is larger than France and Germany combined. As well, it is larger than the combined area of Washington, Oregon, California, and Tennessee and is two and a half times larger than Japan. Comprising 9.5 percent of the

Canadian land surface, it runs 780 miles (1,250 km) north/south and 650 miles (1,050 km) east/west. British Columbia ranks number three in Canada in both population and land mass, behind Ontario and Quebec.

Where *is* everybody?

British Columbia has forty-four cities, fifteen towns, forty villages, fifty-four district municipalities, and one Indian Government District (Sechelt). Sixty-five percent of the population lives on the lower mainland and southern Vancouver Island.

The long and the short of it!

British Columbia's highest **mountain** is Fairweather Mountain, at 15,298 feet (4,663 m), in the northwestern corner of the province. The longest **river** is the Fraser—850 miles (1,368 km)—which drains one-quarter of the province. The longest natural **lake** is Babine Lake—110 miles (177 km). The longest **valley** (which is also the longest in North America) is the Rocky Mountain Trench—870 miles (1,400 km). The highest **waterfall** is Takakkaw Falls—1,650 feet (503 m)—in Yoho National Park. It is also Canada's highest waterfall—almost ten times the height of Niagara Falls—and when measured by vertical drop, the highest in North America.

How many islands did you say?

Approximately 6,500 islands and islets lie off British Columbia's coast.

It's Official!

Flower: Pacific dogwood *(Cornus nuttallii)*

Bird: Steller's jay *(Cyanacitta stelleri),* the cheeky fellow you'll meet in campgrounds

Gemstone: the lovely, dark-green British Columbian jade

Tree: Western red cedar *(Thuja plicata Donn),* which has been known to grow to about 200 feet (60 m)

Tartan: The provincial tartan has five colors (blue, white, green, red, and gold), each with its own significance.

Time out!

Special holidays in British Columbia are **Victoria Day** (Monday preceding May 24), **Canada Day** (July 1), and **BC Day** (first Monday in August).

Wave the flag!

The BC emblem, designed and adopted in 1960 and based on the crest within the coat of arms, consists of a Union Jack (symbolizing British Columbia's origin as a British colony) on the upper third and a gold half-sun (symbolizing its position as Canada's most westerly province) superimposed on three wavy blue bars (the Pacific) on the bottom. The motto is *Splendor Sine Occasu* ("splendor without diminishment").

What time is it?

There are two time zones in British Columbia. Most of the province is on Pacific Time, but near the Rockies, east of Kootenay Lake, the time moves one hour ahead to Mountain Time. Daylight Saving Time for most of British Columbia (yes, there are a few holdouts!) starts on the first Sunday in April and ends on the last Sunday in October.

So, are you saving any?

The average weekly earnings for a British Columbian in February 2003 were $636.36 ($US 418.66), compared with $626.45 ($US 412.13), for the average Canadian.

It's the law!

British Columbia's legal drinking age is nineteen.

You don't like the weather? Wait fifteen minutes!

Because of BC's diverse climates, average temperatures and annual precipitation rates are wide-ranging. In Vancouver January average high and low temperatures range between 42°F and 33°F (5°C and 0°C), and July high and low averages are between 74°F and 55°F (23°C and 12°C). In Prince George (in the northeast), the January ranges are between 24°F and 5°F (-4°C and -15°C), whereas the July ranges are closer to those of Vancouver at 74°F and 45°F (23°C and 7°C).

Vancouver's annual precipitation average is 42 inches (1,069 mm); the average annual snowfall is 21 inches (534 mm); and the average number of days with precipitation is 161. Prince George, on the other hand, averages 24 inches (610 mm) of precipitation, 92 inches (2,341 mm) of snow, and 162 days of precipitation.

In the Beginning: A Peek at British Columbia's History

10,000–13,000 years ago: Carbon dating has confirmed occupation of some BC sites to this period. It is believed that the first people came across the Bering Strait from Asia.

1774: Juan Pérez Hernández saw the coast of British Columbia, did not land, but claimed the region for Spain. (Many of the islands in the Strait of Georgia—Galiano, Valdes, Quadra, for example—bear Spanish explorers' names.)

1778: Captain James Cook, leading two British ships, dropped anchor in Nootka Sound on the West Coast of Vancouver Island.

1789: Spain and Britain disputed ownership of the west coast of North America.

1790–92: The Nootka Sound controversy was settled by the *Nootka Conventions,* which gave equal trading rights to both Britain and Spain but did not establish ownership.

1792–94: Captain George Vancouver mapped the west coast from Oregon to Alaska, naming Vancouver Island "Quadra and Vancouver's Island" and northern Washington and southern British Columbia "New Georgia." The northern coast was called "New Hanover."

1793: Alexander Mackenzie entered the eastern part of British Columbia via the Peace and Upper Fraser Rivers. He reached the Pacific at the mouth of the Bella Coola River.

Early 1800s: Trading posts were established along the Fraser and Columbia Rivers by members of the North West Company and the Hudson's Bay Company.

1849: Vancouver Island was declared the first crown colony, with Fort Victoria as its capital.

1851: James Douglas, an official with the Hudson's Bay Company, became the first governor of the new crown colony of Vancouver Island.

1852: The Queen Charlotte Islands (Haida Gwaii) became a dependency of the colony.

1857: Gold was discovered on the lower Fraser River, resulting in an explosion of gold seekers in Victoria (where they went to obtain permits).

1858: A crown colony was declared on the mainland and given the name British Columbia. James Douglas became the first governor.

1861: The Cariboo Road (from Yale to Barkerville) was completed.

1866: The crown colonies of British Columbia and Vancouver Island were made one, with New Westminster as the capital. The eastern boundary was defined by the Rocky Mountains, between the 49th and 60th parallels.

1868: The seat of government was moved to Victoria.

1871: British Columbia became the sixth province to be admitted to the Dominion of Canada.

Some famous British Columbians who either live or have lived in BC

Artists Emily Carr, Mary Pratt, Bill Reid, Ted Harrison, and Jack Shadbolt; *astronaut* Dr. Bob Thirsk; *environmentalist* Dr. David Suzuki; *first female Canadian prime minister* Kim Campbell; *National Hockey League stars* Gordie Howe, Joe Sakic, Paul Kariya, Mark Recchi, Greg Adams, and Russ and Geoff Courtnall; *championship auto-racing-teams driver* Greg Moore; *golfer* Dawn Coe Jones; *figure skater* Elizabeth Manley; *baseball's* Larry Walker; *basketball's* Steve Nash; *Olympic medalists* Ross Rebagliati (snowboarding); Nancy Greene Raine, Steve Podborski, and Kerrin Lee Gartner (skiing); Silken Laumann and member of parliament David Anderson (rowing); *actors* Michael J. Fox, Brent Carver, Joshua Jackson, and Jason Priestly; *actresses* Pamela Anderson, Meg and Jennifer Tilly, and Alicia Silverstone; *pianist and singer* Diana Krall; *composer and producer* David Foster; *singers* k. d. lang, Colin James, Long John Baldry, Joni Mitchell, Bryan Adams, Burton Cummings, Nellie Furtado, and Sarah MacLachlan; *opera singers* Richard Margison and Benjamin Butterfield; *film director* Atom Egoyan; *authors* Alice Munro, Nick Bantock, Joy Kogawa, Douglas Coupland, Carol Shields, and Wade Davis.

Recommended Reading

Adventuring in British Columbia by Isabel Nanton and Mary Simpson (1998 Douglas and McIntyre, Canada; Sierra Club Books, USA). An excellent guide for the outdoor adventurer; this book is packed with practical information, well researched, and well written.

A Traveller's Guide to Aboriginal BC by Cheryl Coull (1996 Whitecap Books, Vancouver). A comprehensive guide to BC's First Nations' locations, history, and culture.

Ravens and Prophets by George Woodcock (1993 Sono Nis Press, Victoria). First published in 1952, this book describes the BC of postwar days; written by one of Canada's most prolific authors and editors.

The West Beyond the West—A History of British Columbia by Jean Barman (1996 University of Toronto Press, Toronto). A thorough treatment of all aspects that shaped the British Columbia of today.

Nature BC—An Illustrated Guide to Common Plants and Animals by James Kavanagh (1993 Lone Pine Publishing, Vancouver). An excellent layman's guide, beautifully illustrated and simply described.

British Columbia Wildlife Viewing Guide by Bill Wareham (1994 Lone Pine Publishing, Edmonton). Maps show where you'll find what. Tiny, but loaded with information.

The B.C. Fact Book—Everything You Ever Wanted to Know about British Columbia by Mark Zuehlke (1995 Whitecap Books, Vancouver). The consummate fact book on BC.

British Columbia: A Natural History by Richard and Sydney Cannings (2000 Greystone Books, Douglas and McIntyre, Vancouver). A coffee-table book, written by the experts in the field and graced with excellent photographs.

The Birds of British Columbia, Volumes 1, 2, 3, and 4, by Wayne Campbell et al (1997 UBC Press, Vancouver). The BC Birders' Bible! This four-volume set is the culmination of two decades of research and writing.

The Encyclopedia of British Columbia (2000 Harbour Publishing, Madeira Park). Full-color, 824-page print edition and a companion CD-ROM. The publisher, with the help of hundreds of knowledgeable British Columbians, has produced the quintessential work on BC—ten years in the making.

Geology of British Columbia: A Journey Through Time by Richard J. Cannings and Sydney G. Cannings (1999 Greystone Books, Vancouver). Discover the origins of this acutely diverse province.

www.knowbc.com is an excellent on-line resource.

Safety Tips

When traveling on any of BC's logging roads, it's a good idea to visit the local logging company office to find out about activity on the road. Evenings and weekends are the best times to travel. Logging trucks **always** have right-of-way, so drive slowly, keep well to the right, and pull over if unsure of your safety.

About hiking: Always be prepared to stay overnight! You just never know. Carry a rain jacket. (Hypothermia can kill even in summer.) Carry a first-aid kit and water-purifying tablets. (Giardiasis, an intestinal infection often referred to as beaver fever, is not unheard of.) Carry a compass and a map and tell someone of your intended time and route plan. Be aware that bears and cougars are wild animals and should be treated with utmost respect. Always keep to marked trails, make plenty of noise, and keep your food in airtight containers.

Tips for Spending

Unless otherwise stated, prices and rates do not include the 7.5 percent Provincial Sales Tax (PST) or the 7 percent Federal Goods and Services Tax (GST). British Columbia does not offer a PST visitor rebate program, but the federal government offers a GST rebate program for visitors from outside Canada. For more information on GST refunds, write Canadian Tax Refund, Box 42090, Vancouver, V6P 6S6 or claimsdept@canadiantaxrefund.com. To find out what is eligible and to print a Tax Refund Application Form, go to www.canadian taxrefund.com.

The prices and rates listed in this guidebook are quoted in Canadian dollars and were confirmed at press time. We recommend, however, that you call establishments before traveling to obtain current information.

The Islands

Whether it's for the warm Pacific air or the billions of blossoms counted each February in Victoria's *Flower Count,* many Canadians are moving west to the islands. I had lived in three provinces and two territories before I discovered that this 282-mile-long (453-km) island, with its Gulf Island neighbors, is the pièce de résistance of this country I now call home. *Condé Nast Traveler* readers agree—they voted Vancouver Island "Top Temperate Island" in 2002, and the Aerie Resort, in the mountains thirty minutes north of Victoria, "Top North American Resort."

Separated from mainland British Columbia by Queen Charlotte, Johnstone, and Georgia Straits and from Washington's Olympic Peninsula by the 100-mile-long (160-km) Juan de Fuca Strait, Vancouver Island, with more than 2,100 miles (3,400 km) of coastline, is North America's largest island, occupying an area about the size of Maryland. A mountainous spine runs its length, and long fjords on its Pacific west coast cut deeply into the island. Lush forests of large Douglas fir and cedar thrive in the moderate ocean climate. Victoria, on the southern tip of Vancouver Island, is the province's capital, with a population of approximately 78,000. It is part of the Capital Regional District (population 341,563 in 2002), comprising the city of Colwood, the towns of View Royal and Sidney, and nine district municipalities.

After exploring Victoria's Inner Harbor and suburbs, we'll head out to explore the colorful tidepools of Botanical Beach, meet the artists of Salt Spring Island, camp among the giant, old-growth trees at Carmanah Walbran Park, and watch killer whales from aboard a converted mission boat. On an island off Vancouver Island's far north coast, we'll learn of the aboriginal past in a unique cultural center. This is but the tip of the overflowing cornucopia of adventures in store.

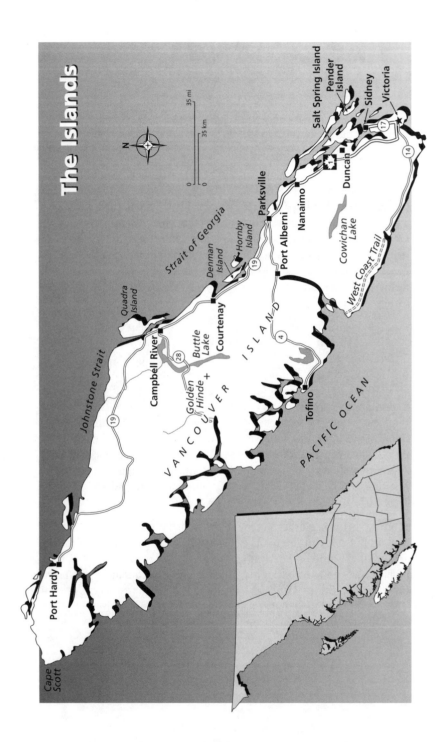

The Islands

Victoria

Rated in *Condé Nast Traveler*'s 2002 Readers' Choice Awards as Canada's number-two tourist destination and number nine in the "Top Foreign Cities" category, Victoria is jokingly called the land of the newlywed and the nearly dead. Perhaps this is but a reflection that younger people, like their grandparents, are now seeing the light and choosing to settle in Canada's Garden of Eden.

On any warm spring or summer day, the downtown core of Victoria hums with activity as both locals and tourists alike head to the **Inner Harbor,** where dozens of mime artists, balloon twisters, didgeridoo players, face painters, bagpipers, fiddlers, and Japanese calligraphers all vie for a spot along the waterfront promenade. Above them, beside baskets of brilliantly colored blooms hanging from nineteenth-century-style street lamps, frightfully English, red double-decker buses, horse-drawn carriages, and kabuki cab pedalers carry tourists from one end of town to the other, giving the city a festive feel.

Victoria is equally exciting at water level. You'll discover this during a three-hour kayak lesson and pleasure paddle ($79) with **Ocean River Sports** (1437 Store Street, Market Square, V8W 3J6; 800–909–4233; 250–381–4233; fax: 250–361–3536; info@oceanriver.com; www.ocean river. com). If you don't need the lesson, rental rates are singles $14 per hour and $42 for the day; doubles $17 per hour and $50 for the day. For

IMAX/Museum

*I*f the weather isn't enticing you outdoors, drop into the **National Geographic Theatre** (250–953–IMAX) at the **Royal British Columbia Museum** (675 Belleville Street, 250–356–7226; 888–447–7977; www.royalbcmuseum.bc.ca) and surround yourself with colossal imagery on a six-story-high IMAX screen. Shows are every hour from 10:00 A.M. to 9:00 P.M. daily. Then step into one of Canada's top museums, where woodblock paved streets bring you back to the late 1800s, and woolly mammoths take you back even further.

Trivia

Contrary to popular belief, Vancouver Island did not break off from the mainland but had its geological birth in the South Pacific. It "docked" with the North American continent about 100 million years ago, somewhere near Oregon or California, and worked its way north along faults similar to the present-day San Andreas fault.

groups of ten or more wishing to learn more about the island's marine life, its old-growth rain forest ecology, or its native peoples' plant use, contact **Coastal Connections Nature Adventures Inc.** (1027 Roslyn Road, V8S 4R4; 250–480–9560 or 800–840–4453; coastcon@island net.com; www.coastalconnections.org). Experienced naturalist guides run fascinating trips ranging from three-hour walks ($49) to ten-hour instructional, sail-kayak-hike Gulf Islands explorations that include gourmet picnic lunches ($199).

Supernatural Sleuth

*M*y late grandmother instilled in me a healthy respect for ghosts. Her tingling tales are imprinted in my psyche, so it was with some apprehension that I set out early one evening in search of Victoria's specters. I'd heard that in Bastion Square the "White Lady" had been seen gliding along Chancery Lane behind the Maritime Museum. But no luck. She'd flown. Night was falling, so I crossed over to the Spirit of Christmas store on Government Street, hoping to catch a glimpse of the dark-haired man sometimes seen in a top-floor window. Whether I was too late and he'd evanesced, I don't know, but while there I did hear a chilling tale.

You see, the building once housed the Bank of British Columbia. One morning, a clerk of Chinese descent, while getting cash from the dark, deep vault, bounded out, hysterically screaming that she'd seen "something down there." It turns out that before it was a bank, a Chinese crematorium operated in the building's depths. The clerk's

assistant saw nothing. Nor did I. The only "spirit" I could find was a fluffy white angel atop a Christmas tree.

I slipped over to Tod House. That's western Canada's oldest dwelling, out in Oak Bay. The story goes that a woman wearing leg chains had been seen inside pleading for help. I peered through the windows, desperate to see at least a suggestion of a shadow. Nothing. Not even a meowing black cat. It was quite dark by now, and I was feeling cheated. Victoria Golf Course was on the way home. I skulked across the fairway in search of Doris Gravlin. She'd been murdered there in 1936, and . . . suddenly, a ghostly figure in a wedding dress drifted by the rocky shore. Seagulls in the mist, you say. No way! Oh YES, Grandma would have been proud.

To learn more about the most haunted city in the Pacific Northwest, join a Ghostly Walks tour with John Adams (250–384–6698; fax: 250–384–2833; discoverthepast@telus.net; www. discoverthepast.com)—if you dare!

With the sea so close, try a tasty seafood lunch. One of my favorites is right downtown across from the **Victoria Visitor Info Center. Sam's Deli** (805 Government Street; 250–382–8424; www.samsdeli.com) piles the shrimp high to produce delicious shrimp-and-avocado sandwiches. Their date squares are made fresh daily from owner Barb Housser's grandma's recipe. Thick clam chowder, freshly squeezed orange juice, and tasty spinach salad are what keeps clients returning. It's open from 7:30 A.M. till 11:00 P.M. in summer (shorter hours in winter) and is a great spot to sit outside and watch the passing crowds while enjoying a cappuccino or a frosty beer. Tell your friends back home to visit www.samsdeli.com/samcam.htm for a view of Victoria with you in it! You could perhaps arrange a time to be on the corner of Government and Humboldt Streets (near the stately and luxurious **Fairmont Empress Hotel** (250–384–8111; www.fairmont.com/empress) to wave to them. See if you can spot the spying live-cam server located at Sam's!

Shoppers looking for the offbeat will enjoy **Market Square** (250–386–2441; www.marketsquare.victoria.bc.ca) on the waterfront between Johnson and Pandora Streets. This funky shopping center borders Canada's oldest **Chinatown,** whose entrance is marked dramatically by the intricate and colorful **Gate of Harmonious Interest**. Don't try to drive down Chinatown's Fan Tan Alley. It's Canada's narrowest street and is but 4 feet wide in places—it was used in the Mel Gibson–Goldie Hawn film *Bird on a Wire*. Often the site of festivals and concerts, Market Square is home to about forty-five stores with such curious names as **Fat Phege's Fudge Factory** (250–383–3435), famous for its fudges and brittles; the **Royal Holographic Art Gallery** (250–384–0123; www.holograms.bc.ca), where $14.95 will buy a matted rose that *holographically* blooms before your eyes (perhaps an appropriate souvenir to take home from Victoria); the **Green Cuisine Vegetarian Restaurant** (250–385–1809; www.greencuisine.com), a vegan restaurant with a self-serve salad bar, dessert bar, and hot buffet, open daily from 10:00 A.M. to 8:00 P.M. (you can download recipes from the Web site); and the **Rubber Rainbow Condom Company** (250–388–3532; 888–423–7193 toll free), where you might be surprised what $6.99 will buy. They glow in the dark!

After dark enjoy a meal at *John's Place* (723 Pandora; 250–389–0711), where my favorite is the Thai chicken. Laced with crunchy cashews, it's awfully addictive, and there's an endless supply of hot, herby bread. But spare some room for an enormous piece of apple pie. Breakfasts are huge, too. A Wurlitzer and great photos give it a fifties feel.

Over in **Oak Bay** (head east along Fort or Johnson Street), just ten minutes from the city, million-dollar Tudor-style waterfront homes with perfectly manicured gardens reinforce the more-English-than-England-itself reputation Victoria has acquired. But this suburb, with the added color of billowing spinnakers, has its own particular charm.

And none more charming than **Chocolate,** a thirteen-year-old harbor seal who spent his first year at Sealand after his mother abandoned him. When Sealand closed in 1990, Chocolate stayed around. If you want to feed him (and his mates), the Marine Store at the top of the ramp at Oak Bay Marina sells a bag of fish nummies for $2.00. You'll find Chocolate and pals salivating at the bottom of the ramp. If they're not around, run the tap in the fish-cleaning sink and they'll appear.

Keep smiling though, as Oak Bay Tourism (www.oakbaytourism.com) has a Web cam aimed at the seal-watching area. (A second Web cam is focused on an eagle's nest behind the Oak Bay Fire Station.)

Trivia

Victoria can lay claim to Canada's longest frost-free period, which stretched over 685 days in 1925–26; so, too, it can claim BC's highest annual amount of sunshine: 2,426 hours in 1970. It must also claim, however, Canada's longest wet spell, beginning on April 19, 1986, when it rained for thirty-three days.

For more scuttlebutt on Chocolate, phone **Oak Bay Marina** (250–598–3369; 800–663–7090 toll free; obm@obmg.com; www.obmg.com) and talk to the local marine-life expert. If you've never tried fishing before, proven fishing grounds are just fifteen minutes offshore. Private fishing charters offer complimentary tea or coffee and come fully equipped with tackle, bait, and rods. Oak Bay is also home to Cadborosaurus Willsi, the legendary sea serpent that has been sighted in the area for decades. **Caddy Marine Tours** (250–514–5070; info@caddytours.com; www.caddytours.com) will take you in a 27-foot navy launch through Oak and Cadboro Bays to Discovery Island, where you can hike through old-growth forests, visit a lighthouse, or just lie on a secluded beach while gazing at majestic Mount Baker and quietly keeping an eye out for Cadborosaurus. To find out more about Caddy, contact a member of the British Columbia Scientific Cryptozoology Club (250–721–3836; caddys can@shaw.ca; www.members.shaw.ca/caddyscan).

While at the marina, there's fine dining at the **Marina Restaurant** (1327 Beach Drive, Victoria, V8S 2N4; 250–598–8555; www. marinarestaurant. com). Ask about their early-bird specials served daily between 5:00 and 6:00 P.M. For more casual dining, the **Café Deli** is right below. Sit out on the sunny deck and watch yachts gently rock, while a great blue heron fishes nearby. Stroll along Beach Drive to Willows Beach, an inviting spot for a family day in the sun, then head up 1 block to Estevan Village for hot and yummy fish and chips (wrapped traditionally in newspaper) at **Willows Galley** (250–598–2711; open Wednesday to Sunday 11:00 A.M. to 6:45 P.M.), then cross the road to the **Willow Tree Cafe** (250–592–8311; open daily from 7:30 A.M. to 5:00 P.M.). For dessert, my favorite is a piece of their apple pie with maple walnut ice cream. Lattes and smoothies are popular, too.

On the way back down Estevan Avenue to the beach, turn left on Heron Street and walk a block to number 2564. You'll be looking at the **John Tod House,** western Canada's oldest house still standing today and reputedly haunted. Construction finished in 1851, some twenty years before British Columbia was brought into the Canadian Confederation.

Up in the village of **Oak Bay,** there's a kaleidoscope of shops, teahouses, and galleries. The **Blethering Place Tearoom** (2250 Oak Bay Avenue, 250–598–1413; www.thebletheringplace. com; open from 8:00 A.M. to 9:00 P.M. daily) is a fine place to meet the locals and enjoy British high tea ($15.95). There's more: Irish music will have you crooning on Fridays, British comedy and music is a charmer on Saturdays, and on Sundays, New Orleans spiritual jazz will set you tapping. It's on the corner of The Avenue and Monterey. In late July the Blethering Place hosts the **Collector Car Festival,** when up to 250 car enthusiasts line The Avenue with their shiny, cherished vehicles. Further down *The Avenue* toward the city, a local favorite, **Blighty's Bistro** (2006 Oak Bay Avenue; 250–592–5111; www.biz-bc.com/blightys; open Tuesday through Saturday from 4:30 P.M.), serves a delicious bowl of Christina & Richelle's mulligatawny soup. For a main item try Richelle's Roast, pork roast stuffed with apples, carrots, parsley, and prunes, complete with gravy, twice baked potatoes, and vegetables of the day. This dish is so popular that it sells out every night. Each menu item is named for staff or regular clients—very young Oak Bay fry get a huge kick when they see their names on the menu. Reservations are recommended. Alternatively, the **Penny Farthing Olde English Pub** (2228 Oak Bay Avenue; 250–370–9008; www.pennyfarthingpub. com) is an exquisitely decorated establishment featuring daily specials and live Celtic music Friday and Saturday evenings. After less than one year of operation, it was voted "Number Two Pub" by the public in the 2002 "Best of Victoria" awards.

Down from the village, near the corner of Newport and Windsor, is the **Windsor House Tea Room and Restaurant** (2540 Windsor Road; 250–595–3135). It sounds British, and if that's what you want, you won't be disappointed! Pick up a London *Weekly Telegraph* at **Windsor Park Place** (250–592–5315) next door and settle in to enjoy your hot buttered crumpets, classic cream scones, butter tarts, finger sandwiches, and a pot of steaming English tea. A full-lunch menu features delicious homemade soups (including ginger carrot soup), plus chicken potpies and spinach feta cheese crepes. It's open Monday through Saturday from 10:00 A.M. to 4:00 P.M. and till 7:30 P.M. Friday. If you're lucky, you'll catch a game of cricket being played on the pitch across the road in Windsor Park. Only in Victoria!

The British theme continues at the **Oak Bay Guest House** (1052 Newport Avenue, V8S 5E3; 800–575–3812 or 250–598–3812; fax: 250–598–0369; stay@oakbayguesthouse.com; www.oakbayguesthouse.com), a 1912-built bed-and-breakfast inn with claw-foot bathtubs, period furniture, and lots of charm. You may even be greeted by a fully dressed butler. Breakfast is a four-course, genteel feast. Rates are from $80 for a single room in off-season to $205 for a double studio suite in high season. If it's a pub-style meal you're after, or just a pleasant waterfront spot for a beer, **The Snug** at the **Oak Bay Beach Hotel** (1175 Beach Drive, Victoria, V8S 2N2; 250–598–4556; 800–668–7758; fax: 250–598–6180; www. oakbaybeachhotel. com) serves light meals in a warm atmosphere, with incredible views of snow-covered Mount Baker from the outdoor deck. There's also fine dining in Bentley's Seaside Grill. Check out the Web site for a variety of accommodation and activity packages at this family-run elegant inn.

You might want to stay more than just a few days to enjoy Victoria's best view.

It's not all Old World charm in this municipality, though. Kids will love the tropical decor at the **Oak Bay Recreation Centre** (near Fort and Foul Bay Roads at 1975 Bee Street; 250–595–7946). With an ozone-purified pool, sauna, hot whirlpool, dropslide, steam room, and a waterslide, you'll leave imagining you've had a trip to Hawaii. View a complete list of their programs at www.recreation. oakbaybc.org. For cyclists, Oak Bay offers splendid roads with brilliant scenery—mountains, oceans, gardens, parks—with just the right mix of hills and flat stretches. You can rent a bicycle ($19 per day) downtown at **Cycle BC Rentals** (747 Douglas Street, opposite the Convention Centre; 250–885–2453; 866–380–2453 toll free; fax: 250–477–9660; info@cyclebc.ca; www.cyclebc.ca) or a second location in the Victoria Marine Adventure Center at 950 Wharf Street. Scooters and motorcycles are also available for rent. Before leaving home, check some of the local cycling Web sites to help plan your trip: www.cyclingvictoria.com and www.simbs.com (South Island Mountain Biking Society).

To return to the city by the most scenic route, take Beach Drive past the gloriously posh **Victoria Golf Course** (250–598–4224; www.victoria golf.com; $160 for a cool eighteen holes for nonmembers plus $35 for a power cart, and don't expect to get a drink at the bar if you're female) to **Clover Point,** where huge ships, paragliders, and high-flying kites are often in view; then continue past **Mile Zero** of the Trans-Canada Highway near **Beacon Hill Park**. Keep to the water. At the breakwater at 199 Dallas Road, join locals at the **Ogden Point Cafe** (250–386–8080; fax: 250–386–8087). It's very popular for its tasty soups, sandwiches, bakery, desserts—and more. It's open daily 8:00 A.M. to 10:00 P.M. (till 8:00 P.M. in winter). There's a full-service dive center below. **Ogden Point Dive Center** (199 Dallas Road, Victoria, V8V 1A1; 250–380–9119; fax: 250–385–9110; info@divevictoria.com; www.divevictoria.com) offers weekend dive charters, daily trips, and scuba diving holidays.

If you're looking for somewhere close to downtown for an excellent meal and delightful accommodation, it's easy walking distance to **Spinnakers Brew Pub and Guest House** (308 Catherine Street; 250–386–2739; 877–838–2739 toll free; fax: 250–384–3246; spinnakers@spinnakers. com; www.spinnakers.com). From the Johnson Street Bridge (the blue bridge) downtown, it's a short walk past Songhees (all those apartments!) to Lime Bay. Spinnakers is a well-known establishment on the waterfront. Noted for their beer, you'll also find luxury bed-and-breakfast accommodation, where double Jacuzzis and fireplaces are but two of the delightful features. Double rates in high season range from $159 to $249; from $129 to $209 in low season.

For more information on Victoria area attractions, contact the *Victoria Visitor Info Centre* (812 Wharf Street, V8W 1T3; 250–953–2033; fax: 250–382–6539; info@tourismvictoria.com; www.tourismvictoria.com; for accommodation reservations only, phone 800–663–3883 or 250–953–2033).

Outdoor enthusiasts can hike, cycle, skate, even ride a horse (anything not motorized) in the Victoria area along the *Galloping Goose Trail,* a 35-mile (57-km) former railway line. Maps and information are available from the Capital Regional District Web site at www.crd.bc.ca/parks/pdf/galgose3.pdf.

From Victoria, a turn south off the Trans-Canada onto Highway 14 brings you to the village of *Sooke,* a haven for fabulous bed-and-breakfasts and artisans. If you're in Sooke the first week of August, be sure to take in the *Sooke Fine Arts Show.* This is the largest juried art show on Vancouver Island. More than 300 artists display and sell their paintings, photography, pottery, carvings, glass, and fabric art. Information on the art show and a comprehensive list of Sooke area accommodations can be obtained at the *Sooke Region Museum* (Box 774, Sooke, V0S 1N0, 250–642–6351; info@sooke.museum.bc.ca; www.sooke.museum.bc.ca). It's located at 2070 Phillips Road on the corner of Highway 14, about forty minutes from downtown Victoria. While at the museum, take a peek in tiny *Moss Cottage,* one of Sooke's oldest buildings. And don't leave Sooke without trying the area's best halibut burgers at *Mom's Café* (2036 Shields Road; 250–642–3314)—when traveling west from Victoria, take the first turn right after Sooke's second set of traffic lights. If you decide to stay overnight here, a popular accommodation in the area is on the beach at Billings Spit. Reservations for the *Billings Spit Beach House* can be made on-line or by phone (877–642–1910 toll free; information@billingsspitbeachhouse.com; www.billingsspitbeachhouse.com). For detailed information on Sooke's attractions and accommodations, visit www.sookenet.com.

Continue west past driftwood-strewn beaches through Jordan River and Port Renfrew to the colorful tidepools at *Botanical Beach.* In all it's about a two-hour journey from Victoria, but don't miss a low-tide visit to this virtual aquarium, with its brilliant red gumboot chitons, giant green sea anemones, purple sea urchins, and blood stars. With the completion of the Juan de Fuca Marine Trail, hikers now have access (four separate entry points off Highway 14 from China Beach to Botantical Beach) to superb wilderness day- and multi-day hiking within easy driving from Victoria.

Sidney

ighway 17 (locals call it the Pat Bay) runs the length of the pastoral Saanich Peninsula, linking Victoria with Sidney and Swartz Bay, where BC ferries connect to the mainland and the Gulf Islands. **Sidney by the Sea** is to many people merely a town you pass when traveling to or from the ferry, but it's worth a closer look.

To see its sheltered waters and close-by rugged islets, try a **Sidney Harbor Cruise** (toll free: 888–634–9096; 250–655–5211; pager 250–480–6930; cruises@bccoast.com; www.bccoast.com). With an onboard marine biologist, a hydrophone, and binoculars, a one- or two-hour cruise in a comfortable, wheelchair- accessible, glass-enclosed boat is in effect a mini-wildlife tour. Pupping seals, nesting eagles, bull kelp, and giant jellyfish are sure to be on the list of what you'll see. Pick up the cruise at the bottom of Beacon Avenue or on E dock at Canoe Cove Marina. Ask about drop-offs at nearby **Princess Margaret Marine Provincial Park (Portland Island).** It has twenty walk-in campsites and features lovely sandy beaches on the northwest and southwest shores.

Filberg Festival, Comox Valley; 334–9242; fax: (250) 334–2899; www.filberg festival.com

Pacific Rim Whale Festival, Tofino; late March; (250) 725–3414 or (250) 726–7742; whalefest@island.net

Brant Wildlife Festival, Parksville/Qualicum; April; (250) 752–9171; fax: (250) 752–9883

Victoria Harbor Festival, Victoria; late May; (250) 953–2033

Nanaimo Marine Festival, Nanaimo; late July; (250) 753–7223

Sooke Fine Arts Show, Sooke Arena; early August; (250) 642–6351

Classic Boat Festival, Victoria; late August; (250) 385–7766; fax: (250) 385–8773; msampson@vreb.org

Festival of Lights, Ladysmith; December; (250) 245–5888

There are a couple of excellent pubs in the Sidney area. Close to the ferry terminal at Canoe Cove's **Stonehouse Pub** (2215 Canoe Cove Road, Sidney, V8L 5V5; 250–656–3498; www.stonehousepub.com), you'll enjoy hearty food in an eighty-year-old stone house cozily converted into a British-style pub and restaurant. At Shoal Harbor's **Blue Peter's Pub & Waterfront Restaurant** (2270 Harbour Road, Sidney; 250–656–4551; fax: 250–655–7044; bluepeter@shaw.ca; www.bluepeters.ca), you can enjoy either pub meals (great chowder) or fine dining with a Pacific Northwest flavor. The special coffees and desserts are tempting, too. With eight different draft beers and more than one hundred wines to choose from, it's a relaxing spot to while away the hours; it's open from 11:00 A.M.

to midnight. *Blue Peter Yacht Charters* (250–655–4312; bluepete@ islandnet.com) operate from the marina in front of the pub. Step aboard a shipshape 40-foot (12-m) sloop and sail through glorious island waterways. Rates are $300 for six hours.

While in Sidney, visit the *Sidney Marine Museum* (9801 Seaport Place; 250– 656–1322; fax: 250–655–6366; info@sidneymuseum.ca; www.sidney museum.ca), where you'll learn the biology and evolution of whales and other marine mammals. It has an echo-location chamber demonstrating how marine mammals orient themselves, and the skeleton of Scar, a 23-foot (7-m) killer whale. Marine ecology and deep-sea research displays from the *Institute of Ocean Sciences,* together with interactive computers and Canadian Coast Guard models, are new additions to the museum. Drive to the end of Beacon Avenue and turn left into Seaport Place. In summer, it's open daily from 10:00 A.M. to 4:00 P.M.; admission is by donation. A second museum, *Sidney Historical Museum* (250–655– 6355; info@sidneymuseum.ca), on the lower floor of the old post office building at 2423 Beacon Avenue (corner of Fourth Street), displays the lives of Sidney and North Saanich pioneers. In summer, it's open daily from 10:00 A.M. to 3:45 P.M.; admission is by donation.

Another museum worth visiting in Sidney is the *British Columbia Aviation Museum* (1910 Norseman Road, Sidney, V8L 5V5; 250–655–3300; fax: 250–655–1611; www.bcam.net). It's by the southeast corner of the Victoria International Airport. Some of the many planes on display include the Eastman E2 Sea Rover (the only one left in the world), the Noorduyn Norseman (restored to airworthy standards by museum volunteers in 2003), and an exact replica of the 1897 Chanute Glider, whose design influenced the Wright brothers.

The *Sidney Spit Ferry* (250–474–5145) runs a foot-passenger ferry to *Sidney Spit Marine Park,* 3 miles (5 km) across on Sidney Island. Here you'll see seabird nesting colonies, fallow deer, and even a few exotic birds. Thirty walk-in (several of them beachfront) campsites are available. Visit www.bc.parks.ca (search word: "Sidney") for more information. The ferry leaves on the hour from the pier at the foot of Beacon Avenue from June 16 to September 4, 9:00 A.M. to 5:30 P.M. daily. Round-trip fares are $10.75 for adults, $8.75 for seniors, and $7.75 for children. Then return to the Beacon Avenue beat and discover some of the unique gift shops and bookstores for which Sidney is renowned.

Salt Spring and Pender Islands

North of Sidney, island-hop by BC Ferry to **Salt Spring Island,** home to many of Canada's best-known artists and writers, and **Pender Island**, where beaches, markets, galleries, hiking, and the Gulf Islands' only disc golf course (a free-eighteen-poler!) make for a quiet but active retreat.

As well as frisbee golf, North Pender Island has an excellent nine-hole golf course, **Pender Island Golf and Country Club** (2305 Otter Bay Road, Pender Island, V0N 2M0; 250–629–6659), very close to the ferry terminal. **Bunkers Licenced Bar & Restaurant** (250–629–6665) in the clubhouse serves tasty soups, sandwiches, and more. For accommodation on South Pender Island (a short bridge connects the two islands), **Brooks Point Glade** (250–598–3607; dgreer@coastnet.com; www.photo-j.com/pender.htm) is a secluded, reservations-only two-day-minimum, all-season cottage a short walk to a quiet beach on Pender's southeastern tip at Gowlland Point. The **Oceanside Inn** (250–629–6691; toll free: 800–601–3284; oceanside@penderisland.com; www.penderisland. com), on the northwestern coast at Bricky Bay, has 4-star accommodation, decadent, private Jacuzzis, and an oceanfront licensed dining room exclusive to inn guests. Gourmet breakfasts are included in the room rates, which range from $139 to $249 depending on the season. Hiking on South Pender at both **Mount Norman Regional Park** and **Beaumont Provincial Marine Park** is superb. For more information on accommodations, dining, and attractions contact the **Pender Island Chamber of Commerce,** Box 123, 3338 Port Washington Road, Pender Island, V0N 2M0; www. penderislandchamber.com.

Lives of the Rich and Famous

When exploring Salt Spring Island, you might bump into one or two famous personalities who either live on the island or who find this gem of a hideaway the perfect escape. Such well-knowns as Robert Bateman (conservationist, naturalist, and artist), Arthur Black (well-known Canadian radio personality and humorist), Randy Bachmann of Bachmann Turner Overdrive and The Who, and Valdy (one of Canada's favorite folk singers) all call Salt Spring Island home. Others who have visited on occasion are Barbara Streisand, Gary "Radar O'Reilly" Burghoff of M*A*S*H fame, Robert DeNiro, Al Pacino, Tom Hanks, Candice Bergen, Steven Spielberg, Tom Cruise, and Robin Williams (no introductions needed).

Trivia

The largest of the Gulf Islands, Salt Spring has a year-round population of approximately ten thousand. From the ferry terminal at Fulford Harbor, Beaver Point Road leads off the Fulford-Ganges Road for 6 miles (9.5 km) to **Ruckle Provincial Park,** with walk-in (not far!) beachfront campsites. There's also a new twenty-site group campsite available. Check www.bcparks. ca (search "Ruckle") for information. The area is still a working sheep farm, with the original 1870 Ruckle homestead at the park entrance.

The Fulford-Ganges Road runs north for 9 miles (14.5 km) to **Ganges,** through what was once BC's largest fruit-growing area. *Mount Maxwell Provincial Park* (day use only), 5.5 miles (9 km) up a steep, rough road, has spectacular views. Take Cranberry Road, about a mile south of Ganges, and follow the signs. You'll bump your way up to Baynes Peak, at 1,932 feet (589 m) the highest point on Salt Spring Island. An observation point at the edge of a vertigo-inducing precipice provides breathtaking views south over the Fulford Valley toward Fulford Harbour and the Gulf Islands and west to Sansum Narrows and Maple Bay. It's worth the wear on your vehicle (or your boots).

On Saturdays you'll find the ferries and highways are full of folks heading to the **Salt Spring Island Saturday Market** (www.saltspringmarket. com), which runs from mid-April to mid-October at the head of Ganges Harbor in Centennial Park. Locals sell flowers, jewelry, and pottery—anything from a slice of watermelon to a sequined frog.

One establishment with lots of pizzazz is **Ruphi Fabrics and Ceramics,** found at the foot of Ganges Hill in the village at 170 Fulford-Ganges Road, SSI, V8K 2T8; (250) 537–1337; ruphi@saltspring.com; www. ruphi.com. Bright hand-painted wall hangings, tablecloths, and checkered or polka-dot ceramic pieces give their factory a colorful, eccentric look. They'll ship pieces home for you, too.

If you missed the Saturday market, the **Naikai Gallery** (3103 Grace Point Square, 115 Fulford-Ganges Road, Salt Spring Island, V8K 2T9; 888–643–9320 toll free; 250–537–4400; naikai@saltspring.com; www. naikaigallery.com) has a huge variety of locals' works. It's open from 10:00 A.M. to 5:00 P.M. seven days a week, from Easter to Thanksgiving, with varying hours during winter. One local artist of note is Carol Haigh. Her acrylic originals and lithographic marine scenes grace the Naikai's walls.

Grace Point Square has more than lovely galleries. The ***Bouzouki Greek Café*** (250–537–4181) looks down Ganges Harbour to the Sisters Islands. Its hosts, Greg and Shirley Keith, serve traditional Greek fare. The Bouzouki is open daily for lunches and dinners from 9:00 A.M. to 9:00 P.M.

A fun spot to enjoy a glass of local Whale Tale Ale is ***Moby's Marina Pub*** (124 Upper Ganges Road, Salt Spring Island, V8K 2S2; 250–537–5559; 800–334–MOBY; mobyspub@saltspring.com; www.mobyspub.com), on the Ganges Harbour waterfront. Live entertainment and an active, pretty harbor, plus first-class pub food, make it a popular haunt.

From Ganges, Lower and Upper Ganges Roads lead northwest to Vesuvius Bay Road and the twenty-minute ferry to Crofton on Vancouver Island. Sunset Drive, running to the northwest tip of Salt Spring, is a pleasant drive where you'll find a high-end bed-and-breakfast, ***Anne's Oceanfront Hideaway*** (168 Simson Road, SSI, V8K 1E2; 888–474–2663 or 250–537–0851; fax: 250–537–0861; annes@saltspring.com; www.annesoceanfront.com). Here you wake to morning coffee delivery followed by a four-course island breakfast in the dining room looking across Stuart Channel. Spend a day canoeing, biking, or shopping, then soak in the en suite hydromassage tub or outdoor hot tub before bed. Prices range from $185 to $210 off-season and $195 to $260 high season. Another luxury B&B with similar rates is ***Aston House B&B*** (205 Quarry Drive, Vesuvius Bay, SSI, V8K 1J2; 866–538–1868; 250–538–1868; fax: 250–538–1868; astonhouse@saltspring.com; www.astonhouse.ca).

Contact the ***Salt Spring Island Visitor Info Centre*** (121 Lower Ganges Road, Ganges, SSI, V8K 2T1; 250–537–5252; 866–216–2936; fax: 250–537–4276; chamber@saltspring.com; www.saltspringtoday.com) for more information about this attractive island, so aptly named in earlier days by its native Cowichan people: *Chu-an,* or "facing the sea."

South Central Vancouver Island

From Crofton, a 6-mile (10-km) drive north along the coast road (43 miles [70 km] north of Victoria) leads to ***Chemainus*** (the Little Town That Did). When faced with a severe economic downturn, the townspeople didn't say "die" but instead came up with an idea that managed to turn Chemainus into the world's largest outdoor art gallery. The ***Chemainus Visitor Info Centre*** (9796 Willow Street, Box 575 Chemainus, V0R 1K0; 250–246–3944; fax: 250–246–3251;

ccoc@islandnet.com; www.chemainus.bc.ca) is open year-round and has maps to help you find the thirty-four first-class murals that depict the town's history, including native culture, Japanese and Chinese heritage, the building of the railroads, and the town's logging beginnings. You could even get a chance to stay in a restored mill house.

The **Olde Mill House** (9712 Chemainus Road, Box 1046, Chemainus, V0R 1K0; 250–416–0049; 877–770–6060 toll free; fax: 250–246–4457; stay@oldemillhouse.ca; www.oldemillhouse.ca) is a century-old historical home constructed for mill employees and is now run as a four-star bed-and-breakfast inn complete with air-conditioning and Jacuzzi. It is centrally located across from the **Chemainus Theatre,** one of British Columbia's favorite professional theaters (800–565–7738 or 250– 246–9820; ctheatre@cow-net.com; www.ctheatre.bc.ca), and near the murals. You'll be invited to sample the Olde Mill House's own fruit wine and to use the barbecue area for dinner. Ask about their dinner/ theater packages.

Just south of Chemainus is Duncan, famous not only as the home of the **World's Largest Hockey Stick** (seen outside the Cowichan Community Center at 2687 James Street) but also for its totem poles, about eighty of which decorate the city. Visit the **Quw'utsun' Cultural and Conference Centre** (200 Cowichan Way, Duncan, V9L 6P4; 877–746–8119; 250–746–8119; fax: 250–746–4143; askme@quwutsun.ca; www.quwutsun.ca) to see them being carved. Here you'll find yourself immersed in the culture of the Coast Salish Natives. Their heritage is depicted in an excellent audiovisual presentation called *Great Deeds.* In the *Big House,* built in the style of a longhouse with huge cedar beams and planks, you'll be treated to a presentation of dancing, native drumming, and singing, while feasting on traditional native dishes. Duncan is 37 miles (60 km) north of Victoria on the Trans-Canada over the scenic Malahat

A Ban on Gift-Giving

*T*he Potlatch is a traditional feast or ceremony common among the Indians of the Pacific Northwest, especially the Kwakiutl. The word is Chinook jargon derived from the Nootka word patschmati, meaning gift. Its traditional purpose was to validate the status of the chief or clan, although individuals also used it to try to enhance their social ranking. Gifts were exchanged, and property was destroyed in a competitive display of affluence. It was prohibited by the government in 1884, but the practice continued in secret. The ban was lifted in 1951.

Range. From the Nanaimo Ferry terminal, it's 32 miles (52 km) south. For more information contact the **Duncan Visitor Info Centre** (April 15 through October 15) at 381A Trans-Canada Highway, Duncan, V9L 3R5; (250) 746–4636 or 748–1111; fax: (250) 746–8222; duncancc@islandnet.com; www.duncancc.bc.ca.

Just 5 miles (8 km) south of Duncan (and 31 miles [50 km] north of Victoria) is the pretty coastal village of **Cowichan Bay.** Here you'll find art galleries, marinas, and a quaint farmhouse bed-and-breakfast called the **Old Farm Bed and Breakfast** (2075 Cowichan Bay Road, Cowichan Bay, V0R 1N0; phone/fax: 250–748–6410; 888–240–1482 toll free; stay@oldfarminncowichan.com; www.oldfarminncowichan.com). This recently renovated, stately, three-story country home was designed by Samuel Maclure of Empress Hotel fame in the early 1900s for a retired English sea captain. Breakfast is a wonderful event and is served elegantly at a large table. All rooms (starting at $95 for a double) have views of evergreens and fruit trees, delightful gardens, and an estuary formed by the Cowichan and Koksilah Rivers, which flow into Cowichan Bay. The high-ceilinged rooms are exquisitely decorated, and all have en-suite bath. Relaxation comes easy in the chaises, gazebo, and hot tub outside, and when you're ready for some exercise, enjoy badminton, horseshoes, a stroll down to the waterfront, or perhaps a game of tennis on one of the oldest grass tennis courts in the world (second only to Wimbledon) at the **South Cowichan Lawn Tennis Club.**

Wild West Side Trip From Duncan

About 3 miles (5 km) north of Duncan, Highway 18 starts its 95-mile (153-km) cut across southern Vancouver Island to **Bamfield,** a town where the main street is the sea—shades of Venice—and half the community is accessible only by water taxi. To get there take Highway 18 west to **Lake Cowichan Village,** a distance of about 19 miles (30 km). The Visitor Info Centre (125C South Shore Road, Box 824, Lake Cowichan, V0R 2G0; 250–749–3244; fax: 250–749–0187; info@cowichanlakecc.ca; www.cowichanlake.ca), open May 24 to September 2, may have maps. You'll find the office in the log cabin at Saywell Park. Wind past Cowichan Lake, either north through Youbou (named for lumber mill owners Mr. Yount and Mr. Bouton!) or south through Honeymoon Bay (March Meadows Golf Course here is the home course of LPGA tour player Dawn Coe-Jones), to the Nitinat Main junction. Twelve miles (19 km) on, turn left onto South Main for 3.5 miles (5.6 km) to the Nitinat General Store, where you can eat a cafe meal, fuel up, and find a bed next door in the **Nitinat Lake Motel**

(250–745–3844). Open year-round; rooms (some with kitchenettes) range from $45 to $65. Cross the Caycuse River Bridge and turn right onto Rosander Main. You're now but 18 scenic miles (29 km) from **Carmanah Walbran Provincial Park,** site of Canada's tallest tree and the tallest Sitka spruce in the world, the **Carmanah Giant.**

A Carmanah holiday with my teenage kids, despite rain and rough roads, is one of my best camping holiday memories. For public safety and environmental protection, the trail to the 312-foot (95-m) **Carmanah Giant** is out of bounds. But the 2.3-mile (3.8-km) trail upstream along Carmanah Creek to the **Three Sisters,** and the 2.9-mile (4.6-km) downstream trail to the **Fallen Giant** are both awesome. For information visit the BC Parks Web site, www.bcparks.ca (search word "Carmanah").

When traveling in this area, be aware that that you will be sharing the road with huge logging trucks—safety checkpoints are often set up—and the operator's directions must be followed; and if continuing on to Bamfield Inlet, keep a close watch for the signs to the village, which can easily be missed. Bamfield is also accessible via a 63-mile (102-km) unpaved logging road south from Port Alberni or via the MV Lady Rose (see Port Alberni section). The Port Alberni route has less unpaved road, is wider, has fewer logging trucks, and is usually in better shape than the road from Lake Cowichan, but from Victoria it's approximately an hour longer. If you're worried about wear on your vehicle (or don't have a good map), take the Port Alberni route. Another option for getting there is to call West Coast Trail Express (250–477–8700; fax: 250–477–8774; bus@trailbus.com; www.trailbus.com) to find out about

The Nuu-chah-nulth

*T*he Nuu-chah-nulth ("along the mountains") people on the west coast used to whale in open seas in cedar canoes—not a very safe occupation. As part of their intensive training program (sexual abstinence, fasting, bathing, and learning how to capture the huge mammals), the whalers also visited sacred shrines made up of skulls and images of whales and deceased whalers. As a further aid, the whaler's wife would lie completely still while her husband was on the kill, to ensure that the whale, too, would be docile. Captain Cook, when he came to the coast in 1778, was seen drifting too close to a reef. The Nuu-chah-nulth called out to him, "Nootka, nootka," meaning "Circle round." His misunderstanding resulted in these people being misnamed as the Nootka.

Hiking the West Coast Trail

*A*t one time considered the world's most difficult hiking trail, the 47-mile (75-km) **West Coast Trail** stretches from Pachena Bay (near Bamfield) in the north to the mouth of the Gordon River (near Port Renfrew) in the south. Boardwalks and ladders have reduced its category now to "one of the most difficult." Needless to say, careful planning, including knowledge of how to read a tide table and possession of good-quality wet-weather gear, is essential. A maximum of sixty hikers are allowed daily on the trail, broken down into forty-eight reserved spaces and twelve (six at each end of the trail) "first-come-first-served" spaces. There is a $25 reservation fee, payable at the time of booking, plus a $70 hiking fee and a $25 ferry fee. Yes, there are a couple of rivers to cross! You can expect to be hiking for about six days, during which time you'll possibly see sea lions, bears, whales, countless seabirds, and incredible Pacific vistas. Check www.sookenet.com and follow the hiking link to a "Hiker Preparation Guide" to the trail, plus several useful links such as a tide graph.

daily buses from Victoria, Port Alberni, and Nanaimo (May 1 through September 30.) This site has information and maps for both the West Coast Trail and the Juan de Fuca Trail.

Once you have reached Bamfield, you have a few comfortable accommodations to choose from, including **Woods End Landing** (380 Lombard Street, Box 108, Bamfield, V0R 1B0; phone/fax: 250–728–3383; 877–828–3383 toll free; woodsend@island.net; www.woodsend.bc.ca). Here you'll find first-class cabin or duplex accommodations in a rustic, beachy setting—a short hike to Brady's Beach or the Cape Beale lighthouse. For the adventurous, experience a kayak trip through the Broken Group Islands with fascinating shoreline caves and abundant marine life. To learn more about what you've seen, the **Bamfield Marine Station** (Bamfield, V0R 1B0; 250–728–3301; fax: 250–728–3452; info@bms.bc.ca; www.bms.bc.ca), near the mouth of the inlet, offers guided field trips.

Hiking the reservations-only **West Coast Trail** (Box 280, Ucluelet, V0R 3A0; 800–663–6000 or 250–726–7721)—or camping beside the world's largest spruce trees in Carmanah Walbran Provincial Park or windsurfing on **Nitinat Lake** are but

Trivia

Nanaimo *is home to both Vancouver Island's tallest building (Cameron Island Development) and its largest shopping center (Woodgrove). You'll also find here the Nanaimo Bastion. Built in 1853 to protect Hudson's Bay Company employees, it is the last free-standing building of its type in North America.*

Rub-a-Dub Tubbers

*I*n one Vancouver Island city, "taking a bath" does not necessarily have the traditional connotations. One of BC's craziest annual events started in 1967 as a wild publicity stunt for the city of Nanaimo. **The Great International World Championship Bathtub Race and Marine Festival,** or more succinctly the Nanaimo Bathtub Race, has grown as fast as its mother city. In the beginning forty-seven "tubbers," kept afloat (or not!) by whatever means possible, made their way from Nanaimo, 36 miles (58 km) across Georgia Strait to Vancouver's Fisherman's Cove. Today tubs are high-tech, and the course is much altered, but the spirit of the original "tubbers" lives on, as can be attested to by Paul Johnson, whose family has raced since 1967: "Insanity is definitely a part of it," says Paul. Further attestation to this dementia can be seen the evening before the race at the traditional **Sacrifice to the Bathtub Gods** boat-burning ceremony in Swy-A-Lana lagoon. So if you're in Nanaimo in July, join the crazy crowds, and perhaps pack along your own bathtub!

three of the activities the outdoor adventurer should put on a list of "west coast things to do."

North to Nanaimo

The Trans-Canada leads north from Duncan to Nanaimo, a city enjoying Canada's mildest climate, and home of the *Bungy Zone Adrenalin Center* (888–668–7874 or 800–668–7771; local numbers: 250–716–RUSH or 250–753–JUMP; jump@bungyzone.com; www.bungyzone.com). The center uses the first legal bungee bridge in North America. Legal or not, whatever you do, don't look down—the drop over the Nanaimo River Canyon is 140 feet (42 m). In February you might try a free Valentine's Naked Love Plunge—definitely one of the more unusual ways to celebrate Valentine's Day. Alternatively, choose between an Ultimate Swing or a Flying Fox (both $50). If you're up for it, a bungee jump costs $95 (or $100 for a lifetime membership, with each jump thereafter $35). To date, 120,000 incident-free plunges have been made into the Nanaimo River Canyon.

The food at Nanaimo's *Dinghy Dock Pub* (250–

Trivia

In 1998 Rodale's Scuba Diving (an American dive magazine) readers' poll chose the coastal waters of Vancouver Island as the **Best North American Dive Destination Overall with the Healthiest Marine Environment.**

Nanaimo's Famous Bar

*I*n 1854 miners from the United Kingdom arrived to work Nanaimo's coal fields. As a comfort, their worried mothers sent this delicious treat, which became known as the Nanaimo Bar. This is the original decadent recipe:

Bottom layer: $^1/_2$ c. unsalted butter; $^1/_4$ c. sugar; 5 tbsp. cocoa; 1 egg, beaten; $1^3/_4$ c. graham wafer crumbs; $^1/_2$ c. finely chopped almonds; 1 c. coconut. Melt butter, sugar, and cocoa in top of a double boiler. Add egg and stir to cook and thicken. Remove from heat. Stir in crumbs, coconut, and nuts. Press firmly into an ungreased 8 x 8 pan.

Middle layer: $^1/_2$ c. unsalted butter; 2 tbsp. plus 2 tsp. cream; 2 tbsp. vanilla custard powder; 2 c. icing sugar. Cream butter, cream, custard powder, and icing sugar together well. Beat until light. Spread over bottom layer.

Third layer: 4 squares semisweet chocolate (1 oz. each); 2 tbsp. unsalted butter. Melt chocolate and butter over low heat. Cool. When cool, but still liquid, pour over second layer and chill in refrigerator.

753–2373) will also give you a rush. Take a ten-minute ($5.00) Protection Connection ferry (250–753–8244) from the dock on Front Street to Protection Island and try Sex in a Dinghy! Relax, it's but a heavenly dessert. For an entree try the Louisiana Blackened Halibut Burger. The burger plus the dreamy dessert will set you back a whole $13. The pub is open 11:30 A.M. to 11:00 P.M. (midnight on weekends) from May to mid-October.

For further information on the Nanaimo area, contact the **Nanaimo Visitor Info Centre,** Beban House, 2290 Bowen Road, Nanaimo, V9T 3K7; (250) 756–0106 or (800) 663–7337; fax: (250) 756–0075; info@tourismnanaimo.com; www.tourismnanaimo.com.

From Nanaimo's downtown harbor the MV *Quinsam* car/passenger ferry runs hourly (approximately) between 6:00 A.M. and 11:00 P.M., taking twenty minutes to reach **Gabriola Island,** famous for its beaches, artists, and prehistoric rock carvings (petroglyphs). You'll see reproductions of these petroglyphs on the museum grounds. Then head southeast for about 8 miles (13 km) down a sometimes very

Trivia

• There are nineteen golf courses within an hour's drive of Nanaimo.

• You'll never guess where the word Nanaimo comes from. It originated when the first non-native settlers tried to pronounce the local Coast Salish people's name for themselves: **Sneneymexw.** The word means "great and mighty people."

steep South Road to the United Church to see the real thing. Dozens of petroglyphs have been uncovered here. Follow a short marked trail to the site, being mindful not to damage these sacred images. If you visit in the early evening when the shadows are long, you're in for some interesting photography. If you head north after the ferry dock, you'll come to *Malaspina Galleries,* sandstone formations that provide hours of fun for the adventurous wishing to dive into the deep waters below. The *Gabriola Visitor Info Centre*—open mid-May to Thanksgiving—in Folklife Village (575 North Road, Box 249, Gabriola Island, V0R 1X0; phone/fax: 250–247–9332; info@gabriolaisland.org; www. gabriolaisland.org) has more information on these attractions, as well as on the four-day Dancing Man Music Festival held in the spring. Although the perimeter roads measure less than 20 miles (32 km), Gabriola has more than four dozen art and craft studios, three provincial waterfront parks, and a campground (250–729–1213) by the beach. It also has a number of moderately priced bed-and-breakfasts. One with spectacular ocean views from a 1,000-square-foot, two-bedroom suite is *Casa Blanca By the Sea* (1707 El Verano, Box 77, Gabriola Island, V0R 1X0; 250–247–9824; casablan@island.net; www.island. net/~casablan). There's also a double-bedroom B&B on the upper level with private bath. Other amenities are a barbecue on the deck overlooking the ocean, a hot tub, and a gourmet breakfast. And the quiet beach is the perfect takeoff spot for kayaking (kayaks available for rental and lessons) to nearby islands. More B&Bs and other types of accommodations are listed at www.gabriolaisland.org.

Parksville/Qualicum Beach and West

P arksville and Qualicum Beach are renowned for having some of the best beaches in Canada, all easily accessible. Add to these beaches the newly designated *UNESCO Mount Arrowsmith Biosphere Reserve* (which encompasses Mount Arrowsmith, Mount Cokely, Mount Moriarty, and all the watersheds that flow from them into the Strait of Georgia), plus a multitude of exciting activities for all ages, and you have one of the world's top recreational areas.

Entering Parksville on Highway 19A from the south, turn right after the railway tracks and stop off at the excellent *Parksville Visitor Info Centre* (1275 East Island Highway, Box 99, Parksville, V9P 2G3; 250– 248–3613; fax: 250–248–5210; info@chamber.parksville.bc.ca; www. chamber.parksville.bc.ca), to find out about accommodations, attractions, and restaurants; then visit *Craig Heritage Park and Museum*

Can't Top This Diner!

*A*s you pass Qualicum Bay, you may find yourself doing a double take at the Marilyn Monroe/James Dean mural painted on the **Cola Diner** *(6060 Island Highway, Qualicum Bay, V9K 2E1; 250–757–2029; fax: 250–757–9789). You see, Marilyn is missing her top. A hot debate on www.colaland.com is being waged to determine whether she should wear a towel or not. Car buffs may be more interested in the '57 Chevy hanging off the front of the building. Inside, you'll find more cola memorabilia and excellent diner-style eating. Modern log cabin accommodations are also available here, set in the woods just steps from the beach. E-mail reservations@colaland.com or phone/fax the above numbers to reserve. Interestingly enough, one of the mural artists, John F. Mortenson, is Marilyn's cousin.*

(250–248–6966; open daily in summer, Wednesdays only in winter) next door to find out about the area's beginnings. If it's the beach you're after, it's right downtown! Fishing, swimming, hiking, and camping (105 sites) are available at **Englishman River Falls Provincial Park,** southwest of Parksville. Take Highway 4A 3 miles (5 km) west, then drive south on Errington Road for 5 miles (8 km). Here you'll find a spectacular canyon situated between two cascades, plus excellent hiking trails that meander through old-growth forest. If you visit in autumn, look for spawning salmon in the Englishman River. Phone (800) 689–9025 or (604) 689–9025 for Discover Camping reservations.

Just north of Parksville the village of **Qualicum Beach** is often bypassed, but its pretty gardens and interesting stores warrant a stop. So glorious are the blooms and gardens here that in 2002 Qualicum Beach won the National Capital Commission Floral Award for the Most Beautiful and Innovative Floral Displays in Canada. Turn off Highway 19A, head up Memorial, and turn right onto West Second Avenue to get to the shopping area. If it's an eclectic restaurant you're after, try **Lefty's** (by Qualicum's only traffic light; 250–752–7530). Also located in Parksville (250–954–3886) next to Thrifty's grocery store, Lefty's offers imported organic coffee, "LeftCoast Cuisine," and Italian sodas.

For more information on the area, contact the **Qualicum Beach Visitor Info Centre** (2711 West Island Highway, Qualicum Beach, V9K 2C4; 250–752–9532; fax: 250–752–2923; info@qualicum.bc.ca; www.qualicum.bc.ca). For comprehensive tourism information on the area stretching from **Nanoose Bay** (south of Parksville) to **Deep Bay** (south of Courtenay), contact the **Oceanside Tourism Association** at Box 374,

Qualicum Beach, V9K 1S9; (250) 752–2388; fax: (250) 752–2392; toll free: (888) 799–3222 or visit www.oceansidetourism.com.

Back on the highway, about 5 miles (8 km) north, is an exquisitely decorated, five-star bed-and-breakfast called *Bahari* (5101 Island Highway West, Qualicum Beach, V9K 1Z1; 250–752–9278; 877–752–9278 toll free; fax: 250–752–9038; relax@baharibandb.com; www.baharibandb.com). The views are outstanding, especially from the hot tub, sitting at eagle-height above basking seals in Georgia Strait. It's a stopover you won't forget in a hurry. Rates, including gourmet breakfast, range from $125 for a queen bed in low season to $275 for a two-bedroom apartment operated as a deluxe bed-and-breakfast in high season. The apartment is also available as a self-cater at $195 ($145 in low season).

From Bahari it's only a mile north to the turnoff to the *Horne Lake Caves Provincial Park.* Look for the Horne Lake Store and Café and follow the signs for about 7 miles (12 km). The caves are open year-round for self-guided exploration. Guided tours are also available. Check out the Web site at www.hornelake.com for information. Choose from a one-and-a-half-hour family tour to a five-hour "Extreme Rappel" expedition, where rappelling down a seven-story underground waterfall is part of the adventure. One of the most popular tours is the "Three-hour Cave Adventure," where explorers see underground waterfalls and ancient fossils. Write: Box 3531, Station Main, Courtenay, V9N 6Z8; phone/fax: (250) 757–8687; adventure@hornelake.com. Anyone planning to "self-explore" the caves should be familiar with caving safety. Expect tight entrances with some rugged climbing inside. Helmets and lights can be rented for $5.00. These caves are some of the most accessible and beautiful of the thousand known caves on Vancouver Island. One in particular, *Riverbend* (a locked cave), is loaded with crystal formations and ancient fossils.

If you've never slept in a teepee, you'll have the chance at the *Horne Lake Teepee Adventure Camp* (contact previously mentioned information). Here you can rent canoes or enjoy a guided sunset paddle, try some rock climbing, and take part in the fun family adventures that run daily in summer.

To unearth more treasures along this bottom third of Vancouver Island, take Highway 4 to Tofino, 107 miles (173 km) west of Parksville. On the way keep an eye out for *Bill Gruff* and friends, the grazing goats on the sod roof at the *Coombs Old Country Market* (Box 219, Coombs, V0R 1M0; 250–248–6272; fax: 248–250–9593; ocm@bcsupernet.com; www.oldcountrymarket.com), walk along jungle paths at *Butterfly World* (250–248–7026), camp at *Little Qualicum Falls Provincial*

Park, and stand in awe in *Cathedral Grove* (MacMillan Provincial Park), where some of the largest Douglas fir trees left on Vancouver Island still stand. Despite the 800-year-old trees misted in moss and sword ferns, you'll quickly realize you're in the heart of logging country as you approach *Port Alberni.*

Tofino, *nominated for a UNESCO Biosphere designation, gets twice as many inches of rain, but only half the hours of rain, as Vancouver.*

Although industry dominates here, outdoor activities are top-rate in the Port Alberni area. One for the very fit (and well-prepared) is a hike to *Della Falls,* at 1,444 feet (440 meters) Canada's second-highest free-falling waterfall (and the sixth highest in the world). It's in Strathcona Provincial Park and can be reached via paved road (look for signs just west of Port Alberni) to Sproat Lake Park and by boating the length of Great Central Lake (northwest of Port Alberni), followed by a 10-mile (16-km) hike beside Drinkwater Creek. Another activity is to join kayakers and hikers heading south to Bamfield, Ucluelet, or the West Coast Trail on the *MV* **Lady Rose** or *MV* **Frances Barkley.** If you join them, expect to see sea lions, whales, eagles, and spectacular scenery. Return trips cost $45–$70, and if you want to stay awhile, you can rent kayaks or stay in the newly decorated *Sechart Whaling Station* lodge accommodation (from $75 per person, including meals) near the *Broken Group Islands,* one of the three physically separated units that make up the *Pacific Rim National Park Reserve* in Barkley Sound. (The other two are Long Beach and the West Coast Trail.) Contact *Lady Rose Marine Services* at Alberni Harbor Quay (250–723–8313 or 800–663–7192 April through September; fax: 250–723–8314; www.ladyrosemarine.com) for information on the Alberni Inlet trip as well as for kayak rentals and lodge information. While there, try the schnitzel at the *Little Bavaria Restaurant* (3035 Fourth Avenue, 250–724–4242 or 800–704–2744). It's tasty and substantial.

The Pacific Rim

Tofino, 21 miles (34 km) to the north, and *Ucluelet,* 5 miles (8 km) to the south, lie at the end of Highway 4, with glorious *Long Beach* between. Information on *Pacific Rim National Park Reserve* can be obtained year-round at the Park Administration Office (P.O. Box 280, 2185 Ocean Terrace, Ucluelet, V0R 3A0; 250–726–7721; pacrim_info@pch.gc.ca). Short films and exhibits of marine biology of the Pacific west coast and the culture of the Nuu-chah-nulth, plus a gift store, make the *Wickaninnish Interpretive Center,* a short distance north of the park entrance sign, worth a stop. While there, enjoy a seafood dinner at the **Wickaninnish Restaurant** (open mid-March to mid-October 11:00 A.M. to 9:30 P.M.; 250–726–7706) and maybe catch a glimpse of Ukee, Ucluelet's gray whale mascot, somewhere in the pounding waves outside. Start your west coast adventure in Ucluelet with an easy walk along the **Wild Pacific Trail,** a soon-to-be seven-phase trail system that skirts the coastline. Accessible to the physically challenged, Phase One starts (or ends) at a parking lot on the corner of Peninsula Road and Coast Guard Road, passes **Amphitrite Lighthouse,** then links to a twenty-minute boardwalk loop through old-growth forest in **He-Tin-Kis Park** just south of Terrace Beach. Several benches add to the relaxing viewpoints found along the trail. Originated through the vision of Ucluelet's "Oyster Jim" Martin, and developed by volunteers and donations to the Wild Pacific Trail Society, the trail will eventually continue northwest 8.7 miles (14 km) along the outer coast to reach the Long Beach section of Pacific Rim National Park. To date, four phases of the trail have been completed. For information on the trail and maps of the area, visit www.longbeachmaps.com. The Pacific Ocean views from this trail are nothing short of spectacular.

Accommodations are fairly spectacular too. A stay at **A Snug Harbour Inn** (Box 318, 460 Marine Drive, Ucluelet, V0R 3A0; 250–726–2686; toll free: 888–936–5222; fax: 250–726–2685; asnughbr@island.net; www.awesomeview.com) will be a stay to remember. Set into woods along a dramatic coastline, every room has a jetted tub, a fireplace, and a private deck for viewing this wild and wonderful west coast. For more

Tofino's Eagle Aerie Gallery

*O*ne of Canada's best-known artists is Roy Henry Vickers of the Tsimshian eagle clan. You may be lucky enough to meet him at the **Eagle Aerie Gallery** (350 Campbell Street, Tofino; V0R 2Z0; 250–725–3235; 800–663–0669; fax: 250–725–4466; eagleaerie@tofino-bc.com; www.royhenryvickers.com) in his self-designed, longhouse-style showroom. Splendid, tall totems support the huge beams of this ethereal building. As you enter through the beaten-copper front doors, you'll notice a strong smell of cedar and be struck by the peaceful feeling inside— what Vickers himself has described as "like walking into a womb, which is what a house should be." Sit in harmony in the carpeted sitting-well, where the longhouse fire pit would traditionally be, and meditate calmly on Vickers's mystical artwork on the surrounding walls.

information contact the Ucluelet Chamber of Commerce (Box 428, 100 Main Street, Ucluelet, V0R 3A0; 250–726–4641; fax: 250–726–4611; info@ucueletinfo.com, www.ucueletinfo.com).

Tofino also has some wonderful attractions, one of which is **Jamie's Whaling Station** (606 Campbell Street, Box 129, Tofino, V0R 2Z0; 800–667–9913 or 250–725–3919; fax: 250–725–2138; info@jamies.com; www.jamies.com). This is the first gray whale tour company on Canada's west coast, and Jamie guarantees his customers a whale sighting and even offers a rain check "forever" if they don't see one. Whales can be observed daily in the waters around Tofino for more than ten months a year! Three-hour trips in the 65-foot *Leviathan II,* with two glass-bottom panels (to check out the abundant sea life), range from $50 to $85, and two-hour trips in a Zodiac range from $50 to $65. After whale-watching, enjoy a bite at the **Alley-Way Garden Café/Costa Azul** (250–725–3105; azul@island.net), behind the CIBC bank just up from the Tofino Co-op. It's open from 8:00 A.M. daily for breakfast, lunch, and dinner, serving vegetarian-style Mexican food as well as absolutely delicious meal-size chowders.

Jamie's (which has recently started tours in Ucluelet—phone 877–726–7444 or 250–726–7444) and several sea kayaking companies and water taxis are available to take visitors to nearby **Meares Island,** the home of the largest Western red cedar in the world. This cedar is more than 2,000 years old, is 72 feet (22 m) round, and is still growing. Meares Island was declared a First Nations Tribal Park in 1984 after the Tla-o-qui-aht First Nations people and other environmentalists successfully lobbied for a court injunction to prevent logging companies from removing timber from there. A boardwalk trail winds and climbs through some of the most spectacular trees in North America. Another of Jamie's tours passes through the gray whale feeding bays in Clayoquot Sound to Hot Springs Cove, 23 miles (37 km) up the coast from Tofino. Here you can hike along a boardwalk through rainforest to **Macquinna Provincial Marine Park.** At the end of a narrow peninsula, stunningly perched right at the ocean's edge, treat yourself to a decadent soak in steaming natural hot springs. It's advisable to make reservations for these tours with Jamie's. Prices range from $69 to $99. Another adventure to try is "Jamie's Sea to Sky," which

- **Lennard Light,** *marking the entrance to Tofino Inlet, was the first high-intensity lighthouse to be established on the West Coast of Vancouver Island.*

- **Opitsaht,** *a native village near Tofino, is (going by carbon dating performed on nearby shell middens) the oldest constantly inhabited village on the west coast of North America.*

takes you to the hot springs by boat, then home to Tofino in a flight over Clayoquot Sound ($139).

Should you be looking for somewhere truly "off-the-beaten-path" for accommodation, try the *Innchanter* (250–670–1149; innchanter@ uniserve.com; www.innchanter.com), a heritage yacht moored near Hot Springs Cove. Luxury staterooms, unbelievable scenery, those glorious hot springs, and memorable gourmet meals prepared by an onboard chef will have you wishing you'd discovered the Innchanter long ago. For those who don't want to simply lie like a lizard on the sundeck, there's plenty to do, such as kayaking, whale watching, and hiking. At $85 per person including breakfast and dinner, you'll probably be returning sooner than you think. The *Tofino Visitor Centre* (Box 249, Tofino, V0R 2Z0; 250–725–3414; fax: 250–725–3296; tofino@island. net; www.tofinobc.org) can also help you find other accommodations and attractions in this area.

If it's blowing a gale when you visit the west coast, throw caution to the wind at the celebrated *Wickaninnish Inn* (Osprey Lane at Chesterman Beach, P.O. Box 250, Tofino, V0R 2Z0; 250–725–3100 or 800–333–4604; info@wickinn.com; www.wickinn.com) with its *Pointe Restaurant, On-the-Rocks Lounge,* and *Ancient Cedars Spa.* Luxuriate decadently in soaker tubs in rooms ranging from $240 to $1,000 and enjoy the truly panoramic, wild Pacific view, often dotted with wet-suited surfboarders. In 2002 "The Wick" was named Top Hotel in North America and third-best hotel in the world by *Travel and Leisure Magazine.* Look for signs on Highway 4 at Chesterman Beach about five minutes south of Tofino.

Denman and Hornby Islands

From the new Inland Island Highway (19) take exit 101, which crosses Oceanside Route 19A (the old Island Highway) to Buckley Bay. A car ferry (250–335–0323) leaves regularly (check www.bcferries. com for details) for Denman Island (affectionately referred to by Hornby Islanders as "The Hornby Speed Bump"). After you cross Denman, a second ferry takes you further east to Hornby Island. These islands are steps back in time, so enjoy them leisurely. Cycling the mostly paved roads is an ideal way to explore the quiet trails through old-growth Douglas fir forests in Boyle Point and Fillongley Provincial Parks. Both are pleasant with driftwood-littered beaches.

Then take the second ferry to Hornby Island, where Tribune Bay Provincial Park has fine white sandy beaches, and Helliwell Provincial

Park has a 3-mile (5-km) circular track with spectacular bluffs. When the herring are running in March, watch for sea lions on nearby Norris Rocks. Bicycle rentals and guides are available at the *Hornby Island Off Road Bike Shop* (5875 Central Road; 250–335–0444), or if you prefer an eye-level view of the sea lions, try some ocean kayaking with *Hornby Ocean Kayaks* (250–335–2726; hikayak@telus.net; www.hornbyisland.com/kayaking). For campers, Fillongley on Denman has ten beach sites, and *Tribune Bay Campsite* (250–335–2359) on Hornby has hot showers and cafes nearby.

As on many of these small islands, artisans and bed-and-breakfast establishments flourish, so drop in to the *Denman Island General Store* (250–335–2293) at the top of the hill after you come off the first ferry and ask about accommodations and anything else you need to know about the islands. While there, be sure to pick up some *Denman Island Chocolate* (info@denmanislandchocolate.com; www.denmanislandchocolate.com). You'll have discovered not only the best tasting chocolate in the world but also Canada's only certified organic chocolate. Just around the corner from the general store near the bakery, you'll find a fine collection of local arts and crafts at the *Denman Craft Shop* (3676 Denman Road; 250–335–0881).There's more useful information on Denman at www. denmanis.bc.ca. Or write the *Hornby/Denman Tourist Association* at Sea Breeze Lodge, Big Tree 3-2, Hornby Island, V0R 1Z0; phone/fax: (250) 335–2321; toll free: 888–516–2321; info@seabreezelodge.com; www.seabreezelodge.com.

Beacon Hill Children's Farm, Beacon Hill Park, Victoria (250–381–2532). Pet baby animals from mid-March to October.

Watch salmon spawning in *Victoria's Goldstream Provincial Park* between late October and mid-December, or learn about their life cycle at the *Quatse River Hatchery* (250–949–9022) near Port Hardy.

All Fun Recreation, at 2207 Millstream Road, Victoria (250–474–3184), has go-carts, water slides, minigolf, and a batting cage.

See the Chemainus murals (250–246–4701) on a steam-train ride through town.

Swim and slide at *Oak Bay Recreation Centre,* 1975 Bee Street, Victoria (250–595–7946).

Drag your parents along the whole 12-mile (20-km) length of surf-swept, sandy *Long Beach,* with a lunch break at the Wickaninnish Centre (250–726–4212), where you'll learn fascinating things about marine life.

Try your skills in the *kid's sandcastle competition* in August on Parksville Beach (250–248–3252).

Sea Breeze Lodge is delightfully set up with families in mind. Guests stay in waterfront (or close) one- and two-bedroom cottages. In summer the rates (which include all meals) are $134 per adult (double) for a waterfront unit, and from September to May, kitchen cottages ($85–$105 double occupancy), some with fireplaces, can make for a very romantic, back to nature getaway, where watching the eagles soar and the herons stand in stately solitude waiting for a fishy meal is part of a normal dreamy day.

For those of you who want to see deeper than the ocean's surface, divers at **Hornby Island Diving** (Ford Cove, Hornby Island, V0R 1Z0; phone/fax: 250–335–2807; info@hornbyislanddiving.com; www.horn byislanddiving.com) will accompany you in search of the elusive sixgill shark. Hornby Island is one of the few places in the world where the primitive, torpedo-shaped sixgill moves into waters as shallow as 50 feet (15 m). As its name suggests, the sixgill has six gills, instead of the five that most other sharks breathe with. They are both graceful and (according to dive masters on Hornby) surprisingly accommodating to the presence of humans. They grow up to 15 feet (4.5 m) long and frequent the waters off Hornby Island from May through September. The sea off Hornby is also known for giant Pacific octopus, sea lions, and harbor seals, as well as colorful nudibranchs, anemones, sponges, sea cucumbers, sea urchins, and particularly large and strikingly colored sea stars. Hornby Island Diving offers diving, accommodation, and meals packages for $165 per person per day. Two-tank day-boat charters are also available for $100 per person. The new dive lodge across from the ocean has great views, a sauna, and basic but pleasant bedrooms. And you don't have to be a diver to stay there. Accommodation and meals are $75 per person for groups of ten to twenty-four. Discounts are available for children under twelve. It's a great place to get together with a group of friends or family to do some beachcombing, craft hunting, hiking, or photography.

One thing you must be sure to visit on Hornby is the **Free Store** at the recycling center on Central Road, where you'll find anything from a glamorous new wig to that old *National Geographic* issue you've been searching for.

The Comox Valley

*C*ourtenay is the city, **Comox** the town, and **Cumberland** the village, three of the communities that comprise the Comox Valley, where some of Canada's tallest fishing tales originate. As well as on the sea, there's plenty to do on land in the Comox Valley. One event that attests to this is the annual **Royal LePage Comox Valley Snow to Surf Adventure Relay,** a grueling 45.4-mile (73.1-km) alpine and cross-country skiing, running, mountain and road biking, kayaking, and canoe race held every April. The course starts high up on Mount Washington and ends at sea level in Comox Marina Park. Check www.snowtosurf.com for details.

From viewpoints in Courtenay and Comox you'll see the *Comox Glacier,* which is part of Vancouver Island's largest ice field. In Courtenay the *Courtenay and District Museum and Paleontology Centre* (207 Fourth Street, Courtenay, V9N 1G7; 250–334–0686; fax: 250–338–0619; museum@island.net; www.courtenaymuseum.ca) is housed in the Old Post Office building downtown. Here you'll see a replica of the only reconstructed *elasmosaur* in BC. It's an eighty-million-year-old prehistoric swimming reptile, found in the nearby Puntledge River where the museum offers guided amateur paleontology day trips. While in Courtenay check out the largest freestanding log structure in Canada—*Native Sons Hall*—which was built in 1928.

In Comox the rustic but stately *Filberg Heritage Lodge* (61 Filberg Road, Comox, V9M 2S7; www.filberg.com) is well worth a visit, especially during the first weekend of August when the *Filberg Festival* (250–334–9242; fax: 250–334–2899; information@filbergfestival.com; www.filbergfestival. com) is held. Arts and craft booths occupy the beautiful nine acres of waterfront gardens set among mature trees with views of Comox Harbour and the Beaufort Mountain range beyond. There is also entertainment and an eclectic array of food. Look for the Richard Krentz totem pole, which is located in the gardens on an ancient Indian midden. It looks out across the water toward *Goose Spit Regional Park,* a popular windsurfing spot and, since 1876, the site of a Royal Navy training base.

Just west of Courtenay is Cumberland, a village whose mining history was at times eventful, even violent. To learn more, visit the *Cumberland Museum and Archives* (Box 258, Cumberland, V0R 1S0; 250–336–2445; fax: 250–336–2411; info@cumberlandmuseum.ca; www.cumberlandmuseum.ca), where you can walk through a replica of a coal mine constructed by retired miners. The village has a population of just 2,800, but in 1914 it was home to the largest Chinese population north of San Francisco.

For more information on the area's attractions, visit the *Comox Valley Visitor Info Center* (2040 Cliffe Avenue, Courtenay, V9N 2L3; 888–357–4471; 250–334–3234; fax: 250–334–4908; visitorinfo@comoxvalley chamber.com; www.comox-valley-tourism.ca).

One attraction 3 miles (5 km) north of Courtenay tweaked my interest. *Outback Emuzing Ranch* (2301 Clark Road, Courtenay, V9J 1T1; 250–338–8227; fax: 250–338–1108; info@emuoilcanada.com; www.emuoil canada.com) is a small emu farm offering tours to the public. Here, just off the Island Highway, Russ and Karen Davis raise these gentle, flightless Australian birds for their meat and hides and for their valuable healing oil.

High above the emu ranch, 19 miles (31 km) west of Courtenay, looms a mountain rated third in British Columbia (after Whistler/Blackcombe and Big White) for the number of skiers it attracts each year. *Mount Washington Alpine Resort* (Box 3069, Courtenay, V9N 5N3, 250–338–1386; ski@mtwashington.ca; www.mtwashington.ca) is number one to more than 360,000 skiers per year. And with an average seasonal snowfall of more than 30 feet (9 m), it's no wonder. (In February 1999 the resort was closed for a day while the staff dug out the chairlifts!) If you need help getting started, you could try one of the resort's "Discover" lessons, where you'll be introduced to skiing (cross-country or downhill), snowboarding, telemarking, or snowshoeing. Their reasonable prices include the lift pass, rental equipment, lesson, and sometimes a hot chocolate or coffee in the lodge to warm you up. And the spectacular view across Georgia Strait to the Coast Mountains is free.

In summer the cross-country ski trails of Paradise Meadows become wildflower-thick hiking trails that wind through a corner of *Strathcona Provincial Park,* Vancouver Island's largest park. No matter what the season, if you need condominium-style hotel accommodation at Mount Washington, contact Central Reservations at (888) 231–1499 or on-line at the address above.

Campbell River and Surrounds

You've seen the view from the top. It's time to return to sea level and head north to the other Salmon Capital of the World (and you were told it was Port Alberni!), *Campbell River*. If you arrive in winter, try a backcountry snowshoe trek with *Paradise Found Adventure Tour Company* (165–1160 Shellbourne Boulevard, Campbell River, V9W 5G5; 800–897–2872; 250–923–0848; info@paradisefound.bc.ca; www.paradisefound.bc.ca). Summer visitors (July to October) can enjoy mountain biking, hiking, whale watching, caving tours, and the ultimate in adventure, a snorkel tour with the massive runs of coho, steelhead, chum, chinook, and pink salmon that spawn in the Campbell River. All equipment, transportation, and expert instruction are provided for this extraordinarily unique three- to four-hour adventure. Ask your guide about *The Spirit of Discovery* video—a visual tour of northern Vancouver Island's outdoor activities and perhaps the perfect souvenir to take home with you. It sells for $15.95 US or $21.95 Canadian.

Not far from downtown Campbell River is the *Discovery Fishing Pier*. For $2.00 a day (from May to mid-October), you can fish off the fully lit,

Ka-BOOM!

*T*he largest ever non-nuclear peacetime explosion occurred in Seymour Narrows near Campbell River on April 5, 1958, when part of **Ripple Rock** was blasted away. Over the years this dreaded hazard to navigation had caused about 114 vessels to sink, with an equal number of lives lost. To complete the task of destroying the rock, a special explosive, Nitramex 2H, was developed. A 500-foot (150-m) shaft was sunk on Maud Island, and a 2,370-foot (722-m)-long tunnel was dug out to the rock. After stuffing the rock with 2,750,000 pounds (1,250,000 kg) of the explosives, the area was cleared for 3 miles (5 km), and the button was pushed. The cost was more than $3 million, and the top 350,000 tons of the rock disappeared in about three seconds. Film footage of the explosion can be seen at the Campbell River Museum.

600-foot (183-m) dock, which sports built-in rod holders, bait stands, fish cleaning areas, and picnic tables. Some huge salmon have been caught off this very pier. The concession stand (250–286–6199) will sell you all the necessary gear, plus bait, licenses, and fantastic ice creams.

For something more substantial than ice cream, head south from the pier to Second Avenue, then right onto Dogwood Street to the *Fusilli Grill* (220 Dogwood Street, V9W 2X9; 250–830–0090; fax: 250–830–0093; info@fusilligrill.bc.ca; www.fusilligrill.bc.ca). The Italian fare here is a huge favorite with locals. Choose from a generous shrimp and scallop fusilli alfredo accompanied by a BC Sumac Ridge Riesling, a healthy grilled chicken focaccia sandwich, and much more. Takeout is also available, and prices are more than reasonable. If you're there on the weekend, the prime rib special is a winner.

I've seen some unusual museum settings, but the *Campbell River Optical Maritime Museum* (102–250 Dogwood Street; 250–287–2052), close to the Fusilli Grill, could be unique. Scattered throughout waiting and examining rooms in a suburban optometrist's office is a fine collection of maritime artifacts. Dr. Robert Somerville was for years a keen auxiliary Coast Guard volunteer. He has brought his love of things nautical into his workplace. From antique diving suits to interesting log books, every nook of his small office is filled. The museum is open during regular business hours, admission is free, and if he's not too busy, Dr. Somerville will give you a personal tour between seeing clients.

With a spectacular view of Discovery Passage, the *Campbell River Museum and Archives* (470 Island Highway, V9W 4Z9; 250–287–3103;

fax: 250–286–0109; public.programs@crmuseum.ca; www.crmuseum. ca) is on the highway at the corner of Fifth Avenue. Look for First Nations culture and art, film footage of the historic Ripple Rock explosion, a replica pioneer cabin and a coastal floathouse, logging and fishing exhibits, and a 200-year-old Sun Welcome Mask. It is wheelchair accessible and is open daily, but it's closed Monday in winter. For more information contact *Campbell River Tourism,* Box 482, Campbell River, V9W 5C1; (800) 463–4386; (250) 286–1616; fax: (250) 286–8336; info@campbellrivertourism.com; www. campbellrivertourism.com

Quadra and Cortes Islands

W hile on Quadra, plan to hike on some of the often-deserted trails. The *Morte Lake* trail is an easy, pleasant hike, and the *Chinese Mountain* trail provides a panoramic view of the island. Tour the *Cape Mudge Lighthouse* (250–285–3351), where Captain George Vancouver went ashore in his exploration of Discovery Passage, or visit *Drahanchuk Studios* (157 Quadra Loop, Box 74, Quathiaski Cove, Quadra Island, V0P 1N0; phone/fax: 250–285–3160; drahan@oberon.ark.com; oberon.ark.com/~drahan). This delightful artists' home and studio is set in picturesque gardens (which are works of art in themselves) with views across Sutil Channel to the Coast Mountains. The studio, where you'll find exceptional paintings and pottery, as well as bronze and soapstone sculptures by Ed and Ethel Drahanchuk, is open most days in July and August, but phone ahead for opening hours.

If you plan to stay, there's accommodation to suit everyone on Quadra Island, even a spot for your boat. *Heriot Bay Inn and Marina* (Heriot Bay Road, Box 100, Heriot Bay, V0P 1N0; 250–285–3322; fax: 250–285–2708; info@heriotbayinn.com; www.heriotbayinn.com) has camping and marina facilities, cycle and kayak rentals, cottages, and a historic bed-and-breakfast inn (rates start at $49 in winter, room only, $80 per room including full breakfast in summer) in pretty Heriot Bay near Rebecca Spit. Mariners can check in on VHF channel 73.

Perhaps the best way to learn about some of Quadra's wildlife is from the quiet of a kayak. *Spirit of the West Adventures* (Box 569, Heriot Bay, V0P 1H0; 250–285–2121; fax: 250–285–2104; toll free: 800–307–3982; spirit1@oberon.ark.com; www.kayak-adventures.com) takes guests in sea kayaks to the Breton Island Archipelago to view seal colonies, porpoises, killer whales, and nesting bald eagles.

From Quadra's Heriot Bay, take a forty-five-minute ferry ride (runs every two hours) to Cortes Island, "where the earth and the sea touch the sky." There's good camping at **Smelt Bay Provincial Park** (800–689–9025 for reservations, but there are also "first-come" sites), 9 miles (15 km) south of the Whaletown Ferry Terminal on Sutil Point Road. The mounds behind the beach are believed to have been built by natives for defense purposes. If you have a valid BC fishing license, at low tide you can help yourself to a few huge oysters, which are delicious cooked on the campsite grill. Take note that this park has only basic facilities—pit toilets, no showers, and RVs to a maximum of 24 feet.

For something more upscale than oysters on a campsite grill (can there be?), try **The Tak Restaurant** (250–935–8555; www.cortesisland. com/thetak; open nightly from 5:00 to 10:00 P.M.) on Sutil Point Road. It's opposite the Cortes Market and the island's only bank machine. If you're arriving by yacht, it's about a ten-minute walk up from the Manson's Landing dock. It's fully licensed and offers the use of a computer to pick up your e-mail. The food is superb. Another good bet for lunch and dinner can be found on the eastern side of the island at **Caffe Suzanne** (250–935–6866). It's on Whaletown Road near the Squirrel Cove Wharf. Just north of Smelt Bay on Potlatch Road there's excellent waterfront bed-and-breakfast accommodation at **Blue Heron B&B** (Box 23 Mansons Landing, Cortes Island, V0P 1K0; 250–935–6584; www.cortesisland.com/blueheron). Rates range from $50.

In Victoria: Spend a day at the Inner Harbor and visit the **Royal British Columbia Museum** *(250–387–3701 or 800–661–5411) and the* **Royal London Wax Museum** *(250–388–4461); cycle the 43-mile-long (70-km)* **Galloping Goose Trail;** *visit* **Craigdarroch Castle** *historic house museum (250–592–5323); view the Italian, Japanese, and rose gardens surrounding* **Royal Roads University** *in Hatley Park, Colwood; enjoy the* **Oak Bay beaches** *and shop for art and antiques in its delightful village (www.oakbay tourism.com).*

In Brentwood Bay: Visit the world-famous **Butchart Gardens** *(250–652–4422) and* **Butterfly Gardens** *(250–652–3822), where the butterflies fly free and the birds are friendly.*

In Duncan: Ride the steam train at the **British Columbia Forest Museum** *(250–715–1113).*

And all over the islands: Do some whale watching, fishing, hiking, and beachcombing.

Cortes is also home to **Hollyhock** (Box 127 Manson's Landing, V0P 1K0; 250–935–6576; fax: 250–935–6424; 800–933–6339; registration@ hollyhock.ca; www.hollyhock.ca), where you can luxuriate in every kind of body, mind, and spirit renewal—an experience that may alter your life forever.

Strathcona Park and the Central West Coast

efore leaving the Campbell River area, head 30 miles (48 km) west on Highway 28 (the Gold River Highway) to **Strathcona Park**. It's British Columbia's first Provincial Park, a hiker's wilderness paradise located almost in the center of Vancouver Island and stretching almost to Nootka Sound on the west coast. At 627,064 acres (253,773 ha), not only is it the largest park on the island, but it also has the island's highest peak, **Mount Golden Hinde,** at 7,218 feet (2,200 m), and Canada's second-highest free-falling waterfall, **Della Falls,** which at 1,443 feet (440 m) is almost ten times higher than Niagara Falls. (See Port Alberni section for hiking details to the falls.) The paved road that hugs the eastern shore of **Buttle Lake** down to **Myra Creek** is spectacular and passes several creeks and waterfalls. Two campsites—Buttle Lake, with eighty-five sites, and Ralph River, with seventy-six sites—can be accessed from Highway 28. Both are located on Buttle Lake. Phone (800) 689–9025 for reservations. Information is available at the entrance to the park (seasonal) or visit the BC Parks Web site, www.bcparks.ca (search word "Strathcona").

As an alternative to camping, you can stay at the **Strathcona Park Lodge and Outdoor Education Centre** (Box 2160, Campbell River, V9W 5C5; 250–286–3122; fax: 250–286–6010; info@strathcona.bc.ca; www.strathcona.bc.ca), where you can also learn a variety of wilderness skills. Everyone is welcome—you're just as likely to see eighty-year-olds perfecting Eskimo rolls as eight-year-olds rappelling down a rocky bluff. Nutritious meals are standard fare, and the package deals are very reasonable.

Gold River, 6 miles (9 km) west of the park border, also has first-class outdoor activities. Fishing in the Gold River and **Nootka Sound**—a 65-pound (30-kg) salmon was taken in 1993—and more than fifty caves within a 30-mile (50-km) radius supplement beautiful views. Enjoy some of these views while hiking the **Peppercorn Trail,** which starts out near the secondary school close to downtown. Steps and a safety rope assist hikers along the trail to Peppercorn Park, where you can cool off in a swimming hole below diving cliffs. For cavers, the **Upana Caves,** located twenty-five minutes northwest of Gold River on the Head Bay Forest Road (toward Tahsis), provide approximately 1,475 feet (450 m) of caving bliss. Gold River Visitor Info Centre can be contacted at Box 610, Gold River, V0P 1G0; (250) 283–2202; fax: (250) 283–7500; goldri@island.net; www.village.goldriver.bc.ca.

THE ISLANDS

Every year on the first Saturday in June, the Tahsis Lions Club hosts the **Great Walk,** undisputedly North America's toughest charity pledge walkathon. The route runs between Gold River and Tahsis. The top time to complete the approximately 40 miles (63.5 km) is four and a half hours. If you think you can beat that, or just want to have some fun, contact the Tahsis Lions Club (Box 430, Tahsis, V0P 1X0; 250–934–6570; fax: 250–934–6576; greatwalk@greatwalk.com; www. greatwalk.com) for information. Afterward, soak your toes in the Tahsis River near **Fern's Place Bed & Breakfast Suite** (379 North Maquinna Drive, Tahsis, V0P 1X0; 250–934–7851; fern@ferns place.biz; www.fernsplace.biz). Accommodation with continental breakfast is in the $45–$65 range. For more information contact the Tahsis Info Centre/Museum (June–September) at 36 Rugged Mountain Road, Box 278, Tahsis, V0P 1X0; 250–934–6667; fax: 250–934–6679; www. villageoftahsis.com.

From Gold River another logging road leads 39 miles (63 km) north through the Nimpkish Valley to **Woss,** just west of the Highway 19 intersection. It's rough, but if you're in Gold River and heading north to Port McNeil, it will cut off 92 miles (148 km). If you don't mind a few corrugations (maybe a lot!) and have good emergency supplies and the appropriate forestry maps, there's lots more to be explored in this wild, northern part of the island. But perhaps the best-kept secret is **Woss Lake**. The views down the lake to the glacier-topped Rugged Mountain Range are breathtaking. To top it off, you can camp by a lovely white-sand beach complete with boat ramp, which is kept in excellent condition by Canadian Forest Products.

From Woss it's about 12 miles (20 km) north to the turnoff to Zeballos, population 200, which is named after Ciriaco Cevallos (close enough!), a Spanish lieutenant under the command of Captain Alejandro Malaspina. Drive for fifteen to twenty minutes along the Zeballos Road and look for the well-marked logging road turnoff to Little

Get Ready for a GREAT Walk

If you're set on doing the **Great Walk***, here are a few very important things to consider:*

- **Socks.** *You'll need a few extra pairs to get you through the forty-odd agony-filled miles (63.5 kilometers to be precise), so bring oodles.*

- **Toilets.** *You'll be sharing the road with about 700 others, so expect long lineups at the potty stops.*

- **Weather.** *Be prepared for any type of weather— cold rain, hot sun, wind . . .*

- **Grades.** *At times the terrain is excruciatingly steep, so train in Everest-like territory.*

- **Earplugs.** *Bring these for the screaming sirens, bright lights, and raucous pot-banging at the end, where you'll be greeted by crowds of high-spirited locals.*

- **Fun.** *Finally, despite occasional torture-filled paroxysms, you can expect to have a ton of this.*

Huson Caves Regional Park. Another fifteen minutes or so on this side road, and you'll be able to explore several caves, rock arches, and a limestone canyon. No, Huson is not a typographical error; you'll see it written as Hustan in maps and government documents (soon to be corrected), but the regional park and the nearby lake are actually named after Mr. West Huson, a North Island pioneer.

We're now back on the road to *Zeballos,* which is 24 miles (39 km) southwest of Highway 19. Ask at the Visitor Info Booth on Maquinna Avenue (Box 127, Zeballos, V0P 2A0; 250–761–4070/4158; fax: 250–761–4331; www.zeballos.com) about guided tours of the village. The booth is open July 1 to September 6. The many false-fronted buildings in Zeballos tell a story of a town with an exciting gold mining history. You can read up on this at the library, which offers an Internet service. Or visit the folks at *Mason's Motor Lodge* (203 Pandora Avenue, Box 10, Zeballos, V0P 2A0; 250–761–4044; fax: 250–761–4074; info@masonslodge.zeballos.bc.ca; www.masonslodge. zeballos.bc.ca). They'll fill you in on this exciting history while you lounge on the large deck below the pretty mountains that edge the Zeballos River and the inlet. And don't be surprised if a black bear snuffles by below in search of his salmon supper, especially in late summer during spawning season. Accommodation at Mason's, a charmingly refurbished, historic hospital building with an attached restaurant, is in the $55–$110 range. Zeballos truly fits the description: "Accessible wilderness."

Rat River Enterprises (250–761–4215) has a 26-foot aluminum boat ready to help you explore *Nootka Island* or *Kyuquot Sound,* where perhaps you'll land a thirty-pound king salmon in this scenic wilderness. Kayakers wishing to get up close and personal with the sea otters, bald eagles, and black bears of the stunning *Nuchatlitz* can contact *Zeballos Expeditions and Kayaks* (115 Maquinna Avenue, Box 111, Zeballos, V0P 2A0; 250–761–4137; kayak@netcom.ca; www.zeballoskayaks.com). Three-day wildlife viewing tours in the *Nootka Sound* area aboard comfortable vessels are also offered.

Another option to consider is to visit Zeballos from Gold River or Tahsis. The *MV Uchuck III,* a 136-foot passenger and freight vessel, makes weekly runs out of Gold River to Zeballos (with a stop in Tahsis) every Monday, year-round. Contact *Nootka Sound Services* (Box 57, Gold River, V0P 1G0; 250–283–2515; fax: 250–283–7582; info@mvuchuck. com; www.mvuchuck.com) for details on this and other trips in the historic Nootka Sound, Esperanza, and Kyuquot Sound areas.

Back on Highway 19 after the Zeballos side trip, the road skirts *Nimpkish Lake* (noted for its world-class windsurfing), with the Karmutzen Range on the opposite side for 40 miles (64 km) to Port McNeill, the ferry terminal for the intriguing island communities of Sointula and Alert Bay.

One more side trip (north off Highway 19) leads to the village of **Sayward** on Kelsey Bay. It's equidistant (50 miles [80 km]) from Campbell River and Port McNeill. From the turnoff, the road follows the **Salmon River,** known for its large steelhead, down the valley to Kelsey Bay in Johnstone Strait, world-renowned for its killer whales (orcas). Don't miss the **Original Cable Cookhouse** (250–282–3433; www.cablecook house.com), made from 8,200 feet (250 m) of old logging cable welded to an iron frame—a wall weight of approximately twenty-six tons. The menu is heavy too—on variety, that is—with the added attraction of homemade pies, pastries, and fresh ground coffee. It's located less than a mile east of Sayward Junction just over the one-lane bridge. Check out the interesting collection of old logging equipment outside. Hikers might try a climb (you'll need a whole day) up **Mount H'Kusam,** a dominating—5481 feet (1,670 m)—feature of the area that often has a mysterious fog ringing its peak. Pick up a map that will direct you to the trailhead at the visitor center. For more information on where to enjoy kayaking, whale watching, caving, and fishing, contact the Sayward Chamber of Commerce (White River Court, Sayward, V0P 1R0; phone/fax: 250–282–3845; www.sayward.com).

The North Islands

Six miles (9 km) south of Port McNeill, just before the Nimpkish River Bridge, a 10-mile (16-km) road leads to **Telegraph Cove** and the **Robson Bight (Michael Bigg) Ecological Reserve,** the most predictable location in the world to see killer whales and one of the most unpredictable to find a place to park! Walk Telegraph Cove's historic boardwalk, perched on stilts over a rocky shoreline, and wander past the folksy, weatherbeaten houses that front the harbor. **Mothership Adventures Inc.** (888–833–8887; fax: 250–384–3750; info@ mothershipadventures.com; www.mothershipadventures.com) will take you right to the whales, as well as to abandoned native villages and the remote rainforests of British Columbia. You'll have a live-aboard, sea-kayaking adventure you won't forget. Former owner Captain Bill McKechnie beautifully refitted the 68-foot (21-m) **Columbia,** a historic mission boat, to take small groups of adventurers to Johnstone Strait, Broughton Archipelago, and the Central Coast (from Port Hardy to Prince Rupert). The new owners, Skip and Teri McPadden, are carrying on the tradition. Costs run approximately $2,500 per week, including kayaks, all meals and wine, hot showers, and comfortable staterooms.

Back on the highway as you head north to Port McNeill on Highway 19, look for an ARTISAN sign after the Nimpkish River bridge that points you to **Henschel Fine Arts Gallery and Studio** (801 Nimpkish Heights Road, Port McNeill, V0N 2R0; 888–663–2787 or 250–956–3539; fax: 250–956–4760; gordon@henschel.ca; www.henschel.ca). Gordon Henschel's delicate North Island scenes grace walls in a handsomely designed gallery.

Just before the gallery, **Roseberry Manor Bed & Breakfast** (810 Nimpkish Heights Road, Port McNeill, V0N 2R0; 250–956–4788; rosemanr@island.net; www.bbcanada.com/roseberrymanorbb) has antique, knickknacky decor straight out of a Victorian dining room. Candlelit gourmet breakfasts plus afternoon tea and evening cappuccinos are all included in the $65–$85 (per double in high season) price range.

If you make the 8:40 A.M. ferry in Port McNeill, it's possible to see both **Sointula** and **Alert Bay** in one day, but give yourself some time or you might miss some of the treasures both Malcolm and Cormorant Islands have hidden away. Check carefully with BC Ferries (888–BCFERRY; www.bcferries.bc.ca/schedules/northern/pmab-current. html); the timetable covering Port McNeil, Sointula, and Alert Bay is complicated, at best!

Sointula, a Finnish word meaning "place of harmony," is aptly named.

Window on a Small Town

*T*he walls were as thin as brothel sheets, the pillow slips thick with bleach. Buses idled below, their sickly fumes filtering into the rain-battered hotel. My dreams involved gas masks. I was beginning to have doubts about Port McNeill.

The next morning, I stumbled sleepily to the town's mall. An adorable teapot in **The Window**, a little hole-in-the-wall studio, tweaked my interest. IT'S MY BIRTHDAY, GONE FOR LUNCH was the greeting on an open door. Of course it

wasn't **really** painter and potter Heather Brown's birthday. She invited me in to see her superb paintings of island gardens and spawning salmon, and her whimsical pottery.

We chatted about the Ronning Gardens (the subject of many of her paintings) near Cape Scott and of the vicissitudes of living in Port McNeill. I left The Window breathing in deeply the sweet smell of a rain-cleansed earth as speckles of blue broke the gray sky.

As soon as you drive off the *Quadra Queen II* thirty-car ferry, you sense the easygoing atmosphere. It wasn't always so, though. The old school building off First Street houses the volunteer-run **Finnish Museum** (250–973–6764), where you can learn about the community's colorful history. It started as a Finnish cooperative community in 1901, but after some dissension and debt, and a fire, which killed eleven people and destroyed the meeting hall, the cooperative disappeared. Many Finns remained, though, and in some of Sointula's back lanes you will still hear a smattering of the old tongue. For more information contact the

Recommended Reading—The Islands

FOR ADULTS:

Island Backroads: Hiking, Camping & Paddling on Vancouver Island, by Richard K. Blier. Orca Book Publishers, 1998.

Hiking Trails 1—Victoria & Vicinity; Hiking Trails II—South-Central Vancouver Island and the Gulf Islands; and *Hiking Trails III—Central & Northern Vancouver Island & Quadra Island* by the Vancouver Island Trails Information Society. Orca Book Publishers, Victoria.

More Island Adventures: An Outdoors Guide to Vancouver Island, by Richard K. Blier. Orca Book Publishers, 1993.

Ghost Towns and Mining Camps of Vancouver Island, by T. W. Paterson and Garnet Basque. Sunfire Publications Limited, 1989. Langley.

Backroading Vancouver Island, by Rosemary Neering. Whitecap Books. Vancouver, 1996. A nitty-gritty approach to exploring Vancouver Island's off-roads, right down to where to buy your ice cream and eggs.

FOR KIDS:

In Like a Lion, by Julie Lawson, illustrated by Yolaine Lefebvre. North Wind Press, Markham, Ontario, 1998. A picture book for kids, grades one and two. Based on a true story about a cougar visiting the Empress Hotel in Victoria.

Jessie's Island, by Sheryl McFarlane, illustrated by Sheena Lott. Orca Books, Victoria, 1992. Ages five to eight. A celebration of West Coast life through a child's eyes.

Ida and the Wool Smugglers, by Sue Ann Alderson, illustrated by Ann Blades. Douglas and McIntyre, Toronto, 1987. The story takes place on Salt Spring Island at the turn of the century. Smugglers row over from the mainland, Ida spots them, and the story continues. For kids at the primary level.

Cougar Cove, by Julie Lawson. Orca Books, 1996. Set on the remote west coast of Vancouver Island. The heroine, eleven-year-old Sam, meets a cougar and two cubs. For kids about the grade three and four level.

Malcolm Island Tourism Association at Box 23, Sointula, V0N 3E0; sointula@island.net; www.island.net/~sointula.

When you arrive at the Sointula ferry landing, you'll see **Choyces** (250–973–6433), where you can rent a bike and pedal around the island to see the old Finnish farms and beachfront homes. Choyces, open Monday to Saturday from 10:00 A.M. to 5:00 P.M., also sells Rogers chocolates, cappuccino, and local arts and crafts. An accommodation choice that's definitely different is **Dunroven Bed & Breakfast Sea Cottage Oxen Farm & Forge** (Box 94, Sointula, V0N 3E0; 250–973–6030; bkbooger@island.net). It features a hands-on history experience with an opportunity to work in a forge (and come away with your own handmade iron article—perhaps a candle snuffer or a dinner gong) and work with the two gentle oxen, Doc and Otter (both 3,000-pound Brown Swiss). The owners, Dan and Lauren Klingbiel, offer a full gourmet breakfast ($50 per person, $55 double), and there's also a self-contained beach cottage ($65 for up to four—weekly rates available). Dunroven is open year-round, is adult-oriented, and is located on Donegal Head, 11 miles (18 km) from the village. Use of a hot tub is another bonus in this seaside haven.

Alert Bay has an equally fascinating but quite different history. To the right a short distance after you come off the ferry is the **Alert Bay Info Centre** (116 Fir Street, Bag Service 2800, Alert Bay, V0N 1A0; 250–974–5024; fax: 250–974–5026; info@village.alertbay.bc.ca; alertbay.ca). Here you'll find a collection of paintings depicting the island's historical waterfront, plus photocopied literature about the island's history and attractions, which will set you off handily on your explorations in the North Island's oldest community.

Head back past the ferry terminal along Front Street and past the Anglican **Christ Church** (built in 1892) to the **U'mista Cultural Center** (Box 253, Alert Bay, V0N 1A0; 250–947–5403; umista@island.net; www.umista.org). The name has an interesting origin. In the early days, if captured people were returned to their villages (possibly after a ransom payment or as a result of a retaliatory raid), they were said to have "U'mista." So, too, the return of treasured artifacts from distant museums is a form of U'mista. First learn about these potlatch treasures from the center's informative brochure, watch the twenty-seven-minute award-winning video *Box of Treasures,* then see the famous **Potlatch Collection** of coppers and masks, originally confiscated by the government in 1921. Allow about two hours for a visit. Regular hours are Monday through Friday 9:00 A.M.–5:00 P.M., and the center is open 9:00 A.M. to 6:00 P.M. daily May Day to Labor Day. Call to arrange group visits and to find out about their special events, guided walking tours, and cultural presentations. And don't miss the interesting gift store.

High up on a hill behind the U'mista Cultural Center, next to a traditional Big House, the 173-foot (53.7-m) *World's Tallest Totem Pole* reaches for the sky. Carved in the late 1960s (although not raised until 1973) by a team headed by Jimmy Dick, the fourteen figures on this pole represent some of the tribes of the Kwakwaka'wakw. Among these figures look for Sun Man, Whale, Wolf, Thunderbird, and a bear holding a salmon, indicative of the native people's pride in the land. Down on the waterfront in the center of town, the *'Namgis Burial Ground* is an imposing reminder of Cormorant Island's aboriginal ancestry. In *Ecological Park*, stark, dead

'Namgis Burial Ground totems in Alert Bay

tree trunks stand amid life-filled reflections, a reminder of the island's commercial past. Check the treetops for eagles, and at the information center learn the interesting history of how this park was formed.

And don't leave without doing some whale watching. *Seasmoke Whale Watching* (Box 483, Alert Bay, V0N 1A0; 800–668–6722 in BC only; elsewhere phone/fax: 250–974–5225; seaorca@island.net; www.seaorca. com) runs five- to eight-hour tours ($55 for children, $75–$140 for adults) from late June to early October. You'll be served scrumptious hot muffins and Devonshire tea, while you enjoy the sights and sounds (via hydrophones) of orcas, Dall's porpoises, harbor seals, humpback and gray whales, river otters, and sea lions. There's also an "On the Beach" self-contained unit where you can relax and enjoy the delightful surroundings. Suitable for up to six, it's a great spot to throw fresh fish on the barbecue while enjoying fabulous sunsets from the large deck. Although private, the shops and restaurants are only a minute or two away. If you're visiting mid-summer check the www.seaorca.com site (or phone) to see if the Foot Ferry between Telegraph Cove and Alert Bay is operating.

Janet's Guest House Bed and Breakfast (Box 229, Alert Bay, V0N 1A0; 250–974–5947; janets@island.net; www.alertbayvacationrental.com), on the waterfront at 667 Fir Street, is another cozy spot. Rates at this turn-of-the-century restored home range from $55 single to $70 double—or $160 for the whole house, which is handy for groups. Several other accommodations (including two campgrounds) can also be found on the island. Check the Info Centre Web site, alertbay.ca, for details.

Back on Vancouver Island, information about Port McNeill and surrounds can be found in the new museum building at the *Port McNeill Visitor Info Centre* (Box 129, Port McNeill, V0N 2R0; 250–956–3131; fax: 250–956–3132; pmccc@island.net; www.portmcneill.net). The excellent Web site is loaded with local information.

From Port McNeill, Port Hardy is a pleasant 27 miles (43 km) northwest. Less than 2 miles (3 km) from Port McNeill's center, the West Main logging road crosses the highway, and a few hundred feet north along this road sits the *World's Largest Burl.* Weighing twenty-two and a half tons, with a circumference of 46 feet (14 m), it's worth stopping simply to take in the immensity of this 360-year-old, 80-foot-tall spruce burl. More burl giants are turning up, so it's only a matter of time before Port McNeill is known as the "Burl Capital of the World." As you approach the Port Alice Road, about 10 miles (16 km) northwest of the burl, you might want to polish up the clubs, as along this very scenic road you'll find two small golf courses. One, the *Seven Hills Golf and*

Country Club (250–949–9818), has a restaurant and is about a mile from Highway 19. You'll find here the remains of the only surviving **Hornsby Steam Tractor,** the direct ancestor of all tracked vehicles. Built in England in 1910, it has had a varied past, having been used both for hauling coal in Dawson City in the Yukon and for hauling logs in Holberg Inlet. The other club, the **Port Alice Golf and Country Club** (250–284–3213), is near the town's pulp mill; it's a steep nine-holer, complete with sand traps and water hazards. For information on the area, or accommodation, contact the village of Port Alice at Box 130, Port Alice, V0N 2N0; 250–284–3391; www.vinva.bc.ca/port_alice.htm.

When you reach Port Hardy, you're at the jumping-off point for *BC Ferries'* fifteen-hour sail through the spectacular *Inland Passage* to Prince Rupert, 305 miles (491 km) north. This journey, at approximately $500 for a car and two adults plus a cabin (one-way summer fare, but check www.bcferries.com/fares/inside_passage.html, 250–386–3431, for updates), is a splendid means of seeing as much of BC as possible without retracing your steps. Check the Web site (www.discoverycoast.bcferries.bc.ca) for a virtual tour of the scenic Discovery Coast Passage trip, which takes you to McLoughlin Bay on Bella Bella, Shearwater, Klemtu, Ocean Falls, and Bella Coola, from which you can drive the Freedom Highway to Williams Lake. (See Cariboo Chilcotin section.) The *Discovery Coast Passage* trip allows plenty of time to explore and enjoy activities in these communities.

In *Port Hardy* the staff and volunteers of the small museum at 7110 Market Street (Box 2126, Port Hardy, V0N 2P0; 250–949–8143) will share their knowledge on the logging, mining, and fishing history of the area. Hours vary "according to available funds!" Considering the small area available, the museum shop is well stocked with books and souvenirs.

The locals all have their favorite eating spots, but these three come highly recommended. *Malone's*

Oceanside Bistro (250–949–3050) is a fifteen-minute walk from the town center. It's near the corner of Highway 19 and Granville Street by Klassens G.M. Dealership. Another choice is the *Airport Inn Restaurant* (250–949–8381). The fifteen-minute drive (it's near the airport off Byng Road) is worthwhile for the best Chinese food in town, as well as good quality Canadian cuisine. If it's seafood you're after, the accomplished chef/owner at *Joe's Bar and Grill* (9040 Granville, 250–949–8187) produces consistently delicious meals. It's at the Port Hardy Inn at the corner of Island Highway and Granville Street, a ten-minute walk from town.

Trivia

Sometimes you don't have to go far to land the big one. One year a boy landed a 100-pound halibut off the Port Hardy dock.

If you prefer a pub-style meal, *I.V.'s Quarterdeck Pub* (6555 Hardy Bay Road; 250–949–6922) has just the right mix of local and marine atmosphere. It's a pleasant fifteen-minute walk from town. Head south along Market Street past the Green Apple Restaurant and turn left on Hardy Bay Road at the Robert Scott elementary school. For accommodation and other information, contact the *Port Hardy Visitor Info Centre* (7250 Market Street, Port Hardy, V0N 2P0; 250–949–7622; fax: 250–949–6653; phcc@island.net; www.ph-chamber.bc.ca). And while you're there, check out the totem poles in and around the building.

If you've come this far north, spare time for *Cape Scott Provincial Park* at the far northwest end of the island. To get there head south from the center of Port Hardy on Highway 19 and turn right (west) onto the Holberg Road. Holberg is 28 unpaved miles (45 km) from Port Hardy, and the park entrance is a farther 12 miles (19 km). Watch for the *Shoe Tree,* a visual pun on the north side of the road about 8 miles (12.5 km) from Highway 19. From Holberg the tiny fishing hamlet of *Winter Harbor* is 12 miles (20 km) south. Here, in September, the tuna fishing fleet enlivens this sleepy port.

If you're heading to Cape Scott, you'll pass the *Bernt Ronning Garden* (Box 105, Holberg, V0N 1Z0; 250–288–3724), a heritage site presently being restored by Julia and Ron Moe. It's off the San Josef Main logging road, about 8.5 miles (14 km) west of Holberg. It's blooming with a collection of plants from all over the world. Look for the pair of monkey puzzle trees at the entrance to the old house site, as well as brilliant rhododendrons, daffodils, and countless squirrels. Bring peanuts!

Unbelievably dauntless Danish immigrants started a colony near Cape Scott in the 1890s; however, the absence of safe boat landings and lack of an access road led to the failure of the colony. Many independent homesteaders followed the Danes, but most left when the First World War began. At present giant Sitka spruce, some settlement remnants, and the *Cape Scott Lighthouse* are but some of the points of interest. Spectacular *San Josef Bay* is an easy thirty-five-minute walk on the 1.5-mile (2.5-km) trail from the parking lot at the end of the road. Be aware that the trail to the cape (as well as the beaches on the north side of the park) is often muddy and requires most of a day to hike one way. Stand on the *Cape Scott sand neck,* from where you can view both sides of Vancouver Island, and think back on those brave Danish settlers. But perhaps think further back to earlier inhabitants who stood on this same sand neck. It was the site of a prehistoric massacre, and it is said that the shifting sands sometimes expose human bones. But the history goes even further back. Native legend has it that Cape Scott is the place where the first people originated. For maps and information (and don't hike here without either), visit the Web site, www.bcparks.ca (search "Cape Scott"). Another Web site that has a wealth of detailed information on hiking at Cape Scott is visit-vancouverisland. com/capescott.html. For information on all areas of the North Island, contact Vancouver Island North Visitors Association, Box 1755, Port McNeill, V0N 2R0; phone/fax: (250) 949–9094; toll free: (800) 903–6660; tourism@vinva.bc.ca; www.vinva.bc.ca. For more information covering all of "The Islands" visit www.vancouverisland.com.

PLACES TO STAY ON
THE ISLANDS

ALERT BAY
On the Beach,
Box 483, Alert Bay,
V0N 1A0; phone/fax: (250) 974–5225; (800) 668–6722 in BC only. Self-contained unit on the water, with ocean and mountain views. Sleeps six.

Janet's Guest House Bed and Breakfast,
667 Fir Street, Box 229,
V0N 1A0; (250) 974–5947.
Waterfront rooms or a whole house.

BAMFIELD
Woods End Landing,
380 Lombard Street,
Box 108, Bamfield, V0R 1B0; phone/fax:
(250) 728–3383;
(877) 828–3383 toll free.
Rustic and beachy cabins and duplex accommodation.

CHEMAINUS
Olde Mill House,
9712 Chemainus Road,
Box 1046, Chemainus, V0R 1K0; (250) 416–0049;
(877) 770–6060 toll free;
fax: (250) 246–4457.
Historic home run as a bed-and-breakfast inn.

CORTES ISLAND
Blue Heron B&B,
Box 23, Mansons Landing,
Cortes Island, V0P 1K0;
(250) 935–6584.
Waterfront, secluded.

COWICHAN BAY
Old Farm Bed and Breakfast, 2075 Cowichan Bay Road, Cowichan Bay, V0R 1N0; phone/fax:
(250) 748–6410;
(888) 240–1482 toll free.
Relaxation plus, with water and garden views.

GABRIOLA ISLAND
Casa Blanca By the Sea,
1707 El Verano, Box 77,
Gabriola Island, V0R 1X0;
B&B and self-contained
suite on the beach; kayak
rentals.

HORNBY ISLAND
Sea Breeze Lodge, Big Tree
3–2, Hornby Island, V0R
1Z0; phone/fax: (250)
335–2321; (888) 516–2321
toll free. Waterfront
cottages.

PENDER ISLAND
Brooks Point Glade,
(250) 598–3607;
dgreer@coastnet.com. A
cozy all-season cottage in
the woods, a short walk to
a secluded beach. Two-day
minimum.

PORT MCNEILL
Roseberry Manor
Bed & Breakfast,
810 Nimpkish Heights
Drive, V0N 2R0;
(250) 956–4788.

QUADRA ISLAND
Heriot Bay Inn and Marina,
Heriot Bay Road, Box 100,
Heriot Bay, V0P 1H0;
(250) 285–3322;
fax: (250) 285–2708.
Bed-and-breakfast inn
with camping and marina
facilities.

QUALICUM BEACH
Bahari Bed and Breakfast,
5101 West Island Highway,
V9K 1Z1; (250) 752–9278.
Waterfront luxury ocean-
front bed-and-breakfast
accommodation.

SALTSPRING ISLAND
Anne's Oceanfront
Hideaway, 168 Simson
Road, V8K 1E2;
(888) 474–2663 or
(250) 537–0851. First-class
oceanfront bed-and-
breakfast accommodation.

SOINTULA
Dunroven Bed & Breakfast
Sea Cottage Oxen Farm &
Forge, Box 94, Sointula,
V0N 3E0; (250) 973–6030;
The name says it all. A
hands-on (if you want)
rural beachy experience;
B&B or self-contained
beach cottage.

SOOKE
Billings Spit Beach House,
(250) 642–1910 or toll
free (877) 642–1910. A
modern oceanfront cottage
in a garden setting. The
welcome basket is loaded
with gourmet goodies.

TOFINO
Innchanter,
Hot Springs Cove; (250)
670–1149. Luxury yacht
accommodation. First-class
menu, too.

VICTORIA
Oak Bay Guest House,
1052 Newport Avenue,
V8S 5E3; (800) 575–3812
or (250) 598–3812. Quality
bed-and-breakfast accom-
modation in quiet suburb
near the water.

ZEBALLOS
Mason's Motor Lodge,
203 Pandora Avenue,
Box 10, Zeballos, V0P 2A0;
(250) 761–4044; fax: (250)
761–4074. Historic hospital
building with an attached
restaurant.

PLACES TO EAT ON
THE ISLANDS

CAMPBELL RIVER
Fusilli Grill,
220 Dogwood Street, V9W
2X9; (250) 830–0090;
fax: (250) 830–0093.
Italian fare. Licensed and
very popular.

CORTES ISLAND
The Tak Restaurant,
on Sutil Point Road,
(250) 935–8555. Classy
healthy food.

NANAIMO
Dinghy Dock Pub,
8 Pirate Lane on Protection
Island; (250) 753–2373.
Seasonal.

OAK BAY
Bentley's Seaside Grill (fine
dining). The Snug (pub
fare) at the Oak Bay Beach
Hotel, 1175 Beach Drive,
V8S 2N2; (250) 598–4556;
(800) 668–7758.

Blighty's Bistro,
2006 Oak Bay Avenue;
(250) 592-5111. Absolutely
delicious food.

Penny Farthing Olde Eng-
lish Pub, 2228 Oak Bay
Avenue; (250) 370-9008.
Features live Celtic music
Friday and Saturday
evenings.

Windsor House Tea Room
and Restaurant,
2450 Windsor Road;
(250) 595-3135. Open
Monday to Saturday 10:00
A.M. to 4:00 P.M.

PORT HARDY
Airport Inn Restaurant,
(250) 949-8381, near the
airport. Chinese and
Canadian cuisine.

Joe's Bar and Grill,
9040 Granville;
(250) 949-8187, at the Port
Hardy Inn. Great seafood.

I.V.'s Quarterdeck Pub,
6555 Hardy Bay Road;
(250) 949-6922.

Malone's Oceanside Bistro,
(250) 949-3050, near the
corner of Highway 19 and
Granville.

SALTSPRING ISLAND
Bouzouki Greek Café,
2104 Grace Point Square,
115 Fulford-Ganges Road;
(250) 537-4181.

Moby's Marina Pub,
124 Upper Ganges Road;
(250) 537-5559;
(800) 334-MOBY, on the
Ganges Harbour water-
front. Live entertainment
and pub fare.

SIDNEY
Blue Peter's Pub and
Restaurant,
2270 Harbor Road;
(250) 656-4551. On the
waterfront in Shoal
Harbour. Impressive
seafood!

The Stonehouse Pub &
Restaurant, 2215 Canoe
Cove; (250) 656-3498.
Casual; by the marina.

TOFINO
Pointe Restaurant at
Wickaninnish Inn,
Chesterman Beach;
(800) 333-4604 or
(250) 725-3100. Great
views, great food.

Alley-Way Garden
Café/Costa Azul,
(250) 725-3105,
behind the CIBC bank.
Breakfast, lunch, and
dinner. Vegetarian-style
Mexican food.

VICTORIA
Charters Restaurant at
McMorrans Beach House,
5109 Cordova Bay Road;
(250) 658-5527. On the
beach. The Sandbar Patio
is a popular spot on a
summer day.

John's Place,
723 Pandora Street;
(250) 389-0711. Best free
bread in the city.

Sam's Deli,
805 Government Street;
(250) 382-8424. Casual,
healthy.

Spinnakers Brew Pub and
Guest House,
308 Catherine Street;
(250) 386-2739. Walking
distance along the water-
front from downtown.
Luxury bed-and-breakfast
accommodation also.

The Southwestern Mainland

Whether you want to be part of the madding crowd or retreat into silent wilderness, this region of British Columbia has it all. Starting out in vibrant Vancouver, rated (out of an international survey of 200 cities) in 2002 for the fourth year in a row as the best city in the world to call home, we'll travel east along the Fraser River to the pretty town of Hope, then north through amazingly engineered tunnels in the Fraser Canyon to the mercifully untouched Stein River Valley. Then it's south through the Coast Mountain peaks and the famous Whistler-Blackcomb ski resort to North Vancouver. From here ferries cross Howe Sound to the warm Sunshine Coast, where from Gibsons Landing, immortalized in the CBC production *The Beachcombers*, we'll pass through laid-back villages and holiday homes to Lund, the last vestige of civilization before the yachting paradise of Desolation Sound.

Vancouver

Vancouver is at the center of a very beaten path. With its eclectic mix of residents, there's little challenge in finding elegant eateries, a variety of accommodations, and a huge range of activities, from sailing to skiing to golfing, often possible all on one day, in any season. But where to start?

From almost anywhere in Vancouver, a look up reveals **Grouse Mountain,** at night a sleeping beauty of twinkling lights giving the city a fairy-tale feel. To get there head north through Stanley Park to the Lions Gate Bridge, then east on Marine Drive, north on Capilano Road, and up Nancy Greene Way to the end. For more than 300 stalwarts (5,000 on weekends!), the 1.8-mile (2.9-km) daily climb, **The Grouse Grind,** to the top of this 3,609-foot (1,100-m) pinnacle keeps them in peak form. This hike is NOT a walk in the park, however, so be prepared (water, sturdy footwear, sunscreen, coat, flashlight) for all eventualities. The grade can be as steep as 45 degrees at times—there are no flat stretches. Occasionally, it is closed for poor weather.

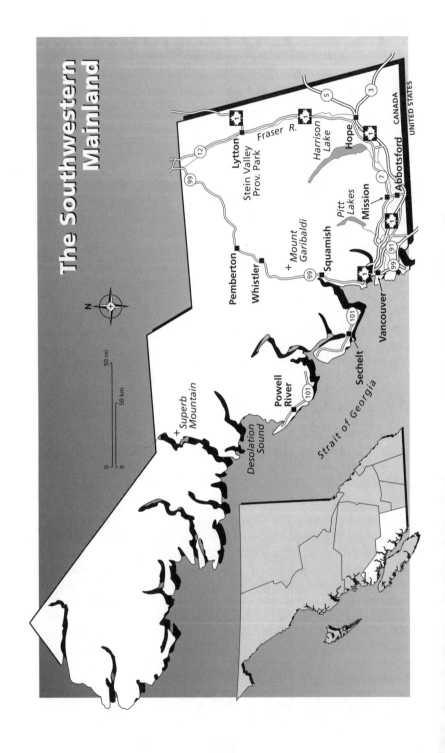

The Southwestern Mainland

THE SOUTHWESTERN MAINLAND

If this is so, or if you're into taking the easy way up, an aerial tramway, *The Grouse Mountain Skyride* (604–980–9311, ext. 6; info@grousemtn. com; www.grousemountain.com), is an eight-minute alternative. At the top view a thirty-five-minute movie *Born to Fly,* Canada's first high-definition video presentation, in the multi-million-dollar *Theatre in the Sky.* Then eat native cuisine in the *hiwus Feasthouse,* impressively decorated with artwork by Coast Salish artist Richard Krentz.

In the cooler months, it's a winter wonderland with skiing, snowboarding, ice-skating, and snowshoeing available. Take advantage of a winter shuttle bus service. *Landsea Tours* makes stops at several downtown hotels. Phone (604) 255–7272 or toll free (877) 669–2277, or visit www. vancouvertours.com for information.

Stop off on the way down at the *Capilano Suspension Bridge* (604–985–7474; fax: 604–985–7479; www.capbridge.com), the world's longest pedestrian suspension bridge, which measures 450 feet (137 m) and sways 230 feet (70 m) above the Capilano River. Here you can enjoy the nature trails or watch native carvers chiseling colorful totem poles at the Big House carving center in *Capilano Park.*

Back at ground level and smack in the center of the city, you'll find a refueling spot at *Harry's Diner* (1078 West Pender Street, near Thurlow; 604–331–0046; www.harrysdiner.com; open weekdays 8:00 A.M.–5:00 P.M.). While sitting beside Billie Holliday and Louis Armstrong photos, enjoy Harry's excellent pizzas, soups, salads, and sandwiches and listen to lively jazz music. For a *loaded* Greek chicken sandwich, try *Uptown Market* (538 West Pender; 604–488–1450). In the Yaletown area, my favorite restaurant is the *Amarcord* (1168 Hamilton Street, 604–681–6500; www. amarcord.ca). Try the sautéed breast of chicken (Petti di Pollo al Whisky) or the marinated salmon (Salmone al Dragoncello). Entrees are in

Trivia

In 1860, four years before the words "In God We Trust" appeared on an American two-cent coin, these same words appeared on New Westminster's coat of arms. Situated 7.5 miles (12 km) south of present-day downtown Vancouver, "New West" was the first town in British Columbia to be incorporated as a municipality.

the $15–$20 range. Or, for something more unusual, **Sushi Bar Wabi Sabi** (4422 West Tenth Avenue; 604–222–8188; www.sushibarwabi sabi.com) is a small restaurant about a mile and a half from the University of British Columbia. Try the Hawaiian Tuna Tatare—a tower of marinated ahi, mango, avocado, and sushi rice—or the Mori-awase Tempura, an assortment of jumbo prawns, scallops, crab, shiitake mushrooms, and vegetables.

While in the university area, visit the **Museum of Anthropology** (6393 N.W. Marine Drive, Vancouver, V6T 1Z2; 604–822–3825; www. moa.ubc.ca), which overlooks the Strait of Georgia and English Bay. The museum houses a fabulous collection of Northwest Coast First Nations artwork, as well as artifacts from around the world. It's open daily in summer from 10:00 A.M. to 5:00 P.M. (till 9:00 P.M. on Tuesday) and in winter Wednesday to Sunday from 11:00 A.M. to 5:00 P.M. Admission is $7.00 for adults, $5.00 for seniors, and $4.00 for students. The family rate is $20.00. Children under six get in free. It's also open Tuesday nights from 5:00 to 9:00 P.M., when admission is free.

A short drive east of the Museum of Anthropology is a cozy yet elegant bed-and-breakfast accommodation. **Escape to the Point B&B** (1318 Cypress Street, Vancouver, V6J 3L2; 604–250–5300; info@ escapetothepoint.com; www.EscapeToThePoint.com) is located on Kitsilano Point, just a five-minute walk to the beaches and the seawall. Choose to eat a gourmet breakfast in your room, or join host Tricia Thomson at the dining-room table. There are endless personal touches, including golf clubs, tennis rackets, and Internet access. It's but a ten-minute walk to cafes, restaurants, bars, and clubs, and a forty-five minute walk to picturesque **English Bay** and Vancouver's famous **Stanley Park.** Close to Escape To The Point B&B is the large, heated **Kitsilano Pool** (2305 Cornwall Street; 604–731–0011), a saltwater pool sloped like a beach; it's open from May through September. Lifeguards are on duty and there are full shower and bathroom facilities as well as a concession stand. At the real (meaning natural) "Kits Beach," seemingly nonstop volleyball games keep players and onlookers amused. For the bagel connoisseur, *Siegel's Bagels* (1883 Cornwall Street; 604–821–0151) is open daily 9:00 A.M. to 5:00 P.M. Siegel's Bagels has been voted Best Place For Bagels year after year in the Georgia Strait's (www.straight.com) *Best of Vancouver* reader's choice.

It's a thirty-minute walk from Kitsilano to the artsy, bustling *Granville Island* (www.granville-island.net), where you'll find a sensuous abundance of eclectic shopping, food, and free entertainment. One of Vancouver's best dining experiences is to be had here at *Bridges Restaurant* (1696 Duranleau Street; 604–687–4400; www.bridgesrestaurant.com). Offering four dining choices (The Restaurant, Bistro Wine Bar, the Pub, and outdoors on the Dock), it's not just the award-winning food that makes Bridges so popular—water, mountain, and city views, especially on a sunny summer afternoon, make for a memorable culinary experience.

Despite all this talk of sunshine, sometimes it rains in Vancouver! Should you need protection from the weather, head over to *The Umbrella Shop* at 1106 West Broadway (604–669–9444), where you'll find an enormous variety of umbrellas—from the foldaway variety, ideal for travelers, to hand-painted originals, an ideal souvenir of your visit.

There's more free entertainment to be found in one of North America's busiest *Chinatown*s. The area, from Carrall Street to Gore Avenue and from Union to Powell Streets, is third in size only to San Francisco and New York's Chinatowns. You'll know you're there by the 15-m *Chinatown Millennium Gate,* which spans East Pender Street between Taylor Street and Shanghai Alley, a block west of Carrall Street near Chinatown's western edge. It's modeled on nineteenth- and twentieth-century inner city gates in Beijing. The gate links Chinatown to Downtown Vancouver and is a portal to the *Silk Road*, where you'll find ancient Chinese remedies, delicious dim sum, and all kinds of exotic teas and spices. Don't miss the *Sam Kee Building* at 8 West Pender Street, listed in the *Guinness Book of World Records* as the world's thinnest office building. Built in 1913 out of spite for the city fathers who had expropriated most of the property, it's all of 6 feet (1.8 m) deep.

Sample refreshing teas at *Ten Ren Tea and Ginseng,* 550 Main Street (at the corner of Keefer), then take your camera along to capture some of the details on the traditional gate framing the entrance to the *Chinese Cultural Center*. It's in front of the *Dr. Sun Yat-Sen Garden* (578 Carrall Street; 604–662–3207; fax: 604–682–4008; sunyatsen@telus.net; www.vancouverchinesegarden.com), an authentic Ming Dynasty garden and

British Columbia is Canada's most attractive film and television location, generating a record $630 million in direct spending to the provincial economy in 1997. More than 25,000 British Columbians are employed in the industry, which produces approximately twenty TV series. Past successes include The X-Files. The largest film production ever completed in the province was Michael Crichton's Eaters of the Dead.

the first of its kind to be built either inside or outside China since 1492. Admission to the garden is $8.25 adults, $6.75 seniors, $5.75 students. Children under five get in free. The family rate is $18.00. These prices include tea and a forty-five-minute tour. The gift shop has some delightful souvenirs.

But if it's Canadian ambience you want to be ensconced in, stay at the 1897 *"O Canada" House B&B* (1114 Barclay Street, Vancouver, V6E 1H1; toll free 877–688–1114; 604–688–0555; fax: 604–488–0556; ocanadahouse@home.com; www. ocanadahouse.com). This Victorian-style heritage home is located in a quiet downtown neighborhood, within walking distance of St. Pauls Hospital, Stanley Park, and the beaches. In 1909 Mr. Ewan Buchan, the original owner, wrote Canada's national anthem here; it was first performed in The Canadian Club in Vancouver on February 9, 1910. At "O Canada" House you'll be served sherry in the front parlor in the early evening, and a three-course gourmet breakfast. Off the dining room, there's a "guest's own kitchen," stocked with complimentary snacks, tea, coffee, and juices. Rates in high season range from $185, or if you want to be totally decadent, spend $255 ($195 in winter) for the Penthouse Suite—all 750 square feet of the third floor—from which you can enjoy Vancouver's superb skyline.

For travelers on a budget, there's a comfortable San Francisco–style, elegantly renovated, hundred-year-old hotel within walking distance of just about everything in Vancouver's heart. At the *Victorian Hotel* (514 Homer Street, Vancouver, V6B 2V6; toll free 877–681–6369; 604–681–6369; fax: 604–681–8776; reservations@victorianhotel.ca; www.victorian-hotel.com) you'll be central to the theater district, Gastown, and the waterfront. If you saw the Tommy Lee Jones's movie *Double Jeopardy,* you've seen the Victorian! Breakfast is included in the reasonable rates (from $59 for a double), which belie the value offered. I particularly loved the hardwood floors, high ceilings, solid wood furniture, and tiled bathrooms that gave it a modern yet 1800s feel.

Before leaving the Vancouver area, discover for yourself how close the wilderness is to this lively city by experiencing a day-paddle (including an impressive salmon barbecue lunch on an uninhabited island) in Indian Arm with *Lotus Land Tours Inc.* (2005–1251 Cardero Street, Vancouver, V6G 2H9; 604–684–4922 or 800–528–3531; fax: 604–684–

4921; info@lotuslandtours.com; www.lotusland tours.com). No experience is necessary. You'll be picked up from your hotel and soon be paddling in romantic wooden canoes, designed both for safety and to put you close enough to water level to give you that eyeball-to-eagle feel. Lotus Land Tours also offers the only orca whale-watching trip from the downtown Vancouver and North Shore areas—where they pick you up from your doorstep. A light lunch is served aboard 42-foot, covered, high-speed Zodiacs (unique on the coast). The trip is three to five hours long, and there's an 85 percent chance of a whale sighting.

For complete information on other city activities, contact the **Vancouver Tourist InfoCentre,** Plaza Level, 200 Burrard Street, Vancouver, V6C 3L6; (604) 683–2000, fax: (604) 682–6839; www. tourismvancouver.com.

East to Abbotsford

From Vancouver the Trans-Canada Highway leads southeast through Surrey to Langley, the Horse Capital of BC. If you're interested in BC history, visit the **Fort Langley National Historic Site of Canada** (23433 Mavis Avenue, Box 129, Fort Langley, V1M 2R5; 604–513–4777; fax: 604–513–4798; fort.langley@pc.gc.ca; www.parks canada.gc.ca/fortlangley). Open to the general public (admission charged) from March 1 to October 31 and to schools and other pre-booked groups weekdays from November 1 to the end of February, this fascinating site will let you discover BC's history. Established in 1827 as

BC-style Recycling

For sixty years two British Columbia sisters, Babe Warren and Dorothea Stafford, have mailed the same birthday card to each other between the Lower Mainland and Victoria. That's 120 trips across the Strait of Georgia via Canada Post, and not once has the card been overdue. Interestingly, the card depicts a penny-pinching Scotsman bragging about a two-for-one card bargain.

Top Annual Events on the Southwestern Mainland

Brackendale Winter Eagle Festival and Count, Brackendale; January; (604) 898–3333

Lytton Days, Lytton; May 24 long weekend; (250) 455–2523

Hope Seabird Island First Nations Festival, May; (604) 796–6821

Alcan International Dragon Boat Festival, Vancouver; June; (604) 688–2382

Annual Mmquam River Whitewater Festival, Squamish; late June; (604) 898–5498

Abbotsford Berry Festival, Abbotsford; July; (604) 850–6547

Harrison Festival of the Arts, Harrison; July; (604) 796–3664

International Comedy Festival, Vancouver; July; (604) 683–0883

Festival of the Written Arts, Sechelt; August; (250) 885–9631

Chilliwack Bluegrass Festival, Chilliwack; September; (604) 792–2069

a Hudson's Bay Company fur trading post, it's also the location where, in 1858, mainland BC was proclaimed a crown colony. You'll find here costumed interpreters ready to guide you through the original storehouse and several reconstructed buildings, as well as exhibits, demonstration vignettes, gold panning, a video/audio tour, a picnic shelter, and a gift shop. You can easily spend a day here lost in BC's engaging history. Take the 232nd Street North exit to the stop sign on Glover Road. Turn right and follow the BEAVER signs to the village of Fort Langley. Just before the railway tracks, turn right and head to the end of Mavis Avenue.

From the history of BC to a winery with a history of nine generations of traditional grape growing—*Domaine de Chaberton Estates* (1064 216th Street, Langley, V2Z 1R3; 604–530–1736 or 888–DDC–WINE [332–9463]; info@domainedechaberton.com; www.domainedechaberton.com) is the only winery in the Fraser Valley. This winery exists where it does because its owner recognized the area's unique wine-growing characteristics. Vintner Claude Violet, whose family has been in the wine-making business since 1644, came from the south of France in 1981 and established the winery both for its closeness to the Vancouver market and its ideal microclimate (it gets 56 percent less rainfall than downtown Vancouver). It started out as a farm gate winery and, after numerous awards, grew to be an estate winery. It is now working on expanding its export business. Claude's wife, Inge, oversees this part of the operation and the on-site wine shop as well as *The Bacchus Bistro* (604–530–9694), which serves such culinary delights as fresh ahi tuna and wild Texas boar rack. Winery tours are held daily at 2:00 and 4:00 P.M. and by appointment for large groups. The shop and a tasting room are open Monday to Saturday from 10:00 A.M. till 6:00 P.M. and from 11:00 A.M. till 6:00 P.M. Sunday. To find Domaine de Chaberton from Fort Langley, take Glover Road to 216th Street, turn left, and stay on 216th till Sixteenth Avenue (approximately twenty minutes). At the junction of 216th and

Sixteenth, you'll see a WINERY sign. It's about 0.6 mile (1 km) farther on. If you're coming directly from Vancouver, take Highway 1 east to the 200th Street exit. Head south on 200 to Sixteenth Avenue. Turn left (east) to 216th Street, then follow the directions above.

Highway 1A travels east to Abbotsford, Canada's raspberry capital, and the place to be in early August when awe-inspiring aerobatics such as the Wall of Fire and incredible wing-walking are performed at the world-famous three-day-long **Abbotsford International Airshow** (604–852–8511; fax: 604–852–6093; info@abbotsfordairshow.com; www.abbotsfordairshow.com). Canada's Snowbirds can be seen here performing loops, rolls, and their famous "Candle Burst" formation, as well as many other thrilling events.

The Fraser River Valley

ross the Fraser River north of Abbotsford to Mission's **Fraser River Heritage Park** (7974 Mary Street, Box 3341, Mission, V2V 4J5; 604–826–0277). Folk festivals, car shows, children's art classes, twilight concerts, and a jam-packed **Canada Day** (July 1) keep the park humming through the warmer months. A concession booth serves light lunches and delicious homemade scones with blackberry jelly (prepared by volunteers in the fall). It's a pretty spot to stop off for a picnic, offering panoramic views of the Fraser River Valley and Mount Baker.

If you want to stay in the area, there's lovely accommodation and delicious home baking at the **Fence Post Lane Bed & Breakfast,** 4 miles (6.6 km) west of Mission at 8575 Gaglardi Street, Mission, V4S 1B2; (877) 833–7009, (604) 820–7009; fax: (604) 820–4974; mperdue@direct.ca; www.bbcanada.com/906.htm. Room rates range from $50 to $75 double in this peaceful four-star country rancher, close to lakes and walking trails. Look for the blue B&B signs on Highway 7.

Three and a half kilometers northeast of Mission, high up over the Lougheed Highway, you'll see (or hear) the distinctive bells in the tower of the **Westminster Abbey Benedictine Monastery** (34224 Dewdney Trunk Road; 604–826–8975). The bells ring for fifteen minutes on Sundays

Trivia

January 1, 1922. Although no injuries resulted, a traffic accident at a Surrey intersection on this date will go down as one of the most bizarre in history. Two cars collided head-on, one on the left side of the road, the other on the right. The driver on the right, a Mr. Claude Harvie who was a Surrey municipal worker, had been up all night placing signs to warn drivers of a change in the traffic laws: Cars were now required to be driven on the right side of the road.

before the 10:00 A.M. Mass and the 4:30 P.M. Vespers. The Benedictine monks invite visitors from 2:00 to 4:00 P.M. Sundays and from 1:30 to 4:00 P.M. weekdays to see their beautiful church. Its 22-foot-high stained-glass windows (sixty-four in all), combined with a tall dome of colored glass rising above the altar, make it an architectural beauty. To get there turn left off Highway 7 onto Dewdney Trunk Road. If you come to the DUCKS CROSSING sign, you've passed it. It's also accessible from Stave Lake Street, just west of Mission's Heritage Park.

Leave the serenity of the monastery and head back to Highway 7. East of Dewdney Trunk Road there's another kind of serenity at the *Hatzic Rock Site,* or, more officially, *XÁ:YTEM Longhouse Interpretive Centre* (35087 Lougheed Highway, Mission, V2V 6T1; 604–820–9725; fax: 604–820–9735; xaytem@dowco.com; www.xaytem.museum.bc.ca/ xaytem/). This national historic site is British Columbia's oldest dwelling—it's even older than the Pyramids and Stonehenge. The remains of a semisubterranean house, between 5,000 and 6,000 years old, were discovered in 1990 by Gordon Mohs, an archaeologist for the Stó:lo Nation. Since then, this Coast Salish Indian group and scientists from the University of British Columbia have uncovered tens of thousands of artifacts, some radiocarbon-dated 9,000 years, revealing a long-term Stó:lo presence and evidence of a ceremonially inclined trader people. Kids can enjoy an archaeology tour during which they can sift for artifacts, and adults can try their hand at working with inner cedar bark; everyone can enjoy the storytelling. Two pit houses (underground circular winter dwellings accessed through the top by a notched ladder), examples of homes used by First Nations people over thousands of years, are open to visitors.

The rock, or *XÁ:YTEM,* (pronounced "hay-tum") is associated with an early period in Stó:lo history when Xexá:ls threw three chiefs into a heap and transformed them to stone for not teaching the people the written language he gave them. The center is open March to June and September to November weekdays from noon to 4:00 P.M. In July and August it is open daily from 11:00 A.M. to 5:00 P.M. Maximum admission for a family of four is $15.00.

There's more history at the *Mission Museum* (604–826–1011, fax: 604–826–1017), where you'll discover the legends of rivers, rails, and robbers. And one more activity in the area that's sure to get the adrenaline flowing is a nail-biting afternoon at *Mission Raceway Park* (604–826–6315; info@missionraceway.com; www.missionraceway.com), just west of town. Quarter-mile drag races, motocross racing, or the sports car road course run most weekends March through October. For more informa-

Sasquatch Madness

S asquatch (from the Coast Salish word sesqac), British Columbia's infamous hairy giant, was not a very popular fellow. His trick was to come down from the mountains, seize young Indian maidens, and seal their eyes with pitch, thus preventing them from knowing their whereabouts. What he did with them is anybody's guess.

Keep your eyes peeled (or pitched) for him as you pass through the Fraser River area. Every May, eyewitnesses, scientists, believers, and nonbelievers gather in Harrison Hot Springs at the Sasquatch Forum to examine the latest evidence. Sasquatch Hikes, Sasquatch Golf, Bigfoot Races, and Sasquatch Parades all add to the craziness.

tion on other activities and accommodations in the Mission area, contact the **Mission Visitor Info Centre,** 34033 Lougheed Highway, Mission, V2V 5X8; (604) 826–6914; fax: (604) 826–5916; mission chamber@telus.net; www.missionchamber.bc.ca.

The Lougheed Highway, or the "Scenic 7" as locals like to refer to it, curls east beside the Fraser toward **Harrison Mills,** "the Home of the Bald Eagle," 24 miles (40 km) past Mission. Hundreds of magnificent eagles frequent the area from November through February, and in spring and summer the Harrison River is a fisherman's paradise, with large runs of coho, steelhead, and sockeye salmon. In late November the area features the **Harrison/Chehalis Bald Eagle Festival.** (Contact the Mission Chamber of Commerce for more information at 604–826–6914, or the organizer at 604–463–2507; driftwood@bc.sympatico.ca.)

Nearby, **Kilby Historic Store and Farm** (215 Kilby Road, Box 55, Harrison Mills, V0M 1L0; 604–796–9576; fax: 604–796–9592; info@kilby.ca; www.kilby.ca), 1 mile (1.6 km) off Highway 7, is a must-stop attraction. It's a 1920s living history site, with a general store museum, surrounding heritage buildings, and a working farm. There's also the Waterloo Farm Gift Shop and Harrison River Restaurant to make for complete visitor services. It's open daily April to October from 11:00 A.M. to 5:00 P.M., but for the rest of the year, only on weekends from 11:00 A.M. to 4:00 P.M.

Continue enjoying the "days of yore" at the small museum run by the **Agassiz-Harrison Historical Society** (Box 313, 6947 Lougheed Highway, Agassiz, V0M 1A0; 604–796–3545). It's open daily 10:00 A.M. to 4:00 P.M. from mid-May until mid-September. There's no charge, but donations are welcome.

The village of **Harrison Hot Springs** lies 4 miles (6.5 km) north. Idylli-cally set on Harrison Lake, southwestern British Columbia's largest lake, below snow-covered 7,825-foot (2,385-m) Mount Breakenridge, Harrison Hot Springs, with fabulous **Sasquatch Provincial Park** (www.bcparks.ca, search word "Sasquatch") just 4 miles (6.5 km) beyond, is a popular spot for a beach holiday.

Every September the words "Ladies and gentlemen, start your buckets" are heard when Harrison Hot Springs hosts the **World Championship Sand Sculpture Competition** (604–796–3425; info@harrisand.org; www.harrisand.org). "Master Sand Sculptors" pit their skills against each other, with solos and international teams competing for $35,000 in prize money and bragging rights to the title of world champion. There's a small fee to view the sculptures. The *Guinness Book of Records* gives Harrison Hot Springs a mention as the site where the world's tallest hand-built sand cas-tle, a 21.5-foot (6.5-m) Christmas tree, was built. With no tides to wash them away, the fantastic sand creations are on display until early October.

Half a block back from the sandy beach, close to shops and restaurants and with a pretty river edging the garden, **Harrison Heritage House and Kottage Bed and Breakfast** (312 Lillooet Avenue, Box 475, Harri-son Hot Springs, V0M 1K0; 604–796–9552 or 800–331–8099; rreyerse @bbharrison.com; www.bbharrison.com) has romantic rooms in the $100–$150 range. Deluxe rooms come with private Jacuzzis and/or fire-places. Separate self-contained riverside cottages are also available.

Nearby, meals at **The Old Settler Pub** (222 Cedar Avenue; 604–796–9722; oldsettler@uniserve.com; www.oldsetter.com) are filling. Humorous chain-saw carvings decorate the log building where, on the patio, I found a pleasant spot to enjoy a generous and delicious salmon dinner. For more information on where to eat and stay in Harrison Hot Springs, contact the Visitor Info Centre, 499 Harrison Hot Springs Road, Box 255, Harrison Hot Springs, V0M 1K0; (604) 796–3425; fax: (604) 796–3188; www.harrison.ca.

Hope

Log carvings also decorate **Hope,** dubbed "the Chain-saw Carving Cap-ital," 20 miles (32 km) east of Agassiz on the south side of the Fraser River. It's an incredibly pretty spot, set on a large, flat plain deep in among the Coastal and Cascade mountains.

Hollywood has discovered Hope's beauty, too. *First Blood* (first of the Rambo series) is the best-known of the movies to emerge from Hope.

THE SOUTHWESTERN MAINLAND

Trivia

Rumor has it that when filming of First Blood *was announced, chaos struck Hope. Hundreds of people wanted to be featured in the film as extras, but out of 550, only 100 were chosen. A rumor circulated that no one taller than Sylvester Stallone was chosen as an extra.*

The Visitor InfoCentre (919 Water Avenue, Box 370, Hope, V0X 1L0; 604–869–2021; fax: 604–869–2160; info@hopechamber.bc.ca; www.hope chamber.bc.ca) has developed a walking and driving tour of the film's key locations.

One of these is in the **Coquihalla Canyon Provincial Park,** site of the **Othello-Quintette Tunnels** (called Chapmans Gorge in the movie), an amazing engineering feat, which, at a cost of $300,000, is perhaps the most expensive mile of railway track in the world. The chain of now-abandoned tunnels was built between 1911 and 1918 to complete the Kettle Valley Railway. Look for the cliff above the stump at Tunnel No. 2, where Rambo's spectacular canyon jump took place. Other movies shot in this area are *Shoot to Kill, White Fang II, K2, Fire with Fire, The Stick Up, New Cardiff,* and *Far from Home: Adventures of Yellow Dog.* To get there take Kawkawa Lake Road from the ball park on Sixth Avenue, passing the cemetery and Kawkawa Lake to Othello Road, a distance of about 3 miles (5 km). Turn right onto Tunnels Road and then into a parking lot. Private campgrounds, such as **Othello Tunnels Campground and RV Park** (67851 Othello Road, Box 2009, Hope, V0X 1L0; toll free: 877–869–0543; phone/fax: 604–869–9448; othello camp@uniserve.com; www.othellotunnels. com) operate year-round.

Trivia

On January 9, 1965, an earthquake, with its epicenter in the Nicolum Valley, caused a devastating landslide about 11 miles (18 km) east of Hope, destroying almost 2 miles (3 km) of the Hope-Princeton Highway. More than 1,600 million cubic feet (46 million m³) of snow, rock, and earth crashed in seconds from the 6,500-foot-high (2,000-m) mountain ridge that formed the north side of the Nicolum Creek valley. Four people in three vehicles were killed—two were never found.

Back in Hope forget movie-mania and spend a quiet minute in **Christ Church** at the corner of Park and Fraser Streets. Consecrated in 1861, this Anglican church is the oldest continuously active church on the mainland still on its original foundations. (But then that's a debatable subject in nearby Yale!) Its builder and first vicar was Reverend Alexander St. David Francis Pringle. He arrived in the midst of the Cariboo Gold Rush, when thousands of young men were gathered in hope of striking it rich. Pringle felt that the men needed access to good reading material, so he began raising funds for a building to carry "respectable and readable newspapers of various nations and politics, together with all the standard reviews and periodicals." The result, on

Toll revenues collected on the Coquihalla Highway during 2002 exceeded $42 million.

December 1, 1859, was the first library on British Columbia's mainland.

With so much history (discover more at the *Hope Museum* next to the Visitor InfoCentre, 604–869–7322) and such a diversity of outdoor activities—everything from rafting to golf to hiking—in this area, stay a while in one of Hope's many motels (check the glass case outside the InfoCentre) or book into the *Evergreen Bed and Breakfast* (1208 Ryder Street, Box 811, Hope, V0X 1L0; 604–869–9918; fax: 604–869–3763; midway@uniserve.com; www.pixsell-bc.ca/bb/2139.htm) with its lovely mountain views. It operates year-round and is at the corner of the Old Hope-Princeton Way and Ryder Street. Rates are $59 to $75. A block away there's a popular cafe called *The Home Restaurant* (665 Hope-Princeton Highway; 604–869–5558), where you'll find thick clam chowder, barbecue back ribs, pies, and other home-style meals in large portions.

Before leaving Hope stop at the *Hope Station House* (604–869–9495) at the junction of Highway 1 and Old Hope-Princeton Way—also known as Rainbow Junction. This smoke-free restaurant, community arts center, and art gallery is located in the restored 1916 Great Northern Railway Station. Specializing in homemade soups and sandwiches and wonderful desserts, it's open between 8:00 A.M. and 8:00 P.M. daily. The *Upstairs Gallery* (located upstairs!) features various artists' work.

From Hope you can either head north through the Fraser River Canyon via the Trans-Canada Highway 1, northeast via the Coquihalla (toll) Highway 5 to Merritt and Kamloops, or east to *Manning Provincial Park* along the Crowsnest Highway 3, a beautiful but winding extravaganza through the Cascades that leads to Princeton and the Okanagan.

"This is Canada!" was my thought as I took the latter choice. I was passing snow-powdered alpine larch at the 4,400-foot (1,341-m) Alison Pass and had read there were 175,440 acres (71,000 ha) more of this delightful park. If you're there in June, take a twenty-minute walk through colorful *Rhododendron Flats,* close to the highway about 6 miles (10 km) east of the marmot carving at the west gate. For park information visit www.bcparks.ca (search word "Manning"). *Manning Park Resort* (Box 1480, Hope, V0X 1L0; 800–330–3321 toll free for reservations; 250–840–8822; fax: 250–840–8848; info@manningpark resort.com; www. manningparkresort.com) offers the only guest services in the park with accommodation (lodge, cabins, and chalets), a store, dining (a cafe, lounge, and dining room), equipment rentals, and programs for a host of summer and winter out-door activities. The easterly route to Princeton continues in the Okanagan-Similkameen sec-tion. Our journey here, though, follows the route the gold seekers took along the raging Fraser River north to Yale.

The Fraser Canyon

At the WELCOME TO HISTORIC YALE sign, 15 miles (24 km) north of Hope in the Fraser Canyon and just south of the town, a steep hike called the *Spirit Caves Trail* begins. The round-trip is about 3 miles (5 km), and the elevation gain is 1,640 feet (500 m). It's worth the climb for the great views of Yale and the Fraser River. Allow about three hours to enjoy it. But if you prefer to just amble through a lush meadow loaded with history, the *Pioneer Cemetery,* directly across from the trailhead, is one of the prettiest old cemeteries in the province. The ages on many head-stones (dating back to 1862) hint at stories of lives prematurely taken.

At the tiny but classy *Yale Museum* (Yale and District Historical Society, P.O. Box 74, Yale, V0K 2S0; 604–863–2324; info@historicyale.ca; www.historicyale.ca) you'll learn of the lives of these pioneers who sought their gold fortunes between the 1850s and the 1880s, when Yale was the head of navigation for the Fraser. The costumed museum staff show a thirty-minute film on Yale's history and arrange guided tours that include an Old Yale Town Tour, a Float trip to Hope (via Fraser River Rafting Expedi-tions), and a Pioneer Cemetery tour. As well, you can learn the fun and skill involved in gold panning. The museum is open Thursday to Monday 10:00 A.M. to 5:00 P.M. from mid-May to early September and only on weekends from September 8 to October 7. Admission prices range from free to $5.50. Tour and gold panning costs are extra.

Included in the town tour is a peek next door at the beautiful *St. John the Divine Anglican Church,* one of the oldest churches on the BC mainland and a designated BC Heritage Site.

To help you enjoy your stay in Yale, there are a couple of bed-and-breakfast establishments in the area ready to pamper you. *Teague House Bed & Breakfast* at 30950 Trans-Canada High-way (Box 10, Yale, V0K 2S0; toll free: 800–363–7238; 604–863–2336; fax: 604–863–2355;

Pioneer Cemetery in Yale

frre@uniserve.com; www.teaguehouse.com) is an 1866 heritage house with lovely views of Fraser Canyon. Get adventurous and sign up for a rafting expedition with **Fraser River Rafting** (www.fraserraft.com; same contact information as the Teague House). Rates for the B&B start at $70 double to $200 for the whole house; a one-day Boston Bar to Yale rafting trip, including lunch, is $105. Another B&B, **Chrysalis Retreat** (31286 Douglas Street, Box 50, Yale, V0K 2S0; 604–863–0055; info@chrysalisretreat.com; www.chrysalisretreat.com), features a hot tub, a sauna, and your own registered massage therapist/hydrotherapist to help relax you on the long journey. Ideal for families or a romantic getaway, this year-round retreat has rates starting at $85.

North of Yale is the wonderfully named **Spuzzum** (from the Thompson Native word meaning "little flat"). Less than a mile north of Spuzzum, you'll find **Alexandra Bridge Provincial Park,** a pleasant, 136-acre (55-ha) spot to stop for a break. In the heart of this park is the historic suspension bridge for which the park is named. First built in 1863, it was twice destroyed, only to be rebuilt in its present form in 1926. A ten-minute walk along parts of the now-abandoned highway brings you to this elegant old bridge.

Back on Highway 1 you're into the spectacular *Fraser Canyon* tunnels. Between Yale and Boston Bar, 26 miles (42 km) north, you'll remove your sunglasses seven times as you pass through these feats of engineering with names such as Saddle Rock, Sailor Bar, Hell's Gate, and the 2,000-foot (610-m) China Bar Tunnel, one of North America's longest. Here enterprising Chinese found their golden mother lode after reworking an old, supposedly exhausted, area.

There's little gold today other than that in the glint of the turbulent rapids seen from the airtram at *Hell's Gate,* the narrowest—110 feet (33 m)—point of the Fraser River. The canyon reminded early explorer Simon Fraser of "The Gates of Hell." It was hell, indeed, for millions of salmon when, in 1914, with the building of the second railroad, the canyon wall slid into the river, causing British Columbia's worst environmental disaster. It almost destroyed the Fraser River salmon run. Several gigantic fishways now assist approximately two million sockeye salmon yearly to reach their spawning grounds.

You can look down on these fishways from the comfortable safety of a twenty-five-passenger cabin run by *Hell's Gate Airtram Inc.* (Box 129, Hope, V0X 1L0; 604–867–9277; fax: 604–867–9279; info@hellsgate

Worth Seeing/Doing on the Southwestern Mainland

Minter Gardens (604–794–7191 or 888–646–8377; minter@minter.org; www.minter.org). *Twenty-seven acres of brilliant show gardens, near Chilliwack; open April through October.*

The Lookout! at Harbour Centre Tower (555 West Hastings Street; 604–689–0421; www.vancouverlookout.com). *Enjoy the 360° view to orient yourself in Vancouver.*

VanDusen Botanical Garden (5251 Oak Street, Vancouver; 604–878–9274). *Glorious gardens. Open year-round from 10:00 A.M.*

Burnaby Village Museum (6501 Deer Lake Avenue, Burnaby; 604–293–6501; mail@burnabyparksrec.org; www.burnabyparksrec.org). *Nine-acre historical village.*

Vancouver Museum (1100 Chestnut Street; 604–736–4431; fax: 604–736–5417; www.vanmuseum.bc.ca). *First-rate museum with great views of city.*

Gulf of Georgia Cannery National Historic Site (12138 Fourth Avenue, Richmond, V7E 3J1; 604–664–9009). *In the village of Steveston, with many excellent seafood restaurants nearby.*

airtram.com; www.hellsgateairtram.com), the steepest nonsupported air tram in North America, which runs mid-April to mid-October. At the lower terminal there's the **Salmon House Restaurant** (excellent salmon steaks and chowder), the **Fudge Factory** (ice creams and more than thirty flavors of homemade fudge), gift shops, and a fisheries display. Fares range from $8.00 for kids six and older to $32.00 for an immediate family. If you watch all three movies, including the award-winning video *Run, Sockeye, Run,* you can easily spend two hours on the *other side.* And you will have passed where, in Simon Fraser's words, "no man should venture."

The tunnels end at Boston Bar, but from here, there's another 26 miles (42 km) of Fraser River views to Lytton. Just before Lytton, located in Nlaka'pamux tribal territory, the Siska (meaning "uncle") Museum, part of the **Siska Art Gallery** (Box 519, Lytton, V0K 1Z0; 250–455–0072; fax: 250–455–2539; siskaib@goldtrail.com) displays soapstone carvings, wooden masks, beaded crafts, drums, and dreamcatchers. They're open year-round. You can't miss the yellow SISKA MUSEUM sign up on the highway.

We leave the Trans-Canada at Lytton, often named on weather broadcasts as Canada's "hotspot." Here the earthy Fraser meets the pretty, aqua-green Thompson River, and we discover another hotspot, the ecologically important Stein Valley, the spiritual home of the Nlaka'pamux Nation. In past years environmentalists and First Nations people have fought to preserve this wilderness area from the logger's ax. In 1995 the 264,865 acres (107,191 ha) of the Stein Valley were permanently protected as the **Stein Valley Nlaka'pamux Heritage Provincial Park.** For day hikers, there's good hiking in the lower Stein Valley near Lytton. More in-depth information (and maps) on the 47-mile (75-km) Stein Valley trail through to the Pemberton area is available on the Web site: www.bcparks.ca (search word "Stein").

Lytton is more than just Canada's hot spot. It's also renowned as the Whitewater Rafting Capital of Canada. Learn more about rafting trips available at the **Lytton InfoCentre** (400 Fraser Street, Box 460, Lytton, V0K 1Z0; 250–455–2523; fax: 250–455–6669; hotspot@goldtrail.com; www.lytton.ca). Next door to the InfoCentre is a volunteer-run museum that houses a portrait of Sir Edward Bulwer-Lytton, for whom the village was named. Several pieces from Lytton's rail and fire department history are displayed outside, and there are picnic tables available for

Trivia

British Columbia's first railway was built between Seton and Anderson Lakes in 1860. This 3-mile-long (almost 5 km), narrow-gauge, wooden railway was powered by mules.

public use. If you'd prefer to eat inside, *Acacia Leaf Cafe* on Main Street next to the bank is open for lunch and dinner, and has healthy soups and hearty suppers in the $10–$12 range.

Kumsheen Rafting Resort (Box 30, Lytton, V0K 1Z0; 250–455–2296 or toll free 800–663–6667; fax: 250–455–2297; rafting@kumsheen. com; www.kumsheen.com), located on the Trans-Canada Highway, 4 miles (6 km) northeast of Lytton, runs thrilling rafting trips that range from three hours to six days long. A Devil's Gorge Run costs $99 ($69 for youths ages ten to sixteen), or a one-day Raging River trip from Spences Bridge to Lytton, during which you'll pass through eighteen adrenaline-pumping rapids with such spine-chilling names as Jaws of Death and Washing Machine, costs $125 (youths $99).

Over the years (since 1973), the headquarters have been enhanced to include a swimming pool, disc golf, hot tub, a restaurant, beach volleyball courts, riverview campsites (stay-over packages from $19 for adults, $12 for youth), and uniquely decorated wood-floor tent cabins. These contain two double beds, all linen, and cost $85. In true rafting fun games boards and ironing boards (must look neat in the rapids!) are set up, ready to use. And the Kumsheen coffee! Stop off for a cup of Kumsheen's best Colombian, or enjoy breakfast (7:30 to 9:30 A.M.) or dinner (5:30 to 7:30 P.M.) at the open-air *Cutting Board Restaurant* and maybe sign up for a rip-roaring trip down a raging river.

The Sea to Sky Highway

*H*ighway 12 (from the green bridge at the north end of Lytton) follows the dizzying, murky Fraser River, past black trampoline-style tarpaulins shading the world's largest ginseng farms for 40 miles (65 km) north to **Lillooet** (see section on Cariboo Chilcotin Coast). Here we leave the Fraser River and join Highway 99 (previously the rough-and-ready but now paved Duffey Lake Road), where stunning views of emerald lakes and icy glaciers lead to Mount Currie and Pemberton. Still on Highway 99, the **Sea to Sky Highway,** we pass North America's number-one ski resort at Whistler. By the time we reach Horseshoe Bay, north of Vancouver, we will have traversed a highway so aptly dubbed "the gateway to the spectacular."

The Duffey Lake Road is tortuous and remote. But, as attested to by movie crews shooting Subaru advertising, its beauty is being broadcast universally. It follows the fast-coursing Cayoosh Creek steeply down to Duffey Lake, Joffre Lakes, and Lillooet Lake.

My favorite photo-op stop-off on this highway is *Joffre Lakes Provincial Park.* The view from *Lower Joffre Lake* of glacier-laden peaks (Mount Matier and Mount Joffre) across the reedy, turquoise lake (1500 feet from the parking lot— a short walk through glorious forest) is spectacular, especially in the late afternoon. A steep trail (with more views of the *Matier Glacier*) leads to Middle and Upper Joffre Lakes. Camping is permitted at the latter. This fireweed-lined part of the highway between Joffre Lakes and Pemberton is extremely steep and winding. Oh to have been riding a motorbike! There are several runaway truck lanes and signs advising trucks to maintain 10-km-per-hour speeds. Several one-lane bridges cross Cayoosh, Gott, and Boulder Creeks. At the Cayoosh Creek bridge, there's an excellent view of the creek.

Organic is the key word at *Sturdy's North Arm Farm* (1888 Sea to Sky Highway 99, Pemberton, V0N 2K0; 604–894–5379; fax: 604–894–6650; northarmfarm@canada.com). Drop in to see what's in season at the Sturdy family's fifty-five-acre (22-ha) mixed farm. Bring your bucket along to load up with delicious raspberries and strawberries, fresh greens and herbs, specialty vegetables, nugget potatoes, garlic, sweet

Kids' Stuff on the Southwestern Mainland

Science World and the Alcan OMNIMAX Theatre (1455 Quebec Street, Vancouver, V6A 3Z7; 604–443–7443; www.scienceworld.bc.ca). Amazing *3D Laser Theatre* with magical visual effects and many more hands-on science exhibits. Kids may even get a chance to create their own cyclone under the silver geodesic dome.

Vancouver Aquarium Marine Science Centre, in Stanley Park, featuring belugas, dolphins, otters, sea lions, and more. Phone (604) 659–FISH (3474); information@vanaqua.org; www.vanaqua.org.

CN IMAX at Canada Place (604–682–IMAX or 800–582–4629; kharvey@imax.com; www.imax.com/vancouver). Huge five-story screen. Films are thirty-five to forty-five minutes.

Trans-Canada Waterslides (53790 Popkum Road S, Bridal Falls; 888–883–8852; 604–794–7455). Thrilling rapids river ride, giant hot tub, blackhole ride. (East of Chilliwack—June to September; www.transcanadawaterslides.com.)

corn, even fresh farm eggs with brilliant yellow yolks. Kids will enjoy the *Wagon Rides* to the pumpkin patch in October. There's a cut-flower garden and farm animals for the kids to enjoy. A commercial kitchen produces bread, cookies, pies, preserves, and treats—fresh from the farm field to the table! They're open daily May to October from 8:00 A.M. to 6:00 P.M., but call ahead to be sure. Look for the green-and-white sign on the highway.

If you're needing accommodation, follow the signs from the highway (go around the roundabout, up the hill, and turn right at the stop sign) to the delightful *Log House B&B Inn* (1357 Elmwood Drive, Pemberton; 604–894–6000; toll free: 800–894–6002; loghouseinfo@loghouseinn.com; www.loghouseinn.com). All seven bedrooms have en suite or private bathrooms and television. It's exquisitely furnished and comes complete with bathrobes for your trip to the outdoor hot tub. There's also a wraparound sun deck, a guest living area with a wood stove, and a reading loft. A full homemade breakfast is served. And you don't have to go far afield for a tasty meal later on. A local favorite with great atmosphere and equally great cappuccinos, bagels, muffins, and tuna melts, as well as excellent evening meals (try the delicious salmon-calzone) is the *Pony Espresso* (1426 Portage Road, Pemberton, V0N 2L0; 604–894–5700). From Whistler, turn left off Highway 99 onto Portage Road, and it's just a few yards north.

In 1967 Pemberton became the first commercial seed potato area in the world to grow virus-free seed potatoes. With that in mind I had to try out the Pemberton Potatoes at the *Pemberton Trail Steakhouse* (604–894–3340). I wasn't disappointed. The prime rib was excellent, too.

But I didn't come just for the meat and potatoes. There's so much to see and do in the Pemberton area. If you'd like a view from above, visit the *Pemberton Soaring Center* (Box 725, Pemberton, V0N 2L0; 604–894–5727; 800–831–2611; fax: 604–894–5776; info@pemberton soaring.com; www.pembertonsoaring.com). A Valley Flight costs $78 for a fifteen- to twenty-minute glide over paradise. The most popular of their flights is a fifty-five minute Glacier Flight ($198), where you'll soar over the higher snow-capped mountain peaks and glaciers.

To find out about other flights, as well as white-water rafting, horseback riding, jet-boat tours, parasailing, fly-fishing, canoeing, and golfing, stop off at the *Pemberton Info Centre* at the junction of Highway 99 and Pemberton Portage Road mid-May to September 30, or off-season write to Box 370, Pemberton, V0N 2L0; (604) 894–6477; fax: (604) 894–5571; shenry@look.ca; www.pemberton.net. The *Historic*

Pemberton Museum and Gift Shop (on Prospect Street; 604–894–5504) has a few original log homes and a collection of artifacts from the Lillooet River Valley, Anderson Lake, and the Pemberton Valley. Every Tuesday is *Toonie Tuesdays* when you can enjoy home-baked goodies and tea or coffee for $2.00. It's open from June to September. About 2 miles (3 km) south of Pemberton, there's a pleasant, short hike to the emerald-green waterfalls in *Nairn Falls Provincial Park.* These stunning falls tumble 200 feet (60 m) into a steep, forested valley creating potholes in the rocks. It's difficult to get a good photo of them as they are fenced off for safety, but they're well worth the hike, which is approximately a 2-mile (3 km) round-trip from the parking lot along a narrow track. Thirteen of the ninety-four campground sites (of which forty can be reserved) are perched high above the raging *Green River.* There's a swimming and play area at *One Mile Lake,* just over a mile north of the campground. For more information, visit the BC Parks & Protected Areas Web site at www.bcparks.ca (search word "Nairn").

Pemberton is just twenty minutes north of North America's number-one ski resort, *Whistler-Blackcomb,* 62 miles (100 km) north of Vancouver. (Readers of Japan's prestigious *Blue Guide* ski magazine voted it the best ski resort in the world four years in a row.) Even in summer you can ski and snowboard at *Blackcomb* on Horstman Glacier. Or if you prefer golf, you have three world-class courses—designed by such prestigious names as Jack Nicklaus, Robert Trent Jones Jr., and Arnold Palmer—each with breathtaking views.

Winter visitors (December to April) might enjoy a little backcountry adventure with *Cougar Mountain Wilderness Adventures* (888–297–2222; 604–932–4086; fax: 604–932–8715; www.cougarmountain.ca). They offer a two-hour ($49) backcountry introductory snowshoeing/nature tour at Cougar Mountain. For $159 there's a combo snowmobile/snowshoe guided tour through 1,200-year-old trees in Whistler's Ancient Cedar Grove. The more adventurous (experienced or not) might try a two- or three-hour snowmobile tour (which start from $119 double or $159 single) including a hearty meal at a cozy lakeside cabin. For those who really want some fun, there's a two-and-a-half-hour ($135 per person based on two per sled) dogsled trip through the Soo Valley Wildlife Reserve. In summer they run fishing trips, ATV tours on Cougar Mountain (two-hour trips start at $99 per person), horseback riding to the Ancient Cedar Grove, and Hummer 4x4 tours into the Soo Valley and Cougar Mountain. Mountain biking and hiking are also offered.

If you need accommodation, contact *Tourism Whistler Activity and Information Centre,* 4010 Whistler Way, Whistler, V0N 1B4. For reservations call (800) WHISTLER (944–7853) within Canada and the United States, and in Vancouver and outside North America call (604) 664–5624; fax: (604) 932–7321; www.mywhistler.com. Other accommodation sites are www.resortac.com and www.whistlerresort.com. For other information contact the **Whistler Visitor Info Centre,** corner of Lake Placid Road and Highway 99, Box 181, Whistler, V0N 2B0; (604) 932–5528; fax: (604) 932–3755.

The Sea to Sky Highway continues south past the western edge of **Garibaldi Provincial Park.** Visit www.bcparks.ca (search word "Garibaldi") for maps and information. To see what "sea to sky" really means, take a drive in the Diamond Head area in the southwest tail of the park. South of Alice Lake, and 2.5 miles (4 km) north of **Squamish,** turn onto Mamquam Road, marked as DIAMOND HEAD (GARIBALDI PARK). It's paved for 2.5 miles (4 km). Finally, after the last switchback and about 10 miles (16 km), you'll get breathtaking views of the Squamish River Valley, the Stawamus Chief, and Howe Sound. From here if you are equipped (and fit!), there's a two- to three-hour hike to Elfin Lakes, with good views of Diamond Head. At this point you are a mere 40 miles (64 km) north of Vancouver. Don't miss **Brandywine Falls** (just west of the park, and 29 miles [47 km] north of Squamish) with its spectacular 230-foot (70-m) waterfall.

Every January at nearby Brackendale, the winter home of the bald eagle, where the Cheakamus and Squamish Rivers meet (halfway between Whistler and Vancouver), hundreds of eagle-eyes gather, cameras and binoculars at the ready, for the annual **Brackendale Winter Eagle Festival.** In 1994 a world-record 3,766 eagles were counted. Enthusiasts leave from the **Brackendale Art Gallery Theatre and Teahouse** (41950 Government Road at Axen Road, Box 100, Brackendale, V0N 1H0; phone/fax: 604–898–3333; brackendaleartgallery@telus.net; www.brackendaleartgallery.com). Eagles or not, stop off here to sample the first-class soups and croissant sandwiches. Located behind a large white unicorn near the corner of Depot Road, the gallery was established in 1973 as a center for the arts in the Squamish Valley. It features a different west coast artist every month and is open weekends and holidays from noon to 10:00 P.M. One interesting gallery, **The Bell Shop,** houses the famous Brackendale bells, made from recycled steel. The folks at the theatre have devised an interesting fund-raising idea with the Casting Wall, where for $100 (and twenty minutes of your time) you can have your face cast into immortality alongside such notables as folksinger Valdy and environmentalist David Suzuki.

You're soon in Squamish—6 miles (10 km) south—where there are so many recreational activities that it's hard to know where to start. Rock climbers go nuts here. They love the cracks and chimneys in the 2,139-foot (652-m) *Stawamus Chief*, a huge exposure of granodiorite, which is part of the coast range batholith. You can view it and, if your lens is long enough, capture some colorful climbing photos from the parking lot on Highway 99.

If you missed the eagles in Brackendale, you might catch a view of them during a leisurely horseback ride through the beautiful Paradise Valley, near Squamish. The eagles are so used to seeing horses in their environs that the rider becomes part of their normal scenery. *Sea to Sky Stables* (Box 1083, Squamish, V0N 3G0; toll free: 866–898–3934; 604–898–3934; fax: 604–898–4190; info@seatoskystables.com; www. seatoskystables.com) offers guided trail rides ($40 for one hour, $60 for two hours, $85 for three hours, and $140 for a day ride with bagged lunch). Accommodation in seven Chuckwagon Bunkhouses (each sleeps twelve—bring your own sleeping bag and pillow) at $15 per person can make for a perfect family (or group) "Old West" experience. The wagons are set around a fire pit next to the *World's Largest Teepee,* with full bathroom facilities nearby.

Horse riding can be a thirsty business, so don't leave Squamish without a visit to the *Howe Sound Inn and Brewing Company* at 37801 Cleveland Avenue, Box 978, Squamish, V0N 3G0; (800) 919–ALES (2537) or (604) 892–2603; fax: (604) 892–2631; hsibrew@howesound.com; www. howesound.com. It opened in 1996 and serves both pub-style meals and moderately priced restaurant meals. The inn's rooms (rates from $95 double) all have panoramic views of Stawamus Chief and the

Finding an Old Friend

I'm addicted to dock strolling. Barely a week goes by that I don't wander down to the local marina to sniff out the new arrivals. From Vancouver I recently sailed on BC Ferries' Queen of Capilano to Snug Cove on Bowen Island and headed for the Union Steamship Company's docks. Back in the twenties, when the company's grand ships cruised these waters, this waterfront buzzed with the summer sounds of dancers and drinkers. I wasn't looking for the ghosts of the booze cruises, though, but for my old mate, the sloop Zeevogel, our family home for three exciting years in the late eighties. From Victoria she had safely sailed to exotic destinations like Tonga's Niuatoputapu, French Guiana's Devil's Island, and Ecuador's mysterious Galápagos. And now there she lies, snugly protected on Bowen Island, while a new young family pampers and primes her, readying the sweet ship for more exciting discoveries ahead.

Coast Mountains. *Shannon Falls Provincial Park* (south of Squamish, immediately adjacent to *Stawamus Chief Provincial Park*) is another "must-see" in the area. The falls are composed of a series of cliffs rising 335 meters (1,100 feet) above the highway—it's the third-highest falls in the province and is the perfect place to stop for a shady picnic. For a view all over the Squamish Valley, stop at the *Tantalus Range Lookout*. It's at a pullout on the highway just south of Squamish.

The *Squamish Visitor Info Centre* (37950 Cleveland Avenue, Box 1009, Squamish, V0N 3G0; 604–892–9244; fax: 604–892–2034; information@ squamishchamber.bc.ca; www.squamishchamber. bc.ca) will help with more information on this exciting area. Their Web site lists several accommodation choices.

The *BC Museum of Mining* (Box 188, Britannia Beach, V0N 1J0; 604–896–2233 or 604–688–8735; fax: 604–896–2260; general@bcmuseum ofmining.org; www.bcmuseumofmining.org) is 7.5 miles (12 km) south of Squamish, is all underground. An electric train takes you into the mountain on a tour of what was at one time the largest copper producer in the British Empire. Its history has not all been happy, though. Back in 1915 the mine was struck by an avalanche, killing thirty-two miners. It's open May to October (or year-round by arrangement for tours but closed December and January). Adult admission is $9.50, students and seniors $7.50; kids five and under are free, and there are family discounts. You can't miss the museum—just look for the 235-ton Super Mine Truck standing in the industrial yard outside.

The Sunshine Coast

ighway 101, the Sunshine Coast Highway, connects pretty coastal communities with attractive names such as Secret Cove, Smuggler Cove, Sechelt, Halfmoon Bay, Garden Bay, Earl's Cove, and Saltery Bay, sprinkled along the sheltered coastline between Howe Sound and the marine-life-rich waters of Desolation Sound.

The ferry from the terminal at Horseshoe Bay at the western end of the Upper Levels Highway in Vancouver takes forty minutes to cross to Langdale, the southern entrance to the Sunshine Coast. Contact BC Ferries (888–BCFERRY or 250–386–3431) and inquire about the Sunshine

BC Ferry approaching Langdale

Coast Circlepac deal, a four-route travel package that gives up to 15 percent off regular one-way fares.

A few minutes west of Langdale (take the more scenic Marine Drive instead of the bypass), fans of *The Beachcombers* (397 episodes of which were aired on the CBC from 1974 to 1990) will want to stop off in **Gibsons** to see some of the haunts made famous by the old television series—such as **Molly's Reach** (604–886–9710), but since 1995 a seafood restaurant. You'll find it down near the "Landing." The **Gibsons Visitor Info Centre** (in the Sunnycrest Mall parking lot in Upper Gibsons, 668 Sunnycrest Road, Box 1190, Gibsons, V0N 1V0; 604–886–2325; fax: 604–886–2379; admin@gibsonschamber.com; www.gibsonschamber.com) has other eateries listed and quite a few bed-and-breakfasts. One of these, **Marina House Bed & Breakfast** (546 Marine Drive, Box 1696, Gibsons, V0N 1V0; 888–568–6688 or 604–886–7888; marinahouse@sunshine.net; www.marinahouse.net), was built in 1931 by local medical legend Doc Inglis. It has lovely view rooms (Molly's and Sarah's) with private baths in the $100 double range, including coffee in your room and a full breakfast in the library. The hosts will also pick you up from the ferry.

Before leaving Gibsons take a look at the Charles Bedford shell collection at the *Elphinstone Pioneer Museum* (716 Winn Road, Box 766, Gibsons, V0N 1V0; 604–886–8232; epm@dccnet.com; www.gibsons library.bc.ca). As well as this world-renowned shell collection, there's a *Beachcomber* series display, which will remind you to take a stroll down *Molly's Lane* and the *Seawalk*. Butterfly fanatics will enjoy the new Don Bland Butterfly Collection. Summer hours are 10:30 A.M. to 4:30 P.M. daily, except Sundays and Mondays. Winter hours are Tuesday, Thursday, and Saturday, 1:00 to 4:30 P.M.

Up the hill from the Landing at *Jack's Lane Bistro* (546 Gibson's Way; 604–886–4898), you'll find specialty coffees, homemade soups and sandwiches, and the best desserts going, as well as fresh Mediterranean food. A tasty Veggie Combo entree for two costs about $14. The *Wild Blueberry Bakery* (604–886–1616) downstairs has a wide variety of breads and sweets.

Head northwest out of Gibsons past thick forests toward Sechelt. Beside the eighteen-hole *Sunshine Coast Golf and Country Club* (800–667–5022; 604–885–9217; fax: 604–885–6212; $30 per round), you'll find a park akin to a small-scale rain forest. *Cliff Gilker Regional Park* consists of an unusual variety of trees, plants, and shrubs, with cedar bridges and waterfalls along pleasant hiking trails.

Turn at the Fire Department building, 6 miles (10 km) from Gibsons, and stop at *Roberts Creek.* Take a walk out along the pier at Rock Point, where unsightly propane tanks used to sit. If you haven't seen it lately, you're in for a surprise. It's now a scenic area "furnished" with driftwood "armchairs." Wander the beach, where you'll sometimes find sea stars, mussels, and oysters, and stay for the glorious sunsets.

Nearby, the *Gumboot Garden Cafe* (1057 Roberts Creek Road; 604–885–4216) serves fresh, tasty foods in keeping with a back-to-the-sixties Roberts Creek atmosphere. It's open daily from 8:30 A.M. till 3:00 P.M. and for dinner Thursday, Friday, and Saturday until 8:30 P.M. *Casual* is the key word at this funky, friendly feast house! Try the locally caught cedar salmon (baked traditionally on a cedar plank) or something off the extensive (from enchiladas to Thai noodle salad) vegetarian or vegan menu. For more information on Roberts Creek check www.roberts creek.com.

The Sunshine Coast Highway 101 continues heading west to the best coffee shop on the coast. *Strait Coffee Traders* (4330 Sunshine Coast Highway, Sechelt, V0N 3A0; 800–893–6646 or 604–885–9757; strait_coffee@ sunshine.net), in the Wilson Creek Plaza, beckons with its rich aroma of roasting beans. The organic lunches (steaming curried lentil-apple

Recommended Reading—The Southwestern Mainland

FOR ADULTS:
A Guide to Climbing and Hiking in Southwestern British Columbia,
by Bruce Fairley. Vancouver: Gordon Soules Publishing, 1986.

109 Walks in British Columbia's Lower Mainland, by Mary and David Macaree.
Vancouver: Greystone Books/Douglas & McIntyre, 1997.

Whitewater Trips for Kayakers, Canoeists and Rafters in British Columbia, by
Betty Pratt-Johnson, 1986.

Fort Langley: Birth Place of British Columbia, by B. A. McKelvie. Beach Holme Publishing Ltd., 1991.

Salmonopolis: The Steveston Story, by S. and D. Stacey. Madeira Park: Harbour Publishing, 1994.

Bicycling near Vancouver: Book 1—Central Fraser Valley, by Margaret Slack.
Vancouver: Gordon Soules Publishing, 1994.

Daytrips from Vancouver, by Jack Christie. Vancouver: Greystone Books/Douglas &
McIntyre, 1997.

Fraser and Thompson Canyons, by Art Downs, ed. Heritage House
Publishing Co. Ltd., 1980.

The Whistler Outdoors Guide, by Jack Christie. Vancouver: Greystone Books/Douglas
& McIntyre, 1997.

Sunshine and Salt Air: An Outdoor Guide to the Sunshine Coast, Karen Southern,
Bryan Carson, Peter Robson (eds.). Madeira Park: Harbour Publishing, 1997.

FOR KIDS:
Breakaway, by Paul Yee. Toronto: Groundwood Books, 2000. The hero is a good
student and soccer player whose Chinese family are poor farmers. Set during the
Depression years in Vancouver. For ages nine to twelve.

soup in winter and cool gazpacho in summer) and dreamy desserts make it a triple-the-value coffee stop.

Continue north past the long, sandy beach and engaging galleries at Davis Bay, and you're soon in Sechelt, home of artists, writers, and retirees. Every August the nationally acclaimed *Festival of the Written Arts* is held at the *Rockwood Centre* (at the top of Cowrie Street; 604–885–9631 or 800–565–9631; info@writersfestival.ca; www.writers festival.ca), just up from the *Sechelt Visitor Info Centre* in the Trail Bay Centre (45–5755 Cowrie Street, Box 360, Sechelt, V0N 3A0; 604–885–0662; fax: 604–885–0691; visitorinfo@dccnet.com; www.thesunshine

coast.com/secheltchamber). Visit the galleries and shops in town and pick up some local artists' works at the **Sunshine Coast Arts Centre** (corner of Medusa Road and Trail Avenue; 604–885–5412).

There's native artwork at the Indian Band Complex, the imposing **House of Hewhiwus** (House of Chiefs), on the highway opposite St. Mary's Hospital as you enter Sechelt. As well as a museum and a 280-seat theater, there's an art gallery in which the raven, an integral feature of the Sechelt Indian band's culture, is a recurring theme. The word *sechelt* means "land between two waters." Indian legend has it that gods carved out the valleys but left a beach along the inlet at nearby Porpoise Bay. Later the transformers—a male raven and a female mink—changed details by carving trees and forming pools of water. Divers love the waters here in Porpoise Bay. In 1992 the 387-foot (118-m) **HMCS Chaudière** was sunk (off Kunechin Point), creating an artificial reef that is now rated as one of the top twenty recreational dives in the world.

If it's the fabulous snow-topped mountain views you're after, stay at the **Beachcomber Marine Spa B&B** (6398 Gale Avenue North, Sechelt, V0N 3A5; 604–885–0900; toll free: 877–399–2929; beachcomber@sunshine. net; www.beachcomberbb.com). This first-class bed-and-breakfast accommodation (also offering massage and other pampering delights) is north of Sechelt in a small community (Timber Creek) edging Snake Bay. To get there from Sechelt, head north along Trail Avenue to the skating arena, turn right on Fairway, and follow this (keeping left) to the end. Turn left onto Gale Avenue North and look for the bed-and-breakfast on the water side. Rates are from $119 per night double.

An unforgettable back-to-nature camping experience can be had with **Tzoonie Outdoor Adventures** (Box 157, Sechelt, V0N 3A0; 604–885–9802; fax: 604–885–9826; camping@tzoonie.com; www.tzoonie.com). You'll hike, camp, and more in a no-road-access wilderness camp on traditional native lands.

On Porpoise Bay Road you'll discover what is possibly Sechelt's best restaurant, **The Blue Heron** (604–885–3847 or 800–818–8977; blue heron@uniserve.com). It's open for dinner Wednesday through Sunday and specializes in seafood, with such delicacies as a bouillabaisse deliciously loaded with fresh fish and shellfish in a lobster bisque broth. The delightful surroundings and high-quality wines, combined with French cuisine, make it very popular with the locals—I suggest you make reservations.

Heading north on Highway 101 from Sechelt, hikers will enjoy **Smuggler Cove Marine Park** (604–898–3678), just past Halfmoon Bay. About 5.5

Statistics show that the number of Canadians traveling to the United States from British Columbia on a single-day automobile trip is strongly affected by the relative value of the Canadian dollar. For every decrease of 1 cent in the Canadian dollar, 30,000 fewer Canadians will make a same-day trip to the United States from British Columbia each month (and the reverse occurs when the currency increases in value).

miles (9 km) northwest of Sechelt (look for the blue-and-white BC PARKS sign), go halfway up a long hill and turn left at Brooks Road, following this gravel road for 2 miles (3 km) to the parking lot. The cove, named for the illegal traffic of Chinese workers to the United States, is an easy 1-mile hike. There are a couple of walk-in campsites with pit toilets but no water.

The highway continues north past Halfmoon Bay to **Pender Harbour,** a puzzling jigsaw of inlets and bays with a few lakes, islands, and reefs thrown in. Here you'll find tiny fishing communities such as Madeira Park, where such signs as BEWARE OF ATTACK SQUIRREL! abound, and you'll find great sandwiches in a hole-in-the-wall cafe called **Jill's Cafe.** Many of the harbor's community-proud residents are there for the good fishing, both saltwater and fresh.

Contact the **Pender Harbour Tourist/Visitor Info Booth** (July–August), 12911 Madeira Park Road, Box 265, Madeira Park, V0N 2H0; phone/fax: (604) 883–2561, for more information on activities and accommodations.

Highway 101 leads north to the ferry at Earl's Cove, but before leaving the peninsula, take a look at the thrilling **Skookumchuck Narrows,** named for a Chinook word meaning "turbulent water" or "rapid torrent." Here, tidal flow associated with Sechelt, Narrows, and Salmon inlets is forced through the narrows to form Sechelt Rapids, perhaps the world's fastest saltwater rapids, with currents surpassing 16 knots. Check current tables (as opposed to tide tables) in the local newspaper (*The Reporter*) for the best viewing times or check with the Chamber of Commerce (they sometimes have a booth on the Langdale ferry) in Sechelt; they display a chart showing the best times and days to view the rapids. (If you go at slack tide, you'll wonder what all the fuss was about!) To get to the rapids, take the turnoff to Egmont (half a mile before you reach the ferry terminal). Drive about 4 miles (6.5 km) to a parking lot marking **Skookumchuk Narrows Provincial Park**. Signs lead you to a 2.5-mile (4-km), easy trail past Brown Lake to North Point (best viewing point on the ebb tide) and Roland Point (best on the flood tide). Allow an hour to walk to the narrows. An alternative to walking is to become one with the whirlpools in a dinner/tour with Bryce Christie of **Sunshine Coast Tours** (RR 1 S9 C1, Garden Bay, V0N 1S0; 604–883–

2280; fax: 604–762–9055; bookings: 800–870–9055; fax: 800–762–9055; info@sunshinecoasttours.bc.ca; www.sunshinecoasttours. bc.ca). If time is on your side, consider a day tour with Bryce to the world-renowned *Princess Louisa Inlet Marine Provincial Park. Chatterbox Falls* at the head of the 5-mile-long (8 km) inlet plunges 120 feet (40 m) into the tranquil waters—undeniably nature's beauty at its best. Tours leave at 10.30 A.M. with two forty-minute stops ashore. Before traveling to the Sunshine Coast, you may want to check out the Web site www.bigpacific. com for an extensive exposé of this wonderful holiday area.

Powell River

The BC ferry takes you to Saltery Bay, 19 miles (30 km) south of Powell River. In *Saltery Bay Provincial Park,* a 10-foot (3-m) bronze mermaid lies at 66 feet (20 m), holding her arms out to the many scuba divers who believe this area to offer the best diving in the world. *Don's Dive Shop* (4552 Willingdon Avenue, Powell River, V8A 2M3; 604–485–6969; fax: 604–485–7609; info@donsdiveshop.com; www. donsdiveshop.com) will take you to the bronze mermaid, as well as to some of the other "best dive sites in the world" aboard **The Shadow,** a customized skiff. It's berthed at Westview Marina, close to the Dive Shop. The Powell River area is renowned for huge ling cod, wolf eels, and giant octopus that thrive in the nutrient-rich waters of this emerald sea. Kayaking, fishing, hiking, diving instruction, or just plain cruising are also part of the scene.

We're almost at the end of the road in *Powell River,* the first pulp and paper town in Western Canada. Despite log booms and steaming chimneys, there's a pleasant *Heritage Townsite,* which in 1995 was designated a National Historic District by the National Historic Sites and Monuments Board of Canada, the only community in Western Canada to receive this prestigious designation. Thirty commercial structures and more than 400 homes were built from 1910–1930 as part of the company town site. At the *Powell River Visitor Info Centre* (4690 Marine Avenue, 877–81–SUNNY [78669]; 604–485–4701; fax: 604–485–2822; info@discoverpowellriver.com; www.discoverpowellriver. com) pick up a Heritage Walk brochure for a self-guided tour. On this walk you'll pass the *Old Courthouse Inn* (6243 Walnut Street, Powell River, V8A 4K4; toll free: 877–483–4777; 604–483–4000; oldcourthouse-inn@armourtech.com; savaryonline.com/oldcourthouse). Steep yourself in the history of Powell River at this former Provincial Building, recently converted to hostel-type accommodation. Rates range from

$20 per person shared to $60 double for a private room with bath. To get there, head north past the breakwater on Marine Avenue, turn left at the first stop sign (Ash Street), and turn right on Walnut Street.

For campers, **Willingdon Beach Municipal Campground** (mailing address: 6910 Duncan Street, Powell River, V8A 1V4; 604–485–2242; fax: 604–485–2162; www.prcn.org/willingdonbeach) at 4845 Marine Avenue just north of town has campsites with plenty of forest surrounding them, and the sunsets are fabulous. Walk the **Willingdon Beach Trail,** about a forty-minute round-trip, winding its way through forest along a beautiful oceanfront. Afterward, you can sit on a driftwood beach to soak up the final rays, eating fresh-out-of-the-sea fish and chips from **The Beach Hut** next door. Campsites range from $15 to $20 (full hookup).

But if you prefer the comfort of a hot tub and a massage, as well as the company of Jetty the cat, stay at **Beacon Bed and Breakfast** (3750 Marine Avenue, Powell River, V8A 2H8; toll free: 877–485–5563 or 604–485–5563; fax: 604–485–9450; stay@beaconbb.com; www.beaconbb.com), a waterfront home where massage technician Shirley Randall knows how to pamper guests. Look for the red-and-white beacons next to the driveway, 3 miles (5 km) south of Powell River. High-season rates range from $80 to $155, including a gourmet breakfast. Massage is extra.

Highway 101 continues north to the coastal village of **Lund,** the last frontier before Desolation Sound. **Cedar Lodge Bed & Breakfast** (C8, 9825 Malaspina Road, RR 2, Powell River, V8A 4Z3; phone/fax: 604–483–4414; erwin@prcn.org; www.prcn.org/cedar), near Okeover Arm Provincial Park, has nature trails that connect to the Sunshine Coast Trail (see end of chapter). Accommodation with continental breakfast starts at $60. Nearby at 2694 Dawson Road, **Desolation Resort** (C36, Malaspina Road, RR 2, Powell River, V8A 4Z3; 604–483–3592; fax: 604–483–7942; desolres@prcn.org; www.desolationresort.com) is a luxurious, dramatically simple resort hidden in the woods; the chalets and apartments seem to hang over the 900 feet (274 m) of wilderness waterfront overlooking the beautiful Okeover Arm. Rates range from $95 to $190 in low season and $120 to $290 for a triple unit in high season. There are canoes and kayaks to use, and the eagles, whales, seals, and sea lions are free to enjoy from your private deck.

Both accommodations are close to **The Laughing Oyster Restaurant** (604–483–9775; falk@prcn.org; www.laughingoyster.ca), where you'll find classic cuisine with a West Coast flavor, served in front of breathtaking views over Okeover Inlet. For lunch try the salmon and spinach crepe, and for dinner don't miss the "hilariously delicious" Laughing Oysters. You'll find the Laughing Oyster at the end of Malaspina Road, just by the Okeover Arm Provincial Park. Another accommodation, the **Oyster Shell Beach House** (self-contained waterfront accommodation—check the Laughing Oyster Web site or write C-4 Vandermaeden Road, RR2, Powell River, V8A 4Z3; 604–414–0231; falk@prch.org), can be found 3 miles (5 km) north of Sliammon Village on the highway to Lund on the west side of Malaspina Peninsula. You can stay for a week ($375 double in high season) or overnight ($65).

A few minutes away is the quiet fishing village of Lund (named after the city of Lund in Sweden), the gateway to Desolation Sound, a sailor's paradise. The historic waterfront **Lund Hotel** (General Delivery, Lund, V0N 2G0; 877–569–3999 toll free in North America; 604–414–0474; fax: 604–414–0476; info@lundhotel.com; www.lundhotel.com), built by the Swedish Thulin brothers in 1889 and refurbished by the Sliammon First Nation in May 2000, provides excellent dining and accommodation, and the views are everywhere. As well as the hotel and restaurant, there's a pub, a general store and post office, an art gallery, a Laundromat, and a fuel dock. Operating out of the hotel are numerous recreational, cultural, and interpretive activities. These include a fleet of charter boats, kayaking rentals and lessons, diving, guided and interpretive hikes, and tours, all designed around and focusing upon the scenic beauty, native heritage, and ecoculture unique to Lund and the Desolation Sound area.

Lund is but a water-taxi ride away (**Lund Water Taxi**, 604–483–9749, reservations appreciated) from British Columbia's largest arbutus tree and the white-sand beaches of one of the prettiest of the Gulf Islands: **Savary Island**.

Stay a while to enjoy Savary's warm waters at **Savary Island Lodge** (604–483–9481; jyuile@armourtech.com), a large log home located directly on one of those endless white beaches. Jean Yuile serves traditional hot English breakfasts that are included in the tariff, which starts at $75 double. Bring your whites for a game of tennis on the wooden-decked court nearby. You'll find a photo of this historic lodge at www.savary.ca, as well as much more about Savary. For tours of the island, phone Rick Thaddeus at (604) 483–3218 or e-mail him at ricky@savary.ca. There are three seasonal restaurants on the island, one of which (Riggers, 604–483–2210) is beside the small general store.

Back on the mainland, experienced hikers can trek the 112-mile (180-km) **Sunshine Coast Trail**, which starts (or ends) at Sarah Point north of Lund, at the tip of the Malaspina Peninsula, the dramatic entrance to

Desolation Sound. Lund Water Taxi (604–483–9749) offers transport to Sarah Point. The other extremity of the trail is at the ferry terminal in Saltery Bay. Learn more about this challenging trail at www. sunshinecoast-trail.com. It nudges a couple of bed-and-breakfasts, which can add a touch of cheer to a sometimes difficult hike.

PLACES TO STAY ON THE SOUTHWESTERN MAINLAND

HARRISON HOT SPRINGS
Harrison Heritage House and Kottage Bed and Breakfast, 312 Lillooet Avenue, Box 475, Harrison Hot Springs, V0M 1K0; (604) 796–9552 or (800) 331–8099; www.bbharrison.com. Rooms $75–$150.

MISSION
Fence Post Lane Bed & Breakfast, 4 miles (6.6 km) west of Mission at 8575 Gaglardi Street, V4S 1B2; (877) 833–7009 or (604) 820–7009; fax: (604) 820–4974; mperdue@direct.ca; www.bbcanada.com/906. html. Room rates $50–$75 double. Four-star rating.

PEMBERTON
Log House B&B Inn, 1357 Elmwood Drive, Pemberton, V0N 2K0; (604) 894–6000; toll free: (800) 894–6002; loghouseinfo@loghouse inn.com; www.loghouse inn.com.

SECHELT
Beachcomber Marine Spa B&B, 6398 Gale Avenue North, Sechelt, V0N 3A5; (604) 885–0900; toll free: (877) 399–2929; beach comber@sunshine.net; www.beachcomberbb.com. Classy bed-and-breakfast plus. From $119.

VANCOUVER
"O Canada" House Bed & Breakfast, 1114 Barclay Street, Vancouver, V6E 1H1; (604) 688–0555; toll free: (877) 688–1114; fax: (604) 488–0556; www.ocanadahouse.com. Downtown. Classy. Rooms from $185.

Victorian Hotel, 514 Homer Street, Vancouver, V6B 2V6; toll free: (877) 681–6369; (604) 681–6369; fax: (604) 681–8776; reservations@victorian hotel.ca; www.victorian-hotel.com. Downtown. Rooms from $59, including breakfast. Newly renovated and great value.

Escape to the Point B&B, 1318 Cypress Street, Vancouver, V6J 3L2; (604) 250–5300; on Kitsilano Point; minutes to beaches; gourmet breakfasts.

PLACES TO EAT ON THE SOUTHWESTERN MAINLAND

GIBSONS
Jack's Lane Bistro and Bakery, 546 Gibson's Way; (604) 886–4898. Great desserts.

HOPE
Hope Station House, at the junction of Highway 1 and Old Hope-Princeton Way; (604) 869–9495. A smoke-free restaurant specializing in homemade soups, sandwiches, and desserts. Open 8:00 A.M. to 8:00 P.M. daily.

SECHELT
The Blue Heron, Porpoise Bay Road; (604) 885–3847 or (800) 818–8977; blueheron@uniserve.com. Open for dinner Wednesday through Sunday. Specializes in seafood. Reservations recommended.

SQUAMISH
Howe Sound Inn and
Brewing Company,
37801 Cleveland Avenue;
(604) 892–2603 or
(800) 919–ALES (2537).
Moderately priced
restaurant and pub meals.

VANCOUVER
Sushi Bar Wabi Sabi,
4422 West Tenth Avenue,
near Forty-second Street;
(604) 222–8188.
Classy; reasonable prices.
Reservations recom-
mended.

Amarcord,
1168 Hamilton Street,
(604) 681–6500.
Excellent Italian dining in
Yaletown.

Harry's Diner,
1078 W. Pender Street
near Thurlow;
(604) 331–0046. Pizza, etc.

The Okanagan

pples and wine, water sports, and lots of sunshine are images that prevail on hearing the words *The Okanagan*. Here in Canada's warmest, driest climate, we'll travel through just 3 percent of British Columbia's 366,275 square miles (948,596 sq km), but our diverse journey will lead us from Princeton, along the once gold-rich Similkameen River, past eccentrically shaped mountains and turquoise lakes in Cathedral Provincial Park, and through orchards of cherries, peaches, pears, apples, apricots, and grapes. Down close to the U.S. border, we'll ride the rolling ranges, where painted turtles and rattlesnakes lurk in Canada's only desert. Farther north we'll look for the mystical Ogopogo in the 90-mile-long (145-km) Okanagan Lake, one of more than 250 lakes in the region. And in fall we'll enjoy world-class wine at the Okanagan Wine Festival, for which this land of plenty is fast becoming famous.

Princeton

tarting in the east at the Manning Park border, the mountainous Crowsnest (Highway 3) winds north to **Princeton,** a town mother-loded with a history of gold and copper mining from the 1880s. Originally called Vermilion Forks, after the nearby bluffs of red ocher, a substance prized by the Similkameen Indians for trading and face painting, Princeton, the southern gateway to the populous BC interior, is in the foothills of the Cascade Mountains, where the Tulameen and Similkameen Rivers meet.

Start your visit to Princeton by stopping off near the bridge over the Similkameen River at the **Princeton Visitor Info Centre** (57 Highway 3 East, Box 540, Princeton, V0X 1W0; 250–295–3103; fax: 250–295–3255; chamber@nethop. net; www.town.princeton.bc.ca) to pick up a *Historic Walk* brochure. Numbered plaques on each historic site correspond with photos and information in the guide.

Trivia

British Columbia's worst road accident occurred July 15, 1975, near Princeton, when a head-on collision caused the deaths of eleven people, including a family of eight.

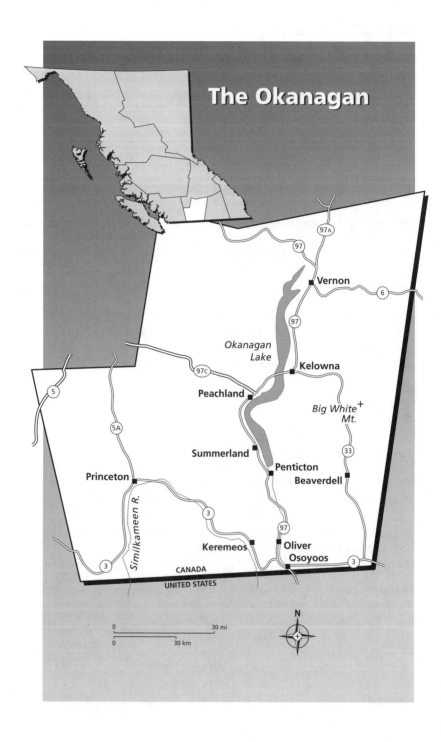

The Okanagan

THE OKANAGAN

AUTHOR'S TOP TEN PICKS IN THE OKANAGAN

Cathedral Provincial Park

The Grist Mill

Princeton Museum and Archives

Haynes Point Provincial Park

Desert Ecological Reserve

Dominion Radio Astrophysical Observatory

Okanagan Pottery Studio

Hainle Vineyards Estate Winery

Myra Canyon

Big White Ski Resort

Historic Site 6, the *Princeton Museum and Archives* (167 Vermilion Avenue; 250–295–7588), is a credit to this population of less than 2,700. It features one of Princeton's more infamous characters, the likable train robber and prison escapee Bill Miner. After doing time in the United States for Pony Express robberies, he moved his talents to the Princeton area and started on the trains, where, as "the Gentleman Bandit," he restricted his robberies to the baggage cars, taking only the payrolls and never the ladies' jewelry. One daring robbery near Kamloops ended in his capture and imprisonment. He escaped and fled to the United States, where, after recapture, he died in a Georgia prison. The museum has a vast collection of rocks and petrified wood, as well as one of the largest collections of fossils in British Columbia. This world-class donated collection necessitated the building of a special wing to house it. The museum is open from 10:00 A.M. to 6:00 P.M. daily in July and August (11:00 A.M. to 3:00 P.M. Sunday and Monday) and 11:00 A.M. to 3:00 P.M. on weekends in May, June, September, and October.

Near the museum enjoy a "Hungry Man Breakfast" at the *Belaire Restaurant* (161 Vermilion Avenue, Princeton, V0X 1W0; 250–295– 7711), also

A Princeton Treasure

*T*he Princeton Museum was closed, so I inquired at the library.

"Find Margaret Stoneberg," was the answer. "She's usually around somewhere."

I found dear Margaret Stoneberg, a wool hat pulled tightly on, a stuffed bag of books by her feet, and her eyes close to a newspaper she was reading. She parted a ring of keys, selected one, rose slowly from her paper, and shuffled me into the museum.

"At first there was just trees and the mountain," she began.

Two hours later, I was still listening eagerly to stories from the gold and copper heydays, learning how during the war all the beer "from here to Alaska" was Princeton beer, and hearing how things haven't always changed for the better. As we left the museum, she was still pointing out artifacts.

"That organ was $29.50 in the 1903 catalogue," she whispered, a note of nostalgia in her tiny voice.

popular for its homemade pies, soups, and delicious full meals. For accommodation to suit all budgets, head out of town to **Princeton Castle Resort and R.V. Park** (Princeton-Summerland Road, RR 1, Site 1, Comp 10, Princeton, V0X 1W0; 888–228–8881 or 250–295–7988; info@ castleresort.com; www. castleresort.com). Outdoor hot tubs add a little decadence at the new log lodge and cottages, which are set behind the racetrack off Osprey Lake Road on the site of an intended cement plant and powerhouse. For some unknown reason, the massive architectural venture didn't pan out (possibly they ran out of limestone), and what is left looks like the ruins of a medieval castle. You may want to spend some time searching for the notorious Bill Miner's lost treasure, rumored to be hidden in his hideout in the hills near the castle. Locals tell me you'll have more luck panning for gold in the creek, though. Or perhaps flying to the moon!

The Princeton Rodeo Club is busy in the spring, with both team roping and rodeo competitions. If you're visiting on the Canada Day (July 1) weekend, you'll catch Princeton Racing Days, and on the second weekend of September, there's the **Little Britches Rodeo** and the **Annual Agricultural Fall Fair**.

From Princeton Castle, continue north along Osprey Lake Road (which is the road to Summerland) for about 15 miles (25 km) to **Pinewood Expeditions.** In summer, guides take you at your own pace through some rugged, dramatic areas on easy-to-ride Yamaha ATVs. In winter, visitors can experience a scenic and exhilarating dog-sled journey along the famous **Trans Canada Trail,** with only the sound of the mushing dogs and the rustle of the pine trees to intrude on the Canadian wilderness in all its winter majesty. Contact Pinewood Expeditions (RR 1, Site 19 C5, Princeton, V0X 1W0; 250–295–7667; fax: 250–295–7657; pine woodexp@uniserve.com; www.pinewoodexp.net) to book summer or winter tours, or to learn to drive your own dog team. All-inclusive weekend tour packages run for $750. Cozy Cabins are available for overnight accommodation, and there's a trapper's wall-tent, adding a touch of realism to this wonderful old-time adventure. The third weekend in January features the Sno-X Races, exciting snowmobile races with contestants from all over Canada and the United States.

Look for the eighteen-hole (newly expanded in 2002) **Princeton Golf Club** (toll free: 888–295–5123; pro shop: 250–295–6123; fax: 250–295–6246; pgc@nethop.net; www.princetongolfclub.com), just three minutes along Highway 3, east of Princeton. Camping is available nearby. The clubhouse has a fully licensed bar and restaurant (the **Sandtrap**

Restaurant—250–295–6656), which serves excellent food on its view patio.

The Similkameen Valley

eaving Princeton, the Crowsnest follows the Similkameen River 41 miles (67 km) east to Keremeos, passing through **Hedley**. Stop here to learn of the area's rich gold-mining history. Perhaps stay in the original 1904 Gold Assay Office, now **The Gold House Bed and Breakfast** (644 Colonial Road, Hedley, V0X 1K0; 250–292–8418; toll free: 866–676–GOLD [4653]; info@thegoldhouse.com; www.thegoldhouse.com). The antique furnishings are luxurious, and there are wonderful views of the valley from the wraparound balcony. In the backyard you'll see ruins of a gold mine. And for a touch of Hollywood, Burt Reynolds was filmed in The Gold House in the 1987 movie, *Malone*. Rates are in the $65 to $85 range. Two miles (3 km) before Keremeos, a 16-mile (25-km) southern side trip on the gravel Ashnola River Road brings you into **Cathedral Provincial Park.** California bighorn sheep, mule deer, and porcupines range in this 81,214-acre (33,272-ha) mountain wilderness, the setting for the movie *Clan of the Cave Bear.*

Past the Ashnola River, a privately owned road leads to **Cathedral Lakes Lodge** (888–255–4453; info@cathedral-lakes-lodge.com; www. cathedral-lakes-lodge.com), Canada's highest full-service hiking and fishing resort, located on Lake Quiniscoe in the very center of the park. From the lodge the most popular hike is the **Cathedral Rim Trail,** which follows a high alpine ridge to unique geological formations such as Devils Woodpile and Smokey the Bear, a jagged gigantic rock looking like a silhouette of old Smokey himself. On a clear day the view is spectacular, as you can see not only Mount Baker and Mount Ranier 200 miles (320 km) to the west but also the Thompson Plateau and the Kootenays to the north and east. It's definitely a top-of-the-world sensation. Glorious wildflowers and the turquoise Cathedral Lakes make the area a wilderness heaven. But keep in mind it's a "be-prepared" park, with no commercial facilities other than the private lodge. Accommodation rates at the lodge include superb meals and transportation from the base camp. Alpine Adventure Day Trips ($75—lunch not included) are available. The pickup is at 8:00 A.M. and the drop-off (back to your car in secure parking at the base camp) is at 6:00 P.M.

Cathedral Provincial Park campsite users who require transportation must reserve ahead (phone 888–255–4453; Visa or Mastercard charged at time of booking) for the one-hour-long ride in a Mercedes Benz Unimog truck from the base camp to the park's center. Costs are $55 per person return June, September, and October or $75 July and August. Children twelve and under cost $30, and under four are free.

For camping information (sixteen sites, open April to October, with fees collected June to September) and a printable overview map, check www.bcparks.ca (search word "Cathedral"). If you're already in the area, *Keremeos & District Chamber of Commerce* (415 Seventh Avenue, Keremeos, V0X 1N0; 250–499–5225) can help with brochure maps and information. A more detailed topographic map (sheet 92H/1) is available for approximately $10 from Nanaimo Maps and Charts (8 Church Street, Nanaimo, V9R 5H4; 250–754–2513; 800–665–2513; fax: 250–754–2313 or 800–553–2313 toll free—include your phone number when ordering) or, in Victoria, at Crown Publications (521 Fort Street, Victoria, V8W 1E7; 250–386–4636; fax: 250–386–0221; crown@pinc.com; www.crownpub.bc.ca). In Vancouver contact World Wide Books and Maps (604–687–3320).

At the route map information sign on Highway 3, 3 miles (5 km) west of Keremeos, the *Login Bed and Breakfast* (C1 Site 27, Highway 3 West, Keremeos, V0X 1N0; 250–499–2781/2664; loginbnb@img.net; www.loginbnb.com) caters to people, pets, and horses, so if you come for the *Chopaka Rodeo* on the Easter weekend or the *Elks Rodeo* on the May long weekend, your horse is certainly welcome, too. The pleasant log home is on 190 acres (77 ha), a short hike away from the Ashnola wilderness. The rooms have lovely views of the Similkameen scenery, and you might see bighorn sheep right outside your window. Breakfasts are excellent, with enough leftovers to stuff your packs for the hike snack. There's a kitchen for your use and a lovely log fireplace. Rates are moderate ($55 to $80 double), and the hosts, Helen and Eric Falkenberg, will let you use their Internet access. Ask them about rides or hikes outside the park to Crater Lake, Barcelo Canyon, and The Columns.

THE OKANAGAN

For those on a tight budget, the *Similkameen Backpack Shack* (C6 S27 R.R.1, Keremeos, V0X 1N0; 250–499–2318; simvalley@hotmail.com; www.hostelbc.com) has dormitory accommodation (eight single beds plus couches) at $20 per night or $50 for three nights (single rates). A u-cook breakfast is available for $4.00. The Shack is an old farmhouse but has a modern kitchen and bathroom; it's set among the trees with a creek and waterfall (and wildlife too!) on the property. It's about halfway between the Login B&B and Keremeos but on the south side of the Similkameen River (1.8 miles [3 km] southwest of Keremeos on East Road), but call ahead for directions. By prearrangement they'll pick you up from the Keremeos bus stop and welcome you warmly, and you can start hiking in the glorious Similkameen Valley right from the back door.

WORTH SEEING/DOING IN THE OKANAGAN

Windsurf on Osoyoos Lake.

Take a wine tour in the Okanagan Valley.

Ride the rails in Summerland on the Kettle Valley Railway.

Ski at Big White (near Kelowna) or Apex Mountain (near Penticton).

Visit the museums in Kelowna and Oliver.

Climb the Skaha Bluffs, one of the best rock-climbing bluffs in the world.

Keremeos, where in-season fruit stands line the highway, has earned the nickname "Fruit-stand Capital of the World." It is also fast earning a name for its many certified-organic orchards and market gardens. Pick up some organic garlic, carrots, and other vegetables, and of course don't miss the organic apples and other delicious fruit the area boasts. In the lovely Similkameen Valley, you'll find lots to see and do, including a visit to the *Orchard Blossom Honey House* (250–499–2821), with its historic beekeeping equipment, and to *Harker's Fruit Ranch* (RR1 Highway 3, Cawston; 250–499–2751), where owners Bruce and Kathy Harker specialize in growing and marketing organic fruits and vegetables. From mouthwatering melons to just-picked peaches to jams, jellies, and juices, the Harkers also offer tours where you can learn the basics of organic farming. They're open daily from July 1 to October 31. Tours should be booked in advance.

But the valley's best-known attraction is British Columbia's only water-powered flour mill, the oldest surviving pioneer flour mill west of Ontario, built in 1877. *The Grist Mill* (RR 1 Upper Bench Road, Keremeos, V0X 1N0; 250–499–2888; fax: 250–499–2434) is well signed 1 kilometer off Highway 3A on Keremeos Creek. It features restored, rare, original machinery driven by a 12-foot waterwheel, *Heritage Gardens* showing the agricultural history of the Similkameen Valley, and hands-on displays depicting this historic milling process. Pioneer lifestyle activities, enacted by costumed interpreters, give you that 1880s atmosphere.

At the *Tea Room*, you can enjoy light lunches featuring fresh-baked goods made from flour milled as it was in 1877 and organically grown vegetables from the Heritage Gardens. In the *Mill Shop* you'll find plant starts from the Heritage Gardens, wheat-straw weavings, corn dolls, dried gourds, and, of course, milled flour. Topical books are a nice addition. The Grist Mill is open formally from May to October and informally the rest of the year. Admission prices are reasonable, with tour discounts available. For more complete information on the Grist Mill, visit www.keremeos.com/gristmill/index.html.

The Okanagan Valley

The Similkameen River winds south to the border, and the highway leaves it to take a northeastern route. Just 5.5 miles (8.8 km) west of Osoyoos, the strange *Spotted Lake* (called *Klilok* by the Okanagan Indians) can be seen from the southern side of the highway. Evaporation and crystallization cause the formation of salty, white circular plates on the surface, hence its name. If it weren't on private land, you'd be able to soak away your arthritic pains in this

Fruity Facts

British Columbia produces 12.1 million pounds (5.5 million kg) of sweet cherries and 2.2 million pounds (1 million kg) of sour cherries a year—about 60 percent of the Canadian cherry crop.

Osoyoos has the earliest fruit season in the Okanagan Valley. The following table will show you when to visit, depending on whether you want to be there for the blossoms (beautiful photography) or the eating (mm!).

Fruit	Blossom	Ripens
Apricots	April 1–30	July 15–August 15
Cherries	April 15–May 1	June 25–July 30
Peaches	April 15–May 10	July 15–August 15
Pears	April 15–May 1	July 15–October 15
Plums	April 15–May 1	August 15–September 20
Apples	April 25–May 20	July 15–September 30
Grapes	April 25–May 20	September 5–October 10

muddy paradise of Epsom salts, calcium, and magnesium, as did the First Nations people in centuries gone by. Instead, be content to enjoy the unusual view from the highway.

Osoyoos Lake, named from *soi'yus,* an Inkaneep Indian word meaning roughly "gathered together" or "where the water narrows," comes into view. "Seems a zealous Irishman added the 'O'," explained former schoolteacher John Wallace, who, with his wife June, was my host at **Haynes Point Lakeside Guest House** (3619 Jasmine Drive, Osoyoos, V0H 1V0; phone/fax: 250–495–7443; www.bbcanada.com/14.html). The Wallaces know and share a remarkable amount of information about the area, even to preparing handouts on birding or arranging golfing or winery tours (there are five fine golf courses and fifteen wineries within thirty minutes), or you can simply enjoy June's delicious breakfasts (where I learned to put cardamom in my coffee for that special flavor) and unwind in one of the hammocks overlooking the 11.8-mile-long (19-km) lake. The more energetic might wish to while away a warm afternoon playing bocce on the lakefront lawn. Their three guest rooms are distinctively decorated to a theme, and the view over the lake and hills is wonderful. In summer boating and swimming in Canada's warmest freshwater lake is popular. (The average summer temperature is 75° F, or 24° C.) To get there turn south from the Crowsnest onto Highway 97; after 2 miles (3 km) follow the HAYNES POINT PROVINCIAL PARK sign south down Thirty-second Avenue. Jasmine Street is a left turn just before the park entrance and lake. Rates in high season range from $90 to $110 (double); the pampered feeling you come away with makes these rates more than reasonable.

Two kilometers south of Osoyoos (take Thirty-second Street off Highway 17) is **Haynes Point Provincial Park** (www.bcparks.ca, search word "Haynes"). Here, a strip of land stretches out into the middle of the lake, narrowing to just a little more than 60 feet (18 m) wide in spots. Forty-one

The Wild Rose

*T*he wild rose held spiritual significance for the Okanagan First Nations people. They ritually placed branches of the bush around a recently deceased person's house to prevent him or her from returning to haunt those left behind. The relatives then drank wild rose tea as an extra protection. Before burial, the grave was swept clean with wild rose branches, to keep mourners from being drawn into the earth and to protect the dead person from bad spirits.

Trivia

In July 1990 Oliver made it into the Guinness Book of World Records *when the World's Largest Cherry Pie—all 37,740 pounds, 10 ounces (17,119 kg) and 20 feet (6 m) in diameter—was baked and eaten by approximately 1,500 people.*

forested campsites line the waterfront, where fishing for trout, kokanee, bass, and lake whitefish is popular. Park personnel offer audiovisual programs and other activities relating to the history of the area. Red-winged blackbirds, ospreys, and eagles are seen regularly. If you're particularly lucky, you may hear the hum of a hovering Calliope hummingbird, Canada's tiniest bird. In summer the park is extremely popular, so reserve a spot up to three months in advance by calling the Discover Camping Campground Reservation Service (800–689–9025), which operates between March 1 and September 15. You'll get to talk to a real person between 7:00 A.M. and 7:00 P.M. weekdays and 9:00 A.M. to 5:00 P.M. on weekends. Because of the park's popularity, campers are allowed a maximum of seven days' stay in a calendar year. The gates are locked from November 1 to late March. For more information on Osoyoos's attractions and accommodation, contact the **Osoyoos Visitor Info Centre** at the junction of Highways 3 and 97 (Box 227, Osoyoos, V0H 1V0; 250–495– 7142 or 888–676–9667; fax: 250–495–6161; tourism@osoyooschamber.bc.ca; www.osoyooschamber.bc.ca).

Still on the lake, but north and east of Osoyoos (across the bridge) is the famous **Desert Ecological Reserve.** Prickly pear cactus, rock rose, antelope bush, and desert creatures such as the endangered burrowing owl, northwestern Pacific rattlesnakes, western painted turtles, black widow spiders, and scorpions all defy human intrusion in this unique terrain. Creatures found nowhere else in Canada include kangaroo rats, praying mantises, a bird called the sage thrasher, and the Great Basin spadefoot toad. Controversy hovers over whether this is a true desert, and whether this "vest-pocket desert" is the tip of the Sonoran Desert extending up from Mexico into Canada. The truth is that because of the variation in ideas on what a desert is or isn't, there will always be this confusion. Xerophytic vegetation of a type rare in Canada exists here, but this alone does not a desert make. It's located on the Osoyoos Indian Reserve and covers approximately 247 acres (100 ha). Contact the Nk'mip Desert and Heritage Centre (1000 Rancher Creek Road, RR1, Site 53, C-1, Osoyoos, V0H 1V0; 250–495–7901; 888–495–8555; nkmipdesert@oib.ca; www.nkmipdesert.com) for permission to visit in the off-season. Between May and September access is via **Nk'Mip Resort** (forty-fifth Street, Osoyoos; 250–495–7279; fax: 250– 495–7281; info@campingosoyoos.com; www.campingosoyoos. com), on Osoyoos Lake's eastern shore. Check the Web site for maps and photos of the desert, campground, and lake. A twenty-minute desert walking trail and an all-day trail have been added to aid persons interested in learning about the desert. Turn off Highway 3 East (Main Street) at Forty-fifth Street, just past the windmill and the **Little Duffer Ice Cream Parlor and Mini Golf** (250–495–6354), and drive north approximately a mile. En route you'll pass the **Indian Grove Riding Stable** (250–495–7555 June 28 to Labor Day, 250–498–4478 off-season; fax: 250–498–4463). Aaron Stelkaia and his staff will lead you through this fascinating desert on mild-mannered horses. You'll wind down into a canyon to underground waterfalls, where you'll be treated to a huge steak dinner—barbecued and ready to eat after you've done some fishing or have had a refreshing swim. You'll possibly see rattlesnakes, deer, bear, coyotes, or bighorn sheep on the way. It's an all-day ride (9:30 A.M. to 7:30 P.M.) and costs $125, but small children can double up with a parent for free. Circular (one hour or so) short rides through the desert cost $25. Ask Aaron, too, about pony rides for the kids. He has operated here for about thirty years and has extensive knowledge about the area's history.

Learn more about the history of the area and its people at **Nk'Mip Cellars** (1400 Rancher Creek Road, Osoyoos, V0H 1V0; 250–495–2985; fax: 250–495–2986; www.nkmipcellars.com). This is North America's first aboriginal owned and operated winery, a joint venture between the Osoyoos Indian Band and Vincor International. The attractive winery is situated on a bench of land overlooking the shores of Osoyoos Lake; the green vineyards and orchards are a stunning contrast to the arid desert nearby.

You'll see the remains of more modern history if you turn off Highway 97 about 7 miles (12 km) north of Osoyoos onto Road 22. Cross a rickety wooden bridge over an irrigation canal ("The Ditch") onto Black Sage Road, a paved but quiet road that passes the old **Haynes Ranch House**. Here you'll find excellent photo opportunities at a historic site.

More dramatic contrast can be seen as you continue north along Black Sage Road, where vineyards again replace the arid pastures. The Okanagan has entered the world arena in wine growing, with many high-quality wines winning national and international awards in recent years. One little gem of a winery along this road is **Carriage House Wines** (Black Sage Road, RR 1, Site 46, Comp 19, Oliver, V0H 1T0; phone/fax: 250–498–8818; carhsewine@cablerocket.com). Keep heading north to just past Orchard Grove Lane. David Wagner, the "only home-grown vintner in the area," works an

> ### Trivia
>
> *Osoyoos* is the Spanish Capital of Canada (based on its climate and buildings), and **Oliver** is British Columbia's Canteloupe City.

Haynes Ranch House near Osoyoos, Okanagan

eight-and-a-half-acre (3.4-ha) small winery with his wife, Karen. A Carriage House specialty is Kerner, produced in both a dry and an off-dry style. Another is a popular white blend called Ebonage Blanc. Fruity Chardonnay, Pinot Noir, Merlot, and Cabernet Sauvignon are all available from the winery. Appreciating the bouquet of a 1996 Kerner, a mandatory prelude before the sip, swirl, and swallow of this delicious wine, even my inexpert nose told me I had found something special. Carriage House Wines, where they "pride themselves on being small," is open daily for tours from 10:00 A.M. to 6:00 P.M. May 1 to October 31 or anytime by appointment. If you're coming from Oliver, take Road 9 left off Highway 97, left again onto Orchard Grove Lane, and left again onto Black Sage Road.

From the winery there's a lovely view of the Southern Okanagan Valley to other larger vineyards, notably *Tinhorn Creek Estate Winery* (Box 2010, RR1 S58 C10, Oliver, V0H 1T0; 250–498–3743; toll free: 888–4–TINHORN; fax: 250–498–3228; winery@tinhorn.com; www.tinhorn.com) and *Gehringer Brothers Estate Winery* (Highway 97 at Road 8; RR 1, S-23, C-4, Oliver, V0H 1T0; 250–498–3537; fax: 498–3510; toll

Trivia

After the First World War, British Columbia's premier, known as "Honest John Oliver," envisioned an irrigation canal, which would bring the dry Sonora Desert region (near the southern Okanagan Lake area) to life. Completed in 1923, the "Ditch" soon transformed this desert region into lush orchards and farms.

free: 800–784–6304), which leads me to understand that there is some truth to the rumor that the Oliver postal code, V0H 1T0, really does stand for "Valley of heaven in the Okanagan." Oliver & District Chamber of Commerce (36205 Ninety-third Street, Box 460, Oliver, V0H 1T0; 250–498–6321; fax: 250–498–3156; info@oliverchamber.bc.ca; www.oliverchamber.bc.ca) is an extensive source of information on this area, including its beaches and parks, the *Fairview Jail,* the *Oliver and District Museum* (located in the former 1924 police station at 9726–350 Street), and the fascinating *McIntyre Bluff* at the south end of Vaseux Lake. Sometimes called Indian Head, it has pictographs depicting legends about rival Indian bands who drove each other over the edge of these 820-foot (250-m) cliffs.

From Oliver take the Fairview–White Lake Road, which runs northwest from the gold rush town of Fairview to the *Dominion Radio Astrophysical Observatory* (Box 248, Penticton, V2A 6K3; 250–493–2277; fax: 250–493–7767; www.drao.nrc.gc.ca). If you're coming from Penticton, turn off Highway 97 at Kaleden junction onto White Lake Road; from the west turn south at the junction of Highway 3A and the White Lake Road and drive 5.6 miles (9 km). Should you still not find it, simply ask a friendly local where the White Lake observatory is.

A tour of the complex (which is part of the National Research Council of Canada) takes you past a row of seven antennae that work together to simulate a giant 1,969-foot (600-m) telescope. The most prominent "dish" antenna is 85 feet (26 m) across. At the visitors' center, displays explain how images from these telescopes are used to probe the invisible gases between the stars. Canadian scientists here are working to understand how stars are born, how they die, and how stars and gas are interrelated in the Milky Way. Beyond the visitors' center is a smaller radio telescope that monitors the radio output from the sun. From these data scientists can research global climate change. Because ignition systems can emit radio waves that interfere with the astronomers' observations, you must leave your car in a parking lot and walk about 600 yards to the observatory grounds. Canada's only radio observatory is open all year. The vistors' center is open weekdays during normal business hours. On weekends from Easter to Thanksgiving, a guide is available in the visitors' center from 10:00 A.M. to 5:00 P.M. Scientists conduct tours of the facility on

Sunday afternoons in July and August from 2:00 P.M. to 5:00 P.M.

North of Oliver, snugged between Vaseaux and Skaha Lakes, lies Okanagan Falls. Try the cinnamon buns at the *Falls Restaurant* (1032 Main; 250–497–5898)—they're legendary.

Just south of Penticton is a world-renowned climbing area known as *Skaha Bluffs.* From the south, turn east off Highway 97 at the northern end of Skaha Lake (site of an annual 7.38-mile [11.8-km] Ultra Swim) from South Main Street (where it meets Lakeside Road at Skaha East Park) onto Crescent Hill Road. At the top of the hill turn south onto Valley View Road, which eventually deteriorates into a winding narrow road, to the Braeside parking lot (locked in winter) at the end. From the parking lot, follow the trail east along the fence to the bluffs. There's an honor-system $5.00 per-day fee here, but climbers attest to the value considering the quality of climbing offered. Don't be put off, though; the Skaha Bluffs cater to all levels of climbing. Look for California bighorn sheep and perhaps a rattlesnake, keeping in mind that this is a fragile wildlife and plant habitat, and that any disturbances can have a serious effect.

As you approach *Penticton,* you'll know exactly where you are by the large sign visible on the east side of the highway on Munson Mountain. Then head for the beach, the most popular area here. Ask at the *Penticton Visitor Info Centre* (888 Westminster Avenue West, Penticton, V2A 8S2; 250–493–4055 or 800–663–5052; fax: 250–492–6119; visitors@penticton.org; www.penticton.org) about the **SS Sicamous,** a nineteenth-century beached sternwheeler, now a heritage site, and the *Rose Garden* next door, with hundreds of varieties of roses. You'll never have to worry about losing the kids at the beach; just tell them to meet you at the *Big Peach on the Beach,* a popular concession stand open on those lazy, hazy days.

Okanagan summers are the warmest in British Columbia, so cooling-off spots between Penticton and Summerland (like *Kickinninee* and *Sun-Oka* [from "Sunny Okanagan"] beaches on Okanagan Lake) are popular spots. With more hours of summer sunshine than Hawaii, though, make sure you're well protected.

Stuffed Chicken with Olives, Sun-Dried Tomatoes, and Mushrooms

*T*hese recipes come from Chef Bennett Manzini at Hainle Vineyards Estate Winery's Amphora Tapas Bar.

½ 12 oz.(350 ml) can black olives (pits in)

½ 9 oz. (266 ml) jar sun-dried tomatoes

10 medium-size button mushrooms

2 cloves garlic

1 package prosciutto ham

4 chicken breasts (bone in)

1 bunch fresh basil

1 cup red wine

Crushed black peppercorns

1. Remove bone from chicken and put bones into pot with 4 to 5 cups of water and bring to boil. Turn heat to simmer until liquid is reduced to half. Skim off foam while simmering.

2. Pit olives and chop. Dice sun-dried tomatoes (save oil for cooking), garlic, and mushrooms. Dice ½ package of prosciutto ham.

3. In a saucepan add sun-dried tomato oil and chopped garlic, olives, mushrooms, sun-dried tomato, and prosciutto ham. Cook about 5 minutes; then add ½ cup red wine and the same amount of chicken stock. Add pepper and ½ bunch of chopped basil. Remove from heat and allow to cool.

4. Take a small knife and insert blade into thick end of breast to make a pocket. Then take a piece of prosciutto ham and insert in pocket followed by a couple of teaspoons of filling. Use your finger to push filling further into pocket. Repeat on all chicken breasts.

5. Preheat oven to 375° F. Heat frying pan and add sun-dried tomato oil and a little olive oil. Dredge chicken in flour and then place skin side down in pan until golden brown, then brown second side. Add the rest of the filling, wine, and remainder of chicken stock; cover and place in oven for 20 to 25 minutes.

SALAD: 1 head lettuce, 4 Tbsp. balsamic vinegar, 2 handfuls sliced almonds, 6 Tbsp. olive oil, fresh Parmesan, salt and pepper to taste. Wash and dry lettuce, tear into bite-size pieces. Add vinegar, oil, salt, and pepper. Sprinkle with almonds. With potato peeler, shave off 10 to 12 large bits of parmesan.

RICE: 3 cups Arborio (or Japanese sushi rice) (short grain), 2 ½ cups chicken stock, 2 cups water. Put ingredients into pot and bring to boil, reduce heat, and simmer 15 to 20 minutes or until done.

Summerland is a major fruit-growing and processing center. Successful orchard and farm development owes much to research, and in this respect the Pacific Agri-Food Research Center (PARC) in Summerland has been a major player. Located on the grounds of this center overlooking Okanagan Lake, and opposite the **Sun-Oka Provincial Park** (8.7 miles [14 km] north of Penticton), is the historic **Summerland Ornamental Gardens and Interpretive Centre** (250–494–6385; www.summerlandornamentalgardens.org), a project of the Friends of the Summerland Research Station Gardens. Wander through, or enjoy a picnic in ten acres of these spectacular ornamental gardens from 8:00 A.M. to dusk daily (9:00 A.M. to 5:00 P.M. December to February); the Hummingbird Visitor Centre and a museum are open 1:00 P.M. to 4:00 P.M. daily in July and August.

The fruit-growing industry was helped in its early days by steam trains. A ride on the **Kettle Valley Steam Railway** (18404 Bathville Road, Box 1288, Summerland, V0H 1Z0; 250–494–8422; toll free: 877–494–8424; fax: 250–494–8452; www.kettlevalleyrail.org) will help transport you back to this time. It departs from Prairie Valley Station (mid-May to mid-October). Phone ahead or check the Web site for location, directions, and operating days and hours. Adult fares are $16, seniors and youths $15, students $14, children three to twelve $10, under three free; the family rate is $53. Entertainment, such as singing and cowboy rope-spinning, is provided on many of the train rides.

There's more railway memorabilia (including an old Kettle Valley Railway ticket booth) at the **Summerland Museum Historical Society** (9521 Wharton Street, Box 1491, Summerland, V0H 1Z0; 250–494–9395; smhschin@vip.net; www2.vip.net/~smhschin) as well as a collection of historical photographs and pioneer tools used in fruit growing. The museum is open year-round: Monday through Saturday in June, July, and August from 10:00 A.M. to 4:00 P.M.; Tuesday through Saturday September through May from 1:00 to 4:00 P.M. For more information ask at the **Summerland Visitor Info Centre** (15600 Highway 97, Box 1075, Summerland, V0H 1Z0; 250–494–2686; fax: 250–494–4039; www. welcometosummerland.com).

If you need accommodation, **Beachside B&B** is located, as its name implies, right on the beach at 15811 North Lakeshore Road, Summerland, V0H 1Z0; (250) 494–8977; carroyl@hotmail.com; www.beach sidebb.net. Head toward the lake from Highway 97 along Peach Orchard Road, just south of Summerland, and turn north on North Lakeshore Road. Rates are in the $85 to $145 (double) range. Ask Carroyl about full facility weekly rental in summer.

From the comfort of the beachfront patio, you might be lucky enough to see Ogopogo, as members of the BC Scientific Cryptozoology Club (cryptozoologybc@yahoo.ca; www.cryptosafari.com/bcscc) did during the summer of 1989. The following is a quote from their report:

> The focus of the investigation turned to Summerland, and a particularly good vantage point was located at Peach Orchard Beach, Lower Summerland, on July 30. All four members of the investigating team were stationed at various points on the beachfront when, at 3:55 P.M., a most extraordinary occurrence took place. A large patch of white water materialised close to a headland at the southern end of the beach, drawing the attention of the BCSCC observers. It was about 1,000 feet distant at this point, and it was clear that a large animal was swimming in a northerly direction against the prevailing wind and slight swell . . . this was the classic Ogopogo, with its humps well above the water level . . . The animal displayed, variously, five and sometimes six humps . . . the animal's skin was whale-like, and there appeared to be random, calcium-like deposits under the skin which appeared to be similar to barnacles in shape. All the team members agree that the animal was between 30 and 35 feet (9–10 m) in length, and was almost 3 feet (1 m) above the surface at its highest point—that being the middle hump.

Cynics and skeptics may laugh, but you just never know . . .

Back on Highway 97 the winding highway climbs past vineyards and rocky cliffs bordering Okanagan Lake to Peachland, 13 miles (21 km) north. Here Peter and Daffnaee Flanagan operate a small bright, family business, **Okanagan Pottery Studio** (6030 Highway 97S, Peachland, V0H 1X0; 250–767–2010; fax: 250–767–2540; dpflanagan@shaw.ca). Here you'll see many of the artists' works decorated in strong purples and greens and with grape-leaf designs inspired by the beauty of the Okanagan. The studio was built by Daffnaee's father, Des Loan, in 1968, and the original kiln is still in operation. Peter's work has been honored with the Special Judges' Award at Mino, Japan. Look for French butter dishes in varying sizes. The butter sits in the "lid." Water in the bottom forms a seal, preserving the butter without refrigeration. The dishes are small, practical, and inexpensive if you're looking for an Okanagan souvenir. The Flanagans have joined forces with Roy and Jean Lysholt to create wrought-iron patio furniture and lamps beautifully combined with pieces of their unique Okanagan pottery.

Another interesting stop heading north along Highway 97 (just past the huge Golf Ball on the roadside) is **Hainle Vineyards Estate Winery**

(5355 Trepanier Bench Road, Peachland, V0H 1X0; 250–767–2525; fax: 250–767–2543; 800–767–3109 for wine orders; info@hainle.com; www.hainle.com), a small, family-run winery producing naturally dry, fully fermented wines. In addition to a tasting room, wine shop, and bistro (*Amphora Tapas Bar*), where tasty lunch specials both complement and compliment their wines, the winery offers a spectacular view of the valley. Their Icewine is a rare wine made by allowing the fruit to freeze on the vine to at least 17° F (-8° C). This requires an early morning workforce frantically picking, crushing, and pressing before the warm sun thaws the grapes. The frozen water from the fruit remains in the press, and from the concentrated juice, wines result that range from sherrylike to fruity and from almost dry to rich and sweet. Hainle Winery boasts several firsts: It's located on what used to be the first peach orchard in the area, giving Peachland its name; it has the first winery-based cooking school (classes started in September 1998); Tilman's father, Walter Hainle, was the first person in Canada to make Icewine (1973), a product that is now making Canadian wines renowned around the world; it's the first winery to label its bottles "certified organic"; and as well, it's the first British Columbia winery to have its own Web site (through which wines can be ordered). Summer hours are Sunday to Thursday 10:00 A.M. to 5:00 P.M., and to 9:00 P.M. Friday and Saturday. At the Amphora Tapas Bar reservations are not necessary but recommended. In winter the winery is open Monday to Friday 10:00 A.M. to 5:00 P.M., but call ahead for Tapas Bar hours.

Recommended Reading—The Okanagan

A Rich and Fruitful Land: The History of the Valleys of the Okanagan, Similkameen, and Shuswap, by Jean Webber (compiler). Okanagan Historical Society: Harbour Publishing Company, 1999.

Ogopogo: The True Story of the Okanagan Lake Million Dollar Monster, by Arlene Gaal. Hancock House. Surrey, 2000.

Exploring the Kettle Valley Railway, by Beth Hill. Polestar Book Publishers, 2000.

McCulloch's Wonder: The Story of the Kettle Valley Railway, by Barrie Sanford. Graphic Arts Center Publishing Co., 1998.

Similkameen and South Okanagan, by Murphy Shewchuk. Surrey: Hancock House, 1987.

Okanagan Trips and Trails: A Guide to Backroads and Hiking Trails, by Judy Steeves and Murphy Shewchuk. Sonotek Publishing, 1999.

THE OKANAGAN

All over the Okanagan, *wine* is the word. The Okanagan Wine Festivals have been recognized as being among the *Top 100 Events in North America* for several years. For four days during the first weekend of every May, the *Okanagan Spring Wine Festival* takes place when valley vintners release their new wines. There are more than eighty events to enjoy over the four days. If you're there the second weekend in August, you can combine the magic of *Silver Star Mountain Resort* (Box 3002, Silver Star Mountain, V1B 3M1; 800–663–4431; 250–542–0224; fax: 250–542–1236; www.skisilverstar.com) and fine wine for three days of wine education, tasting, and dinners. If you time your visit for early October, you'll be inundated with bacchanal choices at the *Annual Fall Okanagan Wine Festival,* a hopping event with more than 150 diverse choices, from grape stomps and pig roasts to a consumer tasting, where you can sample wines from more than forty wineries all under one roof. Winter visitors (late January) can discover the magic and delicacy of icewine at the *Annual Icewine Festival.* Contact the Okanagan Wine Festivals Office (1527 Ellis Street, Kelowna, V1Y 2A7; 250–861–6654; fax: 250–861–3942; info@TheWineFestivals.com; www.TheWineFestivals.com) for information and bookings.

From the west your introduction to *Kelowna* (population 101,592 in 2002 and growing fast) is via a 2,000-foot (640-m) floating bridge, North America's first and largest. You're still in Ogopogo territory, so keep a look out as you cross Okanagan Lake. Long before the first mission settlement by Father Pandosy in 1860, Interior Salish folklore told of a mysterious monster called N'ha-a-itk, the Devil of the Lake. According to the tale, if you see a long, snakelike, humpy, greenish oddity with a horselike head, you'll be the next believer. Could this be the reason Kelowna is labeled "City of Smiles"?

Just past the community of Westbank (home of *Mission Hill Winery* [888–999–1713; www.missionhillwinery.com], which was awarded the International Wine and Spirits Avery Trophy in 1994 for the best chardonnay in the world), both avid golfers and beginners have a chance to play on Canada's first All-Putting golf course at *19 Greens Fun & Sports Centre* (2050 Campbell Road, Kelowna, V1Z 3X7; 250–769–0213; www.19greenskelowna.com), which consists of a natural grass course and an Astro Mini Golf course, both eighteen-hole courses, creatively configured with putting in mind and with a spectacular view of Okanagan Lake. From the south on Highway 97, turn right onto Campbell Road just before the floating bridge. Designed by Les Furber, the course is fully lit for starlight putting. There's also a way-too-much-fun X-treme Bounce facility and a climbing wall.

For a panoramic view of this smiling city, named Canada's most beautiful small city in 1998, hike or bike a route created by the **Kettle Valley Railway** through the horseshoe-shaped **Myra Canyon**. A one-hour bike trip over historic trestle bridges and through two tunnels will reveal breathtaking views of the canyon and Kelowna below. Devastating fires in 2003 destroyed twelve of the eighteen trestles, but nationwide support is behind local enthusiasts (Myra Canyon Trestle Restoration Society, PBC Box 611, Kelowna, V1Y 7P7) to help rebuild them. The railway was first used in 1915, but it was abandoned in the seventies, and the trestles left to rot until their restoration in the nineties. The best time to hike or bike is on the weekend, as the very rough logging roads leading up to the canyon are active. For a guided tour contact **Monashee Adventure Tours** (250–762–9253 or 888–76CYCLE; fax: 250–868–9214; www.monasheeadventuretours. com). They specialize in tours of the Kettle Valley Railroad no matter what level of rider you are; recently the local "tourist watchdog" honored them with a Best of Kelowna rating. Bike tours run mid-May to October, and everything is provided, right down to the water bottle. Depending on numbers in the group, rates range from $60 to $100, including lunch and trail snacks, for an afternoon in the glorious Myra Canyon.

> ### Trivia
>
> *Drive over to Magnetic Hill in northeast Vernon and experience the strange forces involved when you and your car mysteriously seem to be pulled "uphill." The "magnetic" spot is on Dixon Dam Road, between Hughes and Hartnell Roads. Go to Hughes Road and then travel south on Dixon Dam Road past seven alder trees; stop at the second tree, put the car in neutral, and then listen to the kids say: "Oh wow!"*

If you prefer a one-way ride, **Air-Hart Aviation** (1326 Water Street, Kelowna, V1Y 9P3; 250–762–9830; toll free: 877–766–6699; fax: 250–762–9840; www.air-hart.com) will fly you and your bike to McCulloch Lake for a full day's cycle along the Kettle Valley Railway to the Okanagan's oldest orchard, where you'll savor freshly pressed juice and seasonal fruit. The $159 cost includes the floatplane ride, guide, gear rental, snack, and return transport to Kelowna. Contact **Sparky's Lakefront Sports Centre** (1310 Water Street, Kelowna, V1Y 9P3; 250–862–2469; www.sparkysrentals.com) for details.

After a strenuous hike you'll need a restful night. **A View to Remember Bed and Breakfast** (1090 Trevor Drive, Kelowna, V1Z 2J8; 888–311–9555;

250–769–4028; fax: 250–769–6168; info@kelownabandb.com; www. kelownabandb.com) will provide all the rest you may need. This elegant home is decorated with antiques inside and lovely gardens outside. The suites are new, and there's a huge sunny kitchen with a mural and other hand-painted touches by a local artist. Enjoy the fruit from these gardens on a patio with a superb view of the lake and mountains. From Highway 97 take the Hudson exit south, turn right on Guidi Road and left onto Trevor Drive. Rates are in the $89 to $99 (double) range.

Kelowna is fast gaining a reputation as a cultural destination, attested to by the recently completed *Rotary Centre for the Arts* (421 Cawston Avenue, Kelowna, V1Y 6Z1; 250–717–5304; fax: 250–717–5314; www. rotarycentreforthearts.com), a multipurpose venue for special events, theatre, visual art, music, and festivals; it is operated by the Kelowna Visual and Performing Arts Centre Society. Here in the Rotary Centre for the Arts you'll find *The Centre Art Gallery* (250–448–8888), an originals-only venture by well-known local gallery owners featuring paintings, bronze and soapstone sculptures, and many more examples of fine Canadian works. As well, there's the *Kelowna Art Gallery* (1315 Water Street, Kelowna, V1Y 9R3; 250–762–2226; fax: 250–762–9875; kelowna.artgallery@shaw.ca; www.galleries.bc.ca/kelowna), the north terrace of which is graced by *Skagway*, a work by renowned Canadian sculptor Robert Murray.

Nearby, next to the BC Orchard Industry Museum in the historic Laurel Packinghouse, *The Wine Museum* (1304 Ellis Street; 250–868–0441; fax: 250–868–9272) not only offers tastings of world-class Okanagan wines but also displays early wine-making and barrel-making equipment. A feature is a 3,000-year-old clay drinking horn excavated in Iran. The museum is open Monday to Saturday 10:00 A.M. to 5:00 P.M. and Sunday noon to 5:00 P.M.

South of the city, off the KLO Road near Pandosy Street, is the *Tutt Street Square* (3045 Tutt Street). There's more artistry here at the *Tutt Street Gallery* (#9, 3045 Tutt Street, Kelowna, V1Y 2H4; phone/fax: 250–861–4992; jjohnson@tuttstreetgallery.com; www.tuttstreetgallery. com), where oils, raku, bronzes, watercolors, and more—all top-quality works by Canadian artists—are displayed for sale. The gallery is open Tuesday through Friday 10:00 A.M. to 5:00 P.M. and to 4:00 P.M. Saturdays. Just across from the gallery in the square is the *Bonfire Bistro* (250–862–3045) a funky but first-class restaurant. There's an impressive menu for both lunch and dinner. Try the oven-roasted venison rack or the very tasty crab cakes. The wine selection, this being the Okanagan, is tops too.

Whatever your needs in the Kelowna area, the **Kelowna Visitor Info Centre,** just east of the Floating Bridge at 544 Harvey Avenue (Highway 97), Kelowna, V1Y 6C9; (250) 861–1515 or (800) 663–4345; fax: (250) 861–3624; info@tourism kelowna.org; www.tourismkelowna.org, will help you enjoy all aspects of this lovely city.

The staff will probably convince you that wine rules in the Okanagan! Not to be outdone by California's Napa Valley Wine Train, the **Okanagan Valley Wine Train** (888–674–TRAK [8725]; 250–712–9888; fax: 780–478–7666; funtrain@telusplanet.net; www.okanaganwinetrain.com) is one of Kelowna's newest and most popular attractions. It's a five-hour scenic round-trip (Kelowna to Vernon) excursion, which departs from Kelowna every Saturday at 5:00 P.M. between mid-July and mid-October. It combines the beauty of the Okanagan with the romance of the rails passing through **Lake Country** (the Apple Capital of Canada, producing more than 35 percent of Canada's apples), a municipality comprised of **Winfield, Okanagan Centre, Oyama,** and **Carr's Landing,** and past three beautiful lakes: Okanagan, Wood, and Kalamalka. Passengers have a choice of a day coach (adult fare $29.95) or three theme carriages in which meals are served (adult fare including dinner and live entertainment is $79.95). The theme choices are the Hollywood Car with its Big Band sound; the Rock and Roll Car, where you'll hear hits from the fifties and sixties; and the Country and Western Car.

The North Okanagan

From Kelowna take Highway 97 north along the east coast of Okanagan Lake for 29 miles (47 km) north to **Vernon.** *Agri-tourism* is a word often heard in this area; it refers to the many specialty livestock and fruit and vegetable operations open to the public. Just a few miles north of Vernon at Armstrong, Tony and Connie Seale welcome visitors to their llama-breeding establishment at **The Llama Farm** (250–546–3038; llmafarm@junction.net). Take Highway 97A northeast from Armstrong to McLeod Road, then to the corner of Heighton Road. Farther on at the end of McLeod Road you'll find **Chickadee Ridge Miniatures** (1403 McLeod Road, Armstrong, V0E 1B8; 250–546–9323; fax: 250–546–8905; info@chickadeeridge.com; www.chickadeeridge.com), where they invite you to bring the kids to "Come talk to the animals." There are several varieties of miniature animals, a gift store, and a concession stand. It's open seasonally from 10:00 A.M. to 4:00 P.M. At **Little Mountain**

Peruvians (5231 Stepney Road, Armstrong; 250–546–3970; little mountain@telus.net), visitors are always welcome to watch Peruvian *pasos* being trained. Take Highway 97A 3 miles (5 km) north to Stepney Road and follow it for 3 miles (5 km) to the end.

And if you've never seen alpacas, one of Canada's largest herds can be found at **Horizon Adventures Ltd.** (3285A Mabel Lake Road, Enderby, V0E 1V5; phone/fax: 250–838–9559; okalpaca@cnx.net). Visitors are welcome to tour this one-hundred-acre farm on the Shuswap River, 20 miles (32.85 km—hence the address) east of the Enderby bridge in the scenic Monashee Mountains. And it's all free! Children love having their photos taken with these gentle animals, and if visiting between mid-May to mid-September, they may have an opportunity to pet *las crías* (the baby alpacas). You'll see both huacuya and the rare, silky-fleeced suri alpaca—about 125 animals in all—as well as a herd of about eight llamas.

> ### Trivia
>
> **Armstrong**, *known for its cheese, is called the Celery City of BC!*

Plan to stay a few days in the area. As well as a few B&B establishments, next door to the llamas there's a twenty-site campground, **Kingfisher Campground and Store** (3303 Mabel Lake Road, Enderby, V0E 1V0; 250–838–7730; fax: 250–838–6697), where delicious homemade pizzas and other meals are served. About 7 miles (12 km) west of the alpaca farm is the **Kingfisher Environmental Interpretive Centre** (RR2, Site 14A, Comp 6, Enderby, V0E 1V0; 250–838–0004; www.enderbylive.ca/kingfisher.html). Call for more information or a tour of the hatchery, which has one of the most successful salmon enhancement programs in Canada. You'll also see here a half-size replica of a kekuli, the traditional underground home of the Shuswap Indians.

"U-pick" farming is becoming popular in the North Okanagan. At **MacDonald's Pure Beeswax** (250–546–3237; jamesmacdonald@telus.net), between Vernon and Armstrong at 4663 North Grandview Flats Road, you'll find not only prize-winning honey and beeswax candles but also apricots and cherries ripe for the picking. Take Highway 97 north to St. Anne's Road. Continue north to South Grandview Flats Road, then west onto North Grandview Flats Road and look for the HONEY FOR SALE sign. If you'd prefer to pick apples, pears, or plums, call **Cayford's Orchard** (250–546–3411) at 4377 Hallam Road, about 2 miles northwest of Armstrong off the Salmon River Road. Of course, you have to be there in season. Contact the **Vernon Visitor Info Centre** (701 Highway 97 South, Box 520, Vernon, V1B 3W4; 250–542–1415; fax: 250–545–3114; toll free: 800–665–0795; info@vernontourism.com; www.vernontourism.com)

for information on fruit-growing seasons and to find out about other farms involved in this fast-growing agri-tourism industry.

Kettle River Valley

Four miles (6.5 km) east of the Kelowna floating bridge, the lonely Highway 33 winds south from Highway 97 for 80 miles (129 km), following the course of the Kettle River through pretty, pastoral landscapes. A side road (watch out for cattle and deer) brings you to the **Big White Ski Resort** (800–663–2772 or 250–765–8888; fax: 250–765–1822; bigwhite@bigwhite.com; www.bigwhite.com), 34 miles (55 km) from Kelowna and on the edge of the Monashees. With more than 24 feet (7.5 m) of champagne powder annually, expect some superb skiing here. You'll also find Canada's fastest and longest quad chairlift, the Gem Lake Express. It runs at 20 feet (6 m) per second. In summer, the slopes are more peaceful. With beautiful views of the Monashees, good fishing, and lovely walks, consider a stay at the award-winning **White Crystal Inn,** located in the heart of the village. The rooms are large; it's open year-round and offers excellent dining. Double accommodation starts at $69 in summer.

Halfway along Highway 33, at Beaverdell (population about 350), is the historic **Beaverdell Hotel** (Box 40, Beaverdell, V0H 1A0; 250–484–5513), where a wall inscription in The Ladies Parlour reads: "Oh what stories she could tell," and promenades us back to an exciting era invoking memories of the heady days of old. The hotel, built in 1901, claims significance as the oldest operating hotel in British Columbia. Occasionally accommodation is available! Don't leave without trying the very tasty homemade burgers at **Our Place Cafe** (240–484–5529), then get ready to explore the Kootenays when you reach tiny Rock Creek (population fifty-one) 31 miles (51 km) south, just north of the Canada–United States border on Highway 3. We're back on the Crowsnest.

PLACES TO STAY IN THE OKANAGAN

HEDLEY
The Gold House Bed and Breakfast, 644 Colonial Road, Hedley, V0X 1K0; (250) 292–8418; toll free: (866) 676–GOLD (4653); www.thegoldhouse.com. Rates $65–$85.

KELOWNA
A View to Remember Bed and Breakfast, 1090 Trevor Drive, V1Z 2J8; (888) 311–9555; phone/fax: (250) 769–4028; www.kelowna bandb.com. Rates: $89–$99.

KEREMEOS
Cathedral Lakes Lodge, (888) 255–4453; www.cathedral-lakes-lodge.com.

Login Bed and Breakfast, C1 Site 27, Highway 3 West, V0X 1N0; (250) 499–2781/2664; loginbnb@keremeos. com; www.loginbnb.com

OSOYOOS/OLIVER
Haynes Point Lakeside Guest House, 3619 Jasmine Drive, V0H 1V0; phone/fax: (250) 495–7443; www.bbcanada. com/14.html. $90–$110 double.

Nk' mip Resort, Forty-fifth Street, Osoyoos, (250) 495–7279; fax: (250) 495–7281; www.campingosoyoos.com. Open June–September. Serviced sites, store, washrooms with showers, playground.

PRINCETON
Princeton Castle Resort and R.V. Park, Princeton-Summerland Road, RR 1, Site 1, Comp 10, V0X 1W0; (888) 228–8881 or (250) 295–7988; info@castleresort.com; www.castleresort.com. Cottages, lodge, and RV park.

SUMMERLAND
Beachside B & B, 15811 North Lakeshore Road, V0H 1Z0; (250) 494–8977; carroyl@hotmail.com; www.beachsidebb.net. Rates: $85–$145 (double).

PLACES TO EAT IN THE OKANAGAN

KELOWNA
Bonfire Bistro, 3045 Tutt Street, V1Y 2H4; (250) 862–3045. First class—open for lunch and dinner.

Water Street Grill, 1346 Water Street, V1Y 9P4; (250) 860–0707. Casual, interesting menu. Open daily from 11:30 A.M.

KEREMEOS
The Grist Mill Tea Room, RR 1, Upper Bench Road, V0X 1N0; (250) 499–2888. Inexpensive.

PEACHLAND
Amphora Tapas Bar, at Hainle Vineyards, 5355 Trepanier Bench Road, V0H 1X0; (250) 767–2525. Delicious stuff. Reservations recommended.

PRINCETON
The Belaire Restaurant, 161 Vermilion Avenue, V0X 1W0; (250) 295–7711. Popular for its homemade pies and soups.

VERNON
Andy's Added Touch, 3006 Thirtieth Avenue; (250) 549–4706. On Main Street at the Kalamalka Hotel. Full meals.

The Kootenays

The Monashee, Selkirk, and Purcell ranges straddle glacier-fed rivers and lakes to form this scenic area of British Columbia's interior, where the Ktunaxa people trace their unbroken presence back to before the last ice age. In the late 1800s a frenzied rush for precious metals brought newcomers. Many of the towns they built are now but ghostly remnants, but some grew and today, with an excellent system of highways and free ferries, serve travelers wanting to explore this mountainous wilderness.

Our trek through the Kootenays starts in *Boundary County* close to the U.S. border in historic Greenwood and follows the Crowsnest Highway to Rossland, where a tour of a hard-rock gold mine gives us a taste of the fever that shook those early immigrants. We'll experience the Russian influence in the south as we enjoy borscht near a Doukhobor museum, then relive the mining past in a ghost town. We'll meet the interesting people of east Kootenay Lake, where ashrams, weavers, broom makers, blacksmiths, and an embalming-bottle house will arouse our curiosity.

Greenwood

After leaving the Okanagan we rejoin the Crowsnest (Highway 3) and travel east to *Greenwood,* Canada's smallest city, incorporated in 1897. Located near the Washington State border, Greenwood features many historic buildings and sites. As you enter the city from the west, you'll see an old smokestack on the north side of the highway. This marks the ruins of the *BC Copper Company Smelter* that operated between 1901 and 1919. It stands as a reminder of the mining history of the city. A sign indicates a track to the 120-foot (40-m) chimney near *Lotzkar Memorial Park,* where an abandoned underground shaft and slag heaps evoke images of dusty miners. Nearby, the former West Kootenay Power building is being converted into the *Boundary Mining and Power Interpretive Centre.* As part of this

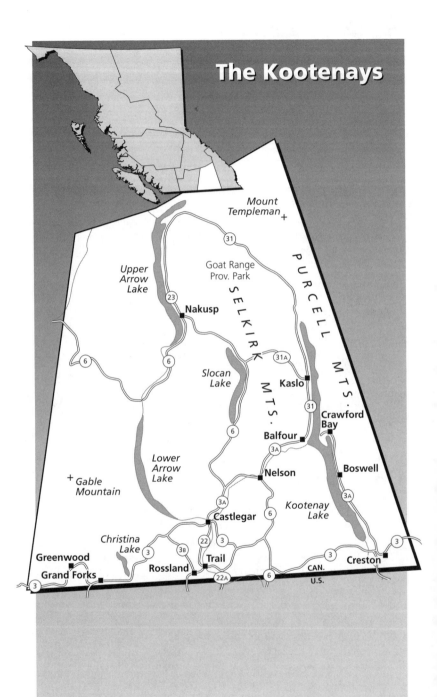

The Kootenays

AUTHOR'S TOP TEN PICKS IN THE KOOTENAYS

Phoenix Forest and History Tour, Greenwood

Red Mountain, Rossland

Doukhobor Village Museum, Castlegar

Ainsworth Hot Springs Resort

S.S. Moyie, in Kaslo

Sandon Ghost Town

Yasodhara Ashram, Riondel

North Woven Broom Company, Crawford Bay

The Glass House, in Boswell

Creston Valley Wildlife Management Area

development alternative energy will be produced at the facility using solar cells and a space-age-looking windmill.

Greenwood is steeped in history, not all of it upbeat. In 1942 more than 1,200 Japanese Canadians were interned here. Memories of this were rekindled in 1997 when part of Greenwood, elevation 2,454 feet (750 m), was transformed into the coastal fishing village of Amity Harbor in the filming of the Oscar-nominated *Snow Falling on Cedars* starring Ethan Hawke.

You're still surrounded by history at the restored **Greenwood Inn Saloon/Restaurant** (321 Copper South; 250–445–6623), where historic photos depict Greenwood at the turn of the century. In those days the city of 3,000 supported one hundred businesses, including fourteen hotels, two newspapers, two banks, and a thousand-seat opera house. In 2002 its population was but 677, with no sign of an opera house. But the wood frame, three-story Greenwood Inn has survived and operated continuously for more than one hundred years. Check out (or perhaps do a little leaning on) the 30-foot-long (9-m) antique bar. Opposite and just down the block at the **Welcome Home Tea Room & Gift Shoppe** (250–445–2234), you'll enjoy home-style breakfasts and lunches surrounded by some exciting artwork. There's more history in the form of a player piano and several other antiques at the **Copper Eagle Cappuccino and Bakery** (325 Copper South, 250–445–6121), where the cinnamon buns and lattes are legendary.

On a city walking tour, take a look at the Hammersly House (perhaps the friendly owners may give you a tour), the City Hall (previously the Court House—there's an excellent display of the original stained glass upstairs in the court room), the Sacred Heart Catholic church (high up on the hill), and the redbrick, towered Greenwood Post Office, with its antique, hourly chiming clock. Ask for directions at the **Greenwood Museum/Visitor Info Centre** (214 Copper Street, Greenwood, V0H 1J0; 250–445–6355; museum@sunshinecable.com; www.greenwood museum.com), at the seasonal Visitor Info Booth. The museum is open daily in summer from 9:00 A.M. to 5:00 P.M. and is worth a visit for its history tours and an interesting collection of mining relics and photos of nearby Phoenix, now defunct, but at one time the highest city in Canada and home of the first Canadian professional hockey team.

Check www.greenwoodcity.com for extensive information on Greenwood and the surrounding area.

If you want to really explore the area, stay awhile at *Country Elegance Bed & Breakfast* (52486 Wallace Creek Road, Box 539, Greenwood, V0H 1J0; 250–445–6677; fax 250–445–2112; husbands@direct.ca; www.bcbnb.com). This beautiful modern home is set in sixteen acres of forest overlooking a lush green valley. Turn onto Boundary Creek Road (Jewel Lake turnoff) 0.6 mile east of Greenwood, then left onto Wallace Creek Road. It's about 3 miles (4.8 km) from town.

The *Phoenix Forest and History Tour* is a two-hour, self-guided driving tour that takes you past the old *Phoenix Cemetery,* where towering Douglas fir trees now grow beside graves of young miners and victims of the 1918–1919 influenza epidemic. A detailed brochure that makes the tour much more interesting is available from the Greenwood or Grand Forks museums or the Chamber of Commerce in Grand Forks. Or for maps, history, and trail descriptions check www.phoenixforest.freehomepage. com. The drive starts (or ends) in Greenwood at the junction of Highway 3 and Phoenix Road, covering 13.6 miles (22 km) of well-maintained road. You'll pass an area around Marshall Lake that is now a cross-country skier's dream, with more than 10 miles (17 km) of trails. Alpine skiing is nearby at the *Phoenix Ski Hill* (250–442–2813; www.skiphoenix. com), where runs are named after the old copper mines. Ask, too (at the museum), for accommodation information and brochures to do hiking/biking/horseback-riding/heritage walk/City Hall tours.

The folks (Faith and Ron) at the *Lind Valley Guest Ranch* (Box 362, Greenwood, V0H 1J0; phone/fax: 250–445–6585; www.lindvalleyguest ranch.com) will also take you to this Phoenix area—on easygoing horses. Take Greenwood Street past the Post Office to Lind Creek Road and drive 3 miles (5 km) to the ranch, where you'll discover more of an adventure than a place to sleep. It's set high up in the mountain valley. Guests see firsthand how an active cattle ranch works and can enjoy trail rides to deserted mining towns. Or if you really want to get into the backcountry, you can try an overnight wagon trip complete with campfire singing and storytelling—a trek into the past.

Grand Forks

Six miles (9.5 km) west of *Grand Forks* along Highway 3, keep an eye out for the abandoned two-story, redbrick *Doukhobor houses* and barns on the south side of the highway. The Doukhobors (or "spirit wrestlers") were a group of Russian pacifists who fled from persecution in Russia to Saskatchewan and Manitoba, only to be evicted again after rejecting the oath of allegiance. In 1908 they arrived in the Grand Forks area, where they farmed simply and were self-sufficient in almost every way. Although the communes are now deserted, the religion lives on.

As does the cuisine! Try a typical Russian meal at the **Chef's Garden Restaurant** (4415 Highway 3; 250–442–0257), 3 miles (5 km) west of Grand Forks at Rilkoff's General Store. "Russian Food from Russian Folks" is the claim, and delicious it is, too. Try the Galooptsi (cabbage rolls) or Nalesniki (Russian crepes filled with cottage cheese) or the Voreniki (potato-based dumplings). They also sell Russian souvenirs. Nearby, off Reservoir Road, enjoy country hospitality and homemade preserves at the **Orchard Bed and Breakfast** (5615 Spencer Road, RR 1, S850C, C3, Grand Forks, V0H 1H0; 250–442–8583; fax: 250– 442–4050).

Continue north along Reservoir Road to the **Fructova Doukhobor Heritage Centre**, open for tours from 1:00 to 4:00 P.M., Monday and Thursday, at 6110 Reservoir Road (250–442–3523), and on to Hardy Mountain Road, where you'll learn more about Doukhobor culture at the **Mountain View Doukhobor Museum** (3655 Hardy Mountain Road; 250–442–8474). Displayed here are handmade household articles, tools, costumes, and photographs. It's open June 1–September 30, but phone first.

Top Annual Events in the Kootenays

Summer Theatre Production: Gold Fever Follies, *Rossland; July/August; (250) 362–5666 or (250) 362–9063*

Winter Carnival, *Rossland; January; (250) 362–5666; chamber@rossland.com*

Silver City Days, *Trail; May; (250) 368–3144; trail@city oftrail.com*

Nelson Artwalk, *Nelson; July/September; (250) 352–2402; ndac@direct.ca*

Kaslo Jazz Etc. Summer Music Festival, *Kaslo; July/August; (250) 353–7538; kaslojazz@netidea.com*

SS Moyie, *Model Boat Regatta, Kaslo; August; (250) 353–2525*

Castlegar Sunfest, *Castlegar; June; (250) 365–3386*

Pass Creek Fall Fair, *Castlegar; September; (250) 365–6313*

Creston Blossom Festival, *Creston; May; (250) 428–4342*

Nelson International Streetfest; *July; (250) 352–7188; streetfest@kics.bc.ca;*

Continue down Hardy Mountain Road into **Grand Forks,** once a lively (perhaps raunchy) hub, with a colorful red-light district and a Chinatown. Rum running, logging, mining, and railroading ruled "The Forks," where the Granby and Kettle Rivers meet. Now the railways are gone, as are the smelters, but you can relive its history at the **Grand Forks Boundary Museum** (7370 Fifth Street, V0H 1H0; 250–442–3737; fax: 250–442–5688; boundarymuse@look.ca) on the main street at the corner of Central Avenue. It's open Monday–Friday 8:00 A.M. to 4:30 P.M. and daily in summer.

Beside the museum at the *Visitor Info Centre* (7362 Fifth Street, Box 1086, Grand Forks, V0H 1H0; 250–442–2833; fax: 250–442–5688; gfchambe@sunshinecable.com; www.grandforkschamber.com), pick up a pamphlet to guide you on an 18-mile (30-km) drive or bike ride past the *Granby Mining and Smelter Company,* at one time the largest non-ferrous copper smelter in the British Empire. Today a couple of slag heaps (now processed as Kleen Blast and used in sandblasting and roofing) are all that remain of the Granby smelter. Take the steel bridge over the Granby River (Granby Road) north to the *Hummingbird Bridge* (a fishing and swimming spot). Cross the bridge and take North Fork Franklin Road, which brings you back south to town past an old Columbia and Western Station, now the *Grand Forks Station Pub* (7654 Donaldson Drive; 250–442–5855), where you can enjoy pub-style meals.

If you're after accommodation in Grand Forks, *The Maples Bed & Breakfast* (931 Central Avenue, Grand Forks; V0H 1H0; 250–442–8182; fax: 250–442–8156) is within easy walking distance to town on the corner of Ninth Street. It's a comfortable heritage home with delightful gardens, and kids and pets are welcome. You'll be treated to a full breakfast, and if you just want to chill out, there are televisions in the rooms. It's open year-round.

Thirteen miles (20 km) beyond Grand Forks, the Crowsnest heads north, hugging the long and lovely *Christina Lake,* one of the warmest and clearest lakes in British Columbia. There are two provincial parks with lakefront sites: *Gladstone,* with sixty-three vehicle-accessible

My Personal Tour Guide

Years ago I lived in the Eastern Arctic, where I knew Trish Exner. Today she lives in a pretty, blue-roofed house on a hilltop in Rossland. Twenty-seven Christmas cards later, we strolled Rossland's San Francisco–like hills, remembering our Baffin days. Trish introduced me to some of the town's colorful characters. I met Lee Flanders, the barber, who joked he'd rather be a barber than one of those "schlubs down in the mine." We said hello to Jack McDonald, Rossland's historian, and Harry Lefebvre, who used to be the mayor. Maurice Samuelson ambled by; he used to be the postman. Trish was the consummate tour guide, taking me from hot pools to osprey nests to beautiful lookouts in the Silvery Slocan, and finally back to the Exner cottage on Kootenay Lake, which was mine to stay in "for as long as you like." That northern hospitality I remembered so well is alive and kicking in Rossland.

campsites at Texas Creek, and *Christina Lake* (no campsites). Check the www.bcparks.ca site (keywords "Gladstone" or "Christina") for maps and information. Several commercial campgrounds (some with cabins) and a number of motels are located along the lake. Reservations for all accommodations at this very popular lake are recommended. You'll find a large choice at www.christinalakevacation.com (866–447–9334). Golfers will enjoy the eighteen-hole *Christina Lake Golf Course* (Box 1106, Grand Forks, V0H 1H0; 250–447–6104; fax: 250–447–6628; www.christinalakegolfclub.com), set among majestic pines next to the Kettle River, with the rugged Christina Range as a scenic backdrop. The course is professionally designed by Les Furber, and with a good sprinkling of bunkers and water hazards, it's a fair challenge. It's on Highway 395 0.6 mile south of Highway 3, and is open April 1 to October 31.

Kootenay South

Fifteen miles (24 km) east of Christina Lake on Highway 3, the highway passes through mountains of scenic forests. Cedar, birch, fir, and hemlock stands lead to the Paulson Bridge, where the views down into McRae Creek are spectacular. *Bonanza Pass,* 6 miles (10 km) farther, cuts through the Monashees at 5,036 feet (1,535 m) shortly before the highway meets the 3B south to Rossland. At the junction winter travelers can enjoy the *Paulson Cross Country Ski Trail* (250–365–3527; www.castlegarnordic.ca), with its 28 miles (45 km) of track-set trails. Adjacent to it, *Nancy Greene Provincial Park* features a subalpine lake and pleasant hiking trails. For more information check www.bcparks.ca (search keyword "Nancy").

Rossland

The Crowsnest follows Blueberry Creek to Castlegar, but first visit *Rossland,* 17 miles (28 km) south on Highway 3B. It sits at 3,398 feet (1,036 m) above sea level in the crater of an ancient volcano. In all seasons it erupts with life. In winter just ask any Red Mountain ski bum, and in spring, summer, or fall, dare to stop a mountain-biker blazing down one of the trails. Of the 3,739 (in 2002) folks who live in Rossland, more than 60 percent are under forty-five, which might explain its lively, small-town feel.

Rossland is Nancy Greene country. A nationally recognized name for Olympic Gold success in alpine skiing, Nancy Greene has had named for her a lake, a mountain, a provincial park, and a recreation area. She started her climb to fame back in the sixties at the fabulous **Red Mountain** (Box 670, Rossland, V0G 1Y0; 800–663–0105; 250–362–7384; fax: 250–362– 5833; 877–969–7669 for reservations; redmtn@ski-red.com; www. ski-red.com), home of Western Canada's first chairlift. The mountain itself is legendary among hard-core skiers and snowboarders for its steep, challenging terrain. But beginners need not fear, as Granite Mountain (part of the complex) features a few easier runs including the seemingly never-ending Long Squaw. Located just a mile north of town, its full-tilt diamond runs tower over Rossland. Nordic enthusiasts might find the nearby **Black Jack Cross-Country Trails** (www.skiblackjack.ca), with more than 30 miles (50 km) of groomed classic tracks and skating lanes, just as exhilarating.

The Rossland Thriftlodge (1199 Nancy Greene Highway, Rossland, V0G 1Y0; 250–362–7364; fax: 250–362–7315; 800–663–0203 for reservations only; thriftlodge@shaw.ca; thriftlodge rossland.ca), at the junction of Highways 22 and 3B, offers package deals with Red Mountain (accommodation, lift pass, and taxes) from $150 double. Regular double rates are from $59. There's the added convenience of a hearty breakfast included in the rates, plus the decadence of a twelve-person outdoor hot tub. In summer, theRossland thriftlodge offers golf packages and rents out mountain bikes.

At this same highway junction (in summer the Visitor Info Centre site), the **Rossland Historical Museum** (Box 26, Rossland, V0G 1Y0; 888–448–7444; 250–362–7722; fax: 250–362–5379; museum@rossland.com; www.rosslandmuseum. ca) features mining history and, as well, houses the **Western Canada Ski Hall of Fame** (where local champions Nancy Greene and Kerrin Lee-

Trivia

Francis Mawson Rattenbury designed the impressive British Columbia Legislature building and the Empress Hotel in Victoria. His private life was also impressive. A married man, he openly courted his mistress, Alma Packenham. After the death of his wife, he married Alma and left Victoria to settle in Bournemouth, England. Alma soon had designs on the family chauffeur, though, and the pair were charged with murdering Rattenbury. She was acquitted, but her lover, George Stoner, was sentenced to death. Unable to go on, Alma committed suicide. Stoner had his sentence commuted to life imprisonment and was eventually released.

Leroi Mine

Gartner are honored). Open from mid-May to mid-September, it's the site of the *Leroi Mine,* the only hard-rock gold mine in Canada that offers public tours. Try your luck at gold panning during the forty-five-minute guided walking tour, then enjoy a light lunch in *The Tea Room Restaurant,* next to the museum lobby. After being sold for a $12.50 recording fee, the Leroi eventually grossed more than $30 million. In the late 1890s it produced 50 percent of Canada's gold at a time when Ross-land's population was around 7,000. It ran dry in 1929, a black year for Rossland, as it was also the year of a disastrous fire.

Despite fires, in Rossland you'll get that turn-of-the-century feel when you see its heritage buildings. The city has produced a brochure (**Historical Heritage Walking Tour**) to guide you through its architectural history. Contact the Rossland Red Mountain Resort Association (Box 1385, Rossland, V0G 1Y0; 877–969–7669; 250–362–5666; fax: 250–362–5399; chamber@rossland.com; www.rossland.com) or check at the Info Centre to find out more about these thirty designated heritage buildings.

One of the grandest, the **Bank of Montreal,** on the corner of Washington Street and Columbia Avenue, was designed by Francis Mawson Rattenbury. The restored, wooden counters and ornate plaster ceilings sit above the **Golden City Barber Shop** (formerly a telegraph office), where many tales of fortunes won or lost must have been heard. You can still have your hair cut (and talk about lost fortunes) in an original 1926 porcelain revolving chair that was reupholstered with Naugahyde from the old Rossland theater seats.

Next door to the barbershop on Washington Street was once the town bathhouse. It's now **The Cellar Fibre Studio** (2002 Washington Street; Box 1575, Rossland, V0G 1Y0; 250–362–7600) and features kids' clothes, weaving, and pottery, mostly work of Kootenay locals. Drop in and hear tales of miners who hid their gold under the floorboards.

On the other side of Washington Street is a funky bookstore, coffee bar, and micro bakery with yummy, homemade delectables. **Gold Rush Books and Espresso** (open seven days per week at 2063 Washington Avenue; 250–362–5333; 800–668–0140; fax: 250–362–5566; goldrush@ rossland.com) serves delicious coffees, homemade muffins, rustic sourdough breads, cookies, soups, and gourmet teas. An eclectic book selection covers everything from philosophy to cooking.

Other buildings of historic note are the **Post Office,** built in 1910 on the corner of Queen Street and Columbia Avenue, and the **Courthouse,** on the corner of Monte Cristo Street and Columbia Avenue. Completed in 1901 at a cost of $53,000, the stained glass and woodwork in the courtroom are exquisite. The building holds National Heritage status. Then take a look at Saint Andrew's United Church and the **BC Firefighter's Museum** (Box 789, Rossland, V0G 1Y0; 250–364–1194/1126; fax: 250–364–1164), on opposite corners at Queen Street and First Avenue. The museum features a hose tower, horse-drawn hose-and-reel wagons, uniforms, and old fire trucks. It's open May to September and admission is $3.00.

There's no need to pay a mother lode for accommodation in Rossland. West of the Rossland Red Mountain Resort Association at 2125 Columbia

Trivia

Trail is called the Home of Champions. Two of these champions include Olympic Gold medalists Kerrin-Lee Gartner (skiing) and Kathleen Heddle (rowing).

Avenue, **Mountain Shadow Hostel** (Box 100, Rossland, V0G 1Y0; 250–362–7160; 888–393–7160; fax: 250–362–7150; mhostel@look.ca) is but $17 per night for a basic bed, shower, kitchen facilities, TV room, reading room, and storage area. There are three family rooms, as well as seven other rooms that sleep four, six, or eight. Another cozy place in town, one very popular with "powderpigs" (Red Mountain is seven minutes away and there's cross-country skiing from the door), is **Angela's Bed and Breakfast** (1520 Spokane Street, Rossland, V0G 1Y0; phone/fax: 250–362–7790; angela@netidea.com; www.visitangela.com). It's renowned for its relaxing fireplace, outdoor hot tub, delicious breakfasts, private suites, and warm atmosphere. Also available are Internet service and self-catering kitchens. Across from the B&B there's a four-bedroom, fully furnished guest house with mountain views—great for a crowd.

Trail

W hen you've had your fill of Rossland, and that isn't easy, head down Highway 3B east to **Trail.** Here the road drops 2,000 feet (610 m) in 7 miles (11 km) into one of British Columbia's major industrial cities. This is the home of **Teck Cominco,** the world's largest integrated **lead-zinc smelter**. Retired Cominco employees give two-hour tours of the Cominco complex weekdays during summer at 10:00 A.M. and by reservation only the rest of the year. Children under twelve are not admitted, and visitors must wear long-sleeve shirts, slacks, and covered shoes. No cameras, videos, or pacemakers are allowed. Tours are free. Teck Cominco also has an **Interpretive Centre** (a mini-science center) at 200–1199 Bay Avenue (above the TD Bank). Here you'll find exhibits concerning Teck Cominco's history and products, and as well you can watch videos on a big-screen TV or play an interactive computer game called Groundwork—Exploring for Minerals in Canada. Contact the **Trail Visitor Information Centre** (200–1199 Bay Avenue, Trail, V1R 4A4; 250–368–3144; fax: 250–368–6427; tcoc@netidea.com; www.trail chamber.bc.ca) for information.

After the smelter tour enjoy a swim at the **Trail Aquatic and Leisure Centre** (1875 Columbia Avenue; 250–368–6484) beside the baseball park, followed by a spaghetti dinner at the **Colander Restaurant** (1475 Cedar Avenue, Trail, V1R 4C5; 250–364–1816), where all the pasta you can eat, meatballs, salad, a bun, and coffee, costs less than $12. Italian food is not uncommon fare in Trail, a city with a long Italian heritage. It proudly maintains the only Italian archives in North America at **Cristoforo Colombo Lodge** (584 Rossland Avenue, Trail, V1R 3M8; 250–368–8921). The public is welcome here (for free) to learn about Trail's dynamic Italian history. Learn, too, how Trail received its "Home of Champions" designation at the Alan Tognotti Sports Hall of Fame in the Trail Memorial Centre, which is beside the bridge at 1051 Victoria Street. There's a special section featuring the story of the 1939 and 1961 World Champion Trail Smoke Eaters Hockey Team.

And if you need a spot to put up the tent or park the RV, where else in this Home of Champions but **Champion Lakes Provincial Park** (www.bc parks.ca, keyword "Champion"). Located about 12 miles (20 km) northeast of Trail on Highway 3B (and in fact named for James W. Champion, one of the area's earliest orchardists), it features three adjacent lakes, ninety-five campsites, an adventure playground, hiking, boating, and fishing. Phone (800) 689–9025 for reservations. First-come, first-served sites are also available. There's also a spot to park at the City of Trail RV Park beside the Waneta Mall. The park includes a playground, showers, and electrical hookups.

Castlegar

ighway 22 travels north from Trail beside the Columbia River for 16 miles (26 km) to **Castlegar**, where the Columbia meets the Kootenay River and, as in Grand Forks, where the Doukhobors have left their mark.

For a taste of this Russian influence, at the junction with Highway 3 cross the Columbia River Bridge, turn left onto Highway 3A, and left again onto Frank Biender Way, opposite the Castlegar airport. The **Doukhobor Village Museum** (112 Heritage Way, Castlegar, V1N 4M5; 250–365–6622; fax: 250–365–5327; larryewashen@telus.net; kdhs.kics. bc.ca) portrays the history of what was the largest communal enterprise in western Canada until 1938. It's easy to appreciate the turn-of-the-century hardships when you see this reconstructed Doukhobor community. Check out its petch (bread-baking oven), blacksmith shop, and wood-fired banya (sauna). The museum is open daily May 1 to September 30 from 10:00 A.M. to 6:00 P.M. Admission is $5.00 for adults, $3.00 for students and no charge for preschoolers.

Next to the museum the **Kootenay Gallery of Art, History and Science** (120 Heritage Way, Castlegar, V1N 4M5; 250–365–3337; fax: 250–365–

3822; kgal@netidea.com; www.kootenaygallery.com) features regional, national, and international exhibits; admission is $2.00. There's also a large gift shop carrying the work of more than fifty local artisans and craftspeople. It's open Wednesday through Saturday 10:00 A.M. to 5:00 P.M. and Sunday noon to 5:00 P.M.

Castlegar offers more than history and culture, though. Golfers will enjoy the scenically set challenges of the **Castlegar Golf Course** (Box 3430, Castlegar, V1N 3N6; 800–666–0324 or 250–365–5006; fax: 250–365–8832), which *Golf Digest* has given a 3.5 rating, recognizing it as one of the top one hundred courses in North America. You'll find it behind the airport. From Highway 3A, which heads north to Nelson, take Ootischenia Road; turn left onto Columbia Road and left again onto Aaron Road. Contact the Castlegar Chamber of Commerce/Visitor Info Centre (1995 Sixth Avenue, Castlegar, V1N 4B7; 250–365–6313; fax: 250–365–5778; cdcoc@kootenay.net; www.castlegar.com) for information on other recreational activities. These activities include camping at the southern shore of Lower Arrow Lake at **Syringa Provincial Park** (www.bcparks.ca, keyword "Syringa"), with its variegated habitat of sandy beaches, grasslands, steep canyons, and cliffs, an important habitat for Rocky Mountain bighorn sheep, elk, and deer; hiking the **Waldie Island Trail,** which winds along the Columbia River's northern shoreline from the CPR train bridge to Brilliant; exploring the **Zuckerberg Island Heritage Park** (250–365–5511) where, set in beautifully landscaped grounds, you'll see an unusual sculpture of a seated woman carved from a tree stump, one of revered Russian sculptor Alexander Zuckerberg's best-known works; and visiting the **Castlegar Museum** (250–365–6440; fax: 250–304–0062; heritage@kootenay.net; www.castlegar.com/cdhs), located in the old railway station at 400 Thirteenth Avenue in downtown Castlegar. Here you'll find aboriginal history and tales of the beginnings of Castlegar as well as modern history. It's open Monday through Saturday from 9:00 A.M. to 5:00 P.M. throughout the year.

Nelson

Twenty-three miles (38 km) northeast of Castlegar along Highway 3A, **Nelson** graces the West Arm of Kootenay Lake in the heart of the Selkirk Mountains. As you approach from the south, keep an eye out for **osprey nests** on the bridge pylons at Taghum, about 3 miles (5 km) before **Grohman Narrows Provincial Park.** The park is a pleasant picnic spot overlooking Kootenay Lake (just before you enter Nelson), with a pond and walking trails.

Nelson is in a picture-perfect setting. It's long been appreciated for movie backdrops, among them the Steve Martin/Darryl Hannah film *Roxanne*. Martin's Pinocchio-nosed character would have appreciated the clean mountain air of this lovely city of heritage buildings, artisans, and steep streets overlooking Kootenay Lake's West Arm.

At the top of one of these steep streets is the **Nelson Guest House** (2109 Fort Sheppard Drive, Nelson, V1L 6A2; phone/fax: 250–354–0198; toll free: 888–215–2500; nelsonguest@yahoo.com; www.nelsonguesthouse.com), a newly constructed cedar home that is close to town, yet you can ski, hike, or bike from the door, or simply sit on the deck and enjoy the mountain air. Accommodation is either a two- or three-bedroom self-contained suite, with kitchen, deck, and laundry facilities. There's also the choice of two main-house rooms with en-suite baths. Rates range from $89 to $119 double in high season and include a hearty breakfast.

Nelson has several fine coffee shops and restaurants to choose from, including **Oso Negro** (522 Victoria Street; 250–352–7661; toll free: 877–BEANGUY; oso_negro@telus.net), a friendly micro-roastery where you can buy freshly roasted beans or grab a java to go, or perhaps hang out for the day sipping espresso and meeting some of Nelson's many characters. At **Max & Irma's Restaurant** (515A Kootenay Street; 250–352–2332; skirby@netidea.com; www.maxandirmaskitchen.com), they bake their daily specials in a brick oven. Every Monday is Ethnic Night, and on Friday and Sunday enjoy local musicians. Prices are reasonable. **Mazatlan Mexican Restaurant** (198 Baker Street; 250–352–1388) is famous for its gigantic tequila margaritas and authentic Mexican cuisine, available inside or out on the sunny deck. Entrees are in the $10 to $15 range with special kids' meals at kids' prices. **Rickaby's** (524 Vernon Street, 250–354–1919; info@rickabys.ca; www.rickabys.ca) was Dixie's Place in *Roxanne* and is as popular with Nelsonites as it was with the firemen in the movie. Monday is "Pasta and a Movie Night," when you can eat all the pasta you like and receive a movie pass for that night's show at the Civic Theatre—all for $11.99.

If you want to dine a little more upscale, take a detour down a back alley 1 block from Baker Street between Josephine and Hall Streets to the **All Seasons Cafe** (620 Herridge Lane, 250–352–0101; fax: 250–352–7499; www.allseasonscafe.com). The menu changes with the seasons, and the wine list is legendary. Prices for mains range from $13 to $22. Its restored heritage-home, back-alley setting appears at first glance downscale, but you're in for a surprise; it comes complete with pretty mountain views.

Still on the theme of heritage buildings, the **Nelson Visitor Info Centre** (225 Hall Street, Nelson, V1L 5X4; 250–352–3433; fax: 250–352–6355; www.city.nelson.bc.ca) has self-guided tour brochures for an architectural heritage walking (or driving) tour as aids in viewing some of the 350 heritage buildings the city boasts.

During your walk you're sure to pass several arts, crafts, and antiques stores, such as **The Craft Connection Cooperative** (441 Baker Street, Nelson, V1L 4H7; 250–352–3006; fax: 250–825–9329; lhall@netidea. com), where you'll find a selection of some of the work of west Kootenay artisans—everything from raku to wreaths—in the "best little art town" in BC. It's open 9:30 A.M. to 5:30 P.M. year-round (noon to 4:00 P.M. Sundays). This "best little art town" is a draw for many cottage industries, some of which are being lauded internationally. One gem hidden away just north of Nelson is **Rocky Mountain Beadworks** (info@rockybeads.com; www.rockybeads.com). Beautiful glass beads are shaped to smooth perfection in a small rural workshop overlooking Kootenay Lake.

During the snow-free months there's a delightful way to view the Nelson waterfront and the lovely **Lakeside Park,** and that's aboard the historic **Streetcar 23,** built in 1906 for service in Cleveland, Ohio, and then used in Nelson from 1924 to 1949. In those days it ran through the winter, but with a snow buildup it sometimes derailed. After enough shopkeepers complained about the tram crashing through their storefronts, it was discontinued in winter. Pick it up ($2.00 a ride) at several points on the route, which runs between the wharf area and Lakeside Park.

Kootenay Lake West

A 21-mile (34-km) drive northeast from Nelson along Highway 3A beside the Kootenay Lake West Arm brings you to Balfour and the world's longest free ferry ride, but first we'll take Highway 31 north along the west shore of **Kootenay Lake,** renowned for its good fishing. Drop the hook for Dolly Varden, kokanee, and rainbow trout.

Nine miles (15 km) north of Balfour at Ainsworth Hot Springs is the **Silver Ledge Hotel** (250–229–4640), a one-hundred-year-old hotel restored to its late-nineteenth-century glory, but now operating only as a museum. It houses a collection of old photos of the Ainsworth Mining District. Once home to 3,000 silver seekers, Ainsworth now has fewer than one hundred permanent residents. The museum is open 1:00 to 5:00 P.M. from the long May weekend till September (daily in July and August, but only weekends in May, June, and September).

For a hot soak go to the caves at the **Ainsworth Hot Springs Resort** (Box 1268, Ainsworth Hot Springs, V0G 1A0; 250–229–4212; fax: 250–229–5600; 800–668–1171 for reservations; reserve@hotnaturally.com; www.hotnaturally.com). You'll soak in 114° F (42° C) water in a 66-foot (20-m) dripping, U-shaped cave. This hot springs water has reputedly the highest mineral content in Canada. The springs originate in the Cody Caves area, which is directly above and to the west of Ainsworth Hot Springs. The water works its way down deeply through porous rock, increasing in temperature at a rate of 104° F (40° C) per kilometer, until it strikes what is known as the Lakeshore Fault. Hydraulic pressure forces the water up along the fault to emerge at Ainsworth Hot Springs. In the dark patches you may bump into a quietly meditating mortal as you drift through the steamy caves. Cost is $7.00 single entry for adults (day pass $10.00) and $4.50 for kids ages three to twelve (day pass $6.50). Towels and disposable swimsuits are available for a small fee. For the hardy there's a 39° F (4° C) glacier-fed pool to alternate with the sizzling dips. The resort provides fine dining at moderate prices, and the lovely lake views are free. Accommodation rates are in the $120 to $160 range in peak season.

Two miles (3 km) north of Ainsworth, a 6-mile (10-km) rugged and steep forest road leads to **Cody Caves Provincial Park** (www.bcparks.ca, search word "Cody"). Here an underground stream flows for more than half a mile (.8 km) through an ancient limestone system of tunnels and galleries containing stalactites, stalagmites, soda straws, and other cave features. Wear sturdy shoes and warm clothing because although it may be hot outside, the interior temperature is about 42° F (6° C). Also, it's a steep, half-mile (.8-km) walk to the caves from the parking lot, so bring drinks and snacks. Guided one-hour tours (and this is the only way to see the caves) are led daily in the summer by Highadventure Corporation (250–353–7364; caves@netidea.com), which provides helmets, headlamps, and gloves. The fees are $15 for adults and $10 for children. A more extensive three-hour tour ($50 per person; reservations required) is available for groups of up to six people.

Kaslo

Thirteen miles (21 km) north of the hot springs, the plain street names (numbers and letters) of **Kaslo,** located between the Selkirk and Purcell Mountains, belie her prettiness. In 1893, when silver, galena, and gold enriched the mountainsides, Kaslo's population grew to 3,000; at present it's fewer than 1,000. Steamers helped develop the area, and to this memory the Kootenay Lake Historical Society has restored the oldest intact passenger stern-wheeler in the world, the *SS Moyie*. She sits majestically on the waterfront in downtown Kaslo, after having steamed an estimated two million miles between 1898 and 1957. Prefabricated in Toronto, all 830 tons were shipped in sections in 1898. The *SS Moyie National Historic Site* (324 Front Street, Box 537, Kaslo, V0G 1M0; phone/fax: 250–353–2525; ssmoyie@klhs.bc.ca; www.klhs. bc.ca), complete with historic trapper's cabin, is the main museum in town and is open daily mid-May to mid-October from 9:30 A.M. to 5:00 P.M., with admission fees ranging from $2.00 (ages six to twelve) to $5.00 for adults.

There's more history at the *Woodbury Mining Museum* (402 Front Street). Open June through September from 10:00 A.M. to 5:00 P.M., here you'll get a good introduction to those booming mining days. Admission is $2.00 for adults and $1.00 for children.

Across from the Post Office at the corner of Fourth and B, the *Langham Cultural Center* (Box 1000, Kaslo, V0G 1M0; 250–353–2661, fax: 250–353–2820; langham@pop.kin.bc.ca; www.kin.bc.ca/Langham/ Langham.htm), one of sixty officially designated heritage buildings in Kaslo, was a hotel for miners in the 1890s. Now it comprises two galleries, a ninety-seat theater, and an ecomuseum. Poignant photographs on the walls tell the story of Kaslo's 1,200 resilient Japanese-Canadian internees, seventy-eight of whom were housed in the Langham during World War II. It's open daily all year, except January, from 9:00 A.M. to 5:00 P.M. Admission is by donation.

Kaslo was the setting for the Mark Harmon movie *Magic on the Water*. If you stare at the lake long enough, you may see Orky, the movie's odd but genial lake monster. A walking tour of this "Switzerland of the Americas" village and its environs is well worthwhile. It's hard to imagine that it has seen devastation in the form of fire, flood, and even hurricane.

To view Kaslo panoramically take a walk up A Avenue and turn right on Wardner Street. After a block you'll see a trailhead on the left side. Turn right and 300 yards (275 m) up you'll come to a sharp left turn followed by some steep switchbacks. At the top you'll get a breathtaking view of Kaslo and Kootenay Lake. In fall mountain ash trees add flaming color to the scene.

After the hike stop at *The Rosewood Cafe* (213 Fifth Street, Box 1435, Kaslo, V0G 1M0; 250–353–ROSE [7673]; rosewood@netidea.com).

This attractive restaurant serves calamari, Camembert fondue, blackened Cajun shrimp, and tortellini in a curry sauce, at moderate prices. Locals are raving about Grant's cedar-planked salmon topped with crab and shrimp Bernaise served on a specially carved cedar plank.

To appreciate the intimacy and quality of life this little town offers, stay awhile. *Beach Gables Accommodation* (Box 962, Kaslo, V0G 1M0; 250–353–2111; fax: 250–353–2240), opposite the beach, is open year-round. This restored heritage home, beautifully furnished with exquisite antiques, offers private decks and views of the lake and mountains. Rates are in the $75 double range (cash or check only).

The *Kaslo Visitor Info Centre* (324 Front Street, Box 537, Kaslo, V0G 1M0; phone/fax: 250–353–2525) can lead you to other lodgings and fill you in on the history of this charming little town. If you visit in early August, you're in time for the Kaslo Jazz Etc. Festival (250–353–7538; kazlojazz@netidea.com; www.kaslojazzfest.com). Check out www. kin.bc.ca on the Web for up-to-date Kaslo information before you leave home.

From Kaslo you can head north along Kootenay Lake on Highway 31 over mostly unpaved road for 88 miles (142 km) to *Galena Bay.* The road edges *Goat Range Provincial Park* and *Trout Lake.* Ask in Kaslo about road conditions; then set out to explore the ghost town of Gerrard (at the south end of Trout Lake), where in early to mid-May you can watch the Gerrard rainbow trout spawn. This is the world's largest breed of rainbow trout, with some reported up to fifty pounds (23 kg). "No-trace" camping is available in the park, with five drive-in spots and

A Not-So-Friendly Monster

*T*he movie Magic in the Water, filmed in Kaslo, may not have been all fiction. Several reported sightings of a "monster" in Kootenay Lake have occurred over the past hundred or so years. A couple of years ago a highway crew reported sighting "humps and a huge wake, much larger than those made by houseboats and fishing boats." Another sighting by a reputable local who "got a good look at it for at least a couple of minutes before it dove" was described as "a head on the end of a long neck lifted up . . . just like the images of the Loch Ness monster that we have all seen." Unlike the lovable Orky in the movie, this creature does not seem to be friendly and has been blamed for various accidents on the lake, which many locals avoid unless they are in a very large boat. Strangely, the monster has yet to be named.

some wilderness walk-in sites. No potable water is available, and anglers must have a valid nontidal angling fishing license. Stop at the one-hundred-year-old (plus) **Windsor Hotel** (RR2, Site 3, Box 49, Nakusp, V0G 1R0; 250–269–2244; fax: 250–369–2246; windsor@columbiacable. net; www.windsor-troutlake.com) in **Trout Lake** (at the northwest end of the lake) for a piece of great pie. The Windsor offers three-night accommodation and all-meals-included package deals that might feature a cruise on Trout Lake; a four-wheel-drive guided tour to see abandoned mines, ghost towns, and alpine scenery; and a gold-panning excursion to Lardeau Creek. Package rates range from $215 to $295. Room rates start at $30.

From Galena a free ferry crosses Upper Arrow Lake to Shelter Bay, 31 miles (50 km) south of Revelstoke. Highway 23 (now paved) continues for 30 miles (49 km) south to Nakusp.

An easier route to Nakusp is via a paved road, Highway 31A, which leads 29 miles (47 km) west from Kaslo to New Denver on Slocan Lake. Here, between Kaslo and Sandon, you'll pass through the Valley of the Ghosts, with its many abandoned mines and ghost towns. Ask in Kaslo or New Denver to help locate these sites. Twenty-four miles (38 km) from Kaslo—or 5 miles (8.3 km) from New Denver—look for a sign indicating the turnoff to **Sandon**. This junction is known as Three Forks. Here a 3.4-mile (5.5-km) unpaved road leads to this formerly rowdy town that once supported twenty-four hotels, three newspapers, and an opera. It had electricity even before Vancouver. At one time the silver-mining capital of Canada, Sandon's population of 5,000 gradually decreased, only to grow briefly again when the Japanese-Canadians were interned there in 1942. The Sandon Historical Society (Box 52, New Denver, V0G 1S0; 250–358–7920/7215; www.slocanlake.com/ slocan) has put together a collection of historic photographs and artifacts in the visitors center in the restored **Slocan Mercantile Building**. When space ran out in its early days, Sandon was enlarged by building a flume to contain the river, then planking over it to add a boardwalk "street." A washout in 1955 devastated the city center, but the City Hall and western Canada's oldest operating hydroelectric station still remain. The visitors center is open June to October, with tours of the **Silversmith Hydroelectric Station** (with a fine collection of operating, turn-of-the-century machinery) held daily in July and August from 10:00 A.M. to 4:30 P.M. Hikers will enjoy the easy 3.8-mile (6.1-km) walk to Payne Bluffs along the **K & S Historic Railway Trail**. You can even drive the first 1.4 miles (2.3 km). Poke around the old mine sites, admire the views, and then hike back to Sandon, where you can enjoy a homemade meal at the *Tin Cup Cafe.* A 7.5-mile (12-km) steep and winding drive (not for motorhomes) from Sandon brings you to a parking lot from which you can hike (about 1.3 miles) along a ridge trail to *Idaho Peak Forestry Lookout Tower.* The views down onto New Denver, Silverton, Rosebery, Slocan Lake, and the Selkirk and Valhalla mountain ranges are spectacular. It's a popular takeoff spot for hang gliders.

Six miles west of the Sandon turnoff is *New Denver,* where you can visit the *Nikkei Internment Memorial Centre* (306 Josephine Street, Box 273, New Denver, V0G 1S0; 250–358–7288/2663; fax: 250–358–7251), a memorial to the thousands of Japanese-Canadians displaced to the area during World War II. A feature of the center is a splendid Japanese garden. It's open June through September daily from 9:00 A.M. to 5:00 P.M. (other times by appointment). The entry fees are $4.00 adults, $3.00 seniors and students, $2.00 children (age five and under free). For more information on attractions in and around New Denver (population 559 in 2002), phone (250) 358–2316 or e-mail newdenver@net idea.com or check out www.newdenver.ca.

In New Denver Highway 31A meets Highway 6 at Slocan Lake on the edge of the aptly named *Valhalla Provincial Park* (www.bcparks.ca, search "Valhalla"). Access to this isolated, undeveloped wilderness is mostly by boat across the lake or via Little Slocan Lake Road, after crossing the river in Slocan. It's beautiful, with lucid lakes, wild creeks and waterfalls, and majestic stands of timber—a paradise for hikers and climbers. The park has only wilderness/walk-in camping sites (pit toilets and no potable water) and a day-use picnicking area.

If you're a hot-springs zealot, a 29-mile (47-km) side trip from New Denver along Highway 6 leads northwest to Nakusp on Upper Arrow Lake. Here the clear air of the Selkirks is rivaled only by the pure waters of *Nakusp Hot Springs* (Box 280, 92 Sixth Avenue NW, Nakusp, V0G 1R0; 250–265–4528; fax: 250–265–3788, toll free: 800–909–8819; info@nakusphotsprings.com; www.nakusphotsprings. com), 8 miles (13 km) farther east along a paved road. With two pools, one hot at 100.4° F (38° C) and the other hotter at 105.8° F (41° C) to soak in, hot-springs connoisseurs insist it's number one in the Kootenays. Camping is available May to November beside the Kuskanax River, a short walk from the hot springs (no reservations necessary). There are also cedar chalets (ranging from $49 to $78 double) on-site that are open year-round. Phone (250) 265–4505 or fax (250) 265– 3596 for chalet reservations. Contact Nakusp & District Chamber of

Commerce/Visitor Info Centre at 92 West Sixth Avenue (Box 387, Nakusp, V0G 1R0; 250–265–4234; fax: 250–265–3808; 800–909–8819; nakcom@columbiacable.net) for more information on Nakusp.

Twenty miles (32 km) north of Nakusp is BC's newest (and perhaps oldest) hot springs resort. Fascinating history, as well as fabulous scenery, surrounds **Halcyon Hot Springs Resort** (Box 37, Nakusp, V0G 1R0; 888–689–4699; 250–265–3554; fax: 250–265–3887; info@halcyon-hot springs.com; www.halcyon-hotsprings.com), located on Highway 23 along the shores of Upper Arrow Lake. At the turn of the century, it was renowned for its fancy dress balls and as a riotous "in" place to holiday, but after 1924, the drinking and gambling stopped when a sedate and charitable general and doctor, Frederick Burnham, bought the resort. The emphasis turned to making use of the health-restoring waters of the springs. Before long Halcyon's healing powers were touted internationally with mind-boggling claims—one man even claimed his hair grew back. Burnham allowed no bathing trunks in the segregated pools, as he believed clothing interfered in the healing process; stories circulated that the surrounding trails were closed in the mornings, as he used to run naked there "to harden" himself. He was killed in 1955 when the hotel burned to the ground, but the shingle-roofed chapel that he built after his beloved wife passed away in 1945 has been restored and now functions as a museum and chapel. What a romantic spot to tie the knot! Now it's a spectacular holiday spot. The resort has four pools with water temperatures ranging from 107° F (41.6° C) to 85° F (29.4° C), forty RV sites, camping facilities, cabins, chalets, a store, and a bistro-style restaurant set by the lake with a view of Mount Burnham. Bring along your arthritis, osteoporosis, and gout, and return home rejuvenated—and perhaps married!

A third way to reach Nakusp is from the west (from Vernon) along Highway 6, via the 3,900-foot (1,189-m) Monashee Pass and a free ferry across Lower Arrow Lake from **Needles** to **Fauquier.** The ferry leaves every half hour from Fauquier between 5:00 A.M. and 10:00 P.M. (from Needles starting at 5:15 A.M.) or on demand from 10:00 P.M. to 5:00 A.M. The crossing time is five minutes. The distance to Nakusp is 37 miles (59 km).

Just 3 miles (5 km) south of New Denver on Highway 6, as you wind through the beautiful **Slocan Valley,** is historic **Silverton.** You'll find a really pretty campground on the lakeshore right in town, down the road from the **Silverton Outdoor Mining Museum** (408 Fourth Street, Box 90, Silverton, V0G 2B0), which displays forty-eight pieces of vintage mining machinery and is well worth a visit, as is the **Silverton Resort** (Box 107, Silverton, V0G 2B0; phone/fax: 250–358–7157; silverton

Did you know that Spokane became a city because of the Kootenays? The Americans made their money through the silver-mining days in the late 1800s in the Kootenays and founded the city of Spokane.

resort@netidea.com; www.silvertonresort.com), with its lovely log lodge, historic house (Senning House—sleeps seven), and loft-cabins on the shores of Slocan Lake. From November to March a sauna is available, and throughout the year you can rent canoes, motorboats, and kayaks. The 1,500-square-foot lodge will sleep eight and has rates as low as $130 in the off-season; late June to early September rates are $255; its deck overlooks Slocan Lake and the Valhalla Mountain Range. Check the comprehensive Web site for accommodation layouts and rates.

Less than a mile (1.5 km) south of Silverton is a viewpoint on a high cliff overlooking Slocan Lake. Don't miss it, or you'll miss one of the best views in British Columbia.

Slocan (population 349 in 2002) is 17 miles (27 km) south of Silverton, and 5 miles (7 km) south of Slocan is the turnoff to a rustic, year-round guest lodge. The front field of the **Lemon Creek Lodge** (Box 68, Slocan, V0G 2C0; phone/fax: 250–355–2403 or 877–970–8090; lemoncrk@telus. net; www.lemoncreeklodge.com), at 7680 Kennedy Road, was home to hundreds of Japanese-Canadian wartime internees. A photo of the internment camp in the warmly furnished living room in the lodge shows how it looked in those difficult years. Located between Valhalla and Kokanee Glacier Provincial Parks, accommodation at Lemon Creek Lodge offers ten neat and clean bedrooms with five shared bathrooms, two cabins, a fabulous Finnish sauna, a Japanese Garden, a twenty-eight-site campground, and a restaurant serving fresh-from-the-garden

Recommended Reading—The Kootenays

Ghost Towns and Mining Camps of the Boundary Country, by Garnet Basque. Heritage House Publishing Company Surrey, 1999.

West Kootenay: The Pioneer Years, by Garnet Basque. Heritage House Publishing Company Surrey, 1996.

Ghost Towns and Drowned Towns of West Kootenay, by Elsie Turnbull. Heritage House Publishing Co., 1988.

Whitewater Trips and Hot Springs in the Kootenays of British Columbia: For Kayakers, Canoeists and Rafters, by Betty Pratt-Johnson. Vancouver: Adventure Publishing, 1989.

vegetables, home-baked bread, and creative desserts. Double accommodation with breakfast costs $75 in the lodge and $80 in the cabins (breakfast not included).

Our side trip through the Slocan Valley returns via Nelson to Balfour and then back to the world's longest free ferry ride (***Kootenay Lake Ferry;*** 250–229–4215). Sixteen forty-five-minute runs daily (ten in winter), starting at 6:30 A.M., sail between the Purcell and Selkirk Mountains to Kootenay Bay on the eastern shore. Watch for Canada geese on the beach at Balfour. At Lang's Marina & Snack Bar (250–229–4771) near the ferry lineup, you can buy grain (or "cwackers") to feed them. There's also a large osprey colony nearby, so keep the binoculars handy.

Aboard the MV *Osprey 2000* or the MV *Balfour,* the ferry cafe serves inexpensive but tasty food. In winter change your watch back one hour after you disembark at Kootenay Bay. You're now on Mountain Standard Time. Just to confuse you, though, in April, when Daylight Savings Time comes into effect, the time doesn't change because Kootenay Bay maintains Mountain Standard Time year-round. You'll soon learn that time really does stand still on Kootenay Lake's eastern shore!

Kootenay Lake East

Some strange, inexplicable force urged me to take the Riondel Road turnoff after the ferry. Two miles (3 km) from this turnoff, along a gravel road (Walker's Landing), I found ***Yasodhara Ashram*** (Box 9, Kootenay Bay, V0B 1X0; 250–227–9224 or 800–661–8711; fax: 250–227–9494; yashram@netidea.com; www. yasodhara.org), a vibrant spiritual community and educational institution founded in 1963 by the late Swami Sivananda Radha. You'll experience here yoga courses and retreats in an atmosphere of peace and harmony. The ashram also offers programs (by application only) for working guests, and families are always welcome. An attractive study center, a well-stocked bookstore, a beautiful white-domed Temple of Divine Light on the lakefront, and residents working quietly in vegetable gardens make up the tranquil scene. The cedar log guest lodge overlooks the lake and mountains. Stay awhile and luxuriate in the peace at ***Tara Shanti Lodge*** (Box 77, 134 Riondel Road, Kootenay Bay, V0B 1X0; 800–811–3888; info@tara shanti.com; www.tarashanti.com). Casual elegance combined with creative meals make for a relaxing retreat. The hot tub on the deck with views to the lake and glacier add to the peaceful scene.

Back on Highway 3A, a few miles south of the ferry landing at the **North Woven Broom Company** (Box 126, Crawford Bay, V0B 1E0; 250–227–9245; broom@northwovenbroom.com; www.northwovenbroom.com), a pungently sweet odor permeates everything inside an old barn. You can almost feel the time warp as you watch Janet and Rob Schwieger fashion brooms from Mexican unprocessed broomcorn. Their machinery consists of a turn-of-the-century treadle-stitcher to sew the brooms flat and an antique vise for gripping the hand-stitched whisks and crooked-handled brooms. They spend their days listening to CBC radio, peacefully wetting and weaving, tying and treadling, as they turn out these nifty brooms. They're open daily from 9:00 A.M. to 5:00 P.M. from April to October. Winter hours vary, so call ahead.

North Woven Broom Company

Nearby, at the **Purple Door Unique Crafts and Curios** (Box 157, Riondel, V0B 2B0; 250–227–6995 or 250–225–3532; info@purpledoor.ca; www. purpledoor.ca), Jamie Lauritzen makes unique sculpted wizards and twerps and other "trippy" stuff, and sells pretty summer attire and jewelry. As well, the folks at the Purple Door have a funky cabin for rent on the shores of Kootenay Lake. It sleeps six (with room for a tent outside), and rents for $65 double, $10 each extra person, with a two-day minimum rental. It's near the public beach in Riondel. It's also only a short drive to the **Kokanee Springs Golf Resort** (16082 Woolgar Road, Box 96, Crawford Bay, V0B 1E0; 800–979–7999 or 250–227–9226; fax: 250–227–9220; info@kokaneesprings.com; www.kokaneesprings.com), one of Canada's finest eighteen-hole golf courses, magnificently set beneath the Purcell Mountains. Accommodation, RV camping, and fine dining are also available.

A few hundred yards south of the broom "factory," the **Kootenay Forge** artist-blacksmiths (Box 119, Crawford Bay, V0B 1E0; 250–227–9467;

toll free: 877–461–9466; fax: 250–227–9408; info@kootenayforge.com; www.kootenayforge.com) produce practical household accessories such as door knockers, umbrella stands, magazine racks, fireplace accessories, candlesticks, and lamps. John Smith (his real name!) and his staff of traditional smiths have been forging and riveting these timeless articles in their "smithy" for more than twenty years. A sign in the gift shop reads: ON THIS DAY IN 1895, NOTHING HAPPENED. Perhaps this is *black*-smith humor? Next door, Tim Elias transforms sand into glowing molten glass at *Breathless Glass* (Box 85, Gray Creek, V0B 1S0; 250–227–9598; blewglas@netidea.com). Visitors watch mesmerized as he brings the artistry of glassblowing to life in the form of delicate goblets, vases, and flasks. Also in the same building, at *Fireworks Enamelled Copper and Glass* (Box 22, Crawford Bay, V0B 1E0; 250–227–9467), beautiful jewelry, bowls, scenic pieces, and more are created by firing colored glass powders onto a copper sheet. Arts and crafts from these workshops are sold in an on-site gallery, the *Forge and Furnace Gallery* (250–227–9467; fax: 250–227–9408), and according to blacksmith John they have one thing in common—they all like it hot!

Yet another cottage industry in this close-knit Crawford Bay community is *BareFoot Handweaving Studio & Gallery* (Box 160, Crawford Bay, V0B 1E0; phone/fax: 250–227–9655; barefoot@telus.net; www.barefoothandweaving.com), located in a straw bale studio immediately to the north of Kootenay Forge. Owner Janet Wallace and staff weave colorful natural fibers on traditional looms. One-of-a-kind items, from sweaters, vests, hats, and throws, to placemats, prayer shawls, and teddy bears, are woven, sewn, and sold on site. They are open from May to October daily and weekdays in winter. And keeping it in the family, Ted Wallace, a teacher at the Crawford Bay School (the smallest kindergarten-to-grade-twelve school in British Columbia), creates visionary paintings created in pencil, colored inks, and acrylics on a variety of media. His latest "Shield" series is made of acrylic on shaped masonite. Many of his pieces are reproduced on cards for sale at BareFoot Handweaving. Among other cottage industries along this "Artisan Way in Crawford Bay" are *Blown Away Glass* (working alongside Breathless Glass), *The Barn* (250–227–9348), where log and twig furniture is created, and *Mud Mamas* (250–227–9030), a pottery guild across the road from the Forge.

There's a lovely residence (a heritage mansion) just over the Crawford Creek Bridge, 4 miles (7 km) south of the ferry terminal at 16002 Crawford Creek Road. *Wedgwood Manor Country Inn* (Box 135, Crawford Bay, V0B 1E0; phone/fax: 250–227–9233 or, for reservations,

800–862–0022; wedgwood@netidea.com; www. bctravel.net/wedgwood) is lavishly Victorian. Originally built in 1910 by a daughter of the English Wedgwood china family, the inn is entirely set apart for guests, but the accommodation rates ($85–$140) include a hot breakfast and evening tea. You'll feel you're on a country estate as you stroll through its fifty acres (20 ha) of lovely woods and gardens or perhaps as you relax by the parlor fireside, curled up with a mystery from the library shelf. The manor is open from April to mid-October. Even if you don't stay, stop by to take a complimentary tour of this historic house.

At Gray Creek, 7 miles (11 km) south of the ferry dock, a warning of what is to come is right there on the highway. The winding lakeshore highway passes a sign proclaiming POPULATION 354—METRIC FREE. So, of course, gas still sells by the gallon, and the store is like a page out of a *Waltons* television script. But the variety of products in this overstuffed emporium is second to none. At the **Gray Creek Store** (1979 Chainsaw Avenue, Gray Creek, V0B 1S0; 250–227–9315; fax: 250–227–9449), you're likely to trip over wheelbarrows, woodstoves, kitchen sinks, chain saws, of course, and the best darned collection of books on British Columbia this side of Vancouver. Oh, and you can resupply your food stocks here, too.

Store owner Tom Lymbery knows the area well. Ask Tom about the 55-mile (86-km) seasonal (July–October) alpine route from Gray Creek to Kimberley. About 10 steep miles (16 km) from Gray Creek, just before the 6,800-foot summit, you'll pass near an alpine lake (Oliver Lake) that features a path made of split colored stone. This route to Kimberley, deserted for the most part, is a "be-prepared" no-services road.

Three miles (5 km) south of the Gray Creek Store, the **Windwalker Ranch** (Box 146, 14434 Highway 3A, Gray Creek, V0B 1S0; toll free: 800–694–2277; 250–227–9372; fax: 250–227–9610; coach@windwalkerranch.com; www.windwalkerranch.com) provides comfortable, total relaxation. But Dan and Kathryn Cook offer much more than just a place to stay. Trail rides and riding clinics using an ancient breed of Russian horses called Bashkir Curlies and beautiful gardens make a stay here memorable. The cabin ($129.50 per night for a family of five) is secluded and has spectacular views of the mountains and lake. Weekly rates are available.

Twenty minutes south of the Windwalker Ranch and 4 miles (7 km) past Boswell on Highway 3A, which is 25 miles (40 km) south of the ferry terminal, is an extraordinary house made from embalming bottles. Funeral director David Brown's son Eldon had me fascinated with stories of growing up in *The Glass House* (RR1, #1, Boswell, V0B 1A0; 250–223–8372; fax: 250–223–8332; glasshouse@kootenay.com). After thirty-five years in the funeral business, the late David Brown retired and began building this unique house. He collected the square bottles from other funeral directors across western Canada (500,000, weighing 250 tons) and built this 1,200-square-foot cloverleaf-shaped house. Inquisitive passersby started showing up, and soon the Browns started charging them to take a look inside after a minister friend had advised them: "If you want to break up a congregation, either pass the plate or ask them to sing!" Since 1952, when building began, other parts have been added—terraces, patios, a glass bridge, a moss-covered wishing well, and a lighthouse on the lakefront. It's open daily May, June, September, and until the Thanksgiving weekend in October from 9:00 A.M. to 5:00 P.M. and in July and August from 8:00 A.M. to 8:00 P.M.

Creston

At the bottom end of Kootenay Lake, only 7 miles (11 km) north of the U.S. border, lies *Creston,* population 4908 in 2002. Grain elevators and scenic fields of alfalfa and canola give it a prairie look. This "Valley of the Swans" comprises some of the province's most fertile fruit-growing land. Raspberries, cherries, and apricots are ripe in July, peaches, apples, and plums in August. In May, Highway 3 is a sea of color as the town springs to life with its annual *Blossom Festival.*

There are a number of quality bed-and-breakfasts and other accommodations in the area. One, the *Sweet Apple Bed & Breakfast* (3939 Highway 3 East, Box 93, Erickson, V0B 1K0; phone/fax: 250–428–7205; info@sweetapple.bc.ca; www.sweetapple.bc.ca), is a modern country home with a panoramic view (from a 60-foot balcony) of the Selkirk Mountains to the west and the Skimmerhorns to the east. Hot breakfast includes home-baked goodies and fresh seasonal fruits. If you've a penchant for fishing, you might like to drop a fly onto the Goat River, which runs through the property, and perhaps land a trout or kokanee salmon. Accommodation, which is on a separate floor from the hosts, is $65 double; or if you prefer a golf package, double accommodation plus two green-fees at the challenging *Creston Golf Course* (250–428–5515; golf@crestonvalley.com) is $140. The eighteen-hole, par-72 course is just 3 miles (5 km) south of

> ## Trivia
>
> *The Crowsnest (Highway 3) contains Canada's highest paved road, at 5,820 feet (1,774 m). It's between Salmo and Creston at the summit of Kootenay Pass.*

Creston off Highway 21 on Mallory Road. Phone (250) 428–5515 for a tee-off time.

Another accommodation in the area is **Goat River Lodge Bed & Breakfast** (1108 Lamont Road, Creston, V0B 1G1; 250–428–7134; fax: 250–428–4713; allmi@kootenay.com; www.crestonvalley.com/goat river), with a heated swimming pool and lovely mountain and river views. Rates are from $50 to $70 double.

Attractions around Creston include the **Columbia Brewing Company** (1220 Erickson Street; 250–428–9344), brewers of Kokanee beer, which offers tours Monday to Friday mid-May to mid-September, the **Kootenay Candle Factory** (1511 Northwest Boulevard; 250–428–9785), and the **Creston & District Museum & Archives** (219 Devon Street; 250–428–9262; fax: 250–428–3324; info@creston.museum. bc.ca; creston.museum.bc.ca). Open daily from 10:00 A.M. to 3:30 P.M. mid-May to mid-September, this stone-house museum is small but of excellent quality. The building itself, with 18-inch-thick walls made of field stones set into white mortar, four fireplaces, a crypt, animal figurines, and windshields embedded in the walls, is intriguing. Contact **Creston Visitor Info Centre** (1711 Canyon Street, Box 268, Creston, V0B 1G0; 250–428–4342; fax: 250–428–9411; crescofc@kootenay. com; www.crestonbc.com/chamber) for more information on these attractions. Ask about the Creston mural walk, an interesting way of viewing the town and its environs. Another information source is their Web site, www. crestonvalley.com.

Without doubt the main attraction in the vicinity is the **Creston Valley Wildlife Management Area** (Box 640, Creston, V0B 1G0; 250–402–6900; fax: 250–402–6910; info@crestonwildlife.ca; www.crestonwildlife.ca). From Creston travel west along Highway 3 for 7 miles (11 km) to this lush, 17,000-acre (7,000-ha) wetland ecosystem drained by the Kootenay River. It's a staging and nesting area for more than 265 bird species and is a breeding ground for a number of rare species. During March and April ducks, swans, and geese in the thousands transform the area into a chattering, marshy amphitheater. Bald eagles, tundra swans, bank swallows, western grebe, osprey, and the rare Coeur d'Alène salamander are some of the species. Viewing is facilitated by boardwalks, a three-story birding tower, and a trail system. You'll possibly see white-tailed deer and coyotes as you hike, bird-watch, or fish in this ever-changing area, no matter what time of year. An **Interpretation Center,** which includes a gift shop, a library, a theater, and a variety of wildlife programs, opens on Mother's Day (early May) weekend, then in June (on Father's Day weekend) there's the annual *Osprey Festival* celebration. It closes on the Thanksgiving (mid-October) long weekend. Hours in summer (from the long May weekend to Labor Day) are from 9:00 A.M. to 5:00 P.M. daily. September and October hours are from 9:00 A.M. to 4:00 P.M. Wednesday to Sunday. Also available from the center are interpretive walks and guided canoe rides ($5.00) through the marsh.

PLACES TO STAY IN THE KOOTENAYS

CRAWFORD BAY
Wedgwood Manor Country Inn,
Box 135,
V0B 1E0; (250) 227-9233 or, for reservations, (800) 862-0022;
wedgwood@netidea.com.

CRESTON
Sweet Apple Bed & Breakfast,
3939 Highway 3 East,
Box 93, Erickson,
V0B 1K0; phone/fax:
250-428-7205;
www.sweetapple.bc.ca.

GRAND FORKS
The Maples Bed & Breakfast, 931 Central Avenue,
(250) 442-8182; fax: (250) 442-8156.

GREENWOOD
Country Elegance Bed & Breakfast, 52486 Wallace Creek Road, Box 539,
Greenwood, V0H 1J0;
(250) 445-6677;
fax: (250) 445-2112;
husbands@direct.ca;
www.bcbnb.com.

Lind Valley Guest Ranch,
Box 362,
V0H 1J0; phone/fax:
(250) 445-6585; www.
lindvalleyguestranch.com

NAKUSP
Halcyon Hot Springs Resort,
Box 37,
V0G 1R0; (888) 689-4699 or (250) 265-3554;
fax: (250) 265-3887;
info@halcyon-hot springs.com;
www.halcyon-hotsprings.com.

NELSON
Nelson Guest House,
2109 Fort Sheppard Drive;
(888) 215-2500;
phone/fax:
(250) 354-0198;
nelsonguest@yahoo.com;
www.nelsonguesthouse.com.

ROSSLAND
Angela's Place Bed and Breakfast,
1520 Spokane,
Box 944,
V0G 1Y0; (250) 362-7790;
angela@netidea.com;
www.visitangela.com.

SLOCAN
Lemon Creek Lodge,
7680 Kennedy Road,
Box 68,
V0G 2C0; phone/fax:
(250) 355-2403;
lemoncrk@telus.net;
www.lemoncreeklodge.com.

PLACES TO EAT IN THE KOOTENAYS

GRAND FORKS
Chef's Garden Restaurant,
4415 Highway 3,
V0H 1H0; (250) 442-0257.

Grand Forks Station Pub,
7654 Donaldson Drive,
V0H 1H0; (250) 442-5855.

GREENWOOD
Copper Eagle Cappuccino and Bakery,
325 Copper South;
(250) 445-6121.

KASLO
The Rosewood Cafe,
213 Fifth Street,
Box 1435,
V0G 1M0; (250) 353-ROSE.

NELSON

Mazatlan Mexican Restaurant, 198 Baker Street, (250) 352–1388.

Max & Irma's Restaurant, 515A Kootenay Street, (250) 352–2332.

Rickaby's, 524 Vernon Street, (250) 354–1919.

ROSSLAND

Gold Rush Books and Espresso, 2063 Washington Avenue, V0G 1Y0; (250) 362–5333; (800) 668–0140; goldrush@rossland.com.

TRAIL

Colander Restaurant, 1475 Cedar Avenue, V1R 4C5; (250) 364–1816.

The Rockies

No matter where you stand in this rugged southeastern corner of British Columbia, there's a good chance that if you close your eyes and spin around, when you open them, you'll be facing a mountain. From rolling hills to crenelated, snow-covered peaks, the Rockies contains twenty-six provincial parks bearing names like Top of the World Park and Height of the Rockies Park. Two national parks, Yoho and Kootenay, occupy most of the northeastern section. The heart of the region is the Rocky Mountain Trench, the longest valley in North America, where the Columbia River begins its 1,245-mile (2,005-km) meandering journey to the Pacific.

On the Rockies adventure list, we'll start with a mix of railway history and marshlands wildlife viewing in the "Key City of the Rockies," Cranbrook, followed by a side trip to the southeastern corner of the province, the Elk Valley, where *wilderness* is the key word. In Kimberley, where yodelers in the Platzl sing out a Bavarian theme, we'll eat German fare and ski in powder-perfect snow, followed by a trip back to 1897 frontier life at Fort Steele Heritage Park. Following the Columbia River, our journey passes through the Windermere Valley, famous for hot springs and golf courses, to Radium Hot Springs, where Rocky Mountain bighorn sheep walk the streets. We'll finish our adventure with a trip through the fabulous Kootenay National Park. Finally, we'll kick our way out of the Rockies with some white-knuckle, white-water rafting on the Kicking Horse River at Golden.

The Crowsnest to Cranbrook

As with the Okanagan and the Kootenays, we begin close to the U.S. border on the Crowsnest Highway 3, which at Yahk joins Highway 95. With the Rockies to the east and the Purcells to the northwest, the highway cuts and weaves northward beside the Moyie River on its path toward Cranbrook, passing en route four provincial parks (Yahk, Ryan, Moyie Lake, and Jimsmith Lake).

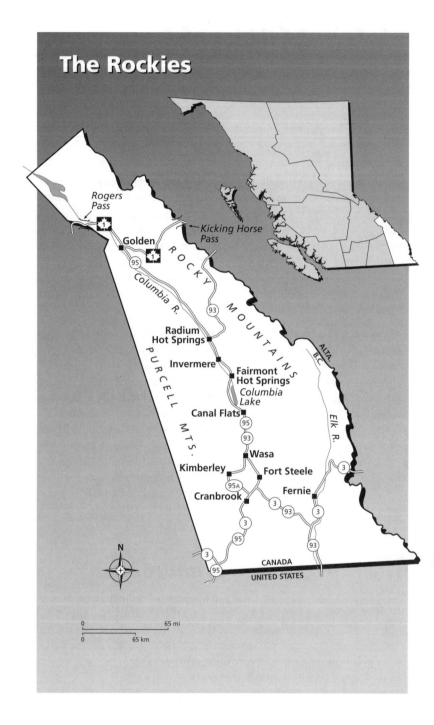

The Rockies

Rogers Pass

Golden

Kicking Horse Pass

ROCKY MOUNTAINS

Columbia R.

PURCELL MTS.

Radium Hot Springs

Invermere

Fairmont Hot Springs

Columbia Lake

Canal Flats

ALTA.

B.C.

Elk R.

Wasa

Kimberley

Fort Steele

Fernie

Cranbrook

N

CANADA

UNITED STATES

0   65 mi
0   65 km

THE ROCKIES

Moyie Lake Provincial Park is a 222-acre (90-
ha), forested playground 13 miles (21 km) south
of Cranbrook, with a good swimming lake and a
sandy beach. It has more than one hundred well-
shaded campsites, pleasant picnic shelters and
showers, and lots of room on the lake for boaters,
windsurfers, and fishing enthusiasts (the Dolly
Varden and rainbows bite well). Reservations can
be made ahead by calling the seasonal Discover
Camping number (800–689–9025 or, in Vancouver, 604–689–9025). For information on this
(and all other provincial parks in this section),
visit www.bcparks.ca and enter the appropriate
park name in the search box. Closer to Cranbrook, *Jimsmith Lake Provincial Park* (twenty-
nine campsites, no reservations) is extremely
popular with canoeists, campers, and picnickers
and has wheelchair access to a table and toilet
facilities. Powerboats are prohibited here.

Author's Top Ten Picks in the Rockies

Elizabeth Lake Wildlife Sanctuary

The ghost on Hosmer Mountain

Chef Bernard's Restaurant

Skiing in Kimberley

Sailing on Wasa Lake

Exploring Fort Steele Heritage Town

Golfing at Fairmont Hot Springs

Soaking in Radium Hot Springs

Sight-seeing in Kootenay and Yoho National Parks

Rafting the raging Kicking Horse River

On the southwestern outskirts of Cranbrook
(population 19,653 in 2002) near the *Splash Zone Water Slides* (250–
426–3389), the 249-acre (100-ha) *Elizabeth Lake Wildlife Sanctuary*
(250–489–8540; fax: 250–489–8506 for more information) is a must-
stop for bird-lovers. Walking trails lead to blinds at different spots
around the lake, allowing excellent bird-watching. You're likely to see
Canada geese, mallard, teal, bufflehead, and ruddy ducks. In summer
the *Cranbrook Visitor Info Centre* is located at the entrance.

Cranbrook has a long railway history. Displays at the *Canadian
Museum of Rail Travel* (Box 400, Cranbrook, V1C 4H9; 250–489–3918;
fax: 250–489–5744; office@trainsdeluxe.com; www.trainsdeluxe.com)
feature, among others, seven original cars from the luxurious transcontinental *TransCanada Limited* of 1929, built by the Canadian Pacific
Railway (CPR). This set of cars (dining, parlor, sleeping, and business
cars), possibly the only surviving set of this vintage in the world
designed as a traveling hotel, once provided service from Montreal to
Vancouver. Tea and scones are often served in the inlaid walnut-paneled
dining car, the *Argyle.* Other earlier trains, such as the 1907 *Soo-
Spokane Train Deluxe,* feature stained glass and art nouveau–style
inlays. The museum is located in the town center at 57 Van Horne Street
(Highway 3/95), an apt position considering that Cornelius Van Horne
was the famous railroad-building pioneer. The centerpiece of the new

(2002) museum facility, though, is the restored *Royal Alexandra Hall,* the original three-story-high, 3,000 square-foot, oak-paneled "Cafe" from the former Royal Alexandra Hotel in Winnipeg, Manitoba, which was built by the CPR in 1906 but demolished in 1971. The Cafe was miraculously saved. As a millennium project the museum reconstructed the Cafe piece by numbered piece. The story of this reconstruction (on the Web site) makes for fascinating reading for anyone interested in Canadian railway history. At the museum ask for a map to do a self-guided tour of Cranbrook that includes many historic buildings, notably the 1888 home of Colonel Baker, the city's founder. These maps are also available at the *Cranbrook Visitor Info Centre* (2279 Cranbrook Street North, Box 84, Cranbrook, V1C 4H6; 800–222–6174 or 250–426–5914; fax: 250–426–3873; cbkchamber@cyberlink.bc.ca; www.cranbrook chamber.com). As well, you'll find here information on eateries and accommodations.

Of a number of pleasant accommodations in Cranbrook, the *Cedar Heights Bed & Breakfast* (1200 Thirteenth Street South, Cranbrook, V1C 5V8; 250–426–0505 or 800–497–6014; fax: 250–426–0045; cedar heightsbc@shaw.ca; www.bbcanada.com/cedarheights) is hard to beat. A beautifully built executive home with spectacular mountain views and an outdoor spa, it has all the class and comforts you'd expect with a Canada Select 4½ Stars–rated B&B. To add to these comforts, artistically presented delicious breakfasts turn a memorable stay into an unforgettable one. Rates are $90–$115 double. From the highway take Third Street South, turn south on Eleventh Avenue South, then east on Thirteenth Street South.

Four miles (6 km) north of Cranbrook on Mission Road heading toward the Cranbrook-Kimberley airport, a scenic detour leads to the *St. Eugene Mission and Church.* The 1897 church was restored in 1983 by the St. Mary's Band and the East Kootenay Historical Association. It is viewed as the finest Gothic-style mission church in British Columbia and has beautiful, hand-painted stained glass.

At the same location the Ktunaxa/Kinbasket Tribal Council has redeveloped the buildings associated with the former Indian Residential School into the *Delta St. Eugene Mission Resort* (7731 Mission Road, Cranbrook, V1C 7E5; 250–420–2000; fax: 250–420–2001; toll free: 866–292–2020; deltanet@deltahotels.com; www.deltahotels.com). A feature of the resort is the *Casino of the Rockies* (7777 Mission Road, Cranbrook, V1C 7E5; 250–417–2772; www.casinooftherockies.com), which has 225 slot machines and twelve gaming tables. It also features a recreation center, the Ktunaxa Interpretive Centre, and the Ktunaxa Arts and Crafts Centre. One of the former residential school buildings is now the clubhouse of the **St. Eugene Mission Golf Course** (7725 Mission Road, Cranbrook, V1C 1E5; 877–417–3133 or 250–417–3417; info@golfsteugene. com; www.golfsteugene.com), a championship course designed by Les Furber that opened in May 2000; it was selected as the third-best new Canadian course for 2001 by *Golf Digest*. Visit the comfortable 19th Hole for a meal and a drink. Tee times can also be booked on the Web site.

The Southeastern Corner

Tucked into the extreme southeastern alcove of British Columbia are the towns of Fernie, Sparwood, and Elkford (the highest community in Canada at 4,500 feet [1,400 m]), lined up south to north in the **Elk Valley** near the Albertan border. To do a side trip to this hunting-fishing-skiing utopia, follow the Crowsnest Highway 3 east from Cranbrook 62 miles (100 km).

The largest of the three towns, **Fernie** (population almost 5,000), is proof that from adversity hope occasionally springs eternal. Two fires in 1904 and 1908 destroyed the city, leaving thousands homeless. The reconstruction in brick and stone has resulted in a city full of beautiful, turn-of-the-century buildings, some of which can now be toured. Contact the Fernie Chamber of Commerce, (102 Commerce Road, Fernie, V0B 1M5; 250–423–6868; 888–754–7325; fax: 250–423–3811; info@ferniechamber.com; www.ferniecham ber. com) to obtain a self-guided walking-tour map to see these architectural beauties.

The fires were just part of a series of disasters to hit the city. Floods and a horrifying coal-mining

---

Top Annual Events in the Rockies

Wings over the Rockies Bird Festival, *Invermere/Radium Hot Springs; late April/early May; (888) 933–3311 or (250) 347–2207*

Golden Wildlife Festival of Birds and Bears, *Golden; second week of May; (800) 622–GOLD or (250) 344–7125*

Sam Steele Days, *Cranbook; June; (250) 426–4161 or (800) 222–6174; www.samsteeledays.org*

Pro Rodeo, *Cranbrook; August; (250) 426–5792*

Elk Valley ArtWalk, *Fernie; July/August; (250) 423–6868*

Coal Miner Days, *Sparwood; late June; (250) 425–2423 or (250) 425–0552*

Wildcat Charlie Days, *Elkford; late June; (250) 865–2241*

Marysville Daze, *Kimberley; June; (250) 427–3666*

Kimberley JulyFest, *Kimberley; (250) 427–3666*

Golden Rodeo, *Golden; August; (800) 622–GOLD*

British Columbia Fact

British Columbia's most easterly point is Akamina Pass in the Rocky Mountains.

explosion in 1902, in which 128 men died, added to its woes. According to Indian legend a curse was placed on Fernie to revenge the coal-mine developer, William Fernie, who spurned a young Indian woman of the Tobacco Plains band. Perhaps the proof of this curse can be seen some evenings at dusk when you look up at *Hosmer Mountain,* just north of Fernie. Some people have even heard the ghostly hoofbeats filling the mountain air as a horse and rider gallop down the sheer, rocky walls. Fortunately for the city, Chief Red Eagle of the Tobacco Plains band lifted the curse shortly before he died in 1964, but the specter is still up there. I asked my waitress at *Rip'n Richard's Eatery* (301 Highway 3, beside the West Fernie Bridge; 250–423–3002) about this famous "ghost." She immediately stopped what she was doing and led me outside to point out where (and when) to look. The Wile E. Coyote Burger at Rip'n Richard's was ready when we came back in, and was it ever good! I was camped a mile west of the restaurant at the *Mount Fernie Provincial Park* (800–689–9025 for reservations), a delightful spot to photograph and hike.

What a fantastic part of British Columbia this Elk Valley is. It's difficult to decide which is the best time of year to visit. The *Fernie Alpine Resort,* 3 miles (5 km) south of Fernie on Highway 3, sports everything from dogsled rides and snowmobiling to snowboarding, cross-country skiing, and downhill skiing. In summer there's mountain biking, horseback riding, and hiking—or you can be lazy and ride the quad lift up to enjoy the beautiful wildflowers and the view. Phone (250) 423–4655 or, for reservations, (800) 258–SNOW (7669); fax: (250) 423–6644; info@skifernie.com; www.skifernie.com. Fernie Tourism Destinations (888–754–7325; 250–423–4395; fax: 250–423–9210; info@fernietourism.com; www.fernietourism.com) will also arrange package holidays and provide information.

Trivia

What's in a name? Fernie is the Outdoor Capital of British Columbia, Spar-wood is the Clean Coal Capital of the World, and Elkford is the Wilderness Capital of British Columbia.

There's also golf at *Fernie Golf and Country Club* (250–423–7773 pro shop; 250–423–4115 clubhouse; DougRobb@golffernie.com; www.golffernie.com), where the clubhouse sits right in the center of the course, and the restaurant's wraparound deck allows you to watch someone else dig up the fairways! Perhaps you'd rather practice a little fly-fishing with *Lost Creek Angling* (250–423–7517; fax: 250–423–7598; lostcreekangler@elkvalley.net; www.lostcreekangler.com), where you can float, "walk and wade," or fly in to fish some of the best trout rivers in British Columbia; or if you've ever wanted to try white-water kayaking or rafting, *Mountain High River Adventures Inc.* (1042 Fifth Avenue, Box 221, Fernie, V0B 1M0; phone/fax: 250–423–5008 or toll free 877–423–4555; fun@mountain high.bc.ca; www.mountainhigh.bc.ca) will have your adrenaline flowing as fast as the water. They use inflated kayaks for trips on the Bull, Elk, and Kootenay Rivers. There are three levels of adventure: Wet Your Appetite Scenic Float Trips, Wet Your Friends White-Water Rafting, and Wet Your Pants Inflatable Kayaking.

Stop over awhile to take it all in at *Willow Creek Bed and Breakfast* (5375 Boomerang Way, Box 6049, Fernie, V0B 1M6; 250–423–7731; fax: 250–423–7723; go2far@yahoo.com; www.go2far.com). B&B rates range from $89 to $119 double (ask about ski package specials) in this cozy home located a stone's throw from the base of the ski lifts. Built of tamarack logs, the home has a beautiful river-rock fireplace with a sitting-room loft above and a private hot tub just outside the door. There's also a suite available (breakfast not included) on a nightly, weekly, or monthly basis; it sleeps up to six. From Highway 3, take Ski Hill Road to Highline Drive (first right), then turn right onto Boomerang Way. In town, accommodation is available at *Barbara Lynn's Country Inn B&B* (Box 1077, 691 Seventh Avenue, Fernie, V0B 1M0; 250–423–6027; toll free: 888–288–2148; fax: 250–423–6024; BarbsCountryInn@monarch.net; www.blci.ca). It's just off the highway at the corner of Seventh Avenue and Seventh Street. Rates are in the $45 to $82 double range, with some excellent discounts for cyclists.

Sparwood (population 4,200), 17 miles (28 km) northeast of Fernie, is a little smaller than its neighbor and a lot newer. The residents moved there in 1968 from nearby Michel and Natal, now no longer in existence because of environmental concerns. The National Film Board's movie *That's the Price,* which documents the town move, can be borrowed from the local library.

Artist Dan Sawatzky (of Chemainus murals fame) and several local artists have spruced up Sparwood with some excellent *murals* depicting its mining history. *The Sparwood Visitor Info Centre* (Highway 3 and Aspen Drive, Box 1448, Sparwood, V0B 2G0; 877–485–8185; 250–425–2423; fax: 250–425–7130; administrator@sparwoodchamber.bc.ca; www.sparwoodchamber.bc.ca) can direct you to a *Mining Artifact Tour,* where you'll see a comprehensive collection of mid-twentieth-century,

Heli-hike with guides or take a sight-seeing tour, leaving from Fairmont Hot Springs Airport.

Float down the Columbia River with experienced rafting guides.

Visit the pets or take a ride in a Spin-n-bump car at the Fairmont Fun Park.

Dine at the Eagle's Eye in Golden, Canada's loftiest restaurant.

Hike to the impressive Josephine Falls near Elkford.

underground coal-mining equipment. The full-size murals and interpretive panels portray vividly the history of coal mining in the Elk Valley. It begins and ends at the Info Centre. Next door to the Chamber of Commerce office is the **Terex Titan,** the world's largest tandem-axle dump truck. It weighs in at 350 tons, and its box can stuff in two huge buses and two pickup trucks. It stands by one of Canada's largest open-pit coal mines, where tours (contact the Chamber in advance) are held in July and August.

From Sparwood Highway 43 travels north for 22 miles (35 km) along the Elk River to **Elkford,** the "Wilderness Capital of British Columbia" and the jumping-off point for the **Elk Lakes Provincial Park** (250–422–3212), a walk-in-only camping park. Elkford is truly a wilderness town, with elk, bear, bighorn sheep, and deer sometimes seen in the environs. Inquire at the **Elkford Info Centre** (4A Front Street, Box 220, Elkford, V0B 1H0; 877–355–9453 or 250–865–4614; fax: 250–865–2442; ecofc@titanlink.com; www.chamber.elkford.bc.ca) for details about accommodation, restaurants, and the many hiking trails (notably one to the breathtaking Josephine Falls) in this spectacularly scenic area.

North to Kimberley

Kimberley, at 3,652 feet (1,113 m), is BC's highest incorporated city. It lies 20 miles (32 km) north of Cranbrook along Highway 95A. Four miles (7 km) before Kimberley, in **Marysville,** look for a sign indicating a boardwalk track to **Marysville Falls,** a thundering 100-foot (30-m) cascade quite near the highway. It's just before the turnoff to the scenic **Kimberley Golf Course** (250–427–4161; www.kimberley golfclub.com), which is set among Ponderosa pines with the Purcell Mountains as a backdrop.

If you're feeling particularly energetic, a 3.7-mile (6-km) nature and fitness trail developed by the Kimberley Rotary and Lions Clubs starts at the bridge at the north end of Main Street in Marysville and leads north to Kimberley along Mark Creek. Walk quietly and you may see mule deer, Rocky Mountain elk, northern flickers, sometimes great blue heron, and lots of wildflowers. Occasionally in summer a moose and calf can be seen in the marshes.

In Kimberley the **Platzl** monopolizes center stage with a brilliant red and green theme. You may enjoy (or not!) Happy Hans's yodeling as the **world's largest cuckoo clock**'s doors pop open at the drop of a quarter.

The clock sits in front of the amazing **Chef Bernard's Platzl Inn and Restaurant** (170 Spokane Street, Kimberley, V1A 2E4; 250–427–4820; fax: 250–427–4829; chefbernards@cyberlink.bc.ca; www.cyberlink.bc.ca/~chefbernards). Why amazing? First, the food is delicious. Second, the confusion of knickknacks inside will keep you gawking for the length of your dinner and then some. Model trains "toot-toot" around the ceiling, sometimes carrying birthday greetings for an unsuspecting diner. Originally the restaurant was fondue-only, until Bernard could afford a stove. His cuisine has won several awards. After many years on *Love Boat* Sunprincesses and serving the rich and famous (from Alfred Hitchcock to the King of Tonga), this Hamburg-born immigrant displays his cosmopolitan past through an eclectic menu—from Cajun Two-Step Jamabalaya to Szechwan ginger crab pot and Drunken Black Tiger Shrimps, all delicious. My lobster-and-steak special went down very well as I sat below accordions and beer steins, while trophy goatheads watched clown fish swim by in colorful aquariums. No kidding!

Upstairs, reasonably priced accommodations, with a hot tub on the outside deck, make Chef Bernard's Inn and Restaurant a one-stop shop.

The ever-expanding **Kimberley Alpine Resort** (800–258–7669 or 250–427–4881; fax: 250–427–3927; info@skikimberley.com; www.skikimberley.com), only a few minutes' drive from the city, has seventy-five runs, ten lifts, one of the longest lit runs in North America, and, consistently, 15 feet of pure white powder each year. Other winter activities at the resort are winter bonfires, snowshoeing, cross-country skiing, skating, helicopter sight-seeing tours, and snowmobiling. In the summer, quad-chair-access mountain biking, hiking, river rafting, horseback riding, fly-fishing, and scenic chairlift rides are offered.

Next door to Chef Bernard's is the **Yodeling Woodcarver Arts and Crafts Shop** (140 Spokane Street, Kimberley, V1A 2Y5; 250–427–7211). If you aren't quite yodeled to death, Adi Unteberger will complement your purchase with one of his famous yodels. If it sounds familiar, it's because his is the voice of Happy Hans of cuckoo-clock fame.

Still on the Platzl, **The Snowdrift Café** (110 Spokane Street, Kimberley, V1A 2Y5; 250–427–2001; snowdrift@cyberlink.bc.ca) is a friendly, lively place to go for a beer or wine, play cards, or read a newspaper, while you enjoy the best Manhattan clam chowder this side of the Rockies. Roy Cimolai serves "natural" foods at supernaturally low prices. His lentil soup, served with homemade whole wheat bread and his freshly baked pies make a great lunch between exploring Kimberley's nooks

OFF THE BEATEN PATH

and crannies. Oversized muffins and huckleberry bars make for a delicious snack. Roy buys huckleberries from local pickers and occasionally picks them himself with his authentic Norwegian plastic berry rake. The Snowdrift Café, almost entirely vegetarian, but with some meat entrees added to satisfy all tastes, is a favorite among the locals, who come not just for the great cheesecakes and the best coffee in Kimberley but also for the daylong, small-town chatty ambience. It's open Monday to Saturday, 10:00 A.M. to 6:00 P.M. and Sunday from noon to 6:00 P.M. The Snowdrift also sells Kicking Horse Coffee (roasted in the Kootenays) and will grind it to your liking.

The warm Kimberley summers may entice you to head for the river. Just a block from the Snowdrift, drop in to the Technosport shop to book a rafting trip with **Canadian Rockies River Expeditions** (250 Spokane Street, V1A 2Y3; toll free: 877–777–RAFT; 250–427–3266; fax: 250–427–4666; www.riverraftkimberley.com). They'll take you to the **St. Mary's and Elk Rivers** to teach you some river basics, while ensuring three hours of fun at the same time. The more adventurous may want to try some cliff jumping and body-surfing during a riotous one-day white-water rafting trip, followed by a full riverside gourmet buffet that will have you hooked and back for more in no time. Kayaking lessons are also offered—choose from three-hour, one-day, or two-day formats.

A short, steep walk from the Platzl via Howard Street (about fifteen

History and Hot Tubs

*I*t was one of those crisp, Rocky Mountain November days when I serendipitously arrived in Wasa Lake. I meandered around the lake and happened upon the Wasa Lakeside Bed and Breakfast Resort. I was a stranger at the door, but that didn't concern James Swansburg, who invited me in and introduced his family, insisting I return for a longer visit. I then drove down to nearby Fort Steele. As it was winter, it was almost deserted, but an enthusiastic groundsman unlocked doors first opened in the 1890s: The Prospector *newspaper office, its*

antique presses still reverberating with sounds that once pumped out the dramatic and the mundane; Bleasdell's Pioneer Drug Store advertising NOTHING CHEAP HERE, BUT YOUR MONEY'S WORTH EVERY TIME. Shadows from the past. With history permeating every pore, I headed back to Wasa. My evening ended with a game of badminton with locals in the school gym, followed by a decadent soak in the Swansburgs' hot tub amid the silence of the dark mountains and the occasional call of a distant wolf. And only the day before, I had never heard of Wasa Lake!

minutes) brings you to the **Cominco Gardens** (306 Third Avenue; 250–427–2293). In season 48,000 blooms overwhelm your optical and olfactory senses. First planted in 1927 to advertise Cominco's Elephant Brand Fertilizer, the two-and-a-half-acre (1-ha) site was later given to the community. It's open dawn to dusk, May through September. You can drive there also from Highway 95A. From the Platzl head north on Wallinger Avenue, following the signs to the hospital; go 1 block farther, and it's on the left. Entrance is free, but a donation for upkeep is welcome. **The Garden Treasures Restaurant and Gift Shop** serves coffee, tea, and light snacks in the original Cominco greenhouse.

According to Ktunaxa (pronounced Tun-ah-hah) legend, hoodoos at the north end of Columbia Lake are the remains of a giant fish that was wounded by a coyote. It tried to travel through the Rocky Mountain Trench but finally died. Its flesh decomposed and its ribs broke up. Half of its ribs became these hoodoos, and the other half became hoodoos located farther south near St. Mary's, just north of Cranbrook.

It's an adventure into the past on the **Bavarian City Mining Railway**, built as a labor of love by volunteers who salvaged the equipment from old mines. The 7.5-mile (12-km) round-trip links downtown Kimberley with the site of the old Sullivan Mine surface facilities. You'll see the Cominco Power House (open for tours), the Orpheum Theatre, the North Star School House, and a miner's cabin, passing through a steep-walled, tight valley. Pick up the train from the downtown station two minutes west of the Platzl. It's not a luxury trip, but it's fun, and the views of the Kimberley Ski Hill and the Thousand Peaks mountain range are spectacular. The train runs on the hour on weekends in June and daily through July to Labor Day. Contact the Sullivan Mine Interpretive Centre Society, 340 Spokane Street, Kimberley, V1A 2E8; (250) 427–5311; fax: (250) 427–3922, for information on the history on this area and information on new developments under way.

For campers **Happy Hans Riverside RV Resort** (Box 465, Kimberley, V1A 3B9; 250–427–2929 or 250–427–4877 off-season; fax: 250–427–2917; www.happyhans.com) has vehicle sites ranging from $16 to $24. This large (140 sites) newly relocated campground is nine minutes south of Kimberley on St. Mary's River Road. As well as the usual conveniences found in large camping parks, plans are under way (2003) to add many more holiday amenities, including a baseball diamond, a children's playground, horseshoes/bocce pits, a group barbecue area, sauna and hot tub facilities, and a hiking trail system within the RV park. It also accesses the 2,000-acre (900-ha) **Kimberley Nature Park** (Box 398, Kimberley, V1A 2Y9; www.rockies.net/kimberley/nature park), one of the largest municipal parks in Canada.

Find out more from the **Kimberley Visitor Info Centre** (Gerry Sorenson Way, Kimberley, V1A 2Z9; 250–427–3666; fax: 427–5378; kimbchamber@ cyberlink.bc.ca) or contact Kimberley Vacations (800–667–0871; kimbvac@rockies.net; www.kimberleyvacations.bc.ca). Another useful site is www.kimberleybc.net.

Kimberley to Canal Flats

ifteen miles (24 km) north of Kimberley, Highway 95A rolls through mysteriously named Ta Ta Creek and then joins Highway 93 heading north to Radium Hot Springs and the Kootenay National Park. A mile south of the Highway 93/95 junction, **Wasa Lake Provincial Park** (www.bcparks.ca, search "Wasa"; 800–689–9025 for reservations) hugs a gem of a lake of the same name. It's a water-sports utopia. A few years ago, a couple of Albertan hang gliders soared off from a road cut in nearby Mount Estella. While ecstatically suspended over **Wasa Lake**, they decided to throw in their tidy nine-to-five Calgary life and head west for some real adventure. Now James and Mary Swansburg operate **Wasa Lakeside Bed and Breakfast Resort** (4704 Spruce Road, Box 122, Wasa, V0B 2K0; 250–422–3688 or 888–422–3636; fax: 250–422–3551; mary@wasalakeresort.com; www.wasalakeresort.com) on the northwest side of Wasa Lake, the warmest lake in the Canadian Rockies. The resort offers Hobie Cat sailing, waterskiing, pedal boating, windsurfing, hot tubbing, hang gliding, paragliding, elegant rooms, and the best "honeymoon" steam shower I've ever experienced. It's decorated beautifully with stained glass and a skylight. Delicious breakfasts are served beside the private 100-foot (30-m) beach. Guests are welcome to use the beachside kitchen, barbecue, or fire pit to prepare lunches and dinners.

Ten minutes south of Wasa, almost to Fort Steele, history buffs can visit the site of the first gold rush—and the first town—in the East Kootenay: **Fisherville**. When a rich gold vein was discovered under Fisherville (a town of 5,000 by 1885), the town site was moved farther up the hill and renamed **Wild Horse**. Stroll through the Wild Horse graveyard, following a trail past a Chinese burial ground, along Victoria Ditch to Walker's grave, and back through the site of Fisherville. The East Kootenay Historical Association (Box 74, Cranbrook, V1C 4H6) has prepared a brochure detailing the history of the area and what to look out for on your hike (allow at least an hour). You'll find the brochures at the Fort Steele ticket booth or in the Kimberley and Cranbrook Chambers of Commerce. To get to Wild Horse/Fisherville, turn east off Highway 93/95 at the Fort Steele RV Resort onto Bull River Road, then left onto a logging road for about 4 miles (6 km).

There's much more to discover in the Bull River Road area, including a spectacular gorge on the Bull River (look for the BC Hydro Dam sign) and the **Kootenay Trout Hatchery** (250–429–3214; fax: 250–429–3202) on the Wardner-Fort Steele Road, where six million rainbow, brook, and cutthroat trout are produced annually. Take a free, self-guided tour of the special viewing areas and displays. Located 5 miles (8 km) north of Wardner (20 miles [32 km] east of Cranbrook) on the east side of the Kootenay River, the hatchery is the second largest in British Columbia. It's open daily from 8:00 A.M. to 4:00 P.M.

Just 12 miles (20 km) south from Wasa on Highway 93/95—or 10 miles (16 km) northeast of Cranbrook—is **Fort Steele Heritage Town** (9851 Highway 93/95, Fort Steele, V0B 1N0; 250–417–6000; fax: 250–489–2624; info@fortsteele.bc.ca; www.fortsteele.bc.ca), named after Samuel Steele, a North-West Mounted Police superintendent blessed with conflict-resolution skills and a certain amount of charisma. He dealt successfully with the tension that had been rising at nearby Galbraith's Ferry between the white settlers and the chief of the Upper Kootenay Indians. The resulting settlement was the first North-West Mounted post west of the Rockies. The restored town, set at the confluence of the St. Mary and Kootenay Rivers, with the magnificent Rockies as a backdrop, is a must-see attraction. It's open from early May through mid-October. During the peak summer months the hours of operation are 9:30 A.M. to 6:00 P.M. and for the spring and fall months, 9:30 A.M. to 5:00 P.M. In summer it operates as it would have in its heyday, with fresh bread coming from a baker's wood-fired oven, chickens pecking in the dust, lambs gamboling in the fields, and transport provided by steam train or Clydesdale-drawn wagon. Daily from late June to early September check out the Wild Horse Theatre for hilarious musical comedies. Make sure to eat lunch at the **International Hotel,** where you'll be seated in period furniture with nineteenth-century prints gracing the walls. Many of the stores— **H. Kershaw and Son General Store**, the **City Bakery,** the **Pioneer Tinshop,** the **blacksmith,** the **leatherworker,** and **Mrs. Sprague's Confectionery** (hard-candy sticks and yummy Canadian maple sugar)— are working establishments, and the array of old-fashioned goodies for sale will assure you that you really have walked back into another century. Special events, such as an unbelievably spooky **Hallowe'en**

> ### Trivia
>
> *Fairmont Hot Springs is Canada's largest odorless natural-mineral hot springs.*

Extravaganza, Heritage Showcase Thanksgiving Celebration, and the *Great Fort Steele Easter Egg Hunt* are held throughout the year.

Admission is valid for two days and ranges from $8.50 to free for children under six. A family two-day pass is $19.25. Season passes ($24.25 per family!) and group rates are available.

The Windermere Valley

Eight miles (13 km) north of the Highway 93/95 junction lies *Skookumchuck,* where the Lussier and Skookumchuck Rivers meet the Kootenay. Stop for a fill-up at the area's cheapest gas station, Skookumchuck Centre (250–422–3737). Seventeen miles (28 km) north, you're in for some pretty scenery around *Canal Flats,* population 680. This legendary area, according to Ktunaxa Indian elders, is where the giant Natmuqcin molded with his knees the mile-wide portage separating Columbia Lake (headwaters of the north-flowing Columbia River) from the south-flowing Kootenay River. If you have a canoe and a couple of days to spare, a trip down the Kootenay River to Fort Steele will take you through some of the best scenery in British Columbia, with lots of wildlife viewing on the way.

About 3 miles (5 km) south of Canal Flats, a turnoff to the east (Whiteswan Lake Road) leads for 14 miles (23 km) along a gravel road to *Whiteswan Lake Provincial Park* (www.bcparks.ca, search "Whiteswan"), with ninety vehicle camping sites plus three wilderness sites. Just inside the park boundary is the *Lussier River Hotsprings*. This fabulous, 111°F (44°C), undeveloped springs (except for a covered stairway and change room) is maintained by volunteers, so please respect this by taking out what you bring in. It is accessed down a gradual slope from the parking lot.

Two miles (3 km) north of Canal Flats, near *Canal Flats Provincial Park* (no campsites but the perfect setting for a travel break, with swimming, a boat launch, and a picnic area), the remains of the bizarrely conceived Baillie-Grohmann Canal, an 1880s endeavor to link Columbia Lake to the Kootenay River in an effort to reduce flooding (while at the same time opening up a north-south navigational system from Golden to Montana), can be seen. On a windy day, windsurfers flock to the lake.

The highway caresses Columbia Lake's west bank up to the fast-growing golfing community of *Fairmont Hot Springs Resort* (Box 10, Fairmont Hot Springs, V0B 1L0; 250–345–6311 or 800–663–4979; fax: 250–345–6616; info@fairmonthotsprings.com; www.fairmonthotsprings.com). Two

Trivia

classy courses are located here: **Mountainside Golf Course** (800–663–4979), which sits in the shadow of the Rockies and has been awarded the title of Canada's Most Unique Golf Resort, and **Riverside Golf Course** (800–665–2112), Canada's Golf Course of the Year in 1998, which incorporates in its design the Columbia River as a natural hazard. **Fairmont Hot Springs Resort** offers package deals of two nights lodging, two rounds of golf at either course, two breakfasts, and

Because of the canal between the Kootenay River and Columbia Lake, the government, in anticipation of an influx of settlers, built a road from Fort Steele to Golden, thus opening up the valley—so the canal was not all for naught.

unlimited use of the odorless, sulfur-free pools for $236 per person in low season and $299 in high season. There's also the family-friendly **Fairmont Creekside Par 3,** located next to the Mountainside Golf Course. In all more than eight eighteen-hole championship courses and several executive-length and mini-putt courses can be enjoyed in the area known as the **Windermere Valley.**

Another accommodation that is located centrally to all the action in the valley and with a spectacular view is **McMillan Chalet Bed & Breakfast** (5021 Fairmont Close, Box 989, Fairmont Hot Springs, V0B 1L0; phone/fax: 250–345–9553; 800–856–9551; cell: 250–342–5785; Kenmcm@rockies.net; www.bbexpo.com/mcmchalet). Turn east off Highway 93 at the large FAIRMONT HOT SPRINGS RESORT sign; then turn left on Hot Springs Road, right on Falcon Drive, and right onto Fairmont Close. The McMillans serve excellent breakfasts and sometimes refreshments in the evening. Double rates are in the $79 to $114 range.

Ten miles north of Fairmont, on the eastern side of Lake Windermere, tiny **Windermere** (population 450) packs quite a punch. Glassblowers, woodcarvers, artists, and potters make up Artisan's Corner near the 1887 White House Hotel, a popular watering hole complete with a funky three-hole golf course. There's even a **Stolen Church** (on the corner of Kootenay Street and Victoria Avenue). The story goes that the church (St. Peter's) was built in Donald in 1887. When the CPR decided to move their railway divisional point from Donald, 115 miles (185 km) north of Windermere, to Revelstoke, it was agreed that several important buildings, including the church, would be moved, too. Rufus and Celina Kimpton of Donald loved this church. But they were moving to Windermere. So they purloined the church, piece by piece, on wagons and barges and had it reassembled on a lovely hill, where it now stands as Windermere's only church.

Garden lovers visiting Windermere shouldn't miss **Creekside Flower Gardens** (Box 113, 4795 Dell Road, Windermere, V0B 2L0; 250–342–6354; cell: 250–341–1617; fax: 250–342–2556; www.creeksidegardens.ca).

Comprised of twenty-two separate theme gardens, too many to list here, the site has fragrant herb gardens, a sunflower forest walk, rose gardens, a tea house, a gardeners' library, a fresh flower shop, and three bed-and-breakfast suites. The gardens are located on Dell Road, off Sinclair Road and Quartz Street just a few minutes from town.

Stay over and get to know the golf courses and beaches in the valley at **Windermere Creek Bed & Breakfast Cabins** (1658 Windermere Loop Road, Box 409, Windermere, V0B 2L0; phone/fax: 250–342–0356; 800–946–3942; www.bbexpo.com/bc/windcreek.htm). It's a bit of the old and a lot of the new. Five private, secluded log cabins—one (the Heritage Cabin) built in 1887, the other four just recently—all featuring double Jacuzzi tubs and showers, plus a main house set in 107 acres, make up this unique bed-and-breakfast. The new cabins have a loft bedroom and a kitchenette (perfect for longer stays). To top it off there's a small orchard and miles of trails to wander, hike, or ski. Hammocks by the creek running through the property make for complete relaxation. Rates are from $105 to $125 (double) year-round. The Windermere Loop Road is on the eastern side of Highway 93/95, and the Windermere Creek B&B is about 2 miles in (halfway along the loop) across from the fifth tee of the **Windermere Valley Golf Course** (250–342–3004).

Invermere (population 3,030 in 2002) is on the northwestern side of Lake Windermere and was known by the Ktunaxa as *Kyaknuqti?it,* meaning "prairie on top of a hill." It has quite a holiday atmosphere. In 1807 David Thompson, the first European in the area, settled here, calling it Kootenae House. One of its more famous establishments is **Strands Old House Restaurant** (818 Twelfth Street, Invermere, V0A 1K0; 250–342–6344; fax: 250–342–6386; strands@invermere.com). Lovely surroundings and to-die-for food make Strands one of the best places to dine in the Rockies. There are at least four innovative chef's features daily, loads of fresh seafood, and a lobster tank. If you can't decide what to choose from the extensive menu, try the Rack of Lamb Anthony (named for Kiwi chef and owner, Tony Wood) or the pork fusilli bok choy. If you eat between 5:00 and 6:00 P.M., they offer a three-course, four-choice, early-bird special for $13.95. You'll find Strands 1 block west of the Invermere post office between Eighth and Tenth Avenues. To learn more about Invermere, view excellent maps, and find accommodation, visit www.invermere.com.

To experience Canadian adventure in this neck of the woods at its most exciting, call **Kootenay River Runners/Purcell River Odysseys Ltd**. (Box 8, Edgewater, V0A 1E0; 250–347–9210; 800–599–4399; fax:

250–347–6598; info@raftingtherockies.com; www.raftingtherockies.com). You'll be hooked after a four-hour lesson/excursion in one of their inflatable kayaks, where for $64 you'll be introduced to the basics of kayaking-à-la-ducky, followed by a run down a Class III river. River Runners supplies all the necessary kayaking gear. There's also white-water rafting: Try a Toby Creek Odyssey, a two-hour adrenaline-pumping thriller at $45 (less for oldies, youngies, and groupies), sure to be a wild and wet one. They also run four-hour Evening Wildlife Safaris ($39) with a naturalist, beginning at Mineral King, the site of an abandoned silver mine, passing through avalanche meadows and subalpine forests to Earl Grey's Cabin, a Canadian historical site. Wine and cheese completes the adults-only Toby Valley wilderness experience. River Runners' base is at Panorama Resort, just 10.9 miles (17.5 km) west of Invermere.

Panorama Mountain Village (800–663–2929 or 250–342–6941; fax: 250–342–3395; paninfo@intrawest.com; www.panoramaresort.com) is legendary, a recreation utopia both winter and summer. Breathtaking scenery and an intimate mountain-retreat village accompany skiing terrains ranging from double black-diamond glades to wide-open groomed cruising. The mountain features a vertical drop of 4,000 feet (1,200 m), boasts runs more than 2.2 miles (3.5 km) long, and has nine lifts. Some features are "slopeside" lodging, terrain parks, night skiing, cross-country skiing, heli-skiing, skating, snowmobiling, horse-drawn sleigh rides, and giant hot tubs. And that's just in winter. In summer you can golf at the Greywolf Golf course, mountain bike (with access via a chairlift), play tennis or volleyball, swim and waterslide, and participate in many more activities.

When you reach *Radium Hot Springs,* where Highways 93 and 95 diverge, you need to decide whether to head east (Highway 93) to wonderful parks and eventually Alberta or northwest (Highway 95) along the Columbia River to Golden. My suggestion, if you have time, is to do both. To miss either *Kootenay* or *Yoho National Parks* (in one of the world's largest protected areas) would be a shame. But first, let's look at Radium Hot Springs.

Here I discovered the Victorian-style *Village Country Inn & Tea Room* (7557 Canyon Avenue, Box 15, Radium Hot Springs, V0A 1M0; 866–761–9392; 250–347–9392; fax: 250–347–9375; mail@VillageCountry Inn.bc.ca; www. VillageCountryInn.bc.ca). My first clue that I was in a wilderness setting was when a herd of Rocky Mountain bighorn sheep, refusing to let development interfere with their traditional beaten path, thundered by as I ate breakfast. Later I looked up to see an osprey and an eagle fly by. The main living room/dining room area is set around a large stone fireplace, and upstairs, hosts Sasha and Gorm have decorated elegantly twelve bedrooms plus a honeymoon suite. Gourmet breakfasts cost $5.50–$7.00, and there's afternoon tea (don't miss Sasha's decadent desserts) for guests from 2:00 to 5:00 P.M. Room rates range from $105 to $135 in peak season.

Trivia

The Banff-Windermere Road (now called Highway 93, the Banff-Windermere Parkway) was completed in 1922. It was the first motor road to be built through the central Canadian Rockies and is one of the most scenic roads in British Columbia, passing through Kootenay National Park to Banff National Park in Alberta.

Ask at the Village Country Inn about the scenic (gravel but well-maintained) West Side Road, which runs south from Radium Hot Springs on the opposite (west) side of the Columbia River, parallel to Highway 93/95. It passes through beautiful valleys and crosses creeks and rivers before coming to bluffs that overlook the valley, eventually arriving at the small hamlet of Wilmer. It then joins the road to Panorama just north of Invermere. Another road leads from the West Side Road to a trailhead, the start of a three-hour hike leading to the glacier at the Lake of the Hanging Glacier, one of the most spectacular areas in the Canadian Rockies. Detailed maps are recommended.

You'll find an excellent meal in Radium at the new **Helna's Stube Restaurant** (250–347–0047; fax: 250–347–0049; mail@helnas.com; www.helnas.com). The Austrian-style menu has a variety of schnitzels and steaks, as well as delicious homemade desserts; locals swear it's the best meal you'll find in the valley. It's open year-round (except January) from 5:00 to 10:00 P.M. on the corner of Main Street West and St. Mary's Street. It's closed Tuesday and Wednesday in winter.

Just 2 blocks from town along Forsters Landing Road—turn west at the highway junction and follow the signs—is the highly acclaimed **Springs Golf Course** (Box 310, Radium Hot Springs, V0A 1M0; 800–667–6444 or 250–347–9311; www.radiumresort.com), and but a mile away, you might take a dip in the Radium Hot Springs (see next section), where you can soak up the minerals and the stunning view from Sinclair Canyon. Should you be visiting in mid-September, you'll catch the **Show and Shine Columbia Valley Classic Car Show.** To help you find these attractions and more, the Chamber of Commerce in Radium has produced a comprehensive map of the area. Inquire at the **Radium**

Radium Hot Springs

Hot Springs Visitor Info Centre (7556 Main Street East, Box 225, Radium Hot Springs, V0A 1M0; 800–347–9704 or 250–347–9331; fax: 250–347–9127; chamber@rhs.bc.ca; www.rhs.bc.ca).

Kootenay National Park to Golden

From Radium Hot Springs you enter the UNESCO Rocky Mountain Parks World Heritage Site at *Kootenay National Park* (Box 220, Radium Hot Springs, V0A 1M0; 250–347–9615 or 800–748–7275; fax: 250–347–9980; kootenay.reception@pc.gc.ca; www.parkscanada.ca/kootenay). Drop in to the Visitor Information Centre at the south end of Radium Village first, then keep your eyes peeled for bighorn sheep as you pass through the dramatic Sinclair Canyon. Then take a dip at the famous Radium Hot Springs (Box 40, Radium Hot Springs, V0A 1M0; 800–767–1611 in Canada or 250–347–9485) in either the hot pool, which, at an average temperature of 100° F (38° C), is great for a soak, or the cooler 84° F (29° C) pool, ideal for a swim. There's also a small

Jacuzzi-style plunge pool. Don't miss a luxurious massage after your soak. (Phone 250–347–2100 for reservations.) A restaurant and gift shop (250–347–9376) complete the complex. Opening hours in July and August are 8:00 A.M. to 11:00 P.M. but vary the rest of the year.

Head east along Highway 93 following Sinclair Creek, then north through the Kootenay River Valley, where from the safety of your vehicle you may see elk or deer. Drive with care, as there is a significant problem with highway mortality of wildlife. Stop off at the *Kootenay Valley Viewpoint,* 10 miles (17 km) from Radium, and feast on the panorama of the Mitchell and Vermilion ranges. Fifty-three miles (86 km) from Radium a mile-long (1.5-km) trail leads to the *Paint Pots,* natural pools where a vivid orange color is formed by iron-rich springs bubbling up through the pools and overflowing to the ocher beds, thus staining the clay red.

At colorful *Marble Canyon,* 55 miles (89 km) from Radium Hot Springs, there's a half-mile trail through a narrow gorge to a thundering waterfall. It's a great leg stretcher and shouldn't be missed. Four miles (7 km) farther, *Vermilion Pass,* at 5,416 feet (1,651 m), marks the Continental Divide (the rivers now flow toward the Atlantic) and the entrance to *Banff National Park* (www.parkscanada.ca/banff) in Alberta. The Trans-Canada Highway then takes you north to the lovely Lake Louise and through Kicking Horse Pass to Golden, where you again meet up with Highway 95. Contact Canadian Heritage Parks Canada at (800) 748–PARK (7275) from anywhere in Canada; natlparks-ab@pc.gc.ca; www.parkscanada.ca for information on fees (including passes) for all the National Parks.

If instead you continue north from Radium Hot Springs, 7 miles (11 km) along Highway 95 is Edgewater, where every Saturday (from 10:00 A.M. to 2:00 P.M.) for the past thirty or so summers the *Edgewater Open Market* has been the spot for farmers and artisans in the valley to show their wares.

Another 11 miles (18 km) north you'll pass through Brisco, population 140, where you may wonder, *why stop?* The *Brisco General Store* (250–346–3343), built in 1906, is why! It seems to sell everything, including liquor, videos, mousetraps, coffee, groceries, newspapers, and rubber boots. It's also the post office and the one original general store left in the Columbia River Valley that hasn't burned down yet. Like the other small towns in this wonderful valley, Brisco has a beautiful view. And if you should be coming on horseback, the hitching post is right out front.

A 30-mile (48-km) gravel logging road just south of Brisco leads to the *Bugaboo Glacier Provincial Park* (www.bcparks.ca, search "Bugaboo"), famous for its huge glaciers, church-spire mountains, and heli-skiing. Should you ever see pictures of climbers hanging off impossible, jagged, rocky cliffs, chances are they were taken in the Bugaboos in the rugged Purcell Mountains. Hiking here can be steep and demanding, so check with park officials before venturing out.

From Brisco to Golden there's not much other than rambling ranches and beautiful scenery. Some people might ask, "What else do you want?" The Columbia continues its northern pursuit, and at *Golden* it's joined by the wild Kicking Horse River. Seated between the imposing Rockies and the Columbia Mountains, with five National Parks close by, Golden is indeed a crossroads. Here Highway 95 meets the Trans-Canada, from which you can travel east to *Yoho National Park,* (Box 99, Field, V0A 1G0; 250–343–6783; fax; 250–343–6012; yoho.info@pc.gc.ca; www. parkscanada.ca/yoho) with its fabulous canyons and glaciers, exquisite lakes, spectacular scenery, and more than 250 miles (400 km) of hiking trails. Yoho is also one of the four Rocky Mountain parks that form the UNESCO World Heritage Site. Features include the superb *Takakkaw Falls,* one of the highest waterfalls in Canada (and second-highest in BC); the *Natural Bridge,* carved out of solid rock; and the *Burgess Shale,* with fossil deposits of internationally recognized significance. Visit www.burgess-shale.bc.ca for a plethora of information on the Burgess Shale, as well as to find accommodation in *Field* (250–353–6783), 18 miles (57 km) east of Golden on the banks of the Kicking Horse River. This pretty village at the foot of Mount Stephen is the home of the *Burgess Shale Earth & Life Science Learning Centre* (250–343–6006). It's also an excellent base from which to explore Yoho National Park.

Recommended Reading—The Rockies

Yoho: A History and Celebration of Yoho National Park, by R. W. Sanford. Altitude Publishing, 1993.

Classic Hikes in the Canadian Rockies, by Graeme Pole. Canmore: Altitude Publishing, 1999.

Central Rockies Mammals, by John Marriott. Luminous Compositions Ltd., 1997.

The Canadian Rockies SuperGuide, by Graeme Pole. Altitude Publishing, 1998.

BC Parks Explorer, by Maggie Paquet. University of Toronto Press, 1986.

Central Rockies Wildflowers, by Mike Potter. Luminous Compositions Ltd., 1996.

Golden is popular with sports enthusiasts of every ilk, in any season. One very popular activity is white-water rafting. Several companies offer all levels of rafting trips on the Blaeberry and Kicking Horse Rivers, including **Glacier Raft Company** (Box 428, Golden, V0A 1H0; 250–344–6521; fax: 250–344–6591; glacierraft@redshift.bc.ca; www. glacierraft.com); **Alpine Rafting** (888–599–5299; info@alpinerafting. com; www.alpinerafting.com); **Wet 'n Wild Adventures** (800–668–9119; fax: 250–344–7650; info@wetnwild.bc.ca; www.wetnwild.bc.ca); and **Rocky Mountain Rafting Company** (888–518–RAFT [7238]; 250–344–6979; fax: 250–344–6985; info@rockymountainadventure. com; www.rockymountainadventure.com). If you want to experience the true thrill of white-water rafting, try a one-day Kicking Horse River rollick, which is probably one of the wildest one-day raft trips in Canada. It begins fast, and the river never really slows as you accelerate through such exhilarating rapids as Man Eater, Shot Gun, and Twin Towers. Most companies offer transportation, rafting gear, and a riverside lunch at the halfway point, then it's on to the lower canyon, which has more than 2 miles (3.5 kms) of continuous rapids through steep, narrow canyons. Wild, wet, and what a wallop! Full-day rates are in the $85 to $99 range.

You'll need a few days here—or at least one in which to relax after that rafting thrill. **H.G. Parson House Bed & Breakfast** (815 Twelfth Street South, Box 1196, Golden, V0A 1H0; 866–333–5001; 250–344–5001; fax: 250–344–2821; hgparsonhousebb@redshift.bc.ca; www.hgparson housebb.com) is a restored 1893-built heritage house decorated with antiques and conveniently located 1 block west of Highway 95 on Twelfth Street South. Rates are $85.50 to $95.50 double in high season. Check the Web site for rafting, bird-watching, and golf packages in summer, or skiing and snowmobiling packages in winter.

Rafting is not the only outdoor activity in Golden. There's paragliding in tandem on **Mount Seven**, hang gliding, fishing, cycling, mountain biking, bird-watching, golfing, and more. **Golden Mountain Adventures** (Box 296, Golden, V0A 1H0; 250–344–4650; fax: 250–344–4651; toll free reservations: 800–433–9533; info@adventurerockies.com; www.adventurerockies.com) will book your activities.

The **Golden Golf and Country Club** (250–344–2700; fax: 250–344–2922; 866–727–7222; teeoff@golfgolden.com; www.golfgolden.com) is in BC's Top Ten list and Canada's Top Thirty. It's located right by the Columbia River, with each hole built to take in the incredible scenery. There's a restaurant overlooking the ninth hole, and there's an RV park next to the driving range.

Kinbasket Adventures (Box 4137, Golden, V0A 1H0; 250–344–6012; 866–344–6012 toll free; fax: 250–344–6140; kbasket@rockies.net; www. bcrockiesadventures.com) runs two-and-a-half-hour Wetland Tours, a float through the Columbia River wetlands (the largest area of wetlands west of Manitoba, covering 64,246 acres—26,000 ha), to view osprey, bald eagles, great blue herons, and many other species in their natural habitat. Rates are $46 for adults and $20 for kids twelve and under; the under fives are free. They also offer canoeing and fishing, and in winter, snow-mobiling.

Purcell Heli-Skiing (Box 1530, Golden, V0A 1H0; 877–HELISKI [435–4754]; 250–344–5410; fax: 250–344–6076; info@purcellhelicopter skiing.com; www.purcellhelicopterskiing. com) offers helicopter skiing (of course!) as well as heli-boarding, heli-hiking, and heli-sight-seeing.

In early May the *Golden Festival of Birds and Bears* (birdsandbears. redshift.bc.ca) is a hit with bird lovers from all over the world; and throughout the year the old Brisco schoolhouse is a feature at the *Golden Historical Society Museum* (1302 Eleventh Avenue South, Box 992, Golden, V0A 1H0; phone/fax: 250–344–5169; museum@ rockies.net; www.rockies.net/~museum). This Web site is an excellent resource for Golden history. To learn more about these attractions and the area, contact the *Golden Visitor Info Centre* at 500 Tenth Avenue North, Box 1320, Golden, V0A 1H0; (800) 622–GOLD (4653); (250) 344–7125; fax: (250) 344–6688; info@tourismgolden.com; www. tourism golden.com.

The activities Golden offers are mostly energy-eaters, so it has a few good spots for refueling. You'll probably run into fellow rafters or hang gliders at the *Mad Trapper Neighborhood Pub* (1203 Ninth Street South; 250–344–6661; food line: 250–344–6262; madtrap@rockies. net; www.rockies.net/~madtrap). Prices are moderate and the daily specials (halibut and chips or salad on Fridays) are always a bargain. Coming from the south on Highway 95, take a right on Ninth Street at the first set of lights just before the Kicking Horse River. Or walk down the street and try the international cuisine at *The Kicking Horse Grill* (1105 Ninth Street South; 250–344–2330; khgrill@cablerocket.com; www.kickinghorsegrill.com). This popular restaurant was once an old log cabin but the cuisine in the relaxed surroundings is decidedly upscale. From the open-air patio you can watch hang gliders and paragliders soaring and sailing above Mount 7. Or you could sit in the peaceful garden at *Eleven 22 Grill & Liquids* (1122 Tenth Avenue South; 250–344–2443 or 250–348–2591; fax: 250–344–7992; eleven22@

redshift.bc.ca; www.eleven22.ca), a renovated heritage building with views of the Purcell Mountains. Adjoining the restaurant is a guest house complete with sauna and a gallery of local art. Room rates range from $55 to $120, including breakfast.

New to Golden is the **Kicking Horse Mountain Resort** (1500 Kicking Horse Trail, Box 839, Golden, V0A 1H0; 866–754–5425; 250–439–5400; fax: 250–439–5401; www.kickinghorseresort.com), a $200 million all-season resort. Enjoy rides on the eight-person gondola to the top of the mountain, where you can dine (while enjoying a 360° view) at Canada's loftiest restaurant, **The Eagle's Eye,** standing at 7,705 feet (2,350 m) elevation. Your meal price includes a complimentary gondola ticket to experience five-star dining. For viewers only, two-way gondola tickets are $15.00 adults, $11.50 youths thirteen to eighteen, $13.00 seniors, and $6.00 ages seven to twelve.

If you are heading toward Rogers Pass on the Trans-Canada, you will find quiet country accommodation on fifty-nine acres (24 ha) at **Hillside Lodge & Chalets** (1740 Seward Frontage Road, Box 2603, Golden, V0A 1H0; phone/fax: 250–344–7281; info@hillsidechalets.com; www.hillsidechalets.com). It's 8 miles (13 km) northwest of Golden (halfway to Donald) and just 500 yards off the highway on the Blaeberry River. The cabins are new, and the views of the river and the Rockies are spectacular. Guest rooms including delicious breakfasts and chalets with kitchenettes range from $108 to $135 double in high season. There's also a suite with a private sauna, steam room, hot tub, fireplace, and those breathtaking views.

The Trans-Canada follows the Columbia River north through Donald and west to Rogers Pass in **Glacier National Park.** Here at 4,534 feet (1,382 m), Canadian Pacific Railway workers performed the formidable task of pushing a railway line through, while avalanches and rock slides took their toll. At Rogers Pass we head into High Country.

CRANBROOK
Cedar Heights
Bed & Breakfast,
1200 Thirteenth
Street South,
V1C 5V8; (250) 426–0505
or (800) 497–6014;
fax: (250) 426–0045.

FERNIE
Willow Creek B&B,
5375 Boomerang Way,
Box 6049, V0B 1M6;
(250) 423–7731.
Moderate. Near ski hill.

Barbara Lynn's Country
Inn B&B,
Box 1077, 691 Seventh
Avenue, V0B 1M0;
(250) 423–6027; (888)
288–2148. In town.
Moderate. Discounts for
cyclists.

FAIRMONT HOT SPRINGS
McMillan Chalet
Bed & Breakfast,
5021 Fairmont Close,
Box 989, V0B 1L0;
(800) 856–9551;
(250) 345–9553. Near the
springs. Moderate. Great
breakfasts.

GOLDEN
Hillside Lodge & Chalets,
1240 Seward Frontage
Road, Box 2603,
V0A 1H0; phone/fax:
(250) 344–7281. Rooms
$108–$135 high-season
double.

H.G. Parson House Bed &
Breakfast, 815 Twelfth
Street South, Box 1196,
V0H 1H0; (866) 333–5001;
(250) 344–5001. Heritage
house. Hot tub.

RADIUM HOT SPRINGS
Village Country Inn
and Tea Room,
7557 Canyon Avenue,
V0A 1M0; (250) 347–9392;
(866) 761–9392.
Beautifully decorated.

WASA
Wasa Lakeside Bed and
Breakfast and More,
Box 122, V0B 2K0;
(250) 422–3688 or
(888) 422–3636. Action-
packed holiday or a romantic getaway.

WINDERMERE
Creekside Flower Gardens,
4795 Dell Road, Box 113,
V0B 2L0; (250) 342–6354.

Windermere Creek
B&B Cabins,
1658 Windermere Loop
Road, Box 409, V0B 2L0);
(250) 342–0356;
(800) 946–3942.
Year-round. Private. Trails.
Near golf course.

FERNIE
Rip'n Richards Eatery,
301 Highway 3,
(250) 423–3002. Casual
and colorful.

GOLDEN
The Mad Trapper,
1203 Ninth Street South,
V0A 1H0; (250) 344–6661.
Pub style.

The Eagle's Eye,
(250) 439–5400;
Canada's loftiest restaurant.
Five-star dining.

INVERMERE
Strands Old House
Restaurant,
818 Twelfth Street,
V0A 1K0; (250) 342–6344.
Moderately priced classy
food. Reservations.

KIMBERLEY
Chef Bernard's Inn and
Restaurant,
170 Spokane Street,
V1A 2E4; (800) 905–8338.
International menu.

The Snowdrift Café,
110 Spokane Street,
V1A 2E4; (250) 427–2001.
Inexpensive,
healthful foods.

RADIUM
Helna's Stube Restaurant,
corner of Main Street West
and St. Mary's Street;
(250) 347–0047.
Austrian-style menu.

High Country

From the east, entry into High Country through Rogers Pass in Glacier National Park is dramatic. The Trans-Canada Highway leads west through Revelstoke, the site of one of the largest hydroelectric developments in the world, to Craigellachie, where in 1885 a plain iron spike completed the railway line linking Canada from east to west. From Canada's houseboat capital on Shuswap Lake, we follow the North Thompson River from Kamloops, British Columbia's largest city in area, through Wells Grey Provincial Park to Mount Robson, at 12,972 feet (3,954 m), the highest peak in the Canadian Rockies. A region of superlatives and diversity, High Country has something for all wanderers eager to find a road less traveled.

Southeastern High Country

My first trip into High Country through Rogers Pass (50 miles [80 km] west of Golden, and 45 miles [72 km] east of Revelstoke) was memorable. It was November, and the snow was falling thick and heavy. Trucks lined the roadside as they stopped to fit wheel chains; an occasional car lay abandoned in a ditch like highway litter. This was Rogers Pass in all its winter fury. But in warmer weather *Mount Revelstoke National Park* (accessed via the 16-mile [26 km]-long Meadows-in-the-Sky Parkway—open during the snow-free months—which begins a short distance east of Revelstoke) and *Glacier National Park* are a hiking and camping wonderland of more than 400 glaciers, unique cave systems (although restricted), and alpine tundra. Information is available from the Park Superintendent (Box 350, 301 Third Street West, Revelstoke, V0E 2S0; 888–773–8888 or 250–873–7500; fax: 250–837–7536; www.parks canada.ca) or at the *Rogers Pass Information Centre* (250–837–6274; fax: 250–837–7536), just west of the pass. Ask staff guides about joining one of their

Trivia
Between 1885 and 1916, 250 railway employees were killed by the "White Death." The tragedy at Rogers Pass in 1910 was Canada's worst avalanche disaster.

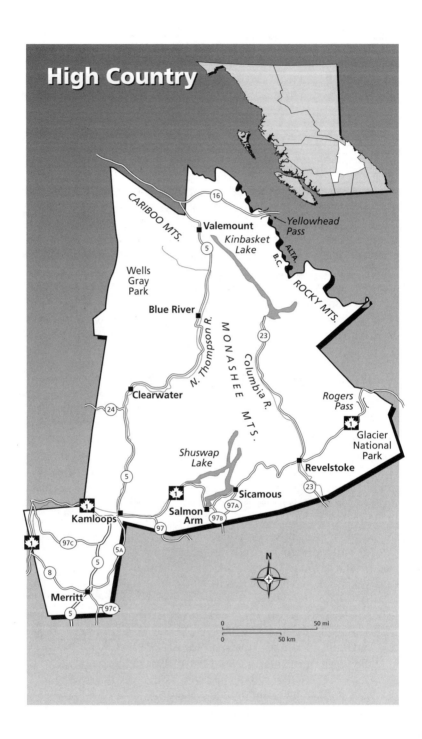

High Country

Yellowhead Pass

16

Valemount

Kinbasket Lake

CARIBOO MTS.

5

Wells Gray Park

ROCKY MTS.

Blue River

MONASHEE MTS.

N. Thompson R.

Columbia R.

23

Clearwater

24

Rogers Pass

1

Glacier National Park

Shuswap Lake

5

Revelstoke

1

Salmon Arm

Sicamous

97A

23

Kamloops

1

97C

97

97B

5A

1

5

8

Merritt

5

97C

N

0   50 mi
0   50 km

AUTHOR'S TOP TEN PICKS IN HIGH COUNTRY

informative hikes or, if necessary, about borrowing an all-terrain wheelchair to enjoy the trail to the Summit Monument. Park passes can also be purchased here. Everyone stopping in national parks must have a park pass, even if just visiting the Rogers Pass Centre. Day passes are available, as are annual passes valid at all western Canadian national parks.

From Rogers Pass the highway threads through snowsheds, erected for protection from all-too-frequent avalanches. One, in 1910, buried fifty-eight railway workers. To learn more about avalanches, visit the **Canadian Avalanche Centre** (Box 2759, Revelstoke, V0E 2S0; 250–837–2435; fax: 250–837–4624; canav@avalanche.ca; www.avalanche.ca). Backcountry hikers and skiers can check snow conditions by calling (800) 667–1105.

Tucked between Mount Glacier and Mount Revelstoke national parks in these spectacular Selkirk Mountains is Albert Canyon Hot Springs. **Canyon Hot Springs Resort Ltd.** (Box 2400, Revelstoke, V0E 2S0; 250–837–2420; fax: 250–837–6160 in winter or 250–837–3171 in summer; info@canyon hotsprings.com; www.canyonhotsprings.com) is set amid 200 acres (81 ha), with superb hiking trails, good fishing, mountain climbing, horseback riding, and river rafting. Open May to September, it's a convenient and relaxing stopover. Watch for the red umbrellas halfway—22 miles (35 km)—between Rogers Pass and Revelstoke. Railway workers enjoyed these soothing waters at the turn of the century. Choose from two pools, a 104° F (40° C) hot pool and an 80° F (26° C) swimming pool. As well as the pools, there are cabins and campsites, a B&B, a laundry, a cafe, and stores.

Renting a houseboat to explore the 621 miles (1,000 km) of Shuswap Lake's shoreline

Touring or horseback riding at Douglas Lake Ranch, Canada's largest working cattle ranch

Hiking to Margaret Falls in Herald Provincial Park, near Salmon Arm

Learning about the bats in Squilax at the Squilax General Store

Learning First Nations traditions at Quaaout Lodge on Little Shuswap Lake

Viewing the Adams River October sockeye salmon run

Exploring Kamloops Wildlife Park

Photographing the alpine meadows at Trophy Mountain, near Clearwater

Heli-skiing or heli-hiking at Blue River

Taking in the awesome views around Mount Robson, the highest peak in the Canadian Rockies

Revelstoke

The Trans-Canada passes **Mount Revelstoke National Park** and follows the Illecillewaet River down into Revelstoke, which lies in the heart of the Monashees, looking like a giant model-railroad

Trivia

In the good old railway heydays, before air-conditioning was invented, 400-pound blocks of ice were placed under the coaches. Air blowing across the blocks cooled the compartments.

town. Here the Illecillewaet joins the Columbia in its southerly sweep to Upper Arrow Lake.

Momma, Poppa, and Baby grizzly-bear stone sculptures guard the entrance to *Grizzly Plaza* in downtown Revelstoke, causing local jokers to call it Sesame Street! From 7:00 to 10:00 P.M. in July and August, the plaza perks up with comedy acts, jazz combos, and bluegrass bands. It's great entertainment and all free!

From the plaza on Mackenzie Avenue, the streets are numbered in order east or west of here, making it easy to find your way around. The city was settled in the 1800s by gold prospectors, but it was the building of the Canadian Pacific Railway that contributed to its becoming the dynamic city of approximately 8,000 that it is today. Learn of the city's history and more at the *Revelstoke Visitor Info Centre,* 204 Campbell Avenue, Box 490, Revelstoke, V0E 2S0; (250) 837–5345 or (800) 487–1493; fax: (250) 837–4223; manager@revelstoke.cc.bc.ca; www.revelstoke.cc.bc.ca. It's open all year, and there's a summer office at the junction of Highways 1 and 23 North. Perhaps request a Virtual Visit CD-ROM containing video footage and photos that will give you a taste of the area in all seasons.

With railway history in mind, follow the tracks (which will inevitably have a train on them, so be patient) to the *Revelstoke Railway Museum* (719 Track Street West, P.O. Box 3018, Revelstoke, V0E 2S0; 877–837–6060 or 250–837–6060; fax: 250–837–3732; railway@telus.net; www.railway museum.com). Here you'll be able to experience the thrill of operating a diesel locomotive via a coin-operated simulated ride and also learn the history of the construction of the most treacher-

Trivia

In 1941 women working on the railways were paid equal pay, 35 cents an hour, to slash brush, tap ties, clean cabs, and wipe down the jackets on the locomotives.

ous section of the transcontinental railway. Volunteers (ex-railway engineers) donate their time to tell you of their experiences on the rails. The museum is open year-round: daily July and August 9:00 A.M. to 8:00 P.M., shoulder season 9:00 A.M. to 5:00 P.M., and December to March weekdays from 1:00 to 5:00 P.M. Admission prices for adults are $6.00, seniors $5.00, youths (ages seven to sixteen) $3.00; children six and under are free. Railway memorabilia is available in the gift shop. On the third weekend in August (biennially), the Railway Museum hosts Revelstoke Railway Days, with tours, hikes, slide shows, and equipment demonstrations.

HIGH COUNTRY

TOP ANNUAL EVENTS IN HIGH COUNTRY

Loggers Day Sports,
Revelstoke; July;
(250) 837–5345

Railway Days, Revelstoke;
August (biennial); (250)
837–5345

Squilax Pow Wow, Squilax;
July; (250) 679–3203

Grebe Festival, The Nature
Bay, Salmon Arm; May;
(250) 832–1389

**Shuswap Whitewater
Rodeo,** Shuswap; June; (250)
838–2367

**Sicamous Moose
Mouse Days,** Sicamous;
August; (250) 836–3313

Valemount Days, Valemount;
June; (250) 566–4846

**Annual Shuswap Lake
Festival of Arts,** Sorrento;
July; (250) 675–3515

Kamloops Cattle Drive,
Kamloops; July;
(250) 372–7075;
(800) 288–5850 toll free;
www.cattledrive.bc.ca

**Kamloops International
Air Show,** Kamloops; August;
(250) 828–1404

Kamloopa PowWow Days,
Kamloops; August;
(250) 828–9708

Mountain Music Festival,
Merritt; July;
(604) 525–3330;
www.mountainfest.com

There's more railway history at the *Revelstoke Museum* (315 First Street West; 250–837–3067; fax: 250–837–3094; rm_chin@revelstoke.net). Housed in the 1926-built original post office, the museum has interesting pieces, such as a 1911 fur press and many artifacts and photographs (more than 3,000) relating to logging, mining, transportation, and farming. It is open 10:00 A.M. to 5:00 P.M. Monday to Saturday June 15 to August 31, and 1:00 to 4:00 P.M. weekdays the rest of the year. Ask about cemetery tours and children's programs held throughout the year.

Outdoor enthusiasts will appreciate that Revelstoke places high in the Top 10 Adventure Towns in North America and is number one in Canada, with the area just outside Revelstoke described as "the heart of heli-skiing in BC's interior," having both the Monashees to the west or the Selkirks to the east to choose from. Another sport gaining popularity, sometimes referred to as "poor man's heli-skiing," is Cat skiing. *Cat Powder Skiing* (877–4CATSKI or 250–837–5151; fax: 250–837–5111; catski@revelstoke.net; www.catpowder.com) boasts " almost too much snow" as they load about a dozen skiers into a modern Sno-Cat (five Bombardier Sno-Cats make up the litter!) for a memorable journey to the summit of Mount Mackenzie. Stronger skiers can descend as much as 18,000 feet (5,500 m) in virgin powder snow. *Powder Springs Resort* (owned by Cat Powder Skiing, 250–837–3199) is the local favorite for regular downhill enthusiasts. This 1,000-foot (305-m) vertical-drop hill has one double chair and a handle tow serving twenty-seven runs. There's a day lodge, ski shop, cafeteria, lounge, rental shop, and ski school. In summer golfers will find the *Revelstoke Golf Course* (250–837–4276) challenging, with its fairways scenically located along the Columbia River. Contact the *Powder Springs Inn* (200 Third Street West, Box 1479, Revelstoke, V0E 2S0; 250–837–5151 or toll free 800–991–4455; fax: 250–837–5111), about two minutes away from the golf course, to

Trivia

arrange golf packages. For more information on any of these activities and accommodation packages, call (877) 4–CATSKI or check out www. catpowder.com.

Revelstoke has a number of historical buildings. A *Heritage Walking and Driving Tour* booklet (available at the museum and Info Centre) adds interest to a walk through the town. The most conspicuous on the list is the ***Revelstoke Court-house*** at 1100 Second Street. It stands prominently about 10 blocks from the plaza, with its 30-foot (9-m) copper-covered dome. Other buildings include the ***Holton House*** (1897), at 1221 First Street West, and Revelstoke's first brick home, the Fromey home, built in 1897 at 912 Second Street West.

Settle yourself in to explore these heritage buildings at ***Christmas Island Bed & Breakfast*** (523 West Third Street, Box 1284, Revelstoke, V0E 2S0; 250–837–3262; toll free: 888–826–5555; bpendrak@rctvonline.net; www.bbcanada.com/ 1974.html), located just 2 blocks from downtown, yet with a wonderful view of Mt. Begbie and Mt. MacPherson and close to the Columbia River. Enjoy the scenery in style from a rooftop Jacuzzi. Rates are in the $70 to $110 range.

There's good coffee (and great desserts) downtown at ***Conversations Coffee House*** (203 Mackenzie Avenue; 250–837–4772). For something more substantial, the ranch-style ***Frontier Family Restaurant*** (Box 1239, Revelstoke, V0E 2S0; 250–837–5119 or 800–382–7763; fax: 250–837–6604; welcome@revelstoke.net; www.revelstokecc.bc.ca/ frontier), at the corner of Highways 1 and 23 North, is a good bet. The Frontier also shouts "Y'all welcome!" if you also need accommodation or gas.

There are a couple of excellent restaurants on the highway just 3 miles (5 km) west of the city. ***The Black Forest Restaurant*** (250–837–3495) is a local favorite—fondues and a variety of schnitzels are popular— it's open daily except Tuesday. On the other side of the highway, ***The Peaks Lodge*** (Box 1061, Revelstoke, V0E 2S0; 800–668–0330 or 250–837–2176; www.revelstokecc.bc.ca/peaks) has much more than just fine cuisine. Accommodation including golf and sledders' packages, guided fishing trips, and a fireside pub are some of the attractions that bring visitors to this cozy resort at Boulder Mountain.

Heritage home in Revelstoke

BC Hydro's **Revelstoke Dam and Generating Station** is five minutes north of the city on Highway 23. Visitors use audio wands to learn about hydroelectricity and the dam's construction. Take the elevator to the Dam Crest Lookout to see over Lake Revelstoke reservoir and the Columbia River. The two-hour free tour runs daily from mid-March to late October. Phone (250) 837–6211 for information or check the Web site at www.bchydro.com (search "Revelstoke").

Twelve miles (19 km) west of Revelstoke is the resort of **Three Valley Lake Chateau Ltd.** and **Three Valley Gap Heritage Ghost Town** (Box 860, Revelstoke, V0E 2S0; 250–837–2109; fax: 250–837–5220; 888–667–2109 for reservations; 3valley@revelstoke.net; www.3valley.com; open mid-April to mid-October). This popular modern holiday spot, situated on a lake in the spectacular Eagle Pass, comes complete with a restored historic town and a theater. Guided tours are held daily, during which you'll see restored cars (1902–1930) and eighty- to ninety-year-old railway coaches. At 8:00 P.M. from mid-May to the end of September, listen to the songs of the Old West and watch a trick roping act at the **Walter Moberly Theatre's** Trails and Rails West Musical

Revue (reservations required). Moberly was the surveyor who chose Eagle Pass for the Trans-Canadian railroad's final stretch through the Monashees. Double accommodation rates at Three Valley Gap are from $115 to $150 in peak season.

Ten miles (16 km) west of Three Valley Gap is the **Enchanted Forest** (Box 2938, Revelstoke, V0E 2S0; 250–837–9477 or 837–9655 off-season; fax: 250–837–9676; enchant@rctvonline.net; www.bcrockies.com/attractions/forest.html). Open mid-May to mid-September, it features a handcrafted Old World Fairyland of dungeons and dragons. You'll explore a Wild Land wonder on boardwalks and boats, and climb a spiral staircase inside a giant 800-year-old cedar, BC's Tallest Grandest Tree House. Six miles (10 km) farther west (27 miles [40 km] west of Revelstoke) is **Beardale Castle Miniatureland** (250– 836–2268; RR1 Malakwa, V0E 2J0; www.beardaleminiatureland. com), a unique attraction featuring multicultural displays and international villages. Here you can experience a 1950s Canadian prairie town, a Swiss mountain village, a German town, and an English Tudor village, all with large-scale model railway layouts. Six of the fifteen trains on display are running at all times. Also featured is a *Last Spike* heritage display, western Canada's largest animated toy-land exhibit, and Mother Goose nursery rhymes in motion. It's open daily May 1 to September 30, 9:00 A.M. to 6:00 P.M., with extended hours in July and August.

West of Beardale Castle is Craigellachie, 28 miles (46 km) west of Revelstoke, the site where on November 7, 1885, Sir Donald Smith, a Canadian Pacific Railway financier, drove in the famous **Last Spike.** A souvenir shop is open from May to October. Attendants will enlighten you with some of the stories surrounding this symbol of Canadian unity. For more information contact Revelstoke Railway Museum (250–837–6060).

The Shuswap

The Trans-Canada moves away from the Monashees and follows the Eagle River past the hiking trails and ancient cedars of the **Eagle River Nature Park** (two picnic areas with walking and cycling trails close to the highway 9 miles [15 km] east of Sicamous) to Shuswap Lake, where more than 600 miles (1,000 km) of shoreline make for a very popular vacation spot. Several arms and channels of the H-shaped lake system appear as tentacles spreading among the intersecting valleys in the

Trivia

Copper Island in Shuswap Lake reminded Sorrento's founder (J. R. Kinghorn) of Sorrento in Italy, where he and his wife honeymooned; hence the name.

Shuswap Highlands. Salmon Arm, Seymour Arm, Anstey Arm, Mara Lake, Shuswap Lake, Little Shuswap Lake, White Lake, and Adams Lake, plus all the hiking trails, sandy beaches, beautiful waterfalls, and friendly people make up this holiday area known as **The Shuswap.**

Sicamous (population 2,906 in 2002), 43 miles (70 km) east of Revelstoke, is Canada's Houseboat Capital. Everything, including the kitchen sink, the hot tub, and a waterslide to keep the kids occupied for days, is provided on a houseboat rented from several companies including **Bluewater Houseboat Rentals** (Box 248, Sicamous, V0E 2V0; 800–663–4024 or 250–836–2255; fax: 250–836– 4955; bluwater@sicamous.com; www.shuswap.bc.ca/bluewater). Contact Sicamous and District Chamber (Box 346, Sicamous, V0E 2V0; 250–836–3313; fax: 250–836–4368; chamber@sicamous.com; www. sicamouschamber. bc.ca) for more information on houseboating and accommodation, plus hiking and fishing opportunities.

From Sicamous Highway 97A leads southwest to Vernon, where it joins Highway 97 to Kelowna. Twelve miles (19 km) south of Sicamous, there's an excellent family private campground at the end of Mara Lake. **Whispering Pines Tent and RV Park** (RR 1, Site 3, Comp 2, Mara, V0E 2K0; 250–838–6775; fax: 250–838–2332; whispines@hotmail.com) has a heated pool, minigolf, and a free daily tractor ride—just a few of the family-oriented friendly features at this 160-site campground.

Salmon Arm

almon Arm, 19 miles (31 km) west of Sicamous on Highway 1, along the southwestern arm (Salmon Arm) of Shuswap Lake, is the main business center in the area. Dubbed the "Gem of the Shuswap," it has a population of about 16,000 and boasts the largest freshwater pier in North America. **Shuswap Lakes Vacation Inc.** (750 Marine Park Drive, Salmon Arm, V1E 4P6; 250–832–2745; fax: 250–832–3384; 800–663–4026; houseboat@twinanchors; www.twinanchors.com) is on the pier and rents boats that sleep up to twenty-two persons. Seadoos and ski boats are also available for a day of water fun.

Also by the pier is the **Salmon Arm Bay Nature Enhancement Center,** a waterfowl sanctuary, where a 2.5-mile (4-km) trail, boardwalks, a viewing platform, and bird blinds are aids in experiencing this very special wildlife area. If you're there between April and June, you might

WORTH SEEING/DOING IN HIGH COUNTRY

Hike in Glacier National Park.

Visit Rogers Pass Centre to see railroad models and learn of the struggles endured by CPR workers in the building of the railroad.

Cruise Shuswap Lake from Sicamous to Seymour Arm aboard the MV Phoebe Ann *(250–836–2220).*

Ski at Sun Peaks Resort.

Canoe on Myrtle Lake in Wells Gray Provincial Park.

catch sight of Clark's and western grebes (the "water dancer" often seen doing his mating ritual on the water's surface) or any of the other 250 species familiar to the area. Visit www.grebe. shuswap.net to learn more about the **Salmon Arm Grebe Festival** held in May. Fishing (Eastern brook and rainbow trout) and hiking are very popular here, too.

Over on the northwest shore of Shuswap Lake's Salmon Arm, **Herald Provincial Park** (119 vehicle campsites; www.bcparks.ca [search "Herald"]; phone 800–689–9025 or www.discovercamping. ca for reservations) is a cooling spot on a hot summer's day (quite common in the Shuswap). Located 9 paved miles (13 km) northeast of Tappen off Highway 1, Reinecker Creek meanders through the park. **Margaret Falls** is at the end of a wheelchair-accessible trail through Reinecker Gorge. It's imperative that visitors stay on this trail, as not only is the area near the falls dangerous (steep, wet conditions) but also increased erosion of the soil and vegetation from foot-traffic will soon alter the environment. Here the cedars are enormous, and the cool moistness of the twenty-minute round-trek is refreshing. For more information on the area, contact the **Salmon Arm Visitor Info Centre** (#1 751 Marine Park Drive Northeast, Salmon Arm, V1E 2W7; 250–832–6247 or 877–SALMON–7 [725–6667]; fax: 250–832–8382; info@sachamber. bc.ca; www.visitsalmonarm.com). Staff have prepared information on golf courses (championship and two executive courses in the vicinity), dozens of campgrounds, hotels, motels, and cabins, and such attractions as a Gouda cheese factory, winery tours, double go-carts, a free viewing zoo, "J" Lanes bowling, and waterslides. **R.J. Haney Heritage Park and Museum** (Box 1642, 751 Highway 97B, Salmon Arm, V1E 4P7; 250–832–5243; fax: 250–832–5291; hpark@ jetstream.net), on the corner of the Trans-Canada and Highway 97B—the road to Vernon. In summer you can take a step back into Salmon Arm's past at a pioneer village. The museum is open Wednesday to Sunday 10:00 A.M. to 5:00 P.M. May through September but daily in July and

Trivia

Need a new hubcap? Tiny Grinrod, southwest of Sicamous and just past Mara Lake on Highway 97A, is home to an eclectic collection of hubcaps and old license plates, as well as books and other paraphernalia. At last count Gordon Packham, owner of Gord's New and Used, had almost 24,000 hubcaps.

HIGH COUNTRY

August. There's also a 1.2-mile (2-km) nature trail to hike, where you're welcome to walk your dog, and where you'll learn about the Shuswap's natural history.

The Trans-Canada heads north from Salmon Arm for 20 miles (32 km) to **Sorrento,** where the air is thick with community spirit.

About 2.5 miles (4 km) before Sorrento, up on a hill with a great view of Copper Island and Shuswap Lake, you can roost for the night at **Pheasant Heaven** (2833 Hilltop Road, Box 202, Sorrento, V0E 2W0; 250–675–4966; fax: 250–675–3420; pheasant@pheasantheaven.com; www.pheasantheaven.com). Here Mandi and Laurier Fleury run a pleasant bed-and-breakfast and aviaries, where they breed and raise more than forty different kinds of pheasants. Their aviaries contain many varieties, including a Monal Impeyan, the national bird of Nepal. They enjoy giving personalized tours, and with plenty of parking space and the free use of their picnic tables, you can make a day of it. There's a small gift shop with displays of exotic bird eggs. Mandi's breakfasts are delicious; for those wanting to cruise or fish the lake, Laurier leads houseboat charters.

While in Sorrento, stop at **Toby's** (250–675–4464), which is on the highway beside the hardware store, for one of Dave and Cherie's homemade

Trivia

Rockhounding is a popular occupation on Squilax Mountain near Chase, the Enderby Cliffs, and Mount Ida near Salmon Arm. Blue-gray and banded agate, crystalline geodes, and amethyst are some of the sought-after stones.

Life in the Bat House

*H*ere's a tale of love that needs to be told. When the historic Squilax church burned to the ground, 2,000 female yuma bats (Myotis yumanensis) lost their home. Concerned for the welfare of the bats, students from Haldane elementary and NorKam secondary schools, with the aid of a wildlife biologist, erected bat houses in the vicinity. Interestingly, with a total of thirty-eight houses to choose from, at first most of the bats squeezed into the few houses at the original church site. Lately, they have been moving from house to house, favoring nine houses, three of which are on the old church site. Today these bat houses are an aid in counting the bat population and are part of a North American Bat House Research Assistance Program. Local volunteers count the bats once a week. Visitors are invited to come out—divesting themselves of whatever bat phobias they may have—and help count the bats. The Squilax site is recognized by Bat Conservation International in Austin, Texas, and is listed in their Vacationer's Guide to Viewing Bats in North America.

Kamloops and the famous Kamloops rainbow trout are well known around the world to fishers. A giant fish, weighing 1,246 pounds (565 kg) and measuring 15 feet (4.5 m), was carved out of a single cedar log to commemorate the World Fly-Fishing Championships in 1993.

pizzas and Caesar salads. Learn about Sorrento's history through a series of murals decorating some of the buildings.

Down behind the Sorrento elementary school on the northern side of the highway, *The Evergreens Bed and Breakfast* (2853 Vimy Road, Box 117, Sorrento, V0E 2W0; 250–675–2568; fax: 250–675–3100; evergreens@jetstream.net; www.bbexpo.com/bc/evergreens.htm) is just a short walk to Shuswap Lake's southwestern shore. Berry-filled gardens provide food for delicious breakfasts as well as afternoon teas, served in a gazebo on Wednesday and Thursday, or by reservation for parties. The gazebo has made the Evergreens a popular wedding spot, so hosts Linda and Verna have added a tiny chapel and an antique buggy for ambience! The accommodations consist of four bedrooms and a suite, which features a soft heat sauna. There's also a hot tub and an exercise room. With an aviary full of chirping canaries and finches, a waterfall, and a fish pond, it has a laid-back holiday atmosphere. Take Passchendaele Road to Vimy Road; the Evergreens is on the left. Rates, which include an excellent breakfast, are $75 double and $120 for the suite. Health spa packages are also available.

Tiny Sorrento is full of pleasant surprises. The **Sorrento Centre** (Box 99, Sorrento, V0E 2W0, 250–675–2421; fax: 250–675–3032; info@ sorrento-centre.bc.ca; www.sorrento-centre.bc.ca) is an ecumenical conference, retreat, and holiday center on Shuswap Lake just off the highway on Passchendaele Road. Here children, teens, and adults can sign up for courses including such wide-ranging topics as wilderness recreation, meditation, social and environmental justice, and therapeutic touch. It can accommodate up to seventy persons in two modern lodges year-round, and as well, there are private rooms, cabanas, and camping facilities. The meals are cafeteria-style with a set menu. Check the Web site for a full description of courses available.

For more information on the friendly communities along the southern shore of Shuswap Lake (Sorrento, Squilax, Blind Bay, Eagle Bay, Tappen, Carlin, Sunnybrae, Notch Hill, and White Lake), contact the South Shuswap Chamber of Commerce (Box #7 Sorrento, V0E 2X0; 250–675–3515; fax: 250–675–3516; sorrentochamber@telus.net; www.south shuswapchamberofcommerce.org).

The highway follows Shuswap Lake, and about 6 miles (10 km) farther west, the historic **Squilax General Store and Caboose Hostel** (Trans-Canada Highway, Squilax, RR 2, Site 2, Comp 11, Chase, V0E 1M0; phone/fax: 250–675–2977; squilax@jetstream.net; www.hihostels.ca) sells "funky foods and groovy groceries." Stay in renovated cabooses overlooking Shuswap Lake for $20, or if you're a Hostelling International member, a mere $16 per person.

From the store take the bridge over the river and turn left onto Little Shuswap Lake Road to the Little Shuswap Band Reserve. Every summer drummers, singers, and dancers from all over North America arrive for the **Squilax International Pow Wow** (Box 1100, Chase, V0E 1M0; 250–679–3203; fax: 250–679–3220). Traditional native food is served, arts and crafts are displayed, and generally a good time is had by all. There used to be a colony (or was it a congregation?) of about 2,000 female **Yuma bats** living in the attic of the old church nearby. In 1994 the church burned down, so some local enthusiasts built bat houses on 14-foot poles near the old church site. The bats are returning, so the mission was successful! Ask at the band office or the Squilax Store for up-to-date information.

Exceptional accommodation is available at **Quaaout Resort and Conference Centre** (Box 1215, Chase, V0E 1M0; 800–663–4303 or 250–679–3090; fax: 250–679–3039; quaaout@quaaout.com; www.quaaout.com). This hotel, owned by the Little Shuswap Indian Band, emphasizes its aboriginal heritage. Traditional native cultural activities, canoeing, a sweat house, and a kekuli, as well as First Nations cuisine in the restaurant, add to the modern lake-view rooms, half-mile of sandy beach, pool, Jacuzzi, fully equipped gym, and steam room at this architectural marvel, inspired by a native pit house. Renowned native dancer and storyteller Ernie Philip is the cultural advisor. He freely gives of his time to explain the traditions behind the features at Quaaout Resort. Double accommodation in high season ranges from $120 to $180.

From Squilax Bridge the Squilax-Anglemont road leads north about 3 miles (5 km) to **Roderick Haig-Brown Provincial Park** (no camping) and the **Adams River**, famous for its October sockeye salmon run, possibly the largest on the continent. The river was called Chu Chua on early maps but was renamed after a Shuswap Indian Chief, Selhowtken, who had been baptized Adam. Every four years (1998–2002, etc.), the river sees a boom run. A slide at Hell's Gate during railway construction in 1913 all but

Trivia
Peter Wing, elected mayor of Kamloops in 1966, was the first mayor of Chinese descent in North America.

wiped out the run, but through the building of fishways and hatcheries, and upgrading habitats, the runs are gradually coming back to their historic numbers. To see this tide of salmon after their 305-mile (490-km) Fraser and Thompson River run, their battered crimson backs thrusting compulsively to return home to spawn and die in the gravel reaches of the Adams River, is a stirring experience. Writer, poet, avid angler, and conservationist Roderick Haig-Brown saw it thus: "River-borne fugitives, red muscled under sheathing silver. . . ." Trained staff are in attendance during the run to explain this incredible phenomenon. For more information on this park and all other provincial parks in the Shuswap or Kamloops area, check www.bc parks.ca and use the park name as a search key.

Before leaving the area explore the northern shore of Shuswap Lake, where the tiny communities of Lee Creek, Scotch Creek, Celista, Magna Bay, Anglemont, and St. Ives serve visitors who come to enjoy a wide variety of outdoor activities. The North Shuswap Chamber (Box 101, Celista, V0E 1L0; phone/fax: 250–955–2113; 888–955–1488; requests@northshuswapbc.com; www.northshuswapbc.com) has the pertinent information.

As you pass *Chase* (population 2,548 in 2002), just past the western end of Little Shuswap Lake, watch for Rocky Mountain bighorn sheep on the hills east of town. A small herd was transplanted to Squilax in 1927. A number of hiking trails are found in the area. One that is a bit of a climb, but with excellent views of Shuswap and Little Shuswap lakes and the South Thompson River, begins near the cemetery. Turn south at the *Chase Country Inn* (250–679–3333). Contact *Chase Visitor Info Centre* (400 Shuswap Avenue, Box 592, Chase, V0E 1M0; 250–679–8432; fax: 250–679–3120; chccom@cablelan.net) for directions. Ask, too, about Chase Falls, not far off the Trans-Canada Highway, and *Neskonlith Meadows,* where you'll find glorious wildflowers in late April. For the meadows, though, you must check first with the Adams Lake Band office (Box 588, Chase, V0E 1M0; 250–679–8841) and purchase a permit.

Kamloops to Merritt and the Nicola Valley

Where the North and South Thompson Rivers meet sits Kamloops, 130 miles (210 km) west of Revelstoke. In the Shuswap (Secwepemc) Indian tongue, it means "meeting place." It's also where three highways and two railroads meet, making it a very reachable city for the many forestry workers, miners, and ranchers who call this area home. It's big—at 144 square miles (373 sq km), BC's largest city in area—it's growing fast, and it has all the facilities you would expect to find in a city of 81,443 (in 2002).

One such facility is just 10 miles (16 km) east of Kamloops. The **Kamloops Wildlife Park** (Box 698, Kamloops, V2C 5L7; 250–573–3242; fax: 250–573–2406; info@kamloopswildlife.org; www.kamloopswildlife.org) is home to two Siberian tigers (Zef and Czarina) and Sheba and Shardic, two orphaned grizzly bears. The park is the largest captive breeding center in North America for the endangered burrowing owl. As well, there are seventy species of local and endangered wildlife, a miniature train ride, a gift shop, farmyard animals, and a walking trail leading to waterfalls. Prices of admission are adults $8.95, youths and seniors $7.95, and children $5.95. The park is open from 8:00 A.M. to 4:30 P.M. daily year-round (except Christmas Day) and until 8:00 P.M. in July and August. Throughout December, hours are extended to 9:00 P.M. for the largest festive light show (200,000 lights) in BC's interior. Tractor wagon rides and entertainment, including a giant outdoor movie, add to the "Wildlight" winter fun.

Right next door, in this area of Mojave-like, weirdly shaped hoodoos and rocky hills, is the **Kamloops R.V. Park & Dolphin Waterslides** (250–573–3789; fax: 250–573–3933). On a blazing hot, western summer day, these 2,000 feet of cool-water dips and curves may be the best place to hang out. It's 9 miles (15 km) east of Kamloops on Highway 1 and is open from May to Labor Day. For more information on the area, contact **Kamloops Visitor Info Centre** (1290 West Trans-Canada Highway, Kamloops, V2C 6R3; 250–374–3377 or 800–662–1994; fax: 250–828–9500; tourism@kamloopschamber.bc.ca; www.adventurekamloops.com). The staff there can guide you to the **Farmers Market,** held downtown every Saturday morning from mid-April to October; or you could spend a day at the **Secwepemc Museum and Heritage Park** (202–355 Yellowhead Highway, Kamloops, V2H 1H1; 250–828–9801; fax: 250–372–1127; museum@secwepemc.org; www.secwepemc.org). Trails here pass archaeological remains of 2,000-year-old Shuswap winter and summer villages, as well as reconstructed winter pit houses. The Museum Store sells arts and crafts, many of which are traditional to the Shuswap area, such as pine-needle and birch-bark baskets, moccasins, dream catchers, and beaded and silver jewelry. Other attractions include a tour of the **Sunmore Ginseng Factory** (925 McGill Place, Kamloops, V2C 6N9; 250–374–3017; fax: 250–374–3011; sunmore@ sunmore.com; www.sunmore.com) and a cruise on the **Wanda-Sue Stern-wheeler** (250–374–SHIP; wandasue@sageserve.com; www. wandasue.bc.ca) to enjoy a cool sunset dinner cruise. Departures are from the old Kamloops Yacht Club on River Street. Check the "Plan a Vacation" link at www.adventurekamloops.com for excellent printable maps and brochures, and to discover the dozens of accommodation, dining, and activity choices available in this adventure-filled crossroads area.

Another cooling-off idea is to head south toward the thriving city of **Merritt,** where the slogan "A lake a day, as long as you stay" would still hold true if you stayed almost half a year. Centrally situated where four major highways meet, Merritt is less than three hours from Vancouver via the Coquihalla (sounds almost like "Coca Cola") Highway 5. But coming from Kamloops, you can take a more leisurely drive down Highway 5A, past forested peaks and rolling, grassy ranch lands, and (nearer to Merritt), the deep, azure, and lovely Nicola Lake.

> ### Trivia
>
> *The Nicola Valley gets its name from a respected Okanagan Salish chief from Douglas Lake, Walking Grizzly Bear, or* Hwistesmetxequen. *The fur traders of the early 1800s were unable to pronounce this and referred to him as Nicholas. Ironically, the natives, in turn, had trouble with the anglicized word and shortened it to N'kuala, or* Nicola.

All the lakes in the **Nicola Valley** are popular fishing spots. Kamloops trout, a wild strain of rainbow trout, makes a splendid catch. Ice fishing for burbot during the winter months is popular, too. Other nearby fishing spots are **Marquart** and **Lundbom** Lakes, a few miles east of Merritt off Highway 5A. They both have forestry service campsites with boat launches. Local enthusiasts tell me that the best time to land rainbow, Kokanee, and brook trout is during spring and fall.

Stop off at the historic and charming **Quilchena Hotel** (Highway 5A North, Quilchena, V0E 2R0; 250–378–2611; fax: 250–378–6091; info@quilchena.com; www.quilchena.com), sitting regally on the edge of Nicola Lake and at the center of one of BC's largest working cattle ranches. It's open early spring through late fall and serves excellent meals in its elegant dining room. In 1908 the hotel's builder, Joseph Guichon, believed the railway from Spences Bridge to Princeton would pass through Quilchena, and although this didn't happen, the hotel was still a success. It was closed between 1921 and 1958, but today, Guichon's grandson, Guy Rose, continues to maintain the splendor and antique originality of this lovely hotel. The sixteen rooms are furnished with antiques. There's fine dining and a 1900s saloon—look for the bullet holes in the bar! Tennis, hayrides, windsurfing, swimming, barbecues, horseback riding, and mountain biking are but some of the activities to enjoy. Rates are $71 to $125 double. Next door, the **Nicola Valley Golf Course and R.V. Park** (General Delivery, Quilchena, V0E 2R0; 250–378–2923; fax: 250–378–2920; www.nicolavalleygolf.com) has a pleasant nine-hole course offering inexpensive golf and comfortable camping services. Golf from your front door! Quilchena Creek winds through the property crossing five fairways, thus creating some of the course's hazards in the process.

Just before Quilchena on Highway 5A is the turnoff to the famous **Douglas Lake Ranch** (800–663–4838; resort@douglaslake.com; www. douglaslake.com), Canada's largest working cattle ranch. The ranch runs close to 20,000 head of cattle over almost 500,000 acres (200,000 ha). It also boasts eleven private lakes with world-class fly-fishing, conducts ranch tours (by reservation), and offers horseback riding to guests. You'll find more information on Nicola Valley activities—ranging from hiking, cross-country skiing, sailing, and windsurfing to, of course, fishing—at the **Visitors Information Booth** (2185 B Voght Street, Box 1649, Merritt, V1K 1B8; 877–330–3377; 250–378–5634; fax: 250–378–6561; info@ merritt-chamber.bc.ca; www.merritt-chamber.bc.ca).

Another major highway that meets in Kamloops is Highway 5, the Yellowhead South, named for the fair-haired Iroquois trapper Pierre Bostonais (known as *Tête Jaune,* which means "yellow head" in French) who, as a Hudson's Bay Company guide, frequently crossed through the spectacular Rocky Mountain pass that also bears his name. The Yellowhead begins in Winnipeg, Manitoba, and completes its route in Masset in the Queen Charlotte Islands. It covers 1,973 miles (3,185 km), including the 211 miles (340 km) of the Yellowhead South between Kamloops and Tête Jaune Cache, which we shall now begin.

The North Thomson River

The first part of our Yellowhead journey hugs the eastern bank of the North Thompson River for 39 miles (63 km) to **Barriere.** On the way, about 11 miles (19 km) north at Heffley Creek, is the turnoff to the famous **Sun Peaks Resort** (800–807–3257; info@sunpeaksresort. com; www.sunpeaksresort.com). *Father's Country Inn B&B* (3240 McGillivray Creek Road, Box 152, Heffley Creek, V0E 1Z0; 800–578– 7322 or 250–578–7308; fax: 250–578–7334; mmfathers@telus.net;

www.dconover. com/bedandbreakfast) is located near the resort and has all the luxuries of a resort. Imagine an indoor pool with a fireplace at one end, a wood stove and a hot tub at the other, all in a tropical setting. The decadence, which includes breathtaking mountain views, in-room fireplaces, candlelit Jacuzzi tubs, and four-poster beds, doesn't match the $75–$125 (double) rates. "Father's" refers to David Conover Sr., father of the owner, who "discovered" Marilyn Monroe. His original photos of the lovely lady are displayed in the B&B, and some prints can be ordered on-line.

Barriere, 27 miles (44 km) north of the Sun Peaks junction, is a farming and forestry town, where every Labor Day weekend the **North Thompson Fall Fair and Rodeo** (Box 873, Barriere, V0E 1E0) is held. To find out more about the area, visit www.barrierebc.com or call the Barriere Chamber of Commerce at (250) 672–9221 or e-mail barriere chamber@ntvalley.com.

There's excellent riverside camping 34 miles (55 km) north of Barriere at the **North Thompson River Provincial Park** (250–587–6150 or 250–851–3000), 3 miles (5 km) south of **Clearwater.** The park is situated where the muddy brown North Thompson River meets the green Clearwater River. There's Poggy Playground for the kids and excellent fishing. At times the rivers can be swift and powerful, so children should always be supervised; swimming alone is not advised. Near the river's edge in the picnic area, look for **kekuli sites,** winter pit-house depressions used by the Chu Chua or Simpcw (pronounced "sim-kwhoo") people.

Before heading north to **Wells Gray Provincial Park,** first drop into the **Info Centre** (425 East Yellowhead Highway, Clearwater, V0E 1N0; 250–674–2646; www.bcparks.ca, search "Wells;" www.ntvalley.com). Here you'll find park information and see displays of its geology, wildlife, and natural history. There's also a gift and book shop, coffee and refreshments, and **Bearfoot Outdoors** (250–674–3537; bear-foot@wellsgray. info), an outdoor-equipment store for new gear or those forgotten items. The center is open seasonally; it's located 22.2 miles (35.8 km) from the park entrance at the junction of Highway 5 and the Clearwater Valley Road.

Right outside the Info Centre, **Jerry the moose** stands guard. He's possibly the most photographed moose in Canada. He started life as a shiny steel creature, refusing to rust for many years. Finally, the sculptor from Victoria urged him along using saltwater-soaked cloths, and today he's a fine-looking brown beast.

Just a couple of hundred yards along Clearwater Road toward the park in a leafy grove on the right is **Flour Meadow Bakery & Cafe** (Box 1715, Clearwater, V0E 1N0; 250–674–3654; fax: 250–674–2625; flour meadow@ntvalley.com; www.ntvalley.com/flourmeadowbakery). Stop off for gourmet coffee, decadent pastries and muffins, quiches, soups, delicious sandwiches, and more. It's fully licensed and is turning into a popular outdoor entertainment spot in summer.

If you're looking for a place to stay, 2 miles (3 km) up the road toward Wells Gray from the Info Centre, there's year-round self-catering and bed-and-breakfast accommodation at **Tanglewood Lodge** (1048 Clearwater Valley Road, Box 1785, Clearwater, V0E 1N0; 250–674–3537; info@tanglewoodlodge.net; www.tanglewoodlodge.net). This family-friendly home was built with sunsets and spectacular views of the surrounding hills and valleys in mind, and is a good base for hiking the alpine meadows, paddling the lakes and rivers, biking the trails, or cross-country skiing and snowshoeing in winter. There's no need to bring all that gear either as ski and bike rentals are available at the lodge.

In the **alpine meadows** at **Trophy Mountain,** you'll see subalpine daisies, cow parsnips, Indian paintbrush, Lewis's monkey flowers, and arnica. To get there take the signposted turn on the right 6 miles (10 km) up the Clearwater Valley Road, just inside **Spahats Creek Provincial Park** (twenty campsites). Late June, July, and August are the months when you'll see the wildflowers at their most brilliant.

Just 2 miles (3 km) before the park gates is a chalet located right on a wildlife migration corridor. **Moose Ridge Woodland Chalet** (Box 247,

A Centennial Trek

*C*learwater's inhabitants include some pretty gutsy folk. Back in 1967, a young woman named Ida Dekelver, aged forty-four and a mother of six, set out with her two donkeys, Bill and Jack, to walk the Yellowhead Highway to Wadena, Saskatchewan. That's more than 890 miles (1,434 km)! She wanted to visit her aunt. Newspapers from all over the country covered her trek, giving publicity to Clearwater and Wells Gray Park. Ironically, she and her donkeys got a ride back home in a truck driven by two Saskatchewan men, also named Bill and Jack. Until recently, Mrs. Dekelver ran the Yellowhead Museum, which consisted of two rustic cabins on the Clearwater Valley Road, full of artifacts and natural history displays, as well as memorabilia collected during her centennial-year trek.

Clearwater, V0E 1N0; 250–674–3271; fax: 250–674–3271; smcgrath@
mercuryspeed.com; www.darfield.com/mooseridge) is equally exciting to visit in summer or winter, depending on whether it's snow-
based activities and the Aurora Borealis (Northern Lights) you're after,
or the wildlife you're wanting to photograph. The folks at Moose Ridge
will introduce you to the folks at *Alaska Husky Adventures* (Dunn
Lake Road, Box 236, Clearwater, V0E 1N0; 866–587–0037; 250–
587–0037; fax: 250–587–0006; info@dogsleddingadventures.com; www.
dogsleddingadventures.com) who run a variety of short and long
mushing adventures, a great Canadian experience. Or you can contact
Wells Gray Chalets & Wilderness Adventures Ltd. (Box 188, Clearwater, V0E 1N0; 250–587–6444; fax: 250–587–6446; 888–SKI–TREK;
info@skihike.com; www.skihike.com) if you'd prefer multiday hut-to-
hut hiking, paddling, or ski-touring trips.

In this wilderness area it's always a bonus to find good food. Near the
park entrance 22 miles (35 km) from the turnoff, *Helmcken Falls
Lodge* (Box 239, Clearwater, V0E 1N0; 250–674–3657; fax:
250–674–2971; info@helmckenfalls.com; www.helmckenfalls.com)
serves hearty meals with a reputation for high standards of excel-
lence. They also offer wilderness camp trips, white-water rafting,
guiding and outfitting services for horseback riding, hiking, berry-
picking rides, sight-seeing tours, and canoeing. The recently upscaled
lodge accommodations in this reach-out-and-touch-nature setting
range from $120 to $150 double. Campsites are also available.

We're finally at *Wells Gray Provincial Park,* with its breathtaking
scenery in all seasons. You'll see snow-covered peaks, glaciers, extinct
volcanoes, old-growth cedar forests, and dozens of waterfalls, the most
famous being the 450-foot (137-m) *Helmcken Falls* (more than two
and a half times higher than Niagara), 6 miles (10 km) inside the park.

A few miles past Helmcken Falls is a naturally carbonated cold-water
mineral spring, where you can add juice crystals to the water and presto!
You have pop. At *Bailey's Chute,* a few miles farther up in the park, forty-
four-pound (20-kg) salmon (in season) leap up the rapids. Park your car
just past the mineral springs, and it's about a fifteen-minute walk.

Back on the Yellowhead Highway in Clearwater, the road now runs
slightly south and east to *Birch Island,* formed by an eddy in the North
Thompson River. Either take the back road east to *Vavenby,* which runs
from Birch Island via an old, one-lane wooden bridge (lots of character)
and Lost Creek Road, or turn right off the highway at Vavenby, 16 miles
(26 km) east of Clearwater. Here you can experience a working ranch at

Recommended Reading—High Country

FOR ADULTS:
Hiking Yoho, Kootenay, Glacier and Mt. Revelstoke National Parks, by Michelle Gurney and Kathy Howe. Falcon, Guilford, Conn. 2001.

Shuswap Pathways—A Trail Guide, by Estelle Noakes. Sunshine Studios, Chase, BC. 1993.

Kamloops: One Hundred Years of Community 1893-1993, by Wayne R. Norton and William Schmidt (editors). Sonotek Publishing Ltd, 1992.

Exploring Wells Gray Park, by Roland Neave. Sandhill Books.

FOR KIDS:
Goldstone, by Julie Lawson. Stoddart Kids, 1998. Based on a true incident in the Rogers Pass area when an avalanche in 1910 killed sixty-six railway workers. The heroine is Karen, whose Swedish father works for the railway. For grades five and up.

Bats, by Gail Gibbons. Holiday House, 2000. Ages nine to twelve (see the section on Squilax). Learn about their protection and the myths surrounding them. Beautifully illustrated.

Vavenby Trail Rides (Box 250, Vavenby, V0E 3A0; 250–676–9598; edshook@hotmail.com; www.ntvalley.com/trailrides). The Shook family takes small groups on guided rides through open pasture, woodlands, and hay fields along the scenic North Thompson River. Help herd the cows or just hold the reins and enjoy the scenery. Rides are $20 per hour. In May and June they have several cattle drives, to which they invite up to six guests ($100 per person) to join. Or there's the *Ride and Stay* package ($125 per person per day) for "like-minded guests," which includes a full day's riding, home-cooked meals, and comfortable beds. The following day could involve any number of activities for a real ranch experience. Vavenby Trail Rides operates from April to late October.

Comfortable accommodation is just a five-minute drive away at *Aveley Ranch* (250–676–9574; fax: 250–676–9575), one of the largest sheep ranches in Western Canada. A specially built bed-and-breakfast log cabin in the woods sleeps six. Double rates range from $90.

Back on the Yellowhead, heading north, there's another entrance to the *Wells Gray Provincial Park* 62 miles (100 km) north of Clearwater. Turn onto a 17-mile (27-km) narrow, winding, gravel forestry road (not suitable for large RVs—four-wheel-drive recommended) just past Blue River. A 1.5-mile (2.5-km) portage from the parking lot will bring you to **Murtle Lake,** North America's largest "no-motors-allowed" freshwater lake. With more than 62 miles (100 km) of shoreline to explore and only the call of the loon to listen to, if you have a canoe, you can really get away from it all. A dawn paddle may bring you face-to-face with black or grizzly bears, eagles, moose, beavers, deer, or wolves. And if you have a BC fishing license (and don't leave it in the car!), the trout are huge. You must pick up a permit in Blue River for camping at Murtle Lake. You'll find information about permits and the lake on the western side of the highway in Blue River at the **Blue River Campground and R.V. Park** (Box 38, Murtle Lake Road and Highway 5, Blue River, V0E 1J0; 250–673–8203; off-season: 780–852–5756; www.bluerivercampground.ca). They also provide canoe rentals, fishing licenses, showers, heli-fishing, full hookups, and if you'd like to spend the night on a bed of cedar chips in a Blackfoot or Cree tipi or a cozy cabin after a friendly evening sitting around a campfire listening to music and sharing stories, that's available, too. An on-site store sells the necessary topographical map for Murtle Lake and a guidebook on Wells Gray Park (also available at the Info Centre in Clearwater). The campground operates May 1 through October 15.

But if tipi camping, portaging canoes, and roughing it on Murtle Lake is not your thing, check into the luxurious year-round resort at **Mike Wiegele Helicopter Skiing** (Harrwood Drive, Box 159, Blue River, V0E 1J0; 250–673–8381; fax: 250–673–8464; 800–661–9170 for reservations only; reservations@wiegele.com; www.wiegele.com) for some backcountry hiking through alpine wildflowers, fly-fishing, biking, skiing, helicopter sight-seeing, or picnicking (gourmet picnics at 7,000 feet!). The luxuries include a health club, a private beach, fireplaces—and the list goes on. There's a choice of accommodation ranging from $75 (double occupancy) at Saddle Mountain Lodge to $395 in the luxury chalet.

Northern High Country

Fifty-five miles (88 km) north of Blue River is Valemount, the midpoint between Edmonton and Vancouver. It sits in a valley where the Cariboo, Monashee, and Rocky Mountains meet, where the views become spectacular, and where the birds flock in the millions.

Just 2 miles (3 km) south of town, the **Robert W. Starratt Wildlife Sanctuary** (Cranberry Marsh) is the site of a Ducks Unlimited project to improve waterfowl habitat. The Canada geese love it here, as do northern harriers and red-tailed hawks. You can hike the whole 600-acre (243-ha) marsh in an hour and a half. Contact the Valemount Visitor Info Centre, open May 15 through September 15 (99 Gorse Street, Highway 5, Box 168, Valemount, V0E 2Z0; 250–566–4435; fax: 250–566–4249; tour@ valemount.org; www.valemount.org) for year-round information. They'll also direct you to the *Valemount Museum* (Box 850, Valemount, V0E 2Z0; 250–566–4177/4324; fax: 250–566–8411; museum@ valemount.com) to discover some valley and railroad history or, if you're visiting in late summer, to Swift Creek in the George Hicks Regional Park, where the world's longest chinook salmon migration occurs.

If you'd like to stay awhile and explore the Valemount area, the *Dream Catcher Inn* (Box 1012, Valemount, V0E 2Z0; 250–566–4226 or 800–566–9128; fax 250–566–9128; dream@valemount.com; www.dream catcherinn.ca) has log chalets as well as bed-and-breakfast accommodation. There's an outdoor hot tub and delicious breakfasts. My hot apple cereal, blueberry muffins, and poached eggs on toast kept me going well into the afternoon. In the bed-and-breakfast, you have a choice of five Indian-named rooms, each with a dream catcher (to catch your dreams before they float away) hanging above a comfortable bed. The inn is located in a ten-acre (four-ha) wooded setting just north of Valemount, within walking distance of the Swift Creek Chinook salmon spawning grounds in George Hicks Park and the nine-hole *Valemount Pines Golf Course* (250–566–4550) on the west side of the highway.

Check with the village of Valemount or visit its Web site at www.vale mount.org/tourism for more information on the many outdoor activities in the area. Also Doreen and Bert Van Asten at the Dream Catcher Inn can put you in touch with guides to do some backpacking, canoeing, rafting, and fly-in/hike-out activities in the vicinity of the *Berg Lake Trail,* considered by many to be the most spectacular hike in North America. Imagine standing at cool, blue Berg Lake, mesmerized by a spectacular view of Mount Robson and Berg Glacier and listening to chunks of ice calving from the glacier into the lake.

Five miles (8 km) north of Valemount is the *Mount Terry Fox Viewpoint.* In Canada the name Terry Fox is a household name. Having lost a leg to a rare form of bone cancer, twenty-two-year-old Fox attempted to run across Canada to raise funds for cancer research. After running at a pace of almost a marathon a day, covering 3,339 miles (5,373 km), he had to retire after the cancer returned. He died ten months later, and today yearly runs are held throughout Canada to continue the fund-raising effort and honor his memory. Look to the east at the viewpoint and you'll see the 8,694-foot (2,650-m) Mount Terry Fox.

To access the Terry Fox Trail, cross the highway from the viewpoint and follow the trail sign at Stone Road. Take this road for a little more than a mile to the trailhead. It's 4.5 miles (7 km) to Mount Terry Fox—easily a full-day hike by the time you get back to the parking lot. It's quite steep, but the alpine views are worth the effort.

It's now time to leave the Yellowhead South (Highway 5) and join the Yellowhead Highway 16 at Tête Jaune Cache, once a thriving town of 3,000, complete with pool halls and flophouses in the early 1900s when the Grand Trunk Railway was under construction. Now it's all but deserted. At this point we are 63 miles (101 km) from Jasper in Alberta and 150 miles (240 km) from Prince George. The easterly drive is spectacular, especially when Mount Robson comes into view just near the Mount Terry Fox Provincial Park. The road to the northwest is a long and lonely drive into BC's north, which we'll explore in the section on the Northeast.

PLACES TO STAY IN HIGH COUNTRY

CHASE
Quaaout Lodge Resort, Box 1215, Chase V0E 1M0; (800) 663–4303; (250) 679–3090; www.quaaout.com. Deluxe rooms on the shores of Little Shuswap. Restaurant also.

CLEARWATER
Tanglewood Lodge, 1048 Clearwater Valley Road, Box 1785, Clearwater, V0E 1N0; (250) 674–3537; www.tanglewoodlodge.net.

REVELSTOKE
Canyon Hot Springs Resort Ltd., Box 2400, V0E 2S0; (250) 837–2420; www.canyonhotsprings. com. Camping, cabins, hot springs.

Christmas Island Bed & Breakfast, 523 West Third Street, Box 1284, V0E 2S0; (250) 837–3262; (888) 826–5555; www.bbcanada.com/1974. html. Downtown views, hot tub.

SALMON ARM
The Log Bog Friendship Farm B&B, 540 Highway 97B NE, Salmon Arm, V1E 1X5; phone/fax: (250) 832–5581; logbog_bb@hotmail.com. Beautifully crafted log home on nineteen acres.

SORRENTO
The Evergreens Bed and Breakfast, 2853 Vimy Road, Box 117, V0E 2W0; (250) 675–2568; www.bbexpo.com/bc/ever-greens.htm. Near lake.

Sorrento Center, Box 99, V0E 2W0; (250) 675–2421; www.sorrento-centre.bc.ca. Camping, cabanas, and lodge accommodation. On Shuswap Lake.

VALEMOUNT
Dream Catcher Inn, Box 1012, V0E 2Z0; (250) 566–4226 or (800) 566–9128; dream@valemount.com; www.dreamcatcherinn.ca. Bed-and-breakfast accommodation.

PLACES TO EAT IN HIGH COUNTRY

CLEARWATER
Helmcken Falls Lodge, Box 239, V0E 1N0; (250) 674–3657. Buffet. Wilderness location.

KAMLOOPS

This Old Steak & Fish House, 172 Battle Street; (250) 374–3227; steakhouse.kamloops.com. Romantic, garden setting. West end.

Storms Restaurant, 1502 River Street, V2C 1Y9; (250) 372–1522; storms.kamloops.com Riverside deck; excellent dining.

REVELSTOKE

Black Forest Restaurant; (250) 837–3495. Fondues and a variety of schnitzels; 5 km west of Revelstoke.

Conversations Coffee House, 203 Mackenzie Avenue; (250) 837–4772. Good coffee and great desserts.

Frontier Family Restaurant, corner of Highways 1 and 23 North; (250) 837–5119 or (800) 382–7763. Fast foods.

The Peaks Lodge; (800) 668–0330 or (250) 837–2176. Fine dining and pub fare. 5 km west of Revelstoke. Accommodation also.

SORRENTO

Toby's Restaurant, Trans-Canada Highway, V0E 2W0; (250) 675–4464. Good pizzas. Open from 7:00 A.M. to 9:00 P.M.

Cariboo Chilcotin Coast

The Cariboo Chilcotin Coast area is located in central British Columbia, with the Pacific Coast to the west and the Cariboo Mountain Range to the east. Hudson's Bay fur traders, who were among the earliest European settlers here, could never have anticipated the gold-hungry throngs that would stampede into the area after the first bright nuggets reached San Francisco in the late 1850s. Thousands marched north to the beckoning land in hopes of filling their pokes with the brilliant booty. And so it all began.

But in less than thirty years, towns like Barkerville, once the gold capital of the world, were empty of both the gold and its seekers. Roadhouses that had catered to exhausted travelers spread their wings to become centers for rambling ranches, and another way of life began.

South Cariboo

Mile Zero of the old *Cariboo Waggon Road* is at Lillooet at the junction of Highways 99 and 12, majestically perched above the muddy Fraser River. It started out as a landing point for mother-lode seekers who had come north through Harrison and Anderson Lakes. Other roadhouses like 100 Mile House and 70 Mile House emerged, their names originating from their distances from Lillooet. A cairn on Main Street marks the Mile Zero spot. A busy town of 16,000 in the gold-rush days of the 1860s, Lillooet was at one time the second-largest settlement north of San Francisco and west of Chicago. It also holds the unenviable claim to the hottest recorded spot in BC, when it reached 111.9° F (44.4° C) in 1941, and the more enviable claim as the best location outside of Myanmar (Burma) to find jade.

Opposite the cairn, at 790 Main Street, *St. Mary's Anglican Church* houses the seasonal (open May to October) *Lillooet Museum and*

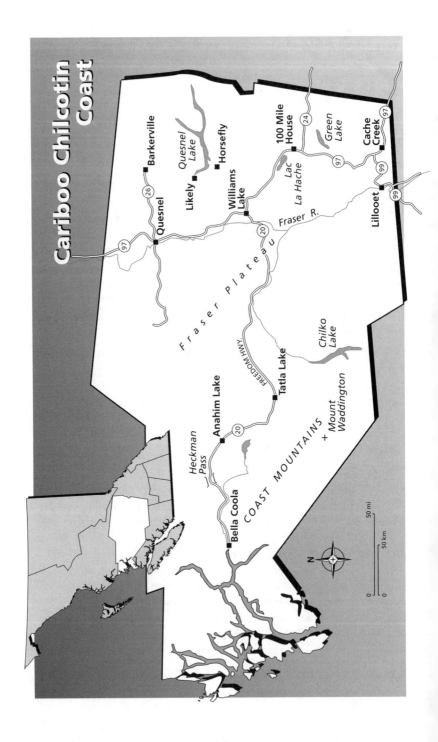

Cariboo Chilcotin Coast

AUTHOR'S TOP TEN PICKS IN THE CARIBOO-CHILCOTIN

Sheep Pasture Golf Course
Green Lake
Historic Hat Creek Ranch
Lookout on Cornwall Mountain
Painted Chasm
Barkerville Historic Town
Xats'ull Heritage Village
Bowron Lake
Lac la Hache
The Freedom Highway

Visitor Info Centre (Box 441, Lillooet, V0K 1V0; 250–256–4308; fax: 250–256–0043; lillmuseum@ lillonet.ca). The Lillooet & District Chamber of Commerce (Box 650, 989 Main Street, Lillooet, V0K 1V0; 800–217–3847; 250–256–4364; fax: 250–256–4315; www.lillooetbc. com) is your best bet for obtaining information from afar. *The Ma Murray Collection* in the church basement is a display of newspaper and printing equipment owned by straight-talking publisher Margaret "Ma" Murray and her politician husband, George. Founded in 1934, the *Bridge River-Lillooet News,* laced with her crusty commentaries, made Ma (who was honored with an Order of Canada medal) a household name. Outside the museum there's a rusty little jail jumbled among antiquated farming machinery. Ask at the Info Centre about Lillooet's Golden Mile of History from the Bridge of 23 Camels to the Old Bridge, made more interesting if you walk or bike along it using a self-guided tour brochure.

A block north of the museum at 690 Main Street, enjoy Greek or Italian food at *Dina's Place* (250–256–4264).

Ma Murray

*M*argaret "Ma" Murray was a mighty woman. Born in Windy Ridge, Kansas, in 1887, she arrived in Lillooet in 1933 with her politician husband, George. To fulfill a campaign promise to his constituents, George established the Bridge River-Lillooet News. Before long, his wife's candid (and often damning) views on the Canadian political situation (and society in general) were widely quoted; she was soon a household name. She also took every opportunity to inform the world of Lillooet's virtues, thus putting it on the map.

In fact, her name became synonymous with that of Lillooet. The flag on page two of the Bridge River-Lillooet News always stated: "Printed in the sage brush country of Lillooet every Thursday, God willing. Guarantees a chuckle every week and a belly laugh once a month or your money back. Subscriptions $5.00 in Canada. Fur-riners $6.00. This week's circulation 1,726 and every bloody one of them paid for." Ma Murray died in Lillooet on September 25, 1982, at the age of ninety-five, and is buried beside her husband in Fort St. John.

At the **Lillooet Bakery** (719 Main Street; 250–256–4889), *bäckermeister* Axel Sterrmann and his wife, Elke, serve European-style breakfasts, delectables such as eclairs and rum balls, wonderful bread, and excellent coffee, attested to by the busloads of tourists who stop by.

If you need a place to stay, in addition to three or four hotels, there's a comfortable spot down on the river, where, if it's fishing or gold panning you're after, you've come to the right place. **Sturgeon Bay Bed and Breakfast** (130 Haylmore Place, Box 1130, Lillooet, V0K 1V0; 250–256–7792; sturgeonbaybb@lillonet.ca; www.sturgeonbaybb.com) has a two-bedroom suite with a private entrance for $90 double. Another popular B&B is **Bountiful Gardens,** also on the Fraser River at 5 Sundial Drive, (250) 256–4355. Owner Cindy MacDonald has four beautiful guest rooms. Yet another accommodation is **Melvins on Main** (P.O. Box 1837, 1103 Main Street, Lillooet, V0K 1V0; phone/fax: 250–256–7135; melvins@lillonet.ca; www.melvinsonmain.com). Downtown hotel accommodation can be found at the **4 Pines Motel** (108 Eighth Avenue, Box 36, Lillooet, V0K 1V0; 250–256–4247; fax: 250–256–4120; reservations: 800–753–2576; 4pines@lillonet.ca; www.4pinesmotel.com). It's modern and clean with friendly service.

There's also a comfortable campground ten minutes' walking distance from town at **Cayoosh Creek Campground** (Box 1548, Lillooet, V0K 1V0; 250–256–4180; fax: 250–256–4174; info@cayooshcampground. com). It's located at the junction of the Fraser and Cayoosh Rivers. While there, plan on doing some gold panning on the Fraser River or perhaps fish for trout in the Seton River. Several times a day **Fraser River Jet Boat Adventures** (1–877–RIVBOAT; fun@rivboat.com; www.rivboat. com) runs trips from the campground along the Fraser River through some impressive scenery.

There's still gold in them thar hills, so if you'd like to try gold panning, **McNal Placer Gold** (250–256–4384) will show you how it's done. Or you could try **Moha Placer Mines** (250–256–7101/7711) at Bridge River. At the **U-Pick Old Airport Gardens** (Box 161, Lillooet, V0K 1V0; phone/fax: 250–256–7051), approximately 400 yards south on Highway 12 (the road that leads to Lytton) just off Highway 99, Arnold, Aggie, and Bobby Malm sell fresh produce—it's very popular with the locals. U-pick is open June to November. For a little horsing around, perhaps visit **Red Rock Trail Rides** (250–256–4495; www.bcpassport.com/lillooet) on Moha Road. The experienced wranglers there will outfit you with the perfect horse for a variety of trips.

Before leaving the area, check out the **Seton Reservoir Recreation Area**

CARIBOO CHILCOTIN COAST

Top Annual Events in the Cariboo Chilcotin Coast

Williams Lake Stampede, *Williams Lake; July; (250) 398–8388 or (800) 71RODEO*

Billy Barker Days, *Quesnel; July; (250) 992–1234*

Gold Nugget Music Festival, *Likely; July; (250) 790–2287*

Bella Coola Rodeo, *Bella Coola; June/July; (250) 982–2766*

Gold Rush Sled Dog Mail Run, *Quesnel; January; (250) 992–9143*

Quesnel Rodeo, *Quesnel; July; (250) 249–5170*

Horsefly River Salmon Festival, *Horsefly; September; (250) 398–8532*

Fall Harvest Fair, *Williams Lake; September; (250) 392–4410*

Gymkanas, *Watch Lake and Green Lake; July; (250) 456–7741*

Wells Winter Carnival, *Wells; (877) 451–9355*

(www.bchydro.com), 3 miles (5 km) southwest of Lillooet on the Duffy Lake Road. The stupendous view of the glacial green waters of Seton Lake and the surrounding Chilcotin mountains is a must-see in BC. The nearby Seton Dam Campground is provided by BC Hydro. It's free! Look for the Chinese bake oven in the campground area—a relic from the gold mining days.

Leaving town as you head north on Highway 99 toward Cache Creek, you cross the Fraser at the *Bridge of 23 Camels,* named for the poor Bactrian beasts of burden (purchased in San Francisco in 1862 for $300) used and abused during gold rush days. It's worth a stop just past the bridge to view the town and the railway line that snakes along the river.

But before heading north, check out Canada's most unusual golf course. *Sheep Pasture Golf Course* (Texas Creek Road, Box 217, Lillooet, V0K 1V0; 250–256–4484; www.teeoff.ca/courses/bc 214.htm), 5 miles (8 km) south of Lillooet on the Texas Creek Road (turn south before the bridge), is a par-35 nine-holer with quite a few moving, bleating hazards, as well as panoramic views of the mountains and river. Owner David Jones built the course after years of losing his sheep to predators; he figured if he had two-legged animals walking around, the predators would disappear! As well as the living hazards, there's water on the course—but no bunkers "because the sheep dig in"—and a few apple trees. Feel free to pick an apple as you play.

Heading up Highway 99 North, *Lori's Lookout* (250–256–7805) is a great spot to stop for a photograph. Ask Lori when the train is due so you can watch it weave through the tunnels below. There's usually plenty of local fruit, and the ice creams are refreshing on those hot Lillooet days.

Once north of town on Highway 99, you'll twist and climb along the Fraser benchlands toward the 4,987-foot (1,520-m) Pavilion Mountain. Until recently, you could stop at the *Pavilion General Store,* at one time a one-day trip away from Lillooet by horse and buggy. Unfortunately, it has now been destroyed by fire. Here the horses were watered before

Cache Creek is the home of the last stop sign that existed on the Trans-Canada Highway. The sign was taken down and replaced with a traffic light on February 4, 1984, and is now on display in the Village Office.

continuing up over the mountain. The slope was so steep that they would have to use log "anchors" to help them down the hill, some of which can still be seen. Passengers would have to get out and push the wagons on the uphill sections.

Farther on, after passing a few shimmering lakes, you'll approach Marble Canyon, about 30 miles (48 km) east of Lillooet. Watch for ***Chimney Rock*** on the north side of the highway and other Utah-like towering cliffs of colored limestone. Camping at ***Marble Canyon Provincial Park*** is available (twenty-six high-density sites on turquoise Crown Lake), and there's also first-class swimming in Pavilion Lake. For information on Marble Canyon visit the BC Parks Web site at www.bcparks.ca, keyword "Marble Canyon." The Pavilion Indian band operate ***Sky Blue Water Resort*** (250– 256–7663; fax: 250–256–7993) on Pavilion Lake; here you'll find rustic cabins with separate washrooms—bring your own bedding. Campsites are available also.

As you leave the dramatic scenery of Highway 99, you'll come to ***Historic Hat Creek Ranch*** (Box 878, Cache Creek, V0K 1H0; 800–782–0922 or 250–457–9722; fax: 250–457–9311; hhcr@goldtrail.com; www.hat creekranch. com) at the junction of Highway 97, which leads south 7 miles (11 km) to Cache Creek or north 18 miles (29 km) to Clinton. Hat Creek Ranch, originally the property of the murderous Donald McLean and his three horse-stealing sons, was an overnight stop for early travelers on the Cariboo Waggon Road. Today it's a holiday attraction, complete with stagecoach and wagon rides. A blacksmith demonstrates his trade, pigs snuffle in the troughs, and chickens scratch in their coop. A reasonably priced full buffet lunch is available. The ranch is open daily from mid-May to late September from 9:00 A.M. to 5:00 P.M. Admission cost, which includes a guided tour of the Roadhouse, the Blacksmith Shop, and the Native Interpretation Center, is $18 for a family of four. Overnight camping is available.

Before heading north to follow the old *Cariboo Waggon Trail,* take a look around Cache Creek and Ashcroft, a few miles to the south on Highway 97. Tune into 105.9 FM to find out what's happening first; then just before Cache Creek visit ***Horsting's Farm Market*** (open daily in summer 8:00 A.M. to 7:00 P.M. and in winter 9:00 A.M. to 5:00 P.M.; phone/fax: 250–457–6546), colorful with fresh berries, vegetables, and hanging flower baskets. Try a piece of Donna Horsting's berry pies or buy a bottle of her delicious Saskatoon berry jam and a loaf of homemade bread.

The kids can play on the trampoline, go for a wagon ride, or visit the goats and rabbits after a picnic in Horsting's park. *The Country Cafe,* next to the market, serves sandwiches (circle your favorite ingredients) and homemade soups.

From jam to jade: British Columbia is the Jade Capital of the World. You can watch jade being cut, polished, and mounted, as well as buy jade souvenirs at the *Cariboo Jade and Gift Shoppe* (1093 Todd Road, Box 280, Cache Creek, V0K 1H0; 250–457–9566; fax: 250–457–9669; jadeshoppe@goldcountry.bc.ca; www.goldcountry.bc.ca/jadeshoppe) in Cache Creek. It's opposite the bus depot and is open late daily in summer.

The streets of Cache Creek are lined with neon signs and flowers. Some businesses and residents display antique cars in keeping with a "Nifty Fifties" theme. Here in Cache Creek, where the Trans-Canada crosses Highway 97 and the rolling grasslands of the Bonaparte River Valley combine with a semi-desert climate, you'll get that Old West cowboy feel. For more information contact the Cache Creek & District Chamber of Commerce (Box 460, Cache Creek, V0K 1H0; 250–457–9566; fax: 250–457–9669; cachechamber@goldcountry.bc.ca). Details on several accommodations in the area are listed on www.exploregoldcountry.com.

From Cache Creek head south along Highway 97 past the tumbleweed and cactus to historic Ashcroft on the Thompson River. Cross the bridge into town, and stop at the bright red *Ashcroft Fire Hall.* This building is a replica of the first fire hall, which was built in 1889. Go down the hill toward the riverbank to a small campground at *Legacy Park* (Box 183, Ashcroft, V0K 1A0; 250–453–2642). The sites

From Canned Cream to Claim Staking

*W*hen I arrived in Ashcroft, one of those special little towns where everybody knows everybody and conversations come easy, I headed down to the River Inn for a piece of blueberry pie and a coffee. A chat with a stranger about canned whipped cream ended with a visit to a remote cabin on a hillside. Sweet-smelling wildflowers, wandering bears, and serenity are what brings Trevor Parker, a ship's captain from Vancouver, back

regularly to where he grew up. Trevor introduced me to how to stake a claim, to esoteric pictographs and hidden ice caves, and to the friendliness of Ashcroft's people. We dropped in to the Irlybird, where he bought two wooden garden chairs. When they wouldn't fit in his small Toyota, it was "no problem" for the lovely woman who served him to drop them off on the way home. That's the kind of friendly little town it is.

are right on the bank. Next door is the *Ashcroft River Inn* (Box 1359, Ashcroft, V0K 1A0; 250–453–9124; fax: 250–453–2565 or 800–465–4800), where you can enjoy a meal or spend a night overlooking the river. Rates start at $51 double. The restaurant opens at 7:00 A.M., and there's often live entertainment in the pub.

If you're interested in Cariboo history, the *Ashcroft Museum and Archives* (Box 129, Ashcroft, V0K 1A0; 250–453–9232/9161; fax: 250–453–9664; www.goldcountry.bc.ca/museum), built in 1916 on the corner of Brink and Fourth Streets, is, as I was told by several residents, "definitely worth a visit." Along with a collection of tools, lamps, and Indian and Chinese items, there's a gift shop. It's open daily from 10:00 A.M. to 5:00 P.M. in the summer. Admission is by donation. Next door you'll find the *Ashcroft Journal,* started up in 1895. Originally called the *BC Mining Journal,* it was one of British Columbia's first papers and still churns out the news today. For more information on Ashcroft, contact either the museum or the Village of Ashcroft (Box 129, Ashcroft, V0K 1A0; 250–453–9161; fax: 250–453–9664; villageofashcroft@telus.net; www.village.ashcroft.bc.ca.

Trivia
Ashcroft has a Superman connection. The parents of Margot Kidder, who played Lois Lane in the movie, live there. The actress herself has purchased 245 acres in the Ashcroft area.

If you head back across the bridge and turn south on Cornwall Road, you'll reach the *Ashcroft Manor* site (Box 127, Cache Creek, V0K 1H0; 250–453–9983; fax: 250–453–9600). If you're coming from Cache Creek, it's 7 miles (11 km) south on the Trans-Canada Highway. Developed by the Cornwall brothers in the early 1860s, these historic buildings, about seven in all, are a must-stop attraction. There's the *Teahouse,* with possibly the best restaurant food in the area, and the *Manor,* which houses a gift shop (excellent selection of jade), a museum (free), and an art gallery. Hours are from 9:00 A.M. to 5:00 P.M. daily from May 1 till October 31. This building was one of BC's oldest roadhouses, which has served also as a post office and a courthouse—the "hanging judge" Matthew Begbie once presided here. An RV campground is on site.

Follow the sweet smell of ponderosa pine and sagebrush for about 9 miles (14 km) south and take a drive up the Hat Creek–Oregon Jack Road to *Cornwall Mountain*. The alpine meadows are thick with wildflowers, but this beautiful drive is really only recommended for 4x4s. There are no services, no campgrounds, a few bears, and if you're as lucky as I was to be guided by an immensely hospitable local, you'll find pictographs and a

Trivia

Clement Cornwall, who with his brother built Ashcroft Manor, was one of British Columbia's first senators. He became lieutenant governor of British Columbia in 1881.

hidden ice cave containing ice stalagmites, seeming to grow like delicate ferns from the cave floor. But that's my secret!

Five miles (8 km) south of Ashcroft off Highway 97C South, the Rowe family at **Sundance Guest Ranch** (Box 489, Ashcroft, V0K 1A0; 800–553–3533; 250–453–2422; fax: 250–453–9356; sun dance@wkpowerlink.com; www.sundance-ranch. com) offers a genuine bit of the old West. With a herd of more than ninety buckskins, bays, chestnuts, pintos, and Appaloosas—horses to suit all levels—and miles of scenic trails, combined with a heated pool, a tennis court, a kids' wing, games room, dances, and barbecues, and with a nine-hole golf course and excellent fishing nearby, you're assured of an unforgettable holiday. Rates (including all meals in the licensed dining room, riding, and use of all ranch facilities) range from $195 per person double occupancy in high season. Children's rates are lower, with kids under three free.

Pictograph near Ashcroft

Circle back to Cache Creek on the Trans-Canada and rejoin Highway 97 heading north to the copper-colored mountains and rolling hills surrounding laid-back Clinton, 25 miles (40 km) north of Cache Creek. A popular spot halfway between Clinton and Cache Creek is Loon Lake. From Cache Creek drive 13 miles (21 km) north and turn east. Six miles (10 km) along the paved Loon Lake Road see kokanee-salmon and rainbow-trout fry at the **Loon Creek Hatchery** (974 Loon Lake Road, RR1, Cache Creek, V0K 1H0; 250–459–2454). A farther 10 miles (16 km) on is the **Loon Lake Provincial Park** (www.bc parks.ca, search "Loon"—no campsites). The 7.4-acre (3-ha) park, set in a forest of Douglas fir and ponderosa pine, is midway along the 7-mile-long (12-km) lake. The rainbow trout usually bite well here, especially during June and September. There is an undeveloped small boat launch.

From the Loon Lake Road, Clinton is another 12 miles (19 km) north. **Cariboo Lodge Resort** (Box 459, Clinton, V0K 1K0; 250–459–7992; fax: 250–459–0060; 877–459–7992, cariboo-lodge@goldtrail.com; www. cariboolodgebc.com) is on the highway in town. It's conspicuous as it is one of the largest log structures in British Columbia. Wonderful old photos on the walls will give you a feel for the past, and with its pretty hanging baskets, swimming pool, pub, and a restaurant with tasty lodge-burgers, it's an inviting rest stop. Room rates (double) start at $80. Ask about riding, sledding, rafting, skiing, and other tours the resort offers.

Across the road at the tiny **South Cariboo Historical Museum** (Box 25, Clinton, V0K 1K0; 250–459–2442/2533; fax: 250–459–0058), built in 1892 from locally made bricks, check out the backyard with displays that include a bull-press (which was used to keep the beast from doing the blacksmith in as he bravely shod it), a model of the now-burnt-down Clinton Hotel, and a BC Express Company sleigh. In winter the museum closes, but you can still see the displays in the back. In summer it's open daily 9:00 A.M. to 5:00 P.M.

Walk along to **Robertson Square** and have a giggle at the Bucking Ham Palace Hotel, where you can "Eat and sleep like a king for $2.00 a day." Perhaps you'd prefer to try "Fitzwillies purifying black paste" for your "painful piles, pustules, pimples of acne, pox, bunions, tonsils, and teething grief." If you're still a mess, at **Hickory Daiquiri Doc's,** you can get "mouthwash, whitewash, hogwash, distilled water, toilet water, tonic water, holy water, bones set, blood let, holes patched, and babies hatched." It's right beside the **Clinton Grill Restaurant** (250–459–2343). Enjoy a Chinese meal on the rustic tables in "the square."

Next door at **Crafts with Class** (1521 Cariboo Highway, Clinton, V0K

CARIBOO CHILCOTIN COAST

**WORTH SEEING/DOING
IN THE CARIBOO CHILCOTIN COAST**

1K0; 250–459–2573) you can buy Vallance pottery, gourmet coffee, and classy sweatshirts. For more than ten years Jill Robinson has featured Bruce Vallance's exceptional pottery, bringing in customers from as far afield as Vancouver. For more information on Clinton, contact The Village of Clinton (Box 309, 1423 Cariboo Highway, Clinton, V0K 1K0; 250–459–2261; fax: 250–459–2227; admin@village.clinton.bc.ca; www. village. clinton.bc.ca). The Web site's tourism page lists several accommodation choices.

Just north of Clinton near Chasm is a northwestern turnoff to wide-open spaces and big ranches, with such cowboylike names as Big Bar, High Bar, Gang Ranch, Dog Creek, and Alkali Lake, stretched out along a road that edges the Fraser River and ends in Williams Lake via the back door. Stay on one of the guest ranches in the area to appreciate the varied terrain and wildlife along this unpopulated pathway, in former times a busy gold rush wagon route.

Any traveler to this part of British Columbia should not miss the spectacular **Painted Chasm,** Canada's Grand Canyon, located in **Chasm Provincial Park** (www.bcparks.ca, search "Chasm"). The turnoff is 9 miles (15 km) north of Clinton; then drive 2 paved miles (3 km) east off Highway 97. There's no fanfare of garish signs announcing its coming, just a small blue PROVINCIAL PARK sign on the roadside. But don't be fooled. This geological wonder, a mile wide and almost 400 feet (120 m) deep, will dazzle you with its display of bright orange and pink rock. Take note of the individual lava flows in the horizontal layering. One modern legend going the rounds is that a Scottish gold digger lost a penny and, in his effort to retrieve it, dug the mighty chasm. If you saw the movie *Grey Fox,* then you've seen scenes shot at the Chasm.

An unplanned turnoff at 70 Mile House, 19 miles (31 km) north of Clinton, led to some unexpected finds. Turn east onto Old Bonaparte

Cruise the spectacular Discovery Coast Passage between Port Hardy and Bella Coola with BC Ferries.

Drive the Gold Rush Trail (at one time the Cariboo Waggon Road) from Vancouver to the historic goldfields near Barkerville.

Take part in a cattle drive at a guest ranch.

Check out the Norwegian heritage in the hand-tooled, square-timbered buildings in the Bella Coola Valley.

Visit 108 Heritage Site, with nine turn-of-the-century buildings.

Visit Cottonwood House, between Quesnel and Barkerville, one of the region's best-known road-houses.

Stay at the famous Tyax Mountain Lake Resort (250–238–2221) on Tyaughton Lake amid the Chilcotin Mountains.

Trek the 260-mile (420-km) Alexander Mackenzie Heritage Trail, the ultimate Canadian hike, which starts northwest of Quesnel and ends near Bella Coola on the coast.

Road, and less than 5 pleasant miles (8 km) later, you're at **Green Lake.** Many locals have their own reasons for the color of the lake (a reflection of the trees), but the one that makes a lot of sense is that it has no outlet; hence, it has accumulated large deposits of soda, salt, and sulfur, which combine to create its glorious shade of green. It's more than just a pretty green lake, though. There are three campgrounds—on both sides of the lake and all with beach sites—plus a plethora of guest ranches surrounding both Green and Watch Lakes, which means you'll probably find somewhere pleasant to stay. For campers **Green Lake Provincial Park** (www.bcparks.ca, search "Green") has 121 camping sites. The park entrance is 10 miles (16 km) northeast of 70 Mile House. Of the three campgrounds at the provincial park (Emerald Bay, Sunset View, and Arrowhead), only Emerald Bay (fifty-one sites on the northeast shore) and Sunset View (fifty-four sites on the southeast shore), which are both well treed, can be reserved ahead (800–689–9025). Arrowhead (sixteen high-density sites on the northwest shore) is in an open waterfront area—you're likely to see owls and golden eagles.

Little Horse Lodge (6143 Green Lake Road North, RR 1, Comp 1, Site E, 70 Mile House, V0K 2K0; 250–456–7524; fax: 250–456–7512; info@littlehorselodge.com; www.littlehorselodge.com), a year-round resort, has everything from a rural agency liquor store and a restaurant (excellent German cuisine) to a general store and a laundry, as well as a host of activities from fishing and canoeing in summer to snowmobiling and ice fishing in winter. Gymkhanas and fishing derbies are held regularly. The hospitality is a mix of true-blue Canadian and *deutsche Gemütlichkeit.* Accommodations are varied: five log cabins, fourteen camping sites, and three bed-and-breakfast guest rooms in the lodge, with rates starting at $45 double.

Discover some of the history of the area at the **Flying U** (Box 69, 70 Mile House, V0K 2K0; 250–456–7717; flyingu@bcinternet.net; www.flyingu.com), a cattle ranch since 1849. It's an international destination with its own BC Rail whistle stop and is Canada's oldest and largest guest ranch with a history and spirit of the early West. Here meals are eaten ranch-style and are announced by the clanging of a bell. There's a two-day minimum stay April to June (adults $140 per day, children from $110 to $80 per day) and a three-day minimum in July and August (adults $160 per day, children from $130 to $100 per day). These rates cover everything from three square meals to unsupervised trail riding to square dancing. Take the northern fork at Green Lake; the ranch is 4 miles (6 km) farther on.

Tall Timbers Resort (RR#1, Site 3, C-8A, 6304 Pioneer Lane, 70 Mile House, V0K 2K0; 888–228–8255; phone/fax: 250–456–7668; info@ talltimbers-resort.com; www.talltimbers-resort.com), *Ace High Resort* (Site 2C, C28, RR#1, 70 Mile House, V0K 2K0; 250–456–7518; acehigh@ bcinternet.net; www.acehighresort.com), and *Watch Lake Lodge* (RR 1, Watch Lake Road, 70 Mile House, V0K 2K0; 250–456–7741; fax: 250– 456–7492; www.watchlake.com) are three more accommodation choices a little farther along on Watch Lake. At Watch Lake Lodge, 3 miles (5 km) on from Little Horse Lodge, you can ride trail, roll your own, and wear a straw hat with Shorty, Enid, and Dimps Horn, who've been doing it for more than fifty years. Just pick a pair of boots that fit from the thirty or so lined up on the veranda, and it's Happy Trails time.

Head north from Green and Watch Lakes to *Lone Butte,* named for the prominent flat-topped rock that is all that remains of the plug of an ancient volcano that once erupted in the Cariboo. Climb the butte for an excellent view of the surrounding area. Park at the corner of Watch Lake Road and Highway 24 and take the trail up the east face.

An easterly turn on Highway 24 will take you through the *Interlakes District* to *Little Fort,* 57 miles (92 km) north of Kamloops on Yellowhead Highway 5. Highway 24 is also known as the *Fishing Highway,* such is the profusion of well-stocked lakes in the area. Fly-fishers and photographers shouldn't miss Lac Des Roches, a few miles east of Bridge Lake. You can stay here at a fishing resort that comes complete with its own Italian restaurant specializing in northern Italian and Tuscan cuisine. *Lac Des Roches Canadian Resort* (C19 Cottonwood Site, RR 1, Lone Butte, V0K 1X0; phone/fax: 250– 593–4141; info@lacdesroches.com; www.lacdesroches.com) is on the western end of Lac Des Roches, 25 miles (40 km) east of the Highway 97/Highway 24 junction. There's a beautiful view from the eastern end of the lake at the Pioneer MacDonald Ranch rest area. Anglers can try for rainbow trout, kokanee, or brook trout. If you're after a trophy rainbow, stop off at Sheridan Lake and perhaps land one in the ten-pound (4.5-kg) range. Licenses, tackle, and hand-tied flies are available at *Loon Bay Resort* (C1 Airmail Road, Lone Butte, V0K 1X0; 250–593–4431; fax: 250–593–4188; loonbay@bcinternet. net; www.loonbayresort.com) on Sheridan Lake. Cabin accommodation is also available at Loon Bay, as well as campsites near sandy beaches. Rent a canoe for a quiet paddle on the lake and wonder at the stunning scenery. From May to September, the Saturday Market at Loon Bay Resort features local crafts, woodworking, and baking for sale.

You'll find more works by some of the area's artisans, of which there are many, at **Country Pedlar Too** (250–593–4133) in the Sheridan Lake Store Complex. Pottery, folk art, and toys are a few of the items here.

Head east and north via the Old Cariboo Gold Rush Trail (Highway 97) into "town," which is **100 Mile House,** and you can't miss the **South Cariboo Info Centre** (422 Cariboo Highway 97 South, Box 340, 100 Mile House, V0K 2E0; 250–395–5353; 877–511–5353 toll free; fax: 250–395–4085; visitors@bcinternet.net; www.tourism.100mile.com) with the 36-foot-long (11-m) **World's Largest Cross Country Skis** standing outside. This is a reminder that every February, 100 Mile House hosts Canada's second-oldest cross-country ski race, the **Cariboo Ski Marathon,** a 30-mile (50-km) race that brings up to a thousand Nordic enthusiasts from all over the world.

Less obvious than those gigantic skis, but ever so lovely, are the **Bridge Creek Falls** near Centennial Park. They're so close to downtown, but even some locals, unfortunately, have never appreciated their beauty. Turn east on Fourth Avenue (opposite the Visitor Information Centre), take a right on Cedar, and turn immediately left by the school to the parking lot. A chip-trail leads to the falls, where a 30-foot (9-m) pipe, once used by a sawmill to harness the power of the water, still stands erect. Look out for mule deer near the falls. From the pipe, trails continue upstream to the **100 Mile Village Campground** (385 South Birch Avenue, Box 340, 100 Mile House, V0K 2E0; 250–395–2434) on Horse Lake Road. This municipal RV park is a pleasant close-to-town campsite with several shaded spots.

There's more natural beauty in 100 Mile House at the **Marsh Wildlife Sanctuary,** beside the Visitor Information Centre. This twenty-acre (8-ha) wetland marsh, surrounded by grassy meadows and bluffs of aspen and white spruce, is a nesting ground for Canada geese and several species of ducks. Informative signs help with identification.

Head up the highway toward (where else?) **108 Mile House,** famous for its internationally acclaimed resorts. The **Hills Health Ranch** (Box 26, 108 Mile Ranch, V0K 2Z0; 250–791–5225; fax: 250–791–6384; info@ hillshealthranch.com; www.thehillshealthranch.com) is the best known. Check out the photo-board inside the main lodge to see some of the celebrities who have enjoyed cross-country skiing, horseback riding, aerobics, and other activities "The Hills" offers. Sign up for a weeklong "lifestyle adjustment" vacation package of Smoking Cessation, Stress Reduction, Weight Loss, and several other wellness programs held in a large, well-equipped fitness center. Ride 'n' Spa Adventures, Golf 'n'

Williams Lake Field Naturalists Volunteers, who have interactive exhibits set up in *The Nature House.* It's full of interesting displays, showing small wildlife, waterfowl, birds, fish, and shells, all indigenous to the Williams Lake area. There's also a bee colony on display. An observation deck and walking trails aid in viewing the beaver lodge, native pit house, otters, muskrats, birds, and ducks that inhabit this conservation area. Reached via a causeway at the west end of Williams Lake, the center is open from 8:00 A.M. to 5:00 P.M. Monday to Friday, May to August, and on Sunday afternoons April through October, but the trails are open daily from 8:00 A.M. to dusk. Bring a picnic lunch and a swimsuit to make use of the tables and sandy beach.

Near the City Hall at the *Museum of the Cariboo Chilcotin* (113 North Fourth Avenue, Williams Lake, V2G 2C8; phone/fax: 250–392–7404; mccwl@uniserve.com; www.cowboy-museum.com), rodeo and ranching history is the theme. Displays include a working model of the Pacific Great Eastern Railway, which brought the first stockyards to Williams Lake in 1919. It is also the home of the *BC Cowboy Hall of Fame,* honoring working cowboys who made contributions to the ranching community. Learn here of the history of western Canada's first cattlemen. Admission is $2.00, and children are admitted free. It's open Monday to Saturday from 10:00 A.M. to 4:00 P.M., May to August, and in winter Tuesday to Saturday from 11:00 A.M. to 4:00 P.M.

The museum also features the *Williams Lake Stampede,* which is held over the July 1 weekend, offering barrel racing, calf roping, steer wrestling, wild-horse racing, bull riding, and other events included on the Canadian Professional Rodeo Association circuit. This four-day event was originally started in the 1920s and is now a major professional rodeo. For more information contact the Williams Lake Stampede Association at (800) 71RODEO (717–6336) in BC only, or (250) 392–6585; fax: (250) 398–7701; office@williamslakestampede.com; www.williamslakestampede.com.

Hikers can take advantage of the easily accessible *Williams Lake River Valley Trail*, a 9-mile (14-km) hiking trail that takes you from downtown to the Fraser River. It's a scenic, easy family hike passing through varying ecosystems. It starts by the highway near the cemetery, and as it nears the Fraser River, the valley narrows with spectacular cliffs rising over 500 feet (150 m) with deep gullies on each side. To get directions, drop in to the *Williams Lake Visitor Info Centre* (1148 Broadway

South, Williams Lake, V2G 1A2; 250–392–5025; fax: 250–392–4214; visitors@telus.net; www.bcadventure.com/wlcc) at the crossroads of Highways 97 and 20 and pick up even more information on the area.

If it's delicious specialty coffees, salads, soups, wraps, desserts, or frittatas (and more) that you're after, you won't go wrong at the **Beanstalk Coffee Company** (phone/fax: 250–392–5656; www.the beanstalk.com) at 180 Third Avenue North. An armchair-friendly atmosphere plus local entertainment at 8:00 P.M. every Saturday night (jazz, blues, acoustic folk music, etc.) is what's offered. Pick up a book in the adjoining new library near the corner of Third Avenue and Borland and settle back for a truly relaxing (and delicious) respite.

Golfers can play till they drop at the **Williams Lake Golf & Tennis Club** (104 Fairview Drive, Box 4006, Williams Lake, V2G 2V2, 250–392–6026/6548), where a special daily eighteen-hole rate is offered. The fairways overlook the town and the attractive lake with the Chilcotin hills in the background. Nongolfers can take in the view and enjoy a meal in the dining room. It's close to town—take Highway 20 south to Fairview Drive.

As you drive farther north in the Cariboo, you have a chance to experience hands-on both the native history and the more modern gold rush history. First, at **Xats'ull Heritage Village** (Soda Creek First Nation Site 15, Comp. 12, RR 4, Williams Lake, V2G 4M8; 250–989–2323; fax: 250–989–2300; heritagevillage@xatsull.com; www.xatsull.com), 23 miles (37 km) north of Williams Lake near Soda Creek Reserve, you'll be able to experience the spiritual and cultural magic of a Shuswap heritage village set a few miles south of highway down a narrow, winding, unpaved road. There are one-day programs (Tuesday, Thursday, and Saturday 10:00 A.M. to 4:00 P.M. from June to fall) at Xats'ull (pronounced "hat-shul"), where you can learn beading, basketmaking, and traditional food preparation. Stay in teepees and reconstructed pit houses (*kekulis*) on the high banks of the Fraser River and become spiritually cleansed and rejuvenated in sweat lodges. Ancient petroglyphs can be found near the teepee circle, where you can listen to traditional storytelling and discuss the old ways with Shuswap elders for an experience different from any other you're likely to have in the Cariboo.

Quesnel

From Xats'ull Heritage Village Highway 97 continues north, parallel to the Fraser River for another 51 miles (82 km) to Quesnel. This is where the hands-on gold rush experience starts—where the Fraser and Quesnel Rivers meet. From here, back in the 1860s, thousands of gold seekers left the Fraser and trekked east to historic Barkerville. *Quesnel* is dubbed "Gold Pan City," loudly proclaimed by the *World's Largest Gold Pan,* located north of the city at the junction of Highways 97N and 26E. The *Quesnel Visitor Info Centre* is downtown in LeBourdais Park at 703 Carson Avenue, Quesnel, V2J 2B6 (250–992–8716 or 800–992–4922; fax: 250–992–2181; qvisitor@quesnelbc.com; www.northcariboo.com). Ask there about gold panning in the Quesnel River, or phone the Gold Commissioner (250–992–4313) for details first, or you could unwittingly become a claim-jumper. At low water during fall, you're most likely to strike it rich!

Next door to the Info Centre is the *Quesnel & District Museum and Archives* (705 Carson Avenue, Quesnel, V2J 2B6; 250–992–9580; fax: 250–992–9680; rstubbs@city.quesnel.bc.ca; www.sd28.bc.ca/museum/), one of the best small museums in BC. The museum houses a rare collection of nineteenth-century Chinese items and the enigmatic Mandy—see below for details. The major fun event in Quesnel is held the third week of July with four days of revelry called *Billy Barker Days.* If you're visiting in late January, don't miss the *Gold Rush Trail Sled Dog Mail Run,* which ends with festivities in Wells at the *Wells Winter Carnival.* For more information visit www.wellsbc.com.

Mysterious Mandy

Since 1991, staff at the **Quesnel Museum** at 705 Carson Avenue have been feeling a little creepy. Several antique dolls reside there, but none so unusual as the eighty-year-old Mandy, who came to live at the museum after many years in a local resident's basement. The resident had often heard a baby's cry coming from the basement but on investigation could find nothing. Mysteriously, after the doll's departure, the resident was no longer disturbed by the crying. Today Mandy sits in the museum, smiling awkwardly, several deep cracks disfiguring her head, and one eye wandering disconcertingly. Before she arrived, the aura in the museum was tranquil, even fun. But after she arrived, that aura was disturbed and "things" started to happen until the curator, both to contain the doll's ghostly spirit and to prevent more havoc than she had already caused, placed her in another room inside her own special glass case. On two separate occasions attempts were made to develop photos of Mandy in two different labs. In one case contact sheets mysteriously disintegrated, and in the other the lab was found in disarray! Things are tranquil now. Could Mandy have calmed down when she realized that the museum was safe? Who knows, but many visitors to the museum are still spooked.

With two rivers passing through Quesnel, how could it help but be attractive? But it wasn't always so. The town has been spruced up now with the very attractive ***River-Front Trail*** system, which consists of the 3-mile (5-km) North Quesnel Trail and the 2.6-mile (4.3-km) West Side Trail (along the shores of the Fraser River and Baker Creek). Here you can see the city at your leisure and meet a few locals at the same time. Ask at the Info Centre for a guide.

Six miles (10km) north of Quesnel there's a very popular campground. ***Ten Mile Lake Provincial Campground*** (www.bcparks.ca, search "Ten") has sixty lakeside (camping) sites and eighty-two touring (RV parking) sites. The camping sites are reservable (800–689–9025; www.discovercamping.ca). It's a relaxing spot to watch beautiful sunsets over the lake while the locals fish in float-tubes. The showers here are excellent—one looney ($1.00) for five minutes. Sites cost $15.00 plus $7.50 for each additional vehicle.

From Quesnel a turnoff 3 miles (5 km) north at the junction of Highways 97 and 26 leads 55 miles (88 km) to ***Barkerville Historic Town*** (Box 19, Barkerville, V0K 1B0; 250–994–3332), now fully restored and surely one of British Columbia's most remote, yet biggest, tourist attractions. It's a walk back into those fascinating gold rush days of yore. In summer (when admission is charged) all activities, from live theater to guided tours, are in full swing. Barkerville is open 8:00 A.M. to 8:00 P.M. year-round.

Between Wells and Barkerville on Highway 26, a 14-mile (23-km) road leads northeast to ***Bowron Lake Provincial Park*** (www.bcparks.ca, search "bowron lake"; 250–398–4530 for information), one of North America's premier canoeing circuits. Six major lakes connected by several smaller lakes provide solitude and scenery unsurpassed, with plenty of wildlife as well. To paddle in the park, you need a park permit, which costs from $60 per one-person canoe/kayak or from $120 per two- or three-person canoe/kayak. Voyageur canoe permits cost $60 per person. In summer phone (800) HELLOBC (435–5622); outside North America phone (250) 387–1642. Payment must be made at the time of reservation (there is an $18 non-refundable fee applied) by Visa or Mastercard only.

You could take the easy way out by staying at ***Becker's Lodge*** (Highway 26, Bowron Lake, Box 129, Wells, V0K 2R0; 250–992–8864 or 800–808–4761; fax: 250–992–8893; radio phone: N698552 Wells

Channel; info@beckerslodge.ca; www.beckers lodge.ca). Relax in one of the cabins or go completely "wild" and sign up for a weeklong canoe trip. You'll camp in such idyllic spots as Indian Point Lake, Wolverine Bay, Rum Lake, and Spectacle Lake. The all-inclusive guided tour costs $1,650 plus GST, or stay overnight at rates starting at $70. Perhaps rent a canoe for the day. Park permits are not needed for day rentals. Keep in mind that there are no regular phone lines to Bowron Lake. To get there go through Wells, and 0.6 miles (1 km) before Barkerville, turn left to Bowron Lake. After 13 miles (24 km) along a good gravel road, you'll see the BECKERS sign and their Trading Post Store. A transfer service is available from Quesnel.

The Freedom Highway

I t was the summer of 1953, and the folks in the Chilcotin were tired of hearing that a road couldn't be put through to the coast. George Dalshaug started from the west, and Alf Bracewell pushed downward from the east. They would show them. And show them they did. On September 26, 1953, Dalshaug and Bracewell touched bulldozer blades and shook hands; thus, BC's last frontier, the vast Chilcotin, was laid open. Today the *Freedom Highway* (Highway 20—also known as the Bella Coola Road) is a tribute to those stubborn souls who said it *could* be done. To describe the whole of the enormous, dramatic Chilcotin Coast area, which is served by the Freedom Highway, is a book in itself. This small section will hopefully give you enough of an adventurous nudge that you'll be tempted to explore it. As services on the highway are limited, careful planning is in order: Before you set out make sure that your vehicle is in top-notch order and that you have adequate safety equipment and a good map. Staff at the Williams Lake Visitor Info Centre (250–392–5052) have prepared a two-page pamphlet on Highway 20 (*The Chilcotin—Highway 20 Guide)* outlining services and interesting spots along the road. For up-to-date information from afar, phone the Cariboo Chilcotin Coast Tourist Association at (800) 663–5885; (250) 392–2226; fax: (250) 392–2838; or write to 118A North First Avenue, Williams Lake V2G 1Y8; cta@landwithoutlimits.com; www. landwithoutlimits.com.

From Williams Lake to the west coast at Bella Coola, you'll cover 288 miles (463 km), of which 212 miles (341 km) are paved or sealcoated. Without question the section most talked about is *The Hill,* a 27-mile (43-km) steep, narrow stretch, the most memorable part of which is a 5.5-mile (9-km) series of gravel switchbacks (with grades to a nail-biting 18 percent) that descend through the 5,000-foot (1,524-m) Heckman Pass in *Tweedsmuir Provincial Park* (BC's largest) into the *Bella Coola Valley.* You might ask yourself, why risk this baptism of fire? There are three answers.

The first is that the views in the Chilcotin of wide-open spaces, crystal-clear lakes, thick-forested mountains, marshes, and meadows, palettes of wildflowers, and the majestic Bella Coola Valley, home of the mythical thunderbird, are second to none. You're also likely to encounter wandering bears and head-knocking California bighorn sheep.

Trivia

In 1935 in an area just above Taseko Lake, seven men were left working in a gold mining camp, well-stocked with supplies for the winter. At breakup runners who were sent in to make a routine check were astonished to find the camp empty. Everyone had disappeared—but there were some human bones lying about. Then a body, presumably that of the cook who may have been collecting supplies, was found in a root cellar. Apparently, an avalanche had occurred while he was in the cellar, sealing it off from the air and preserving the only body of the seven.

The second reason is the people you will meet: people who are not "chicken" to try a new venture and who love their Chilcotin. People like the Christensens of Anahim Lake, who for more than one hundred years—three generations of the family—have provided service as *A. C. Christensen General Merchants* (Box 3449, Christensen Road, Anahim Lake, V0L 1C0; 250–742–3266). Outside, the store is decorated with a mural of rearing stallions. The Christensen motto is "If we don't have it, you don't need it." Present owners, the McLeans, give a double-or-nothing guarantee with purchases. Flip a coin, and if you win, it costs nothing; if you lose—well, you did agree to double or nothing!

A detour south of Tatla Lake will bring you to folks like the Bracewells at Circle X Ranch. The family runs *Bracewell's Alpine Wilderness Adventures* (Box 8, Tatlayoko Lake, V0L 1W0; 866–476–1169; phone/fax: 250–476–1169; alex@bracewell.com; www.bcadventure.com/bracewell; www.bracewell.com). During the day they'll take you riding the ranges and in the evening may show home movies of Alf Bracewell's impressive road-building feat. Ask Alex and Connie about their new houseboat venture on Tatlayoko and Chilko Lakes. These piloted boats are suitable for two couples or a family of four. A two-night stay aboard, followed by an exciting ATV guided tour, could make for the most incredible wilderness holiday of your lifetime.

Recommended Reading—Cariboo Chilcotin Coast

FOR ADULTS:

Cabin at Singing River, by Chris Czajkowski. Raincoast, 2002. Modern pioneering adventures in BC's Coast Mountains.

Backroads Explorer Volume 1, Thompson Cariboo, by Murphy Shewchuk. Maclean Hunter, Vancouver, 1985. This book is a wonderful in-depth source with detailed maps and historical snippets.

Looking Back at the Cariboo-Chilcotin, by Irene Stangoe. Heritage House Publishing Company, Surrey, 1997.

Stein Valley Wilderness Guidebook, by Gordon R. White. Stein Wilderness Alliance, 1991.

Gold Panning in the Cariboo—A Prospector's Treasure Trail to Creeks of Gold, by Jim Lewis and Charles Hart. Heritage House Publishing Ltd., 1997.

Cariboo Chilcotin, Pioneer People and Places, by Irene Stangoe. Heritage House Publishing Company, Surrey, 1994.

They Call it the Cariboo, by Robin Skelton. Sono Nis Press, Victoria, 1980.

Stagecoach and Sternwheel Days in the Cariboo and Central British Columbia, by Willis J. West. Heritage House Publishing Company Ltd., Surrey, 1985.

FOR KIDS:

Three Against Time, by Margaret Taylor. Orca Books, 1997. Three boys are taken back in time to the great Barkerville fire—a gold rush story. For grades four to seven.

Chilko Lake is in Ts'yl-os Provincial Park (250–398–4414). It is the largest natural high-elevation freshwater lake in North America. Fishing enters a new realm here, with rainbow and Dolly Varden trout reaching twenty-two pounds (10 kg). You'll find exciting rafting on the Chilko River (featured in the Alan Alda movie *The White Mile*), with thrilling rapid drops that thunder through spectacular scenery, including one section through Lava Canyon that provides an adrenalin rush for 12 miles (19 km).

Contact **Chilko River Expeditions** (3831 Loloff Crescent, Quesnel, V2J 6E3; 250–398–6711; rafting@chilkoriver.com; www.chilkoriver. com) and get set for a true wilderness rafting trip that will leave you exhilarated. Ts'yl-os (sounds like "sigh-loss") Provincial Park (www. bcparks.ca, search "Ts") is situated about 100 miles (160 km) south-west of Williams Lake and is one of BC's newest (1994) parks. There are two main routes into the park, and two campgrounds—one at the end of each route. Both routes take four to six hours (depending on weather) from Williams Lake. Keep a sharp eye out for bald eagles and peregrine falcons. Accommodation is available at **Chilko Lake Resort** (Box 17, Tatla Lake, V0L 1V0; 250–481–3333; fax: 250–481–3334; holiday@chilkolake.com; www.chilkolake.com), located a four-hour drive west of Williams Lake. Rates at this luxury wilderness resort start at $145 and include the use of the swimming pool, sauna, hot tub, tennis court, games room, canoes, pedal boats, and fishing rods. There are also packages available that include air transportation to and from Vancouver, just over an hour away.

Nearer the coast, halfway between Hagensborg and Bella Coola, you'll meet people like Barb of **Barb's Pottery** (Box 363, Bella Coola, V0T 1C0; 250–799–5380; www.bellacoola.ca). Barb's studio, where she creates lovely stoneware, raku, and porcelain pottery, is in an early 1900s log heritage building of a type constructed by Norwegian settlers who arrived in Bella Coola in 1894. Note the hand-hewn cedar logs and dovetailed corners. Look for the ARTISAN sign on the highway.

Hagensborg has an attractive, shady RV park, **The Gnome's Home** (Box 730, Bella Coola, V0T 1C0; 250–982–2504; fax: 250–982–2448; gnome@belco.bc.ca; www.gnomeshome.ca) that is just a few minutes' walk to the store, pub, and swimming pool, and is just a ten-minute drive to Bella Coola. It has hot showers, a laundry, a cooking shelter, hookups, and free firewood. If you're up for a little back-roading, ask at the campground about the 12-mile (20-km) West Nusatsum Forestry road to the impressive **Odegaard Falls Recreation Site.** You'll also see a few glaciers on the way. An easy walk through old-growth forest brings you to a viewpoint with the awesome spray-filled falls cascading about 600 feet (200 m) down into the East Nusatsum Valley, right in front of you. It's a don't-miss sight, of which there are many in this area, including the **Odegaard Glacier,** visible above the timberline at the head of the east fork of the **Nusatsum River.**

The third tongue-in-cheek reason for driving the Freedom Highway is that you can then honestly flaunt a bumper sticker (if they don't exist, they soon will): I SURVIVED THE HILL!

You finally emerge from the lushly forested Bella Coola Valley, home of the Coast Salish Nuxalk nation, to the fresh ocean smells and dockside activity of Bella Coola, attractively decorated with native art, at the head of North Bentinck Arm, in total contrast with the dramatic pinnacles, blessed with names like Stupendous Mountain and Matterhorn Peak, so recently passed. Valleys, fjords, countless islands, and thousands of miles of wilderness coastline are waiting to be explored. Breathe in the clean ocean air while hiking the *Gray Jay Lake Trail,* which crosses wetlands to scenic fjords, or the *Big Cedar Tree Forest Recreation Site,* which protects a magnificent 16-feet-across red cedar. It's off the South Bentinck Arm Road, 29 miles (47 km) south of Bella Coola. Take a run along North Bentinck Arm through the Labrouchere and Dean channels into Cousins Inlet for 60 miles (97 km) to Ocean Falls, where lodges such as *Walls' Fish Camp* (66 Highland Drive, Ocean Falls, V0T 1P0; 800–656–7476; fax: 250–289–3307; www.westcoastfishing.com) bring keen fishers from all over the world in search of freshwater trout, chinook salmon to sixty pounds, and halibut to ninety pounds. There's more information on the area at www.centralcoastbc.com, www.bellacoola.ca, and www.oceanfallsbc.com.

And finally, if you're reluctant to retrace your Freedom Highway steps, consider booking a passage aboard BC Ferries (888–BCFERRY; www.bcferries.com). Ships leave from Bella Coola every two days from June to September (early morning) on a fourteen- to twenty-four-hour sail (depending on stops). You'll land in Port Hardy, from which you can drive the length of Vancouver Island to Victoria.

PLACES TO STAY IN THE CARIBOO CHILCOTIN

70 MILE HOUSE
Little Horse Lodge,
Green Lake Road North,
Comp 1, Site E,
RR 1, 70 Mile House,
V0K 2K0; (250) 456–7524.
fax: (250) 456–7512;
www.littlehorselodge.com.
Lodge, cabins, or
campsites.

108 MILE RANCH
The Hills Health Ranch,
Box 26, 108 Mile Ranch,
V0K 2Z0; (250) 791–5225;
fax: (250) 791–6384;
www.thehillshealthranch.
com

BOWRON LAKE
Becker's Lodge,
Highway 26, Bowron Lake,
Box 129, Wells, V0K 2R0;
(250) 992–8864;
(800) 808–4761;
fax: (250) 992–8893;
radio phone: N698552
Wells Channel;
www.beckerslodge.ca.
Wilderness
accommodation.

CHILKO LAKE
Chilko Lake Resort,
Box 17, Tatla Lake,
V0L 1V0; (250) 481–3333;
fax: (250) 481–3334;
holiday@chilkolake.com;
www.chilkolake.com.
Wilderness accommodation four hours west of
Williams Lake.

CLINTON
Cariboo Lodge Resort,
Box 459, Clinton,
V0K 1K0; (877) 459–7992;
(250) 459–7992; fax: (250)
459–0060;
cariboo-lodge@
goldtrail.com;
www.cariboolodgebc.com.

LILLOOET
Sturgeon Bay Bed & Breakfast, 130 Haylmore Place,
Box 1130, V0K 1V0; (250)
256–7792; www.sturgeon
baybb.com.

Bountiful Gardens,
5 Sundial Drive, V0K 1V0;
(250) 256–4355.

LONE BUTTE
Loon Bay Resort,
C1 Airmail Road,
Lone Butte,
V0K 1X0; (250) 593–4431;
fax: (250) 593–4188;
loonbay@bcinternet.net.
Cabins and campsites on
Sheridan Lake.

OCEAN FALLS
Walls' Fish Camp,
66 Highland Drive, V0T
1P0; (800) 656–7476;
fax: (250) 289–3307;
www.westcoastfishing.com.

WILLIAMS LAKE
Rowat's Waterside Bed and
Breakfast,
1397 Borland Road,
Williams Lake,
V2G 1M3; (250) 392–7395;
(866) 392–7395;
www.wlakebb.com.

PLACES TO EAT IN THE CARIBOO-CHILCOTIN

BELLA COOLA
Valley Inn Restaurant,
(250) 799–0045. Seafood,
burgers, chow mein.

CACHE CREEK
Ashcroft Manor Teahouse,
Box 127, Cache Creek,
V0K 1H0; (250) 453–9983.
Excellent meals in a
historic roadhouse.

HAGENSBORG
The Bentinck Arms Pub at
The Bay Motor Hotel,
Highway 20,
Box 216,
Bella Coola,
V0T 1C0; (888) 982–2212
or (250) 982–2212;
fax: (250) 982–2330;
bayhotel@bcadventure.com;
www.baymotorhotel.ca.
Nine miles (14 km) east of
Bella Coola. Patio cafe and
coffee shop. Free shuttle to
ferry terminal or airport.
Accommodations, too.

LILLOOET
Dina's Place,
690 Main Street;
(250) 256–4264.
Greek and Italian food.

Lillooet Bakery,
719 Main Street;
(250) 256–4889. European
style; baked goods.

WILLIAMS LAKE
Beanstalk Coffee Company,
180 Third Avenue North,
phone/fax: (250)
392–5656. Near the library
at Third and Borland, offering soups, salads, wraps,
desserts, and specialty
coffees.

The Northeast

*O*nly since the completion of the Alaska Highway in 1942 has even a scant section of this huge, beautiful region been easily accessible to tourists. From the Yellowhead/Trans-Canada Highway junction at Tête Jaune Cache, we'll follow the Fraser River northwest to Prince George, British Columbia's fourth-largest city. From here we'll head to the big skies of the Peace River district and Dawson Creek, where we'll tackle the legendary Alaska Highway to the Yukon border. In total the journey will be more than 930 miles (1,500 km) through some of the most spectacular scenery the province has to offer.

Following the Fraser to Prince George

*A*bout twenty minutes northwest of Tête Jaune Cache on Highway 16, there's an easily missed sign to *Dunster.* Go down the hill and just after a one-lane Bailey bridge, take the first right to the end of the road. Another right and you're at *Bonnie and Curtis Culp's farm*; perhaps just follow the smell of the wool. Peacocks, llamas, and sheep roam near antique sheep wagons built for herders one hundred years ago. The Culps have redecorated the wagons to operate a unique bed-and-breakfast business. The double beds are covered with Bonnie's quilts, filled with wool from their sheep. Some wagons have woodstoves, and all are decorated and repainted in their original brilliant colors by the Culps' daughter Kitty. Double accommodation (by pre-booking only, no drop-ins) is $50, including breakfast. If prearranged, other meals can be served. In early June join lilac lovers on the free annual *Lilac Walk and Tea Party*. The property boasts more than one hundred lilac cultivars. Call ahead for exact dates. You can contact the Culps at Station Road, Dunster, V0J 1J0; (250) 968–4309.

Another choice for get-away-from-it-all accommodation is *The Mother Land Inn* (River Road, Dunster, V0J 1J0; 250–968–4356; arlene@bcnorthweb.com; www.bcnorthweb.com/motherland). Turn right before

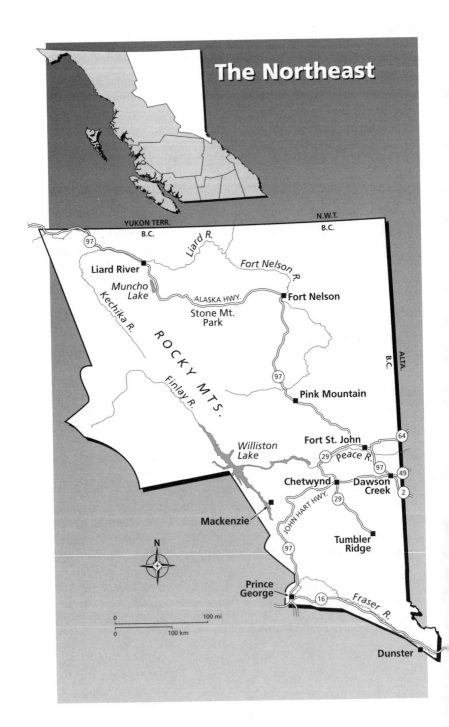

The Northeast

YUKON TERR.
B.C.

N.W.T.
B.C.

97

Liard River

Liard R.

Fort Nelson R.

Muncho Lake

ALASKA HWY.

Fort Nelson

Kechika R.

Stone Mt. Park

R O C K Y   M T S.

ALTA.
B.C.

Finlay R.

97

Pink Mountain

Williston Lake

Fort St. John

64

29

Peace R.

97

49

Chetwynd

Dawson Creek

2

Mackenzie

JOHN HART HWY.

29

97

Tumbler Ridge

N

Prince George

16

Fraser R.

0   100 mi
0   100 km

Dunster

**AUTHOR'S TOP TEN PICKS
IN THE NORTHEAST**

*Strider Adventures
llama treks*

*Fraser–Fort George
Regional Museum*

*Huble Homestead, north of
Prince George*

Peace Canyon Dam

W.A.C. Bennett Dam

*Kinuseo Falls near
Tumbler Ridge*

*Fort St. John–North
Peace Museum*

*Stone Mountain
Provincial Park*

Muncho Lake

Liard River Hot Springs

the bridge and drive to the end of River Road. This remote but cozy log house property, which sleeps eight, is available for rent at $1,000 per week (one-week minimum July and August), including the use of a wood-fired sauna. It's a wonderful getaway for a family, group, or a romantic twosome wanting some space. Gourmet meals can be arranged. There's a fully equipped kitchen (seats twenty-four), showers, and bathroom available for camp-style living for larger groups, as well as bed-and-breakfast accommodation ($75 double). With 168 acres (68 ha) and more than 2.5 miles (4 km) of river frontage, there are plenty of activities offered—canoeing, birding, hiking the ridges and riverbank trails, or simply relaxing in pristine, awe-inspiring surroundings.

Back on the road into Dunster, drive for a mile or so to the **Dunster General Store** (250–968–4488). Cathy Greenhough and partners sell everything and anything in this eclectic grocery-cum-post-office-cum-hardware store. It's the epicenter for a community of about 150 families who ranch, farm, log, and create in this quiet rural area. Ask Cathy about the **Dunster Farmers' Market,** held

Fur-Out Friendliness

*A*n old black car sat abandoned in a field, a television intriguingly propped on its hood, encouraging me to explore more of this laid-back area in BC's northeast. It was 1996. I stopped at the nearby Dunster store and met Claude Hill. He has loved this Robson Valley since he came here hunting in the sixties and has worked at everything from logging to highway construction. But he has "never looked back" since he "picked up the store" in 1973.

"It's a fantastic community," he enthused, between selling eggs and stamping mail.

He told me of a board game called Fur Out, for "Ages 10–110," invented by local trappers Rod and Deb Reimer.

"A whole bunch of us invested, thinking we had the new Trivia," he joked. When I left Hill's Store, Claude was explaining how he was happily anchored to this neighborly community.

"Someone will always need a rat trap, so you just can't go away," he said, insistently tucking a game of Fur Out under my arm.

in the parking lot of the Community Hall most Saturday mornings in July, August, and September. Locals bring fresh produce and home-baked goods, and as well there's a friendly old-fashioned flea market. Across the street from the store is the old *Dunster Train Station,* one of the last of the original CNR train stations built in the early 1900s.

Continue south on gravel road, watching on the right for *Terri's Attempts* (Box 20, Dunster, V0J 1J0; 250–968–4468). Terri creates hand-stitched teddy bears, reverse appliqué wall hangings, dream catchers, and other craft items.

Seven and a half miles (12 km) southeast of Dunster is an area called South Croydon. When the railways were being built, the village of South Croydon was a lively spot. Now only a few stalwarts remain. At the foot of the Old South Croydon Ferry Road is *Mountain Pottery* (250–968–4310), where Stefi McLean's studio overflows with aesthetic, medium-fired porcelain. It's an unlikely discovery on a sheep farm set in the fertile Robson Valley.

If you don't mind a little dust or mud on your vehicle, you might want to drive farther south and try your luck at hooking a few rainbow trout in *Shere Lake.* This recreation area makes for an excellent picnic spot. It's about 14 miles (23 km) from Dunster. A mile or so on, hikers can enjoy a ninety-minute steep hike from Kiwa Lake to the forestry lookout tower on Shere Point. The superb views extend to Valemount and McBride. And yet another valley viewpoint is found 6 miles (10 km) farther southeast at Watertank Hill. Watch for wildlife in the slough by the road as you continue on toward Tête Jaune Cache. If you're visiting between mid-August and mid-September, don't miss the McLennan River salmon spawning area, just past the original village site of Tête Jaune Cache, once a busy hub for both railroad and riverboat traffic near the confluence of the Fraser and Robson Rivers.

You're back on the tar now. Nine miles (14 km) northwest of the junction is *Terracana Resort and Chalets* (12155 Yellowhead Highway 16 West, Box 909, Valemount, V0E 2Z0; 866–968–4304; 250–968–4304; fax: 250–968–4445; chalets@terracana.com; www.terracana.com). Located on the Fraser River, and with views of the mountains second to none, this resort is much more than just a place to sleep. Jet-boat tours, guided canoeing, horseback riding, and hiking as well as several winter sports are but the beginning of a host of activities offered. Rates for double accommodation in modern chalets start at $89. The chalets are available year-round.

Robson Valley Fall Fair,
McBride; August; (250) 569–0321

**Prince George and District
Music Festival,**
Prince George; February/March;
phone/fax: (250) 962–7927/7020;
www.pgmusicfestival.com

Prince George Rodeo, Prince George;
August; (250) 964–0389 or
(800) 668–7646;
www.pgwhatson.ca/pgrodeo

**Saulteaux First Nations
Pemmican Days,** Moberly Lake;
June/July; (250) 788–3345

Alexander Mackenzie Day,
Mackenzie; June; (250) 997–5775

Peace County Bluegrass Festival,
Dawson Creek; July;
(250) 782–9325;
www.peacebluegrass.ca

Tumbler Ridge Grizfest,
Tumbler Ridge; August;
(250) 242–4246;
www.grizfest.com

**Dawson Creek and District Fall
Fair Exhibition, Stampede, & Pro
Rodeo,** Dawson Creek; August;
(250) 782–9595 or (888) 645–3022

**World's Invitational Gold Panning
Championship,** Taylor; August;
(250) 789–3004/3392

North Peace Fall Fair, Fort St. John;
August; (250) 785–2020/6037

Fort Nelson Rodeo, Fort Nelson;
August; (250) 774–1035

Snow Daze, Prince George; February;
(250) 564–3737

McBride, a town that owes its beginnings to the Grand Trunk Railway, is 41 miles (66 km) northwest of Tête Jaune Cache. Logging and farming are the main industries in this scenic Robson Valley location. A display of local art, crafts, and photography can be seen at the **Whistle Stop Gallery** (Main Street and First Avenue, McBride, V0J 2E0) in the newly renovated historic CN railway station. Hours are from 9:00 A.M. to 4:00 P.M., but phone (250) 569–8891 for extended hours in summer. Bird lovers will enjoy the **Horseshoe Lake Bird Viewing Station,** where swans, Canada geese, blue herons, and goldeneye ducks can be observed. It's but a short distance from downtown. A wheelchair-accessible viewing platform leads out over the lake. To get there, turn left off Main Street onto Second Avenue, then left onto Horseshoe Lake Road. There are few services on the lonely Yellowhead Highway after McBride, and as Prince George is another 125 miles (202 km), make sure to top up the gas tank. For information on restaurants and accommodation in the area phone the **McBride Info Centre** at (250) 569–3366 or e-mail mcbride@mcbridebc.com.

Prince George

Prince George (PG to northerners) has all the amenities of a modern city. With a population of 76,008 (2002), the city enjoys first-class live theater, its own symphony orchestra, a university, and modern museums and art galleries. But with 1,500 lakes in the area (it's dubbed the "Lakes and Rivers District") and 140 parks in the city alone, PG has managed to maintain a laid-back, northern atmosphere.

You'll see what I mean if you have a day or two to spend with *Strider Adventures* (17075 Perry Road East, Prince George, V2K 5E3; 800–665–7752 or 250–963–9542; fax: 250–963–8446; strider@bcgroup.net; www.pgweb.com/strider). They'll take you packing out onto alpine trails with calm, inquisitive llamas on either half-day hikes or two-, three-, six-, and seven-day camping adventures. The llamas do all the work; you just have to walk and enjoy the scent of the wildflowers and the superb scenery. The turnoff to Strider Adventures is at the WILLOW RIVER AND UPPER FRASER sign on the Yellowhead Highway, 10 miles (16 km) east of the Yellowhead Bridge in Prince George. Take the first turn right for 2 miles (3 km) to the A-frame at 17075 East Perry Road. Phone to book or check Dan and Dorothy's Web page for details.

Prince George is conveniently located where two major highways, two prominent rivers, and two railway lines intersect, making it a lively transportation hub. Restaurants are plentiful, as are accommodations—in fact, you might call it Bed-and-Breakfast City. Phone (888) 266–5555 or (250) 561–BEDS or visit www.princegeorge.com/bnb to link to a large selection of B&Bs in PG.

One of the newer sights to take in is the $5 million *Two Rivers Art Gallery* (725 Civic Plaza, Prince George, V2L 5T1; 888–221–1155 or 250–614–7800; fax: 250–563–3211; www.tworiversartgallery.com), which has displays of local and regional artists exhibited in a state-of-the-art gallery next to the *Civic Center Plaza,* which is opposite *Connaught Hill Park* (a good spot for a view of the city and a picnic). If you're interested in native arts and crafts, try the *Prince George Native Art Gallery* in the nonprofit Native Friendship Center. Here, while learning some First Nations' history, you can also purchase a souvenir of the true north directly from the artists—items range from mukluks and moccasins to beaded jewelry and original paintings. The gallery is at 1600 Third Avenue, V2L 3G6; (250) 614–7726. Or for more information visit the Web site at www.pgnfc.com.

If you're still seeking history, visit *Fort George Park* on the banks of the Fraser River and *The Exploration Place,* operated by the **Fraser–Fort George Regional Museum** (333 Becott Place, Box 1779, Prince George, V2L 4V7; 250–562–1612; fax: 250–562–6395; info@theexplorationplace.com; www.the explorationplace.com). This is the site of the original Hudson's Bay Trading Post. Displays give a good overview of the area's history, and as well there's a hands-on **Northwood Explorations Gallery**. The Discovery Boxes are educational and fun for the kids. In summer a miniature 1912 steam train chugs around, picking up kids at the historic station in the park. For the true trainaholic the **Prince George Railway and Forest Industry Museum** (850 River Road, V26 5S8; 250–563–7351; fax: 250–563–3697; trains@ pgrfm. bc.ca; www.pgrfm.bc.ca) is a hands-on railway experience. It's next to Cottonwood Island Park, where the Nechako and Fraser Rivers meet.

There's lots more to do in PG, so much so that the **Prince George Visitor Info Centre** has set up two offices: one on the corner of Victoria Street and Fifteenth Avenue (250–562–3700) and a summer site (250–563–5493) at the junction of Highways 16 and 97. They also regularly update an events Web site: www.afterhours.org. Contact them from outside the area by phoning (800) 668–7646; (250) 562–3700; fax: (250) 563–3584; or by writing to them at 1198 Victoria Street, Prince George, V2L 2L2. The e-mail address is tourism@initiativespg.com, and the Web site is www. tourismpg.com.

Worth Seeing/Doing in the Northeast

Watch beavers swimming in the pond at Forests for the World Park in Prince George.

Visit the Little Prairie Heritage Museum in Chetwynd (beautiful antique quilts).

Paddle the Fort Nelson River from Fort Nelson.

Float down the Liard River in a raft.

Take a train trip on VIA Rail's The Skeena for a memorable two-day trip from Prince Rupert to Jasper, Alberta.

Enjoy colorful skies as the northern lights (aurora borealis) dance over Fort Nelson.

Hike the 7-mile (11-km) Heritage River Trails in Prince George.

Join a forestry or mill tour in Fort St. John.

Tour Walter Wright Pioneer Village in Dawson Creek. See the log school-house, the smithy, general store, two churches, and a trapper's cabin.

See the best fossil collection in the Peace River area at Hudson's Hope Museum.

North to Peace River Country

From Prince George we leave the Fraser River and cross the Nechako River past thinning suburbs and rolling farmlands along the John Hart Highway (97 North). Twenty-five miles (40 km) north is the **Huble Homestead**, now part of a regional park. In 1900 a trapper named Albert Huble operated a trading post from here. The business

Trivia

became a regular stop for steamboats running the Fraser River to Tête Jaune Cache. Today the steamboats are gone, but Huble Homestead remains as a historic site and a popular hiking area. To get there follow the signs from the highway for 4 miles (6 km) along Mitchell Road. The site includes the Giscome Portage Interpretive Centre, the original 1912 log house, the 1914 general store, farm animals, a blacksmith shop, and other heritage buildings. Costumed staff work at the site, gardening and demonstrating tasks from the May long weekend to the Labor Day weekend in September. Contact the Huble Homestead/Giscome Portage Heritage Society (202–1685 Third Avenue, Prince George, V2L 3G5; phone/fax: 250–564–7033; hublehomestead@mag-net.com) for more information. From the homestead, a pleasant hike, the *Giscome Portage Trail,* runs for 5 miles (8.5 km) northwest to a pull-out on Highway 97. Eighty miles (130 km) north of Prince George is the tiny community of *McLeod Lake,* the longest continuously occupied European settlement in BC. About 6 miles (10 km) south of the community is a beautiful water playground with a sandy beach—*Whiskers Point Provincial Park* (www.bcparks.ca, search "Whiskers"). It has sixty-nine sites (about ten of them on the lake), flush toilets, an excellent playground, trails, and a covered eating area. It's the perfect summer holiday spot.

Ninety-eight miles (158 km) north of Prince George on Highway 97, there's a turnoff to Mackenzie, which is located on the shores of *Williston Lake,* North America's largest man-made reservoir. A 2-mile (3-km) drive north of town takes you up *Morfee Mountain* for a spectacular view of the lake through the unpolluted crystalline air of the Rockies. Mackenzie was named for fur trader and explorer Alexander Mackenzie, who camped nearby in 1793, during his historic journey to Bella Coola on the coast. The town is a pulp, paper, and lumber manufacturing center, surrounded by countless logging roads to access the multitude of rivers and lakes. It's also home to the world's largest *tree crusher,* weighing 177 tons (160 metric tons), which was used to clear timber to form the 746-mile (1,200-km) shoreline of Williston Lake. It sits in state on Mackenzie Boulevard. For information on the area, contact the Chamber of Commerce (88 Centennial Drive, Box 880, Mackenzie, V0J 2C0; 877–622–5360; 250–997–5459; fax: 250–997–6117; mchamber@macbc.com; www.mackenzie chamber.bc.ca) year-round.

The next town traveling northeast along Highway 97 is **Chetwynd,** The Gateway to the Peace Country, 190 miles (306 km) north of Prince George. It's here that you decide whether to go north to Fort St. John via the **Bennett Dam** or east via Dawson Creek. The former is very scenic, following the Peace River to join the Alaska Highway 8 miles (13 km) north of Fort St. John; the latter is slightly longer but will take you to Mile Zero of the Alaska Highway.

Those traveling to Alberta might consider doing a circle tour through Chetwynd along Highway 29 north to Hudson's Hope and Fort St. John, then south through **Taylor** to Dawson Creek, west 11 miles (17 km) on Highway 97 to **Arras,** and south along the **Heritage Highway** 60 miles (98 km) to Tumbler Ridge. Then head north on Highway 29 back to Highway 97 (near Chetwynd), then east for 60 miles (98 km) back to Dawson Creek and on to Alberta. You'll have covered it all, and in 330 miles (532 km) of paved roads, you'll have retraced your steps only 11 miles (17 km).

While in Chetwynd try out the **Leisure Pool,** which includes a wave pool, a hot tub, and a dry sauna. Another activity is to take a walk round to seek out the **Chetwynd Chainsaw Sculptures**. After being greeted by three huge bears at the entrance, you're sure to want to see more of the two dozen or so carvings that decorate the town. Ask at the **Visitor Info Centre** on Highway 97 next to the three bears (Box 594, Chetwynd, V0C 1J0; 250–788–1943; fax: 250–788–1846; chetinfo@pris.ca; www.gochetwynd. com) for a brochure showing sculpture locations. Learn some of the area's history at the tiny **Little Prairie Heritage Museum,** (Box 1777, Chetwynd, V0C 1J0; 250–788–3358), which is Chetwynd's oldest building, once having served as the first post office. Quilters will enjoy seeing the antique quilts. It also has an interesting collection of more than 2,500 jugs and pitchers, a caboose, and a trapper's cabin. It's just off Highway 97 on Westgate Road. Look for the sign about a mile west of Chetwynd. It's open July and August, Tuesday through Saturday from 10:00 A.M. to 5:00 P.M. Admission is by donation.

Moberly Lake Provincial Park (www.bcparks.ca, search "Moberly"), 16 miles (25 km) north of Chetwynd on Highway 29, is set on the south side of Moberly Lake. It's a beautiful park, with a boat launch, nature trails, and a playground. It has 109 sites, thirty of which are reservable. Swimming is excellent, as is fishing for northern pike, bull trout, lake trout, and lake whitefish.

Highway 29 from Moberly Lake heads west and north to the **Peace Canyon Dam**. Drop in at the Visitor Centre (see below for contact information), open daily Victoria Day (the Monday before May 24) to Labor

Day from 8:00 A.M. to 4:00 P.M. (and on weekdays the rest of the year) to learn here, via self-guided tours, of dinosaur evidence discovered when the Peace River was dammed. You'll see two life-size dinosaurs plus photographic displays of the building of the Peace Canyon Project.

Fourteen miles (23 km) upstream from the Peace Canyon Dam is the **W.A.C. Bennett Dam,** an enormous structure—1.2 miles (2 km) wide— constructed from glacial moraine left over from the last ice age. This damming formed the 225-mile-long (362-km) Williston Lake, which took a whole five years to fill. Take the Dam Access Road (Canyon Drive) just west of Hudson's Hope and drive along good road for 15 miles (24 km). In the Visitor Centre, there are numerous exhibits and an audiovisual theater. Guided tours of the powerhouse, 500 feet (152 m) underground, are available daily from Victoria Day to Labour Day from 10:00 A.M. to 6:00 P.M. and by appointment the rest of the year. For information on both dams, contact Box 359, Hudson's Hope, V0C 1V0; (250) 783–5048/5000; fax: (250) 783–9470, or call the toll-free number at (888) 333–6667. Admission is free.

The **Hudson's Hope Museum** (9510 Beattie Drive, Box 98, Hudson's Hope, V0C 1V0; 250–783–5735; fax: 250–783–5770; hhmuseum@ pris.ca) is housed in a 1942 Hudson's Bay Company store opposite Beattie Park and the Hudson's Hope Visitor Info Centre (9555 Beattie Drive, Box 330, Hudson's Hope, V0C IV0; 250–783–9154; fax: 250–783–5598; info@dist.hudsons-hope.bc.ca; www.dist.hudsons-hope. bc.ca). If you're interested in fossils, the museum has an excellent collection including a rare baby ichthyosaur, a prehistoric turtle, and hadrosaur tracks. Also of note is an 11,600-year-old mammoth tusk. The town has adopted a dinosaur called Dudley as its mascot. **St. Peter's Shared Ministry Church,** built in 1938, is next to the museum (which is by the highway near the dam access road). The church is of log construction, very small, and quite beautiful. This highway spot is near where explorer Simon Fraser wintered in 1805.

The pretty, 55-mile (88-km) drive along Highway 29 between Hudson's Hope and Fort St. John follows the **Peace River.** Cast a line for rainbow trout, arctic grayling, Dolly Varden, or northern pike. And keep the camera handy, as the views of the island-stippled Peace River are lovely. The road twists and bends sharply as it approaches the Alaska Highway north of Fort St. John.

Should you choose the southern route from Chetwynd—Highway 97—62 miles (100 km) to Dawson Creek, you'll cross the Pine River at the entrance to the **East Pine Provincial Park,** a pleasant picnic spot, where you can cast for a fish or launch your boat.

But there's yet another side trip to consider before starting the journey north along the Alaska Highway.

A mile or so east of Chetwynd, Highway 29 South leads to **Tumbler Ridge,** a town that opened in the 1980s to serve two mines, one of which was the world's largest open-pit coal mine. One mine closed in 2000, and the second in 2003, but the town's scenically wild surroundings and modern facilities (including a beautiful Aquatic Centre) have made it the center of an exciting off-the-beaten-path tourist destination.

> ### Trivia
>
> *Traditional Indian pemmican consists of a mix of chokecherries, blueberries, moose meat, and a few other energy-filled ingredients that combine to produce a food similar to a granola bar.*

En route to Tumbler Ridge, you'll pass the turnoff to **Sukunka Falls Provincial Park,** which is 12 miles (21 km) along a forest service road. Stay on the highway and you'll come to **Gwillim Lake Provincial Park** (www.bcparks.ca, search "Gwillim"), located midway between Chetwynd and Tumbler Ridge in the Rocky Mountain foothills. There are excellent camping facilities (forty-nine sites) and miles of wilderness blue-lake shoreline to explore.

Twelve miles (20 km) south of the park—42 miles (68 km) south of Chetwynd—is the site of the old Bullmoose Mine. The roads in this area lead to some wonderful wilderness destinations, including a mountain with a long tunnel near the top, but it's a two-day adventurous trail blaze to get to it. The town of Tumbler Ridge is 23 miles (37 km) south of the mine, but the jewel of the area is even farther south.

Monkman Provincial Park is a 79,000-acre (32,000-ha) wilderness park, where the 210-foot-high (64-m) **Kinuseo Falls** provides excellent photographic opportunities. In summer jet boats take tourists up the Murray River to visit this unspoiled wonder, which is higher than Niagara Falls. If you don't mind about 30 miles (45 km) of gravel with occasional apple-size rocks, an industrial road leads from Tumbler Ridge to the falls, where there are trails to a viewing platform and other vantage points. The **Kinuseo Falls Campground** (www.bcparks.ca, search "Monkman") has forty-two sites. The **Stone Corral Interpretive Hiking Trail** (2.5-mile [4-km] return) leads past scenic ponds via small caves and interesting plants, fossils, and magnificent viewpoints. Interpretive brochures are available at the trailhead, or you can arrange for a guided trip with *Mista-haya Wayatinaw Ecotourism Cooperative* (Box 1363, Tumbler Ridge, V0C 2W0; 800–891–0566; 250–242–GRIZ [4749]; fax: 250–242–5095; www.grizzlyvalleyco-op.com). They'll also help you discover why Tumbler Ridge is rewriting BC's paleontology history after a series of finds, which are deemed to be Western Canada's best outdoor collection of dinosaur tracks.

Recently the southern border of Monkman Park has been extended to include upper Fontoniko Creek and the Limestone Lakes area, thereby protecting ecosystems, old-growth spruce forests, wildlife, and other important recreation aspects of the park. The unbelievably beautiful scenery here is inaccessible other than a 15-mile (24-km) trail to Monkman Lake, with some short trails near the end heading down to the Cascades—a series of ten waterfalls on Monkman Creek all within a few short miles. Contract the *District of Tumbler Ridge* (305 Founders Street, Box 100, Tumbler Ridge, V0C 2W0; 250–242–4242; fax: 250–242–3993; edo@dtr.ca; www.tumblerridge.ca) for more information. The Web site lists several accommodation choices. Close to town, a day hike will give you a top-of-the-world view of Tumbler Ridge from Bergeron Cliffs on *Bergeron Mountain.* From the *Bergeron Cliffs* trailhead, it is a little more than an hour's hike to reach the 330-foot (100-m) *Bergeron Falls,* the highest falls in Northern BC.

A paved road (Highway 52 North) heads 60 miles (98 km) northeast from Tumbler Ridge to Arras, where you rejoin Highway 97, 10 miles (17 km) west of Dawson Creek. Nineteen miles (30 km) along this road there's a pullout at the trailhead of the *Murray Canyon Overlook Interpretive Trail.* This 1-mile (3-km) hike leads to excellent views of the Murray River. Several more trails leading to yet more waterfalls in the area are proof that Tumbler Ridge is indeed the "Waterfall Capital of Canada."

The Alaska Highway: Dawson Creek to Fort Nelson Section

The *Alaska Highway* has its official beginning in *Dawson Creek,* so the popular thing to do there is to have your photo taken at the *Mile Zero Alaska Highway* post. Many of the sites of interest to tourists are found in this general area. The *Dawson Creek Visitor Info Centre* (900 Alaska Avenue, Dawson Creek, V1G 4T6; 250–782–9595; fax: 250–782–9538; www.tourismdawsoncreek.com) is housed in the *Railway Station Museum.* Throughout the day, the video *The Alaska Highway,*

THE NORTHEAST

1942–1992 is shown. The **Dawson Creek Art Gallery** is housed in the renovated annex of a prairie elevator and is situated in a municipal park (NAR Park) in the center of Dawson Creek. A free visit to the elevator is an excellent learning experience for kids (adults too!) who see these buildings throughout Canada and don't understand how they work. On Saturdays, the **Farmers' Market** is in full swing. Ask at the Info Centre about other

> ### Trivia
>
> *The Peace River is named for Unijigah (Peace Point), where the Cree and Dunneza peoples smoked peace pipes and drew up an agreement to stop the warring between these two sovereign nations.*

sites in town: **McQueen Slough** (a waterfowl refuge); the **Walter Wright Pioneer Village** in **Mile Zero Rotary Park**, where you can take a virtual trip back to the 1940s; the **Zip and Dip** at Centennial Pool, where kids can enjoy a swim and a slide; and the local golf course and driving range.

In March 1942 Dawson Creek's population went from about 500 to 10,000 in a few short days when the United States military started arriving in droves. Eight months and three weeks later, the highway was officially opened, an amazing feat considering that the distance covered was 1,421 miles (2,288 km), and it traversed impossible terrain to its end in Fairbanks, Alaska. At present the Canadian and Yukon governments spend about $40 million annually on its maintenance and reconstruction, and it is now a fully paved highway.

Before heading north, you'll find an extensive menu at the **Alaska Cafe** housed in what was originally the Dew Drop Inn at 10209 Tenth Street, but now called the **Alaska Hotel** (Box 246, Dawson Creek, V1G 3T5; 250–782–7998; fax: 250–782–6277; www.alaskahotel.com). The antique furniture in the cozy rooms breathes old-world charm.

> ### Trivia
>
> *Back in the early 1800s, the trappers and traders in the Fort St. John area learned to depend on one another for meat, furs, guns, wire for snares, traps, etc. They had, in effect, a kind of unwritten contract. When Fort St. John closed in 1823, the dependent trappers reacted by killing five employees and destroying the fort. This led to the closure of all Upper Peace forts, and much starvation ensued.*

If you're heading east to Alberta, stop off in Pouce Coupe, a pretty village surrounded by undulating hills overlooking the Pouce Coupe River, and once the terminus for the Northern Alberta Railway. The old (1931) NAR station was moved to the center of the village and now serves as the museum (250–786–5555; fax: 250–786–5216). It's open mid-May to August 31. Just south of the village there's overnight camping (twenty-six sites, some with hookups) in **Pouce Coupe Regional Park,** located on the banks of the Pouce Coupe River and Bissette Creek. For more information on this pioneer community, contact the *Pouce Coupe Visitor Centre* (5006 Forty-ninth Avenue, Box 293, Pouce Coupe, V0C 2C0; 250–786–5555 open May 15 to September 15 or, off-season, 250–786–5794; fax: 250–786–5257).

As you head north, definitely don't miss what is possibly the world's longest curved wooden bridge; it's the only one in Western Canada. It was built over nine months during 1942–43 as part of the original Alaska Highway and can be found now just 3 miles (5 km) off Highway 97 on the Old Alaska Highway, 21 miles (34 km) north of Dawson Creek. You can camp near this historic *Kiskatinaw River Bridge* at the *Kiskatinaw Provincial Park,* which provides twenty-eight pretty campsites on the banks of the Kiskatinaw River. All campsites are on a first-come, first-served basis. Fishing for pike is good, and there are some bull and rainbow trout to be hooked, too.

Trivia

Down near Dawson Creek is a village called Pouce Coupe. This means "cut thumb" in French, but the origins of the village's name are vague, ranging from a story of a French voyageur who cut his thumb skinning a buffalo, to that of a Sekanni trapper who lost a digit in a gun accident, to meaning an "abandoned chief's lodge by a deserted beaver dam" in the Beaver language. The real answer, so I hear from local Pouce Coupians, is that it is named after the Puscapi Indians, who inhabited the area when white settlers first arrived. Whatever the origin, the area is rich with rustic views and colorful grain fields.

At *Taylor,* whose motto is "Where Peace and Prosperity Meet," you'll quickly notice evidence of the major industries: oil and gas, forestry, and agriculture. The corn here is considered some of the best in the province and is exceptionally sweet and crunchy. Taylor is very proud of its high placings in the "Communities in Bloom" competitions in 1997–98, and there is abundant proof of this throughout the district. The old Peace River Suspension Bridge, built in 1943, collapsed dramatically in 1957. Today there's an excellent view of the *Peace River Bridge* (built in 1960) from the highway, just south of Taylor.

The city of *Fort St. John* is 45 miles (73 km) north of Dawson Creek and just 12 miles (19 km) north of Taylor. It's the site of the first European settlement on the British Columbia mainland. (It started with twelve men, four women, and five children.) In 1793 Alexander Mackenzie marked it as an excellent fur-trading center during his journey to the coast. There's a monument to him in Centennial Park on One Hundredth Street. Since the first settlement in 1794, the city has occupied six different sites. But it was the *Alaska Highway* (then the Alcan Military Road) that in the early forties caused Fort St. John's great growth spurt. Discovery of oil and gas south of the city in 1951 was the icing on the cake for this Energetic City. The *Fort St. John*

Visitor Info Centre (9923–96 Avenue, Fort St. John, V1J 1K9; 250–785–3033 or 250–785–6037; fax: 250–785–7181; fsjchamber@ awink.com; www.fortstjohnchamber.com) has a wealth of information on this thriving city, including where to eat—Boston Pizza seems the most popular of several fast-food restaurants just off the highway. The *Fort St. John–North Peace Museum* (9323 One Hundredth Street, V1J 4N4; 250–787–0430; fax: 250–787–0405) is easy to find, located beside a 136-foot-high (41-m) oil derrick. The museum traces the region's development from fur-trapping days to road-building days to oil-rich days. Interestingly, although the Peace-Liard Region has only 15 percent of the total farming units in BC, the region contains nearly all (90 percent) of BC's cereal grain and seed crops, 100 percent of canola crops, and 28 percent of all forage crops. For information specific to the *Alaska Highway Parks,* visit the BC Parks District Manager at 150–10003 110th Avenue, Fort St. John, V1J 6M7; (250) 787–3407; fax: (250) 787–3490 or check the www.bcparks.ca site.

About 7 miles (11 km) north of Fort St. John, near the junction of Highways 97 and 29, is *Charlie Lake Provincial Park* (fifty-eight sites; 800–689–9025 to reserve; www.bcparks.ca, search "Charlie"). The sites are about a half mile from the lake; pit/dry toilets only. Archaeological findings from caves here show evidence of huge bison having occupied the area. A 10,500-year-old bead was found here, the oldest evidence of human adornment in North America. You can see a replica on display in the museum.

Between Fort St. John and Fort Nelson, you have only the scenery and the occasional moose or caribou to entertain you for 240 miles (387 km). These long, desolate stretches give the Alaska Highway its mystery and magic and, occasionally, its boredom. After *Wonowon* (at Mile 101 of the Alaska Highway!), the road follows the Blueberry River through densely forested areas as it slowly climbs to 3,600 feet (1,100 m) at *Pink Mountain,* the halfway point between Dawson Creek and Fort Nelson. Services here include *Mae's Kitchen* (Mile 147, Alaska Highway, Box 35, Pink Mountain, V0C 2B0; 250–772–3215; fax: 250–772–5147), a restaurant/motel combo, specializing in homemade bread and pastries, and, 4 miles south of Mae's on the east side of the highway, *Pink Mountain Campsite,* Box 73, Mile 143, Pink Mountain, V0C 2B0; phone/fax: 250–772–5133). Here, there's a full-service gas station, a liquor store,

> ### Trivia
>
> *In 1898 a group of gold seekers who were heading for the Klondike were stopped at Fort St. John from continuing their journey by 500 Dunne-za natives. It wasn't until a land treaty with the Indians was promised that the would-be miners were allowed to pass.*

Animal Checklist

❑ bison   ❑ lynx

❑ black bear   ❑ moose

❑ caribou   ❑ mountain goat

❑ coyote   ❑ mule deer

❑ deer   ❑ stone sheep

❑ elk   ❑ white-tailed deer

❑ fox   ❑ wolf

❑ grizzly bear   ❑ wolverine

hunting and fishing supplies including licenses, a post office, and a convenience store ("the Mall of Pink Mountain"). The campsite is open year-round. There's a sani-dump, plug-ins, a laundry, and more; reasonably priced cabins are also available). You'll often see wildlife, mainly moose, on the roadside around here.

A side trip at Mile 147, just south of the Beatton River, heading west on Road 192 for 10 miles (16 km), brings you to a summer road that ascends steeply to a communications tower and lookout at Pink Mountain. When the fireweed is blooming, sometimes at sunrise it actually looks pink. The lowlands to the north and west sides of the mountain are the only areas in the province where you are likely to see wild Plains bison, but this pretty area has another distinctive claim with its high population of rare Arctic butterflies.

About 15 miles (24 km) north of Mae's, you'll find gas and lodging at Mile 160 at *Sikanni River RV Park* (Box 4, Pink Mountain, V0C 2B0; 250–772–5400). Cabins, hot showers, toilets, and laundry facilities complement grassy campsites along the river. There's also gas and propane, a gift shop, and groceries. Ask here for directions to *Sikanni Chief Falls,* located 9 miles (15 km) west of the Alaska Highway. Access to a viewpoint adjacent to these splendid falls is via a 4x4 gravel road followed by a 1-mile (1.5-km), well-marked hiking trail. Back on Highway 97, at Mile 172 (Km 277), the *Buckinghorse River Provincial Park* has a campground (thirty-three sites, no flush toilets) with nice views across the river, where moose occasionally appear. *Buckinghorse River Lodge* (Box 21, Pink Mountain, V0C 2B0; 250–773–6468), at Mile

173 (Km 278), is a full-service stop with impressive views and free RV parking. Next stop north, located at Mile 217 (Km 350) of the Alaska Highway, approximately 78 miles (125 km) south of Fort Nelson, is at the **Prophet River Wayside Provincial Park** (no camping); watch for the many eastern species of birds such as the Connecticut warbler. Another 10 miles (16 km) north, **Lum'n'Abner's** (Mile 233 [Km 375], Alaska Highway, V0C 2V0; 250-773-6366) is a roadhouse that has served travelers (originally as Prophet River Services) since 1942. It's a full-service facility with a restaurant.

The Alaska Highway descends steeply down into the Muskwa River Valley and drops to 1,383 feet (411 m) near **Fort Nelson** (at Mile 300 [Km 483]), the lowest point on the Alaska Highway. Here long, hot summers and excellent soil provide good growing conditions. It's not unusual to hear of forty-pound cabbages.

But gigantic vegetables aren't the only "biggests" that Fort Nelson has to boast. It's also home to Canada's largest gas-processing plant and a huge plywood/oriented strand-board operation. Despite all the industry there are still quite a few fur trappers in the area, working mostly as their ancestors have done for centuries.

Locals assure me that one of the best meals in town can be found at **Fran's Place** at the **Fort Nelson Flight Centre,** located by the airport. It's worth the 5.6-mile (9-km) drive from town. It originally catered only to airline personnel, but word of the scrumptious food hit the airwaves, and the rest is history. Homemade soups, breads, sandwiches, and desserts are enjoyed in a small room just like at home, with the kitchen right there. Coffee is always on, and drinks are located in the refrigerator, from which you can help yourself. Talk to the locals, read a book from the shelf, or play one of the games provided in this laid-back atmosphere. To get there, turn east at the Post Office (Airport Drive) and at the airport entrance, turn left to the Flight Centre. Fran's daughter tells me it's the only place in town where you get to yell at the cook.

For those who want to find out more about these offbeat spots and the many hiking areas near Fort Nelson or who want to take tours of the wood-products factories and the gas-processing plant, information is available at the **Fort Nelson Visitor Info Centre,** which is located in the Recreation Centre on the highway at the west end of town. Write Northern Rockies Regional District &

Trivia

Just south of Fort St. John, on the Alaska Highway by the Lone Wolf Golf Club, is the World's Largest Golf Ball, which is constructed from an old fuel tank. It measures 42 feet (12.8 m) across and weighs 37 tons.

Town of Fort Nelson, Town Square, 5319 Fiftieth Avenue South, Bag Service 399, Fort Nelson, V0C 1R0; or, in winter, phone (250) 774–2541, ext. 241; fax: (250) 774–6794; in summer, phone (250) 774–6400; fax: (250) 774–6868; ecdev@northernrockies.org; www.northernrockies.org. The **Fort Nelson Heritage Museum,** across the road from the Recreation Centre, will be of interest to Alaska Highway history buffs. Next door, the **West End Campground** (250–774–2340; fax 250–774–2840; sbrown@ northwestel.net; www.fnbc.net/campground), open April 1 to November 1, has 160 sites, is conveniently located, and has a large display of stuffed animals and birds. You can also have your oil changed, windscreen chips mended, and other minor repairs completed.

The Info Centre can lead you to several accommodations in the $65 double range, including the **Ardendale B&B** (Mile 305, Old Alaska Highway, Lot 7645, Box 427, Fort Nelson, V0C 1R0; 250–774–2433; fax: 250–774–2436), a beautiful log country home on the northern side of the highway 6 miles (10 km) north of Fort Nelson, where the hosts, Frank (once mayor of Fort Nelson and a former sled dog racing champion) and Gail Parker, offer sleigh and wagon rides; and the **Bluebell Inn** (3907 Fiftieth Avenue South, Mile 300, Alaska Highway, Box 931, Fort Nelson, V0C 1R0; 250–774–6961 or, for reservations, 800–663–5267; fax: 250–774–6983), a one-stop motel/RV site/gas-diesel station/bar/restaurant/ convenience store located near the highway.

If you really want to get off the beaten path, visit the **Old Fort.** Getting to

Recommended Reading—The Northeast

FOR ADULTS:
Peace River Chronicles, by Gordon E. Bowes. Prescott Publishing Company, Vancouver, 1963.

The Alaska Highway in World War II: The U.S. Army of Occupation in Canada's Northwest, by Kenneth Coates and W. R. Morrison. University of Toronto Press, 1992.

The Alaska Highway: A Geographical Discovery, by Thomas and Carole Huber. University Press of Colorado, 2000. A travel log detailing cultural and natural phenomena in the area.

Tumbler Ridge: Enjoying Its History, Trails, and Wilderness, by Charles Helm. MCA Publishing, 2001.

FOR KIDS:
Back to the Cabin, by Ann Blades. Orca Books, 1996. Two boys who don't want to go up to their parent's cabin on a lake south of Prince George end up having an exciting time.

the site of the original Fort Nelson is an adventure in itself. You'll need a four-wheel-drive vehicle, though. The trip takes about an hour, and the road is either extremely muddy when wet or very bumpy when dry. It isn't plowed in winter and is often merely a track. To get there take the road to the Helmet Oil Field, just south of the Husky station in Muskwa Heights 6 miles (10 km) south of town. Cross a rickety rail bridge (controlled by a traffic light) and drive until the road forks at a gas-line pumping station called Clarke Lake Central (about twenty minutes). Follow a rough road straight to the Old Fort. In winter access is by an ice bridge across the river. Once there, explore the settlers' first church, now restored, and the rectory and graveyard behind it. I've heard that the only ghost in the Fort Nelson area is the one haunting the basement of this church. A couple of families still live in the vicinity, so respect their private property while you explore.

Fort Nelson to the Yukon Border

As you travel west from Fort Nelson, you'll start to get the feeling of the true north, of its strength, its freedom, and its beauty. There are 326 miles (525 km) of diverse and spectacular scenery ahead of you between Fort Nelson and Watson Lake in the Yukon, so get ready for a little visual ecstasy.

About 16 miles (27 km) northwest of Fort Nelson, the Liard Highway (gravelly Highway 77) leads 270 miles (434 km) to Fort Simpson in the Northwest Territories, passing Fort Liard at 26 miles (42 km), where there are services.

You'll find gas and food at *Steamboat Mountain Lodge* (Mile 350, Alaska Highway; 250–774–3388) a plain-looking stop-off but with spectacular views of the Muskwa River Valley and the Northern Rockies. There's a good view of Indian Head Mountain just south of the *Tetsa River Provincial Park* turnoff, but watch for moose, too, especially near the Tetsa River Bridge. About 11 miles north of the park is *Tetsa River Services Gas and Lodging* (250–774–1005). You're soon (14 miles [23 km] on) in *Stone Mountain Provincial Park.*

In the park, the *Flower Springs Lake Trail* takes you up almost 1,000 feet (300 m) for a 3.3-mile (5.3-km round-trip), hiking through breathtaking scenery along the North Tetsa River, past waterfalls to Flower Springs Lake, looking brilliantly blue in an alpine setting. To get there turn south at the Summit Lake Lodge buildings, where you're likely to see caribou on the highway. About 100 yards past the old lodge there's a left turn, which is an access road to a microwave tower. Keep

Tourist Treasures

Overheard in a gift shop in a small, far-northern town: "Does the Canadian flag come in any other colors?"

Overheard on a tour bus in another far-northern town: "Is that snow on those mountains?" Bus driver: "No, Ma'am, up here we call that angel poop."

an eye out for moose, mountain caribou, stone sheep, and grizzly bears. Stone Mountain is visible across the valley. Though access by vehicle is restricted, a hike up to the tower will give you a spectacular view of the park.

If you have time and wish to explore **Stone Mountain Provincial Park** more thoroughly, there's a list of outfitters, available at the Fort Nelson Info Centre, willing to share their knowledge of the park and hoodoo-filled Wokkpash Recreation Area adjoining the southwestern limit of Stone Mountain Park. These hoodoos (pillars caused by erosion), which reach heights of 100 feet (30 m), give the area an otherworldly aura. There are a couple of close-by hoodoos along a short trail just west of the Summit Lake Campground. Watch carefully for the nondescript EROSION PILLARS sign on the northern side of the highway.

The scenery is very pretty and pastoral just south of Toad River. Stop off for some tasty food at the **Toad River Lodge** (Box 7780, Toad River, V0C 2X0; 250–232–5401; fax: 250–232–5215), where at last count there were about 4,000 caps hanging from the ceiling. Gas, minor mechanical repairs, and towing services are available—if you need a tow after 10:00 P.M. phone (250) 232–5378.

A mile or so on, just inside Muncho Lake Provincial Park, **The Poplars Campground and Motel** (Box 30, Mile 426, Alaska Highway, V0C 2X0; 250–232–5465) has extra-clean cabin accommodations, thirty RV sites, full camping facilities, a souvenir shop, great cinnamon buns, gas, and car repairs.

Your first vision (the word *view* is too tame) of **Muncho Lake** will leave you speechless. I now have to take a deep breath before turning that special corner when I know a lake so blue-green and clear, surrounded by snow-covered Rocky Mountains at their awe-inspiring best, will be revealed. The jade color comes from reflection and refraction of light on the suspended sediments brought into the lake by glacial melt water, but if you prefer, simply enjoy the beauty unhindered by explanations. Keep your eye out for stone sheep (a southern subspecies of Dall sheep) and woodland caribou, attracted to the salt left on roadsides after winter maintenance. **Muncho Lake Provincial Park** (www.bcparks.ca, search "Muncho") has two campgrounds, both on the lake. **Strawberry Flats** is the southern site, and **Macdonald** the northern. They fill quickly in summer, probably because the fishing (lake trout) is excellent and in all likelihood you'll see wildlife (stone sheep, moose, and caribou), but possibly the reason they are so popular is that the views from both campsites are second-to-none. Reservations are not accepted. The impressive **Folded Mountain** towering above the road in the southern section of the park is made up of limestone "folds" caused by tetonic deformations.

At Mile 462 of the Alaska Highway, the **Northern Rockies Lodge** is one of the largest log buildings in British Columbia. Sitting right by Muncho Lake, it has a 45-foot (13-m) stone fireplace that dominates a European-style restaurant. Together with the older **Highland Glen Lodge,** there are a total of forty-five units, open year-round. A campground, RV park, boat rentals, and other facilities are available. Owners Marianne and Urs Schildknecht will organize complete package holidays whether you're into fishing, photography, or mere sightseeing. Urs has bush-piloted in the area for more than twenty years; with their own floatplanes (Liard Air), the Schildknechts can help you explore a large part of this magnificent area. Write Box 8, Muncho Lake, V0C 1Z0; (250) 776–3481; fax: (250) 776–3482 or (800) 663–5269 for reservations; liardair@northern-rockies-lodge.com; www. northern-rockies-lodge.com.

Ask at any of the lodges or parks in the area about access routes for hiking the **Trail of 42** along the "Old Highway," which runs above the present Alaska Highway along Muncho Lake. You'll soon appreciate the driving (and road-building) skills required to traverse the area fifty years ago.

After leaving Muncho Lake, 16 miles (27 km) on is **Liard River Hot Springs,** another spot worthy of waxing poetic. Not only are the waters intensely hot and soothing, but there are also some interesting organisms living here that can be found nowhere else in BC, including the tiny Plains forktail damselfly. There's also a small snail called the hot-water physa, which is unique to these waters. The two pools, Alpha and Beta, are a pleasant stroll along a 760-yard boardwalk (originally built by U.S. servicemen) from the parking lot near the campground. On your walk check the steamy bogs for little lake chub darting about, and several species of orchids, lobelias, cow parsnips, and ostrich ferns. The atmosphere is almost tropical! In fact it's hard to believe that not far from here at Smith River, the province's coldest temperature was recorded in 1947, a chilling -74° F (-58.9° C).

Cold or not, there is nothing quite like a winter stop at Liard River Hot Springs. Not only are there fewer people than in summer, but it's also comical to watch hair turn into spaghetti, as the steam combines with bitter cold air, aging each thread into hoarfrost. The first pool you come to is tiered, with each tier a slightly different temperature, which then runs off in a stream. Take care though, as the waters are so hot—from 100–120° F (38–49° C)—that you can easily become hyperthermic before realizing it. The recommended immersion time is about twenty minutes maximum. The second, deeper, cooler pool is another ten- to fifteen-minute walk through the lush vegetation. Occasionally moose and black bears come to the pools to graze on the aquatic vegetation, so take particular care. A resident park naturalist is a great source of knowledge about the flora and fauna in the area and offers summer hikes. Don't miss the *hanging gardens,* which can be viewed from the boardwalk, just past Alpha pool.

As with Muncho Lake, finding a site in the provincial campground (fifty-three sites, open year-round) can be difficult in summer. If you just want to use the hot springs, you don't have to camp there, though.

A couple of lodges nearby provide rustic accommodation. *Trapper Ray's Liard Hotsprings Lodge* (Mile 497, Liard River, V1G 4J8; phone/fax: 250–776–7349) is a log building with campground, RV park, and attached cafe across the road from the hot springs. It's open year-round. Showers are available to the traveling public for a couple of dollars. *Liard River Lodge* (Mile 496, Alaska Highway, Box 9, Muncho Lake, V0C 1Z0; 250–776–7341; fax: 250–776–7340) provides very friendly service and is just minutes from the hot springs. It's also open year-round and overlooks the Liard River Suspension Bridge. In 2002 it was "parking" or tenting only, as the owners were planning a new building. The *Liard River Hot Springs Provincial Park Campground* is reservable (800–689–9025). Watch for bison on the road twenty minutes north of the hot springs. At Mile 533, at the junction of the Coal and Liard Rivers, there's moderately new lodging and camping at *Coal River Lodge* (9515–95th Avenue, Fort St. John, V1J 1H7; 250–776–7306; off-season: 250–785–8775; drogers@ pris.bc.ca). Canoeing or fishing for Dolly Varden and grayling between Whirlpool Canyon and Cranberry Rapids are wonderful wilderness activities. At *Fireside Car/Truck Stop, Dora's Cafe* (Mile 543, Fireside, V0C 1P0; 250–776–7302) will satisfy your sweet tooth and more. The RV park is pleasant and the motel units fairly new. Near Fireside is evidence of the second-largest burn (1982) in British Columbia, which destroyed more than 400,000 acres.

The Alaska Highway straddles the BC/Yukon border, passing through Watson Lake and Upper Liard before it meets the Stewart-Cassiar Highway, which we will explore in the next chapter.

PLACES TO STAY IN THE NORTHEAST

DUNSTER
Motherland Inn, River Road, V0J 1J0; (250) 968–4356. Whole house, groups, B&B also.

Culp's Farm, Station Road, V0J 1J0; (250) 968–4309. Stay in antique sheepherder's wagons; $50 including breakfast. Reservations only.

FORT NELSON
Ardendale B&B, Mile 305, Old Alaska Highway, Fort Nelson, V0C 1R0; (250) 774–2433. Country home.

MUNCHO LAKE
Northern Rockies Lodge, Box 8, V0C 1Z0; (250) 776–3481 or (800) 663–5269 for reservations; fax: (250) 776–3482; www.northern-rockies-lodge.com. European-style dining too.

PINK MOUNTAIN
Pink Mountain Campsite, Box 73, Mile 143, Alaska Highway, V0C 2B0; phone/fax: (250) 772–5133. Gas, diesel, and propane available; post office and store. Cabins. Open year-round.

PRINCE GEORGE
Bed-and-breakfast lines: (250) 561–BEDS or toll free: (888) 266–5555.

TOAD RIVER
The Poplars Campground, Mile 426, Box 30, Alaska Highway, V0C 2X0; (250) 232–5465. New log cabins, thirty RV sites. Full-facility stop. Great views and cinnamon buns!

TUMBLER RIDGE
Golden Aspen Bed & Breakfast, 175 Kiskatinaw Crescent, V0C 2W0; (877) 883–8835; (250) 242–4415; www.golden-aspen.com. Double rooms or large suite with Jacuzzi and sauna.

PLACES TO EAT IN THE NORTHEAST

DAWSON CREEK
Alaska Hotel, Café and Pub, 10209 Tenth Street, Dawson Creek, V1G 3T5; (250) 782–7998; www.alaskahotel.com. Cozy accommodation, too.

FIRESIDE
Dora's Cafe, Mile 543, Alaska Highway, (250) 776–7302. Motel units also.

FORT ST. JOHN
Anna's Deli & Coffee House, 9600 Ninety-third Avenue, Fort St. John, V1J 5Z2; (250) 785–9741. In the Totem Mall near the Info Centre. Serves appetizing sandwiches, soups, and full meals.

LIARD HOT SPRINGS
Trapper Ray's Liard Hotsprings Lodge and Café, Mile 497, Alaska Highway, Liard River, V1G 4J8; (250) 776–7349. Open year-round. Opposite hot springs.

PINK MOUNTAIN
Mae's Kitchen, Box 35, Mile 147, Alaska Highway, Pink Mountain, V0C 2B0; (250) 772–3215. Homemade bread, pies.

PRINCE GEORGE
Great Wall Restaurant, 2757 Spruce Street and Highway 97 South; (250) 563–8128. Canadian and Chinese cuisine. Open from 11:00 A.M. to midnight.

The Northwest

This huge region, approximately one-third of British Columbia, ranges from the rolling plains of the interior plateau west of Prince George and follows the Yellowhead Highway past myriad fishing lakes and First Nations' villages to the smell of the sea at Prince Rupert. It then heads north along the Stewart–Cassiar Highway, past the stirring Bear Glacier and the Grand Canyon of the Stikine, to the Yukon border.

Vanderhoof

The big-city feel of Prince George is replaced by open country and ranches by the banks of the Nechako River, as the Yellowhead Highway 16 heads to *Vanderhoof* (population 4,603 in 2002), 60 miles (97 km) west, located close to the geographic center of British Columbia. Vanderhoof, Dutch for "of the farm" (but named for its founder, Herbert Vanderhoof, a Chicago publisher), grew quickly as a railway town for the Grand Trunk Pacific Railway, but today it's BC's second-largest agriculture forage-producing area and a gathering-hole for foresters and farmers—the kind of town where trucks sport bumper stickers such as one I saw declaring BEATEN PATHS ARE FOR BEATEN MEN.

Many travelers rush through Vanderhoof, unaware that on the northern edge of town, the *Vanderhoof Bird Sanctuary,* bordering 3 miles (5 km) of the Nechako River, swarms with migrating birds, notably Canada geese. To find out more contact the Nechako Valley Sporting Association (Box 1077, Vanderhoof, V0J 3A0; 250–567–4805) or the *Vanderhoof Visitor Info Centre* (2353 Burrard Avenue, Box 126, Vanderhoof, V0J 3A0; 800–752–4094 or 250–567–2124; fax: 250–567–3316; chamber@hwy16.com; www.hwy16.com/chamber), located 1 block north of the highway.

Vanderhoof's history "lives" at the reconstructed *Heritage Village Museum* on the corner of Pine Street and Highway 16 West (Box 1515, Vanderhoof, V0J 3A0; 250–567–2991; fax: 250–567–2931; museum@ hwy16.com; www.hwy16.com/museum). Here costumed waiters in the

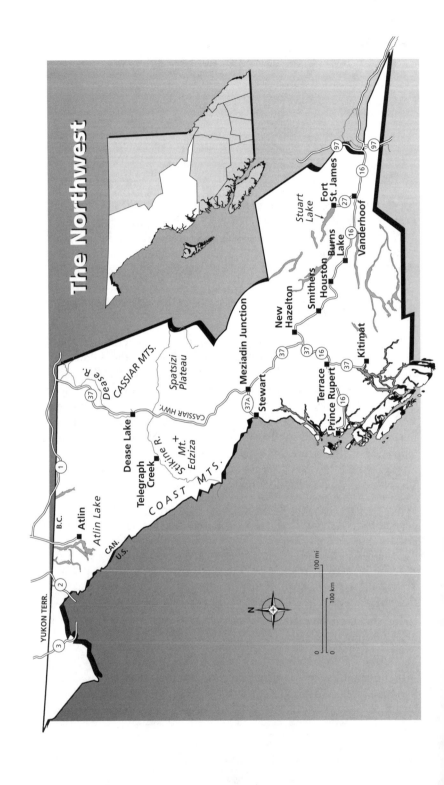

The Northwest

AUTHOR'S TOP TEN PICKS
IN THE NORTHWEST

*Wandering through the
Fort St. James National
Historic Park*

Touring historic Telkwa

*Visiting 'Ksan Village to
see First Nations exhibits
in the museum*

*Adventuring in the Kitlope
with the Na Na Kila
watchmen*

*Hiking the moonscape
at the Nisga'a Memorial
Lava Bed Park*

*Touring the Khutzeyma-
teen River Valley by plane
from Prince Rupert*

*Watching the Stikine River
plunging through the
Lower Grand Canyon*

*Backpacking through
Mount Edziza
Provincial Park*

*Taking tea on the MV
Tarahne in Atlin*

*Rafting in the
Tatshenshini-Alsek
Wilderness Park*

seasonal **OK Hotel and Café** (478 West First Street; 250–567–5252) serve good old-fashioned home cooking in a 1920s environment, just as they would have back in the early part of the century. In those days (1920 to 1942) the cafe was run by two Chinese men, Tim Chow and George Cheuy, and no matter what you ordered it cost five cents. Other displays of interest at this eleven-building heritage site are the hotel room, the medical office, the bottle room, a Carrier Indian display, and natural history displays. Several hotels and motels line the highway strip and beyond, as well as a couple of RV parks and campgrounds. Stay awhile and play at the **Tachick Lake Fishing Resort** (Tachick Lake Road, Box 1112, Vanderhoof, V0J 3A0; 250–567–4929; fax: 250–567–5566; tachick@ hwy16.com). Cabin rates are $50 to $60 twin, and camping is also available. Here you'll find the **Saddle Bar Lodge,** famous for its (weekends only) gourmet dining. To get there head south from Vanderhoof down the Kenny Dam Road for 15 miles (24 km).

Fort St. James

Historic **Fort St. James** (population 2,038 in 2002) is 34 miles (54 km) north along Highway 27. It's in a "don't miss" area and is the oldest continuously inhabited non-First Nations community west of the Rockies.

Before exploring Fort St. James, visit **Paarens Beach Provincial Park** and, 3 miles (5 km) farther on, **Sowchea Bay Provincial Recreation Area** (thirty-six campsites at Paarens and thirty small sites at Sowchea), on the south shore of Stuart Lake. Reservations (800–689–9025) are accepted only at Paarens. For detailed information visit www.bcparks.ca (search "Paarens" or "Sowchea"). Take Sowchea Bay Road just before the bridge over the Stuart River. There is no day-use area at Sowchea Bay, but picnic facilities, change houses, a playground, and a log picnic shelter are available at Paarens Beach, located on a long stretch of wide sandy beach. The campsites on the beach all have excellent views across 62-mile-long (100-km) Stuart Lake. Just before the

Trivia

At the end of Fraser Lake, the Nautley River, at less than half a kilometer, is the shortest river in Canada. It connects Fraser Lake to the Nechako River. Many of the hundreds of trumpeter swans that make Fraser Lake their resting spot during their spring and fall migrations overwinter on the Nautley River.

Sowchea Bay Park entrance, on the corner of Heavenor and Sowchea Bay Roads, the **Big Bay Bed and Breakfast** (Box 1849, Fort St. James, V0J 1P0; 250–996–8857; bigbay@fsjames.com) is a new Victorian-style home that is completely wheelchair-accessible. Jo Anne and Martial Desrochers run five large guest rooms. Double accommodation is in the $65 range and the hot breakfasts are delicious.

The beach across the road is sandy, and there are plenty of hiking or snow-mobiling/ski trails. The nearby **Antimony Mine** 3-mile (5-km) **hiking trail** leads to an old mining site. And for divers there's a **freshwater reef** near Battleship Island, a fortresslike island located 7.5 miles (12 km) from Fort St. James in Stuart Lake.

To get an eagle-eye view of Fort St. James and the surrounding wilderness, do the 3-mile (5-km) hike up **Mount Pope** to T-shaped caves. Inside, the caves are smelly with bat droppings, but from the 4,829-foot (1,472-m) Mount Pope summit, the view of Fort St. James, Stuart Lake, and the snowy Omineca Mountains to the north is spectacular. The trailhead begins along Stones Bay Road, 3 miles (5 km) from town. It starts out steeply, but there are plenty of viewpoint stops on the way, with a total elevation gain of 2,600 feet (791 m). There's a gazebo on top of the mountain, as well as an old forestry lookout. Allow about five hours for the return trip. A hiking map is available at the **Fort St. James Chamber of Commerce and Visitor Info Centre** (115 Douglas Avenue, Box 1164, Fort St. James, V0J 1P0; 250–996–7023; fax: 250–996–7047; fsjchamb@qlynx.com; www.fortstjames.com).

If you prefer riding to hiking, there are three horses available on Pinchi Road for trail rides. Hans Sturm (radio phone: N694633 YL Channel) will take you on guided trail rides, on quiet forest trails.

For skiers **Murray Ridge Ski Area** (Box 866, Fort St. James, V0J 1P0; 250–996–8515; toll free: 888–229–1155), 6 miles (10 km) north of Fort St. James, has almost 20 miles (30 kms) of downhill runs as well as 12 miles (20 km) of groomed cross-country ski trails, a T-bar lift (the longest in North America), and a day-lodge with a licensed lounge and a cafeteria. **Whisky Jack Restaurant** (250–996–8828), just past the mill on North Road near the ski area, is well-known for its great burgers. But there's more. For more than sixteen years Joe (the chef) and Margaret

Holzleitner have served steaks, seafood combos, and European-style cuisine in their licensed (beer and wine) log-building restaurant 5 miles (8 km) from town. To get there, head north and take Germansen Road for about a half mile. It's closed Monday but is open the rest of the week from 8:00 A.M. to 2:00 P.M. and by reservation in the evening.

The big attraction in Fort St. James is the **Fort St. James National Historic Site** (P.O. Box 1148, Fort St. James, V0J 1P0; 250–996–7191; fax: 250–996–8566; www.parkscanada.gc.ca). Here, in an authentic 1896 Hudson's Bay Post, you'll learn about the Carrier Indians (named for their widows who carried the cremated remains of their deceased husbands on their backs until a potlatch could be held). In summer actors become early Hudson's Bay Company officers and Carrier Indians. Chickens and geese run around, and you feel as if you have walked in on a scene from the fur-trading past. "The Fort" is open from 9:00 A.M. to 5:00 P.M. mid-May to the end of September.

Across the road from the fort is the **Nak'azdli Handicraft Shop** (250–996–7368; open seasonally from 9:00 A.M. to 5:00 P.M.). Here an elder's society makes traditional moose-skin crafts and beaded jewelry.

From the fort follow Lakeshore Drive past Cottonwood Park, site of a one-third-scale model of a German Junkers W34 float plane, to one of the oldest Catholic churches in British Columbia. **Our Lady of Good Hope Church** was completed in 1836 by Fr. Blanchet, O.M.I., and was in regular use until 1951. Mass is celebrated on Saturday evenings in summer, but otherwise there is no access to the interior. A graveyard nearby has headstones written in the Carrier syllabics that were developed by

Rose Prince

A very special native event is held every summer at Lejac, just east of Fraser Lake. The Rose Prince pilgrimage honors a Carrier woman who attended the Lejac Residential School more than fifty years ago. A kind, gentle woman, who endured curvature of the spine and several family losses, Rose Prince died in 1949 on August 19 (her 34th birth-day) from tuberculosis. In 1951, during the transfer of several graves, Rose Prince's casket broke open. It was discovered that her body, which had been buried for more than two years, was perfectly preserved. Other bodies were examined, and all were found to be decaying. There is speculation as to whether Rose Prince will be declared a saint.

Our Lady of Good Hope Church

another Oblate, Fr. Morice. Behind the church is an old log hut in which Fr. Morice printed the Carrier books and newspapers, which can be seen in the "Old Fort" museum.

Perhaps stay awhile in the area, canoe and fish the waterways, ride the trails, or in winter enjoy dog mushing. At **Vindsdalur** (Box 1713, Fort St. James, V0J 1P0; 250–996–6129; fax: 250–996–7079; ohm@vinds dalur.com; www.vindsdalur.com). Lisi and Marcus Ohm, who have worked and bred Icelandic horses for more than twelve years, offer canoe and trail-riding trips on their property on the Stuart River.

Fort Fraser, Fraser Lake, and **Endako** dot the highway leading to Burns Lake, approximately 100 miles (161 km) west of Prince George. The main employer in the area is Canada's largest molybdenum mine at Endako, but ranching and recreational fishing are also important. A little-known fact about tiny Fort Fraser is that it is the site of the last spike driven when the east–west connection of the Grand Trunk Pacific Railway was made in 1914. Drop in to the *Last Spike Pub* (250–690–7433) and ask the locals about the railway history. Nearby, *Beaumont Provincial Park* (www.bcparks.ca, search "Beaumont"; forty-nine sites; 800–689–9025 for reservations) is set on the southeastern sandy shores of Fraser Lake. If you camp here, think back to 1806, when explorer Simon Fraser established historic Fort Fraser on this very spot. Fraser chose the site, originally known as Natleh, for its commanding view of the lake and the summer breezes that kept the bugs at bay. Near Fraser Lake watch for trumpeter swans that nest close by. Stop at the *Fraser Lake Visitor Info Centre* (65 Endako Avenue, Box 430, Fraser Lake, V0J 1S0; 250–699–8844/ 6257; fax: 250–699–6469; www.village.fraserlk.bc.ca) to learn more about these beautiful birds, whose booming, trumpetlike call is heard around the 300 or so lakes that dot the area. If you're visiting in late fall or early spring, you'll soon realize why Fraser Lake is called The White Swan Capital of the World. The Info Centre is a log building, just off Highway 16, at the east end of the village. Ask here about tours of the *Endako Mine* (www. endakomines.com). The mine is located 14 miles (22 km) southwest of Fraser Lake. Tours are by appointment (250–699–6211, ext. 313) on Wednesday during June, July, and August. If you're wondering what they do with the molybdenum that is mined there, it is used as an alloy to strengthen and harden steel. Almost all ultra-high-strength steels contain molybdenum in amounts up to 8 percent.

The museum at the Info Centre is an excellent source on the history of the area's earliest inhabitants—from the Carrier people to the early fur traders to the farm settlers—as well as on the history of logging practices and the more recent development of the molybdenum mine. Recreational fishing is very popular in the big lakes as well as in the hundreds of other lakes and rivers in the vicinity. Ask at the *Par 3 Sports in Motion Store* (111 Chowsunkit Street, Box 99, Fraser Lake, V0J 1S0; 250–699–8063; fax: 250–699–8901;

Tweedsmuir Days, Burns Lake; July; (250) 692–3773

Stuart Lake Fishing Derby, Fort St. James; June; (250) 996–7023

Fort St. James Fall Fair Festival, Fort St. James; August; (250) 996–7023

Riverboat Days, Terrace; August; (250) 635–4997

Prince Rupert Seafest, Prince Rupert; June; (250) 624–9118 or (800) 667–1994

Cow Bay Days, Prince Rupert; July; (800) 667–1994 or (250) 627–1808

Smithers Midsummer Festival, Smithers; June; (250) 847–1971; festival@bvfms.org; www.bvfms.org

Bulkley Valley Exhibition, Smithers; August; (250) 847–3816; fax: (250) 847–3626

Pacific Northwest Music Festival, Terrace; April; (250) 635–3215

Nechako Valley Exhibition, Vanderhoof; August; (250) 567–3987

Stewart/Hyder's International Days, July; (888) 366–5999 or (250) 636–9224; stewhyd cofc@hotmail.com par3@flk.auracom.com; www.par3sports. com) in Fraser Lake for information, or else book a fishing guide. Par 3 will also outfit you smartly for the outdoors and has the best selection of fishing gear in the area. **Binta Lake Outfitters** (Box 1092, Fraser Lake, V0J 1S0; 250–699–6980; fax: 250–699–8989; koenig@ bcgroup.net) offers fishing and hunting adventures, and if the guys at Binta Lake can't accommodate you, they'll find someone who can.

Downtown Fraser Lake's best bet for a tasty lunch is the **Lunch Box Deli** in the Fraser Lake Mall. Its walls are lined with local photography and native art objects.

Another area worth exploring is the east end of François Lake, the Glenannan Tourist Area, which starts about 6 miles (10 km) south of Fraser Lake. It is served by several resorts with the added attraction of the nine-hole **Moly Hills Golf Course** (250–699–7761; www.burns lake.net/molyhills) at 1400 East Francois Lake Road. One of these resorts, where you shouldn't miss a delicious Swiss meal (by reservation only, closed Monday and Tuesday), is **Stellako Lodge** (Box 400, Fraser Lake, V0J 1S0; phone/fax: 250–699–6695) on the Stellako River, world-famous for its fly-fishing. The lodge has cabins, RV parking, camping, boat rentals, a store, laundry and shower facilities, and a recreation room. Keen skiers and hikers love the **Fraser Lake–Stuart Lake Pack Trail**, a 28-mile (45-km) link between native villages on the two lakes. At one time it was a Hudson's Bay Company fur-trade route. One more spot you can ask staff at the Info Centre to direct you to is **White Swan Park**. Just north of Highway 16, it has an excellent swimming beach, picnic site, and boat launch.

Lakes District

The area known as the **Lakes District,** with its center at Burns Lake, is another excellent recreation area. In downtown Burns Lake take a drive up **Boer Mountain Road** to a lookout that will give you a panoramic overview of the district. To the south, in **François Lake,** large rainbow trout and char are common. To get to these big fish, take a left just before Burns Lake (Highway 35), passing pretty Tchesinkut Lake (pronounced "te-sink-it"), and drive 15 miles (24 km) south to the ferry landing.

Close to the ferry landing, **Darter's Misty Willows Ranch Bed and**

Bluegrass Ghosts

G oats, turkeys, a curious cat, and a dog or two greeted me as I drove into Darter's Misty Willow farm. Before you could sing "Hot Corn, Cold Corn," I was wearing Marie Darter's gumboots and dragging bales of hay to sheep troughs. Later, over roast dinner and excellent wine, Marie reminisced about when she and her late husband, Charlie, added music to their yearly picnics—and the **Burns Lake Bluegrass and Western Swing** **Festival** was born. Marie told of the history of her home, built by Jacob Henkel in 1906. Before the ferry service, settlers across François Lake would signal with fires, and Henkel would row a canoe over to fetch them. That evening I listened as the ferry crunched through the ice, and I imagined I could hear the stomp and twang of a bluegrass banjo beat. Across the lake a brightly glowing fire sent tingles up my spine.

Breakfast (Colleymount Highway, Box 455, Burns Lake, V0J 1E0; phone/fax: 250–695–6573; mdarter@futurenet.bc.ca) has more than 300 acres (122 ha) of aspen groves, rolling meadows, and waterfowl ponds, as well as a lovely view of François Lake. In this 1906-built home, I enjoyed swapping stories beside a grand old woodstove in the big country kitchen with Marie Darter and her neighbors. Bed-and-breakfast rates start at $65 double in high season.

Free ferries leave the north side of the François Lake on the half hour and the south side on the hour. Fourteen paved miles (22 km) south is **Takysie Lake,** where you'll have no trouble filling your creel with rainbow trout. **Likkel's Lakeside Store and Resort** (Box 11, Takysie Lake, V0J 2V0; 250–694–3403; 877–694–3403 toll free; fax: 250–694–3503; sllikkel@hotmail.com; www.bcnorth.ca/lakeside) has campsites, cabins, a licensed restaurant (popular with the locals after Sunday church), a store, a post office, hookups, a sani-dump, and a Laundromat. You'll also find canoe rentals and pedal boats, a sandy beach, and a playground.

Back in Burns Lake (originally called Burnt Lake because of an enormous bush fire), **Process 4 Gallery** (Box 200, 425 Yellowhead 16 and Third Avenue, Burns Lake, V0J 1E0; 250–692–3434 or 888–990–2298; fax: 250–692–3934; www.burnslake.net/process4gallery) sells local art as well as fine art prints, originals, and collectibles by leading artists such as Ted Harrison (www.tedharrisongallery.com). All purchases are sold G.S.T. free! Owner Wayne Brown, who has fished and explored most of the area, reveals readily his good fishing spots. He tells of the **Fulton River spawning grounds,** where the fish are so thick "you can walk across their backs." The best month to see this run is September. The Department of Fisheries and Oceans **Fulton River Salmon Project** (Box 9, Granisle, V0J 1W0; 250–697–2314) is the largest sockeye artificial spawning channel in the world and welcomes visitors. Take the road north from Topley, 32 miles (51 km) west of Burns Lake, for 25 miles (40 km), keeping a watch out for moose, black bears, and bald eagles.

Before heading west, though, stop at the **China Moon** (250–692–7411) in the Lakeview Mall (on the highway opposite Mulvaneys) and enjoy their Subgum Wonton Soup, loaded with jumbo shrimp, chicken, pork, and vegetables. After eating take a walk along the **Eveneshen Nature Trail**. It starts behind the **Burns Lake Visitor Info Centre** (540 Highway 16 West, Box 339, Burns Lake, V0J 1E0; 250–692–3773; fax: 250–692–3493; staff@bldchamber.ca; www.bldchamber.ca), which is on the highway in town. The staff has information on the many accommodation options in and around Burns Lake. While at the Info Centre, check out the **Bucket of Blood** beside the **Lakes District Museum** (open summer only); once a gambling den, the little building earned its gruesome name after a shootout over a game of poker.

A block west of the Info Centre is Babine Road, which leads for 18 miles (30 km) to the Pinkut Creek Project, an artifical salmon spawning channel 30 miles (50 km) north of Burns Lake; it offers good recreational fishing. Burns Lake is also the northern gateway to **Tweedsmuir (North) Provincial Park** (www.bcparks.ca, search "Tweedsmuir"), an untamed wilderness accessible by floatplane, foot, or horseback via the **Alexander MacKenzie Trail**. You can also get there from the Nechako Reservoir (Ootsa and Whitesail Lakes) by jet boat. Ask at the Info Centre for information on guides who can take you into this magnificent, untouched park. **Tweedsmuir (South) Provincial Park** is accessible via Highway 20 and is located about 250 miles (400 km) from Williams Lake. (See Cariboo-Chilcotin section.)

Houston to the Hazeltons

*H*ouston (population 3,738 in 2002), the self-proclaimed World Steelhead Capital, is 50 miles (81 km) west of Burns Lake. It's the home of the 60-foot-long (18-m), 804-pound (365-kg) **world's largest fly rod,** which is located at the **Visitor Info Centre** (3289 Highway 16, Box 396, Houston, V0J 1Z0; 250–845–7640; fax: 250–845–3682; chamberh@bulkley.net; district.houston.bc.ca). This oversized aluminum rod is perhaps a hint at how to catch the steelhead in the Morice and Bulkley Rivers, which run through town. For a good view of the Bulkley, hike the North Side Community Trails, just around the corner from the Info Centre.

Two miles (3 km) west of Houston is a turnoff (Morice Forest Road) to the **Nadina River Project** (250–697–2314). Follow this road past Owen Lake to the Nadina Lake turnoff, then take this road (Tahtsa Road) for 18 miles (30 km) almost to Nadina Lake. Follow the signs to the artificial sockeye spawning channel. Look for golden eagles in the area. Visitors are welcome, especially in September when the run is at its best.

Thirty miles (49 km) west of Houston is picturesque *Telkwa,* where the Bulkley River meets the Telkwa. It's a tiny village (population 1,440 in 2002), bordering *Tyhee Lake Provincial Park* (800–689–9025 for reservations), also tiny, but a perfect holiday spot set in the Bulkley River Valley with views of the Hazeltons Mountains to the west and the Skeena Mountains to the east. You have fifty-nine shady sites to pick from at Tyhee (which means "fish" in the native Gitxsan language), and as the lake is stocked with rainbow trout, you might want to try your luck. It has both pit and flush toilets, showers, and a coin-operated sani-station. There's a 200-yard sandy beach with a designated swimming area, an adventure playground for kids, a picnic shelter with a wood stove, and an area for volleyball and horseshoe enthusiasts. The 1.5-mile (2.5-km) Aldermere Trail circumnavigates the park. The trail is named after the Collins Telegraph Line town, set on the southwest corner of the lake on the bluff above Telkwa. It consisted of a hotel, livery stables, a newspaper office (*The Interior News*—now based in Smithers), a store, and a post office, but it died out in the early part of the twentieth century when people moved down the hill to Telkwa to be closer to the anticipated Grand Trunk Railway, and a better water source. A fascinating mystery/adventure novel called *The Last Three*

WORTH SEEING/DOING IN THE NORTHWEST

Relaxing by Red Sand and Kitsumkalum Lakes, hoping to catch sight of the Spirit Bear, the rare kermodei.

Cruising the Inside Passage from Prince Rupert to Port Hardy.

Shopping in Cow Bay, Prince Rupert.

Watching Haisla artists at work in Kitamaat.

Driving the Nisga'a circle tour from Terrace.

Panning for gold in Telegraph Creek.

Chartering a plane to see the crater of Mount Edziza, then continuing on to the Spatzizi Plateau Wilderness Park for an unforgettable sightseeing trip.

Renting a boat or canoe to explore the multitude of anchorages in beautiful Atlin Lake.

Learning the history of the Tsimshian First Nations people at the Museum of Northern British Columbia in Prince Rupert.

Touring the eleven beautifully restored early 1900s buildings in the Vanderhoof Heritage Museum.

Fly-fishing for steelhead in the Skeena and Babine Rivers.

Hundred Miles, by G. Stewart Nash, gives a glimpse of the history and geography of northwest BC and the Collins Telegraph Line. On your Aldermere Trail hike, you'll pass a marsh-viewing platform where common loons, redknecked grebes, ruffed grouse, downy woodpeckers, and red-winged blackbirds will satisfy the bird-lovers among you. Occasionally moose (in winter), black bear, and beaver are seen. Maps at the **Telkwa Museum** (located in an old schoolhouse) describe a walking tour of twenty-six historic sites. Accommodation is available in one of these heritage houses, and what was Telkwa's first bank, the Assisted School and Union Bank built in 1908, now **The Old Schoolhouse** self-catering B&B. It is private, self-contained, and sleeps eight. The kitchen comes stocked with breakfast fixings, basic cooking supplies, and spices, and there's a barbecue outside, near the banks of the Bulkley River. Contact Jerry or Jill Schneider at 1617 Riverside Street, Telkwa, V0J 2X0; (250) 846–5939; schoolhouse@highway16.com; www.highway 16.com/schoolhouse. To learn more of Telkwa's history and its accommodation choices, contact the Village of Telkwa, 1704 Riverside Street, Box 220, Telkwa, V0J 2X0; (250) 846–5212; fax: (250) 846–9572; info@telkwa.com; www.telkwa.com. Telkwa is halfway between Prince George—226 miles (364 km) to the east—and Prince Rupert on the Pacific coast. Tiny Telkwa has some hidden dining secrets, one of the best of which is the **Crocodile Cafe** (1116 Fourth Street, Telkwa, V0J 2X0; 250–846–9268; fax: 250–846–9122), open daily and located on the highway. For a tasty breakfast (which is served until 5:00 P.M.) try the huevos rancheros. The dinner menu, with a mainly Mexican flavor, has an international side to it, too. Local crafts and souvenirs are also sold.

Smithers (population 5,710 in 2002), is at the center of the Bulkley Valley, sitting snugly below the towering 8,600-foot (2,621-m) Hudson Bay Mountain. As far as recreation goes, Smithers is it. From hiking and hunting to skiing and sledding, just name it, you'll find it in Smithers. The town has thirty-six downhill ski runs to choose from, so skiing and snowboarding are the big attractions in winter. Hikes to the Twin Falls and Glacier Gulch are a popular summer activity. Ask for trailhead directions at the **Smithers Visitor Info Centre** (1411 Court Street, Box 2379, Smithers, V0J 2N0; 800–542–6673 or 250–847–5072; fax: 250–847–3337; info@tourismsmithers.com; www.tourismsmithers.com), which is easily found by following the signs from the highway. It's located in Central Park, on the corner of Highway 16 and Main, just west of the Mountain Goat Monument, and next to the Bulkley Valley Museum (Box 2615, Smithers, V0J 2N0; 250–847–5322; fax: 250–847–5363; bvmuseum@ bulkley.net). Of special interest at the museum is the re-created Watson Store, which operated as a general store in the twenties and thirties.

Fossil followers mustn't miss **Driftwood Canyon Provincial Park,** 6 miles (10 km) northeast of Smithers—follow the signs on Old Babine Lake Road. It was created in 1967 to protect the fossil beds on the east side of Driftwood Creek. A viewing platform allows a good view of the plant, animal, and insect species within the shale formations that inhabited the area 50 million years ago. Driftwood Canyon is recognized as one of the world's most significant fossil beds.

Check the Smithers tourism Web site for a huge choice of lodgings. One on the eastern edge of town is the family-owned (since 1980) **Hudson Bay Lodge** (3251 Highway 16 East, Smithers, V0J 2N0; 800–663–5040 for reservations or 250–847–4581; fax: 250–847–4878; reservations@ hblodge.com; www.hblodge.com). It has two friendly restaurants and a bar. Nearer the heart of Smithers is the **Stork Nest Inn** (1485 Main Street, Box 2049, Smithers, V0J 2N0; 250–847–3831; fax: 250–847–3852; storknest@telus.net; www.storknestinn.com), where they serve free full breakfasts in a friendly talk-to-the-chef atmosphere. Internet access, local phone calls, newspapers, movie channels, and more are free, too.

As a modern, youthful town, Smithers, with a Swiss Bavarian (check out the life-size alpine herdsman statue in this Little Switzerland) theme, has a wide range of dining choices—from fast food to haute cuisine.

If you can find a few days to enjoy the scenic Bulkley Valley, **Berg's Bed and Breakfast** (3924 Thirteenth Avenue, Box 3235, Smithers, V0J 2N0; 888–847–5925 or 250–847–5925; fax: 250–847–5945; bvtbb@telus. net; www.bbcanada.com/2125.html) is within walking distance to town, has lovely views of the Hudson Bay Mountain and ski hill, and has hiking trails from the door. As experienced former tour directors, Beverley and David Berg can lead you to the best valley and mountain sites, such as historic **Moricetown Canyon,** 20 miles (32 km) west. In fall, fishers armed with gaffs or spears and nets challenge the rushing waters of the Wa Dzun Kwuh (Bulkley River) as it roars through a 50-foot (15-m) chasm. The village has some interesting, original totem poles.

An attractive log building houses the **New Hazelton Visitor Info Centre** (4070 Ninth Avenue, New Hazelton, V0J 2J0; 250–842–6071; fax: 250–842–6271), 22 miles (35 km) northwest of Smithers, at the junction of Highways 16 and 62. It's worth a traveling the 4 miles (7 km) to find out what's *off* the highway in this **Totem Pole Capital of the World,** which comprises two municipalities (the Village of Hazelton and the District of New Hazelton), three unincorporated settlements (South Hazelton, Two Mile, and the Kispiox valley), and four First Nations villages (Gitanmaax, Hagwilget, Glen Vowell, and Kispiox), as well as 'Ksan Village.

Head down the Hazelton High Road (Highway 62) and cross the one-lane *Hagwilget Bridge,* suspended like a tightrope high over the Bulkley River. Built in 1931, it replaced a rickety footbridge of poles lashed together with cedar-bark rope, which was used in the past as a trading route by the Gitxsan and Wet'suwet'en ("the people of the lower drainage").

Cross over the bridge, and about 3 miles (5 km) north, where the Skeena and Bulkley Rivers meet, seven communal houses and some fabulous totems make up the *'Ksan Historical Village* (Box 326, Hazelton, V0J 1Y0; 877–842–5518; 250–842–5544; fax: 250–842–6533; ksan@ksan.org; www.ksan.org). This Gitxsan village has been reconstructed similar in every detail to the village that stood on the site when the first Europeans explored the area some 200 years ago and how it was for millennia before that. Cultural interpreters guide you through the houses and relate the area's history. The museum houses a collection of items that make up Gitxsan material culture, from button blankets to headdresses (both worn by high chiefs) to bentwood books and coppers (valuable possessions). All pieces originate from a 30-mile (50-km) radius of 'Ksan, and some are owned by Gitxsan locals. From October through April 'Ksan Village hosts on-site the Kitanmax School of Northwest Coast Indian Design, a four-year carving and design program. During the months of July and August, the world-renowned 'Ksan Performing Arts Group can be seen. Guided tours are available May through October, but the gift shop and museum are open year-round.

Continue on to Hazelton, sitting like a Western movie set on the banks of the Skeena River. Take time to do a walking tour of this restored pioneer village, which includes a riverboat replica and an original steam donkey. Nine miles (14 km) north, the Kispiox River joins the Skeena at *Kispiox.* Here you'll find some of the best totems in all of BC. Kispiox's fourteen poles have been moved from their original sites in the village to a spot by the water's edge. The *Kispiox Cultural/Information Centre* (RR 1, Site K, Comp 25, Hazelton, V0J 1Y0; 250–842–7057; fax: 250–842–0157) sells local arts and crafts; it's open seasonally. Ask here about totem pole tours, hatchery tours, and the *Friday Salmon Barbecues,* where from June to September you can enjoy traditional Gitxsan food: half-smoked salmon, potatoes, onions, fried bread, salad, and a beverage. In the Cultural Centre there's a display of historical photos and artifacts. Products such as moccasins, beaded vests, chokers, necklaces, medicine bags, earrings, and carved silver and gold jewelry by renowned artists are on display for sale.

The all-native owned and operated company, *Skeena-Eco Expeditions* (same contact as Info Centre plus toll free: 877–842–5911; info@ kispioxadventures.com; www.kispioxadventures.com) offers river rafting, jet boat tours, hiking, canoe rental, and fishing trips, all with a cultural tie-in. Try for spring salmon from June to August and steelhead from July to October.

About twenty minutes up the Kispiox Valley Road from Kispiox, just before the Rodeo Grounds, the *Sportsman's Kispiox Lodge* (Kispiox Valley Road, Box 252, New Hazelton, V0J 2J0; 250–842–6455; fax: 250–842–6458; www.kispiox.com/lodge) is open year-round and has a licensed dining room and lounge. There are also self-contained cabins that sleep five and lodge rooms. The lodge will arrange white-water rafting, canoeing, and scenic river trips, fishing, trail riding, hiking, and natural history tours, as well as winter excursions. The Kispiox River is famous for its huge—in the thirty-pound (14-kg) range—native steelhead as well as for excellent salmon and trout fishing.

Terrace to Kitimat

Twelve miles (19 km) east of Terrace is one of British Columbia's loveliest parks. *Kleanza Creek Provincial Park* (www.bcparks. ca, search "Kleanza") features cascading waterfalls and a hiking trail to a beautiful view spot at the top of a canyon. *Kleanza* in Gitxsan means "gold," so some people like to try a little panning here. Don't laugh—back in 1934 some lucky panner took out a 6.3-ounce (180-gram) nugget. The park fronts the Skeena River and both sides of Kleanza Creek, where in fall you can watch for migrating pink (humpback) salmon.

At the eastern edge of Terrace, Highway 37 leads to *Kitimat,* 36 miles (58 km) south, at the head of Douglas Channel. Kitimat's industry accounts for approximately 10 percent of the province's manufacturing Gross Domestic Product, with the combined value of its industrial products being in the vicinity of $1 billion. Tours of what keeps Kitimat booming—*Alcan Smelter* (250–639–8259) and *Methanex/ Pacific Ammonia* (250–639–9292)—are provided free of charge weekdays from June to August. Reservations are required. For the Methanex tour, no children under twelve, no contact lenses, and no beards are allowed. For information write or phone *Kitimat Chamber of Commerce and Visitor Info Centre* (2109 Forest Avenue, Box 214, Kitimat, V8C 2G7; 800–664–6554 or 250–632–6294; fax: 250–632–4685; info@visitkitimat.com; www.visitkitimat.com). While there pick up information about the many hiking trails that criss-cross

Recommended Reading—The Northwest

FOR ADULTS:
The Skeena: River of Destiny, by Dr. R.G. Large. Heritage House Publishing Company, Ltd., 1996. First published in 1958. A BC classic.

Monkey Beach (A Novel), by Eden Robinson. Houghton Mifflin, 2000. An emotionally thrilling narrative that captures the essence of the Haisla of Kitamaat.

Cassiar's Elusive Gold, by Francis E. Caldwell. Trafford Publishing, 2000. An adventure story about a prospector willing to risk his life to find gold. Provides an in-depth look into early-day wilderness transportation in BC's Northwest.

Atlin's Gold, by Peter Steele. Caitlin Press, Prince George, 1995. The story of the Steele family's experience interspersed with the history of the Atlin area.

Canyon Creek: a script, by Sheila Peters and Meg Hobson. Creekstone Press (www.creekstonepress.com), 1998. Tells the disturbing story of the eviction of a Wet'-suwet'en family from its home site near Smithers in 1920.

Diary of Fort St. James, by Margaret Owen. Owen Enterprises, Box 464, Fort St. James (250–996–8680).

FOR TEENS:
War of the Eagles, by Eric Walters. Orca Books, 1998. Set on the west coast of Northern BC. The hero is a Tsimshian native. His best friend, who is a Japanese-Canadian, was interned in BC's interior during World War II.

the Kitimat area. One beautiful hike (rated moderate to difficult) is the *Douglas Channel Trail.*

In town at the *Kitimat Centennial Museum* (293 City Center, V8C 1T6; 250–632–8950; fax: 250–632–7429; kitimatmuseum@telus.net; www3. telus.net/kitimatmuseum), learn about oolichan trading and the grease trails, and visit the gift shop for some Haisla art and other local arts and crafts. Then head over to the Kitimat River to see BC's largest Sitka spruce tree. It's more than 500 years old, measures 36.7 feet (11.2 m) around, and is 165 feet (50.32 m) tall. There's apparently enough wood in it to frame nine houses. For campers the nearby *Radley Park Campground* (250–632–8955; fax: 250–632–3668) has fifty-six sites by the river. And if you're looking for a spot to eat, the *Chalet Restaurant* (852 Tsimshian Boulevard; 250–632–2662) and the *Ol' Keg Pub* (874 Tsimshian Boulevard; 250–632–6920) are both good bets for a tasty meal.

Kitamaat ("people of the snow" in Tsimshian) *Village,* the home of the Haisla and Henaaksiala people, is 7 miles (11 km) by road from Kiti-

Trivia

mat. You can see it across Douglas Channel from Hospital Beach near Alcan. Watch for killer whales, eagles, and sea lions as you gaze across to the village, where you can learn about the home of the Hudusdawachdu people in the untouched *Kitlope* ("people of the rocks") *Valley,* an area 80 miles (130 km) southeast of Kitimat. In 1994 this 780,000-acre (317,000-ha) valley was set aside as a protected area to preserve the world's largest intact coastal temperate rain forest. Contact the *Na Na Kila Institute* (130 Owekeno Street, Haisla Resource Centre, Box 1039, Kitamaat Village, V0T 2B0; 250–632–3308; fax: 250–632–3384; kevin dobbin@uniserve.com; www.nanakila.ca) for information on Eco-Adventure tours. The recently built *Kawesas Lodge,* a multipurpose 1,800-square-foot, post-and-beam building, which can hold up to forty people, will be used to facilitate ecotourism programs by the Na Na Kila Institute. Na Na Kila is working on a cultural interpretive trail in Kawesas for visitors to access and learn about Haisla traditions, culture, and sites. In the Na Na Kila gift shop in Kitamaat Village you'll find an excellent display of Haisla artwork.

At Mount Layton Hotsprings Resort by Lakelse Lake Provincial Park, south of Terrace, you'll hear tales about the big-tipping, luggage-lacking "Catholic priests," who were guests there for two weeks in October 1928. They turned out to be none other than Al Capone and three of his henchmen, escaping the heat of their rumrunning in the Prohibition-riddled Chicago.

Forty minutes north of Kitimat, and fifteen minutes south of Terrace, the *Mount Layton Hotsprings Resort* (Box 550, Terrace, V8G 4B5; 250–798–2214 or 800–663–3862; fax: 250–798–2478; mountlayton@ kermode.net; www.kermode.net/mountlayton) is a short hike to the lake at *Lakelse Lake Provincial Park* (www.bcparks.ca, search

The Thing

*I*f you're wondering what the large yellow "thing" across from the Terrace Visitor Info Centre is, meet Bertha, the only remaining portable spar pole in the world. This fifty-ton monster has had an up-and-down life as a tree mover. When first unloaded from a flatcar in 1952, it sank 3 feet into the rail-yard mud. After one use it was found to be totally impractical in the Terrace area, so it was parked, never to see service again. Designed to move logs by inserting the cut tree in the iron tube on the top and then attaching cables to lift the logs, Big Bertha was just too huge to move around in the bush; nor would her cables stay taut. So today the huge, bright white elephant exists merely as a curiosity, for tourists to say: "What's that thing?"

"Lakelse"), a 156-site campground thick with old-growth giant cedars, hemlock, and Sitka spruce. The public is invited to use the resort's odorless, open-air hot pools and waterslides ($6.75 slides; $4.50 pools, $2.50 for seniors and children three to twelve). Accommodation, which overlooks the pools, is in the $80 double range, and the sunset views of the snowcapped mountains are wonderful. Cross-country ski trails at **Onion Lake** are just five minutes away. There are two eating areas, the Poolside Restaurant open 7:30 A.M. to 10:30 P.M. for family use, and the Johnstone Dining Room, open 5:00 to 10:00 P.M. for a pleasant evening meal.

> ### Trivia
>
> *Terrace boasts the longest continually running amateur theater group in British Columbia, the Terrace Little Theatre, which was started more than fifty years ago.*

We're almost back to Terrace. Keep your eyes peeled, as you may catch a glimpse of the rare Kermodei, the elusive and mystical Spirit Bear, a white-colored black bear sometimes seen in the Skeena Valley. When two black bears breed, and each of these bears has a double-recessive gene, the result is a Kermodei. It has been chosen as Terrace's municipal symbol. Get your bearings at **Heritage Park** (4011 Sparks Street), where you can tour original log buildings, each depicting a different aspect of pioneer life; a short walk from here takes you to a spot where you can enjoy panoramic views of the Skeena River winding through the city and surrounds. Then check at the **Terrace Visitor Info Centre** (4511 Keith Avenue, Terrace, V8G 1K1; 800–499–1637 or 250–635–0832; fax: 250–635–2573; info@terracetourism.bc.ca; www.terracetourism.bc.ca), where an accommodation book will help you choose a pleasant spot to spend a few days. The staff can also provide a city map and information about hiking. One hike of interest leads round the perimeter of Ferry Island (across the bridge), where a local carver has created about sixty carvings in the trunks of trees—wizards, birds, wolves—there's quite a variety. And don't miss the colorful **Skeena Valley Farmers' Market,** (250–615–0025) held every Saturday (8:30 A.M. to 1:00 P.M.) and Wednesday (3:00 to 8:00 P.M.) from May to October on Davis Avenue behind George Little Park. This is the largest farmer's market in the northwest and illustrates the diversity of community in this fertile Skeena Valley.

The Info Centre has information on the **Kitselas Canyon** area, steeped in history, with settlements going back thousands of years. Archaeologists have been involved in digs here since 1968. Petroglyphs, totem poles, and longhouse remnants will hopefully not be allowed to weather away. Obtain permission from the Kitselas Band Council (4562 Queensway

Drive, Terrace, V8G 3X6; 250–635–5084; fax: 250–635–5335; kitselas. village@osg.net; www.kitselas.bc.ca) before exploring the area, which is accessible by a walking trail. Plans to develop and restore the area 9 miles (15 km) east of Terrace, near Kleanza Creek, are under way.

But the most spectacular, yet devastating, event in this area happened more than 250 years ago, about one hour north of Terrace on the mostly paved Nisga'a Highway toward New Aiyansh. Lava beds, created by a volcanic eruption (Canada's most recent), flowed into the Nass Valley for about 16 miles (25 km) downstream, resulting in an area resembling a *moonscape.* An amazing 330-foot-high (100-m) cinder cone stands in the spot where the eruption occurred, destroying two native villages and killing perhaps 2,000 people. Find out more about the *Nisga'a Memorial Lava Bed Provincial Park* at the Terrace Info Centre or visit www.bcparks.ca, search "Nisga'a." A visitor's center, built along the lines of a traditional longhouse, has displays pertaining to the many features and native legends associated with the eruption. Access to the cinder cone is by guided hike only. Call Steven Bolton (250–633–2991) at Gitwinksihlkw to see the Nisga'a people's homeland and the volcano that had such a devastating effect on their lives and their land. Camping (sixteen mostly shaded sites, no reservations) is available in the park. But if you'd like something more comfortable, *Miles Inn on the T'Seax Bed & Breakfast* (Nass Road, Box 230, New Aiyansh, V0J 1A0; toll free: 800–553–1199; 250–633–2636; fax: 250– 633– 2699) has beautiful accommodation, and the food is superb.

Before heading west to Prince Rupert, stop at the *House of Sim-oi-Ghets* (250–638–1629; fax: 250–635–4622; www.kitsumkalum.bc.ca), another longhouse-style building, where you can buy traditional west coast First Nations artwork, books, and clothing. It's just over the Kalum River west of Terrace on Highway 16 and is run by the Kitsumkalum Native Band.

Prince Rupert and the Coast

From Terrace there are 91 miles (147 km) of lovely twisting Yellowhead Highway to cover as it follows the Skeena River to Prince Rupert. Drive it by day or you'll miss towering snow-covered peaks, waterfalls, and possibly a bear or two.

Don't miss the *North Pacific Historic Fishing Village* (1889 Skeena Drive, Box 1109, Port Edward, V0V 1G0; 250–628–3538; fax: 250–628– 3540; www.district.portedward.bc.ca/northpacific), the oldest and most complete cannery village still remaining on the North Coast. The turnoff to this 1889-built National Historic Site is about 8 miles (12 km) before Prince Rupert. Students act as guides and storekeepers in this restored cannery (open daily May 15 to September 30 from 9:00 A.M. to 6:00 P.M.) where you can eat in the "messhouse" (The *Salmon House Restaurant*) and stay in the "bunkhouse" (*The Waterfront Inn).* Entrance into the sites to see videos on fishing, the restored cannery, displays on salmon enhancement, and one of the largest collections of model railroads in western Canada costs from $9.95 to $11.95 (children under six are admitted free). Visitors will be able to stroll past the twenty-eight cannery buildings lining the two boardwalks and see several exhibits, which include an authentic running canning line, a company store and office, living quarters, a net loft, and two First Nations housing units. As well there's live entertainment—a performance of the *Skeena River Story.*

In the heart of the village, *Macgregor Studio* (2161 Seal Cove Circle, Prince Rupert, V8J 2G4; 250–627–7171 or 250–628–3117; kmacgreg@ citytel.net; www.macgregorstudio.com) has a beautiful collection of one-of-a-kind Fabergé-style eggs, gem jewelry, paintings, sculpture, and more.

Prince Rupert (population 15,420 in 2002) is Canada's deepest ice-free harbor and is a major shipping port. It's the terminus for ferry traffic to Alaska, the Queen Charlotte Islands, and Vancouver Island, and for more than 10,000 years, it has been home to Tsimshian First Nations people. Their culture is depicted in the many totem poles seen throughout the city. Visit the carving sheds near the Court House downtown to watch the creation of these majestic poles.

Back in the eighties I had sailed into Cow Bay. A decade later, I headed straight to the waterfront, keen to see how it had changed. The area was once known as Cameron Cove in the community of Vickersville, but after a herd of cattle was unloaded off a barge into the water in 1909, the name Cow Bay stuck. A new cruise-ship terminal (Atlin Dock) has been built, so now, instead of cows, tourists head down the gangplanks. And instead of a dairy, there's fresh seafood for sale. The cowpatch black-and-white hydrants and fuel drums, though, do give you the impression that you're surrounded by a herd of Holsteins. To get to

Canoe and totem, Prince Rupert

Cow Bay from the highway (McBride Street), turn north on Third Avenue East and follow it across the railway line to Cow Bay Road.

"See You Latte" says the reverse of the business card at ***Cowpuccino's Coffee House*** at 25 Cow Bay Road, Prince Rupert, V8J 1A4; (250) 627–1395. For breakfast try a large, fresh-fruit salad and granola loaded up with yogurt, and a choice of Latte, Moocha, or Cowpuccino coffee. It opens early (from 7:00 A.M. daily except Sunday, when it's open from 9:00 A.M.) and will often play foot-tapping Bob Marley music.

Other interesting restaurants in the area include **Smiles Seafood Café** (113 Cow Bay Road; 250–624–3072), which has been around since 1934 and is famous for its halibut, and **Cow Bay Café** (205 Cow Bay Road; 250–627–1212; cbcafe@citytel.net), serving a colorful menu of fresh halibut with sun-dried tomato pesto, red Thai chicken curry, and vegetarian moussaka. And you can lose yourself in a library of books as you wait for your meal or watch the fleet come in.

There are accommodations at **Eagle Bluff Bed and Breakfast** (201 Cow Bay Road, V8J 1A2; 250–627–4955 or 800–833–1550 [toll free in Canada only]; fax: 250–627–7945; eaglebed@citytel.net; www.citytel. net/eaglebluff), right on the docks overlooking the Yacht Club, perfect for the landlubber with a secret desire to wake up to the sounds and smell of the sea. It was originally a cannery house. Double accommodation with a cozy nautical theme ranges from $55 to $90. Next door and still on the Cow Bay Pier, **Eco Treks Adventures** (203 Cow Bay Road, Prince Rupert, V8J 1A2; 250–624–8311; fax: 250–624–8318; ecotreks@ citytel.net; www.citytel.net/ecotreks) offers kayak rentals ($35 per half day, single; $50 double), evening Harbor tours ($25), two-hour Pictograph Tours ($50), five-hour Lucy Island Tours ($75), overnighters such as the Nass Valley Oolichan Run and the Khutzeymateen Grizzly Trek, and kayaking courses. The guides are all knowledgeable and experienced, and each has an infectious love of the natural environment.

Across from Cowpuccino's on Cow Bay Road, **The Rain Store** (250–627–1002) is full of wet-weather stuff—gumboots with bells attached, umbrellas, rain sticks, and colorful raincoats—which may give you a hint at what to expect from the weather! Above, there's **Opa Sushi** (250–627–4560)—awesome Japanese food.

A rewarding few hours can be spent at the **Museum of Northern British Columbia** (100 First Avenue West, Box 669, Prince Rupert, V8J 1A8; 250–624–3207; fax: 250–627–8009; mnbc@citytel.net; www. museumofnorthernbc.com) in its new quarters at the cedar-beamed **Chatham Village Longhouse.** It's open Monday through Saturday 9:00 A.M. to 5:00 P.M. and till 8:00 P.M. June through August (except Sunday). The museum is well known internationally for its exceptional northwest coast collection, which depicts Tsimshian settlement history, and for its quality display of smooth, black argillite carvings. It offers Heritage Walking Tours and visits to the Kwinitsa Railway Station Museum and the First Nations Carving Shed. Don't miss the opportunity to see (and join) the Quis'amiilgmgigol Dancers as they share their legacy of Tsimshian dramatic and musical performance art at the museum's 'Wiiwabbm Ts'Msyeen (Tsimshian longhouse).

THE NORTHWEST

Tourism Prince Rupert and the Visitor Info Centre (Suite 100, 215 Cow Bay Road, Prince Rupert, V8J 1A2; 250–624–5637 or 800–667–1994; fax: 250–627–8009; prtravel@citytel.net; www.tourismprincerupert.com) are both located in the Atlin Terminal. You'll find here maps for a tour of the city's totem poles; information on the *Firehall Museum* (200 First Avenue West, Prince Rupert, V8J 1A8; 250–624–2211; fax: 250–624–3407; www.princerupertlibrary.ca/fire), where if the firemen aren't out on a call, they'll show you around—ring the buzzer (Note: Operating costs are helped by donations and gift-shop sales—T-shirts, puzzles, photocards, etc.); and information on the *Kwinitsa Station Museum* (Bill Murray Way—named for a long-standing politician, not a comedian), down on the waterfront. This attractive building is one of the last Grand Trunk Pacific railway stations left

British Columbians have a thing about shoes. Port Hardy had the original "Shoe Tree," and now Prince Rupert has followed suit with its "Shoe Tree II, Home for Lost Soles." In 1994 Crystal Fitzpatrick and her family located a large but dead tree along Highway 16, about 2.5 miles (4 km) east of Prince Rupert. They decorated it with a year's collection of old work boots and children's shoes. Today the tree continues to "grow," as more and more passersby hang up their old shoes.

in BC. Summer hours (June–August) are daily from 9:00 A.M. to noon and 1:00 to 5:00 P.M. Several motels and hotels (more than 700 rooms), bed-and-breakfasts, hostels, and lodges are available in the area, but because of high ferry and railway passenger arrivals, accommodations can be tight; it is recommended that you book ahead. Contact the info center for assistance.

There's an excellent photo view of Prince Rupert from the top of Fifth Avenue West, or for a better view you could take a flight-seeing tour of the *Khutzeymateen River Valley,* a protected habitat for one of the highest concentrations of grizzly bears in the world. Contact *Harbour Air* (800–689–4234; 250–627–1341; fax: 250–627–8307; harbour@harbour-air.com; www. harbour-air.com) or *Inland Air Charters* (Box 592, Prince Rupert, V8J 3R5; 888–624–2577 or 250–624–2577; fax: 250–627–1356; info@ inlandair.bc.ca; www.inlandair. bc.ca), two of the companies offering this flight close to the Alaskan border. Flights leave from the seaplane base at Seal Cove. To get there take Sixth Avenue East (off McBride Street) and follow the seaplane signs. The cost for the one-hour Khutzeymateen trip from Inland Air is $218. A thirty-five-minute local tour costs $117 per person (both trips minimum three people). Check www.inlandair.bc.ca for an up-to-the-minute live dock camera view of their planes' activities.

A relaxing way to see the majestic Rocky Mountains and more is by VIA Rail (888–VIA–RAIL [842–7245] in Canada; 800–561–3949 in the

United States; www.viarail.ca) on a two-day 725-mile (1,160-km) day-light excursion on The Skeena. It leaves Prince Rupert three times weekly, stops overnight in Prince George (book your own accommodation), and ends in breathtaking Jasper (just across the Alberta border). The basic one-way fare (not including meals) is approximately $130. Totem Class fares (which include meals and access to the best views in the Park Cars but are only available peak-season) are approximately $480. If you take the westerly route, when you arrive in Prince Rupert you can head south via the Pacific Ocean route. Check details with BC Ferries (250–386–3431; 888–BCFERRIES; www.bcferries.ca).

The Stewart–Cassiar Highway

We return east, following the Skeena River, to Kitwanga, 138 miles (223 km) from Prince Rupert, and join the **Stewart–Cassiar Highway,** which after 454 miles (730 km) joins the Alaska Highway at the Yukon border. Although not as developed as the Alaska Highway, the road is incredibly scenic. Planning your gas and accommodation stops is an essential element to an enjoyable trip up "The Cassiar," but if you fill up every time you come to a gas station, you should have no problems. Most of the route is either pavement or seal-coat, but some portions are gravel. Check conditions at www.th. gov.bc.ca/roadreports.htm (click on "Hwy 16/37").

At Kitwanga cross the Skeena River Bridge and turn east, driving slowly along a very narrow loop road to Gitwangak, "place of the rabbits." Here you'll see twelve totems that tell the story of Kitwanga Fort and its defender, the fierce Nekt, who wore a suit of armor made from grizzly skins lined with pitch and slate. Information is available in **St. Paul's Anglican Church** (1893), across the road from the totems. It's one of BC's lovelier old wooden churches.

The **Kitwanga Fort National Historic Site** is 3 miles (5 km) north on Highway 37. Here, back in the 1600s, the Gitwangak people devised a defense system whereby logs were rolled on enemies who tried to attack the fort. Interpretive panels along a trail up to Battle Hill (Ta'awdzep) describe the history (in English, French, and Gitxsanmx). For more information write Fort St. James National Historic Park (Box 1148, Fort St. James, V0J 1P0; 250–996–7191; www.parkscanada.gc.ca, search "Kitwanga").

Nine miles north of the fort, and appearing on many maps as Kitwancool, is **Gitanyow.** Ask carvers working in the shed near several impressive totem poles to show you Hole in the Ice, believed to be the oldest totem in the world. The original pole was taken down and is in storage, but a new one has been carved and erected. You may have seen some of these poles depicted in paintings by renowned artist Emily Carr, who visited in 1928, and in more recent works by Roy Vickers. The Gitanyow are in the process of completing a historic village project, part of which includes turning the twenty-one *getimgan* (history poles)

Gitanyow, on Highway 37, means "place of many people." It was renamed Kitwancool, meaning "place of reduced number of people," after many people were killed by other tribes, then reinstated to its original name.

around to face east, thus restoring the original look of Gitanyow. A museum showcases repatriated artifacts and existing community collections, and future plans are for an interpretive trail, arts, crafts, and interactive displays, as well as a new carving shed. Check out the Web site at www.kermode.net/gitanyowchiefs—it features the Gitanyow totems. For more information contact: Gitanyow Hereditary Chiefs Office, Hu Wilp Society, Box 148, Kitwanga, V0J 2A0; (250) 849–5373; fax: (250) 849–5375; gitanyowchiefs@kermode.net.

The highway follows the shore of Kitwancool Lake and on to Cranberry Junction, where a westerly turn will take you on a logging road 38 miles (61 km) to New Aiyansh and the Nisga'a Memorial Lava Bed Park (covered in the section on Terrace). Fifty-two miles (83 km) north and you're at *Meziadin Junction.* Take a break about 9 miles (14 km) before the junction at the rest area at the south end of the bridge overlooking the Nass River. A few hundred yards north of the bridge, visit the *Meziadin Fish Ladder.* Information signs give the ladder's history. It's interesting and well worth a stop, especially in July and August, when the chinook are on their homeward spawning run. Don't be surprised to see a thirty-pound (13.5-kg) salmon leaping into the air in an effort to navigate the ladder. Close to the junction, camping facilities at the *Meziadin Lake Provincial Park* (www.bcparks.ca, search "Meziadin"; sixty-two sites), 96 miles (155 km) north of Kitwanga, are excellent. Fish, launch your boat, swim in the cool lake, and rest before the long road ahead.

Side Trip to Stewart

ighway 37 forks at Meziadin Junction, and Highway 37A (the Glacier Highway) travels 40 miles (65 km) to *Stewart,* at the head of Portland Canal. It passes the magnificent *Bear Glacier,* 16 miles (25 km) from Meziadin Junction, just beyond the Strohn Creek Bridge. Here, even on hot days, you can feel the cool air flowing off the

OFF THE BEATEN PATH

glacier. It's a fantastic sight, with the glacier so opalescent and blue that it glows at night. You may recognize these surroundings from the movies, as the final climactic scenes of the 2001 film *Insomnia,* starring Robin Williams, Al Pacino, and Hilary Swank, were staged on a frozen lake in the mountain valley of Bear Glacier. Along the 40 miles (65 km) to Stewart, you'll see more than twenty glaciers amid towering, craggy mountains. This road is definitely one of the most spectacular in North America.

Stewart and its American sister, Hyder, are frontier towns with a history of hard-rock gold, silver, and copper mining, but with such spectacular natural beauty, tourism is fast becoming a mainstay. The area is also valued as a movie backdrop (*Bear Island, The Thing, Iceman,* and *Leaving Normal* as well as *Insomnia*). By 1910 Stewart's population was booming at 10,000; today it's just a little more than 700. Around morning teatime you'll find a good percentage of the population at **The Bakery** (250–636–2777), when the steaming aroma of delicious donuts and pastries wafts from within.

Seaport Limousine (516 Railway, Box 217, Stewart, V0T 1W0; 250–636–2622; fax: 250–636–2633) provides bus service to Terrace and will also take you into the glacier country for a breathtaking trip through the steep Salmon River Valley. Colorful commentary of the valley's interesting history and characters adds to the tour as you travel past alpine meadows, bears, eagles, spawning salmon, and the spectacular **Salmon Glacier.** From mid-July through early September, with the arrival of the spawning salmon, the **Fish Creek Wildlife Observation Site** (one of the few bear-viewing areas in the world that you can drive to) allows visitors to see grizzly and black bears as they fish for chum and pink salmon in the shallow waters of the Fish and Marx Creeks below. The site, operated by the U.S. Forest Service (250–636–2367), is a day-use area only. To get there, follow a well-maintained gravel road (Salmon River Road) through Hyder and continue 3 miles (5 km) north. The parking area is on the left, past the Fish Creek Bridge. To cut down on congestion, owners of larger vehicles are advised to use the shuttle vans from Hyder and Stewart. Contact Seaport Limousine in Stewart (250–636–2622) or the Grandview Inn in Hyder (250–636–9174). For more information, drop into the **Historical Society Museum** and **Stewart/Hyder International Chamber of Commerce Information Centre** (222 Fifth Avenue, Box 306, Stewart, V0T 1W0; 888–366–5999 or 250–636–9224; fax: 250–636–2199; stewhydcofc@hotmail.com; www.stewartandhyder.homestead.com). The friendly staff will sell you a *Salmon Glacier Self-Guided Auto Tour* pamphlet to show you the way. They'll also reveal the good hiking and fishing spots in the area. If you're camping, the **Rainey Creek Campground** (250–636–2537; fax: 250–636–2668; off-season: 888–366–5999) on

Eighth Avenue borders a salmon stream. It's just a few minutes walk to the shops and a mile or so from Hyder, Alaska, where you can get into the "spirit" of things at the *Glacier Inn* (250–636– 9248) bar and earn an I'VE BEEN HYDERIZED certificate. If you're still standing after that jolt, stick with tradition and sign a dollar bill, which you then add to the 60,000-odd papering the walls of this quirky pub. Nothing's too serious in this friendly little ghost town.

In the morning head to *The Wildflour Coffee Shop* (250–636–2875), a very popular bakery and breakfast restaurant.

Extensive information on Stewart's mining history and bios of many of the area's early residents can be found at www.stewartbc.com. Another useful site for travelers is www.stewart-hyder.com.

The Grand Canyon of the Stikine

From Meziadin Junction the Stewart–Cassiar follows the Bell Irving River to Bell II, 57 miles (92 km) north. From Bell II you cross several creeks, then skirt Kinaskan, Tatogga, and Eddontenajon Lakes on the way to Iskut and the Grand Canyon of the Stikine. With so much dusty road to cover, and so many logging trucks, you're advised to drive cautiously.

On Eddontenajon Lake, about 2 miles (3 km) south of Iskut, **Red Goat Lodge** (Box 101, Iskut, V0J 1K0; 888–RED–GOAT/733–4628 for reservations; phone/fax: 250–234–3261; redgoatlodge@aol.com; www.karo-ent.com/redgoat.htm) is open year-round. The $85 double rate includes a full breakfast. There are also cabins and bunk rooms available, as well as a campground with hot showers and a laundry. Canoes can be rented, or perhaps a hike with the llamas is more your style. The lodge is perfectly positioned for hiking, canoeing, and fishing, with *Spatsizi Plateau Wilderness Park* to the east and *Mount Edziza Park,* with its 900,000-year-old crater surrounded by thirty small lava and cinder cones, to the west. For information on both provincial parks, visit www.bcparks.ca. Another recommended place to stay is *Bear Paw Ranch* (Box 69, Iskut, V0J 1K0; 250–234–3005; bearpaw@room42.com; www.room42.com/wilderness), 5 miles (8 km) north of Iskut in beautiful surroundings. Soak in the outdoor hot tub, take a package tour into the scenic wilderness, or simply cozy up around the fireplace with either hotel or cabin accommodation. For those who want to rough it, there's a tipi too. High-season hotel rates start at $85, and cabins, complete with a wood-fired sauna, start at $60.

When you reach Dease Lake, accommodation is limited. The **Northway Motor Inn and Restaurant** (Box 158, Dease Lake, V0C 1L0; 250–771–5341; fax: 250–771–5342) and the **Arctic Divide Bed & Breakfast** (Box 219, Dease Lake, V0C 1L0; 250–771–3119) are your two choices. The B&B rooms have private bath, TV, and access to a shared kitchen, with ample continental breakfast included.

Dease Lake should be renamed Halfway, as it's halfway between Seattle and Anchorage and halfway between Whitehorse and Smithers. It's also 52 miles (83 km) north of Iskut, at the junction of the 74-mile (119-km) spectacularly scenic gravel road (the first built in the Cassiar area) to historic **Telegraph Creek.** Leave your trailer in Dease; then check at the **Dease Lake and Tahltan District Chamber of Commerce** (Box 338, Dease Lake, V0C 1L0; 250–771–3900) for information and road conditions. At about 50 miles (80 km) west, the road starts to twist and roller-coast along narrow canyons, with rock walls almost 1,000 feet (300 m) high, past fish camps and lava beds along the Stikine River, till it reaches Telegraph Creek.

Accommodation here is limited, but you'll find everything you need (including free Internet access) at the original Hudson's Bay Company store, now the **Stikine RiverSong Cafe, Lodge & General Store** (Stikine Avenue, Box 47, Telegraph Creek, V0J 2W0; phone/fax: 250–235–3196; info@stikineriversong.com; www.stikineriversong. com). Double accommodation units are from $65. Talk to Dan Pakula at the lodge about a four-day boat trip down the Lower Stikine to Wrangell, Alaska. Shorter trips are available also, notably a jet boat tour of the breathtaking Lower Grand Canyon of the Stikine. For paddlers, Dan can also arrange kayak or canoe rentals and back hauls from Wrangell, thus cutting down on trip costs, as well as simplifying customs paperwork in Wrangell. The Web site gives all the details. If you have any doubts about driving the road to Telegraph Creek, staff at the lodge are a good source of information.

North to the Yukon Border

The road north from Dease Lake follows the pretty lake and river of the same name. A couple of rest areas at scenic spots, and good char and grayling fishing, make for a pleasant trip. At the Cassiar Junction you can pick up souvenirs at **Jade City Store** (Box A8, Jade City, Cassiar, V0C 1E0; 250–636–2593 or 2M3536 Cassiar channel). Buy raw jade and gold, gold nugget jewelry, semiprecious stones such as rhodonite and bloodstone, and gifts such as paintings done on jade.

Huge jade rocks from the Princess Jade Mine, one of the largest jade deposits in the world, are cut here in Jade City. The **Cassiar Mountain Jade Store and Mine** (Box B8, Jade City, V0C 1E0; 250–478–3905; cassiarmountain@yahoo.ca) is operated by the Princess Jade Mine owners. They offer rooms, a coffee shop, an RV park, and showers. Check out the outdoor interactive mining museum and the jade-mining photo collection. It's open year-round from 7:00 A.M. to 11:00 P.M. Continue north through the Kaska Dene First Nation village of Good Hope Lake for 20 miles (33 km) to one of the prettiest campsites I've ever stayed in, **Boya Lake Provincial Park** (www.bcparks.ca, search "Boya"). The forty-five sites, set beside a turquoise lake, are a boater's and photographer's joy. The clarity and rich color of the lake result from light reflecting from the bottom, which is composed of marl, a mixture of silt and coarse shell fragments. For more information on highway facilities and attractions, contact the Stewart–Cassiar Tourism Council, Box 14, Stewart, V0T 1W0; 866–417–3737; stewartcassiar@hotmail.com; www.stewartcassiar.com.

At Boya Lake, the **60th Parallel** (the Yukon border) is 50 miles (80 km) north, and the Alaska Highway is 2 miles (3 km) farther on. Since we left the Yellowhead, we've covered many a dusty mile, but there's still one little gem hidden way up in the far-northwestern corner.

Atlin is 290 miles (460 km) southwest of the junction of the Alaska and Stewart–Cassiar Highways. The turnoff is at Jakes Corner, 52 miles (84 km) southeast of Whitehorse. Although Highway 7 is mostly gravel, the 60-mile (98-km) scenic trip south along Little Atlin Lake and Atlin Lake, with the stunning, snow-clad Coast Mountains towering splendidly over them, is nothing short of magnificent. In the past it was a thriving gold rush town. Now its streets are paved with creativity, and there's a certain spirituality.

A good starting point for a tour of Atlin is the **Atlin Historical Museum** (Box 111, Atlin, V0W 1A0; phone/fax: 250–651–7522), on the corner of Third and Trainor Streets in a little 1902 schoolhouse. In summer museum staff members conduct walking tours of the town and the historic, elegantly restored **MV Tarahne.** In 1928 it took wealthy tourists on round-the-island cruises, but since 1936 it has lain idle on the shores of Atlin Lake. It's now the site of the annual "Tea on the Tarahne," held the first weekend of July, when period-costumed hostesses serve delicious refreshments and finger foods. On your walk around town watch for St. Martin's Anglican Church, built in 1900, and the Globe Theatre, built in 1917 and now fully restored.

A delightfully rustic place to stay can be found at the *Atlin Inn & Kirkwood Cottages* (Box 377, Atlin, V0W 1A0; 250–651–7546; fax: 250–651–7500; atlininn@atlin.net; 800–68–ATLIN/28546 for reservations) on Lake Street. The eighteen hotel rooms and eight cozy cottages occupy a downtown spot on the lakeshore, where, until the Depression, the three-story White Pass Hotel sat so majestically. Inn rooms in high season are in the $90 double range, and cabins run $103 double, with much reduced rates in winter. The fully licensed *Atlin Inn Lakeshore Restaurant* has recently been added and offers great views over the lake. If the restaurant is closed, try the coffee, soups, sandwiches, etc., next door at Kershaws (250–651–0018).

If you prefer bed-and-breakfast accommodation, try *Quilts & Comforts Bed & Breakfast* (Box 59, Atlin, V0W 1A0; 250–651–0007; 800–836–1818; quiltsandcomforts@clarkmail.com; www.quiltsandcomforts.com). Word has it that the breakfasts are amazing, the quilts (some available for purchase) beautiful, and the view, again, stunning. Afternoon tea, available to the public, is served in the National Award–winning garden. There's also *Win's Place* (Box 1, Atlin, V0W 1A0; 250–651–7490; 867–668–3653; fax: 250–651–7550), a restored, Victorian-style lakefront home built in the early 1900s in Discovery, a gold rush town that a century ago thrived about 5 miles (8 km) from Atlin. The historic cottage has been restored to classy accommodation that sleeps four. Privacy is the key, with home-baked goods supplied for guests to cook their own breakfast.

Log cabins are available from *Sidka Tours* (Box 368, Atlin, V0W 1A0; 250–651–7691), which also rents kayaks and canoes and offers guided tours. *Brewery Bay Chalet* (Box 349, Atlin, V0W 1A0; 250–651–0040; fax: 250–651–0041) offers self-contained two-bedroom units on the lake complete with barbecue. *Atlin Lake Houseboat Tours* (Box 381, Atlin, V0W 1A0, 250–651–0030) at Brewery Bay Marina offers sightseeing and dinner cruises.

The *Atlin Art Centre* (Box 207, Atlin, V0W 1A0; 800–651–8882 or phone/fax: 250–651–7659; atlinart@netcom.ca; www.atlinart.com) offers something entirely different. Overlooking the largest natural lake in BC (Atlin is from *ahtlah,* meaning "big lake" in the Taku River Tlingit people's language), guests here are given the choice of either art workshops or wilderness adventure. *Atlin Quest* is a series of ten-day wilderness adventure vacations, including hiking and canoeing ($1,800). The *Atlin Art Centre* offers creative retreats; ten days cost $980 and three weeks $1,500, tuition and accommodation included. The center operates from June to September.

THE NORTHWEST

Trivia

The lowest temperature ever recorded in British Columbia is -74° F (-58.9° C) at Smith River (in the northwest corner) in 1947.

One of the coolest things to do in Atlin is to pan for gold—legally and with hope! East of town, on Spruce Creek, there's a "keep all you find" panning claim, to which the friendly staff at the *Atlin Museum & Visitor Association* (Box 365, Atlin, V0W 1A0; phone/fax: 250–651–2211; visitors@ atlin.net; located in Happy Trails, Discovery Avenue and McBride Boulevard in summer, and at the south end of Second Street in winter) will direct you; they'll also direct you to the artists and outfitters who make this wild but exquisite part of British Columbia their home. Further information on Atlin can be found at www.atlin.net. Or contact *Bookies "R" Us,* (Box 426, Atlin, V0W 1A0; 250–651–2211; toll free in North America: 877– 399–BOOK [2665]; bookies-r-us@atlin.net) a booking agency experienced in arranging fishing, air, and sight-seeing charters, as well as accomodations and tickets for summer theater events, such as the *Murder Mystery* plays at the *M. V. Tarahne*, the *Vaudeville Revue*, and *Backwoods Story Telling*. Owner Heather Kennedy will also set you up with outdoor gear (retail or rental) and fishing tackle, and will arrange minor bike repairs at *Atlin's Happy Trails.* Ask Heather about the *Book of What To Do*, a good source of, well, what to do in this breathtaking Atlin area.

And to finish your exploration in this utopian northwestern corner, take a guided raft trip on the Tatshenshini and Alsek Rivers with *Tatshenshini Expediting* (1602 Alder Street, Whitehorse, Yukon, Y1A 3W8; 867–633–2742; fax: 867–633–6184; info@tatshenshiniyukon. com; www.tatshenshiniyukon.com). Prices range from $100 per person for a one-day trip on the Upper Tatshenshini River to $2,900 for an eleven-day Tatshenshini/Alsek expedition. (Special group rates are available.) You'll pass through three United Nations World Heritage Sites: *Kluane National Park* in the Yukon; *Tatshenshini–Alsek Wilderness Park* in the most remote corner of BC; and Alaska's *Glacier Bay National Park.* Expect to be overwhelmed as you pass by huge icebergs thunderously calving off Alsek Glacier, and the gigantic peaks of the St. Elias Mountains, which include BC's highest peak, the 15,300-foot (4,663-m) Mount Fairweather. You'll end your journey in Alaska, where the Alsek meets the Pacific's pounding surf at Dry Bay, and from here, fly by charter to Whitehorse in the Yukon.

The final adventure in our BC journey takes place on the magical Queen Charlotte Islands, as the eagle flies, about 400 miles (640 km) south of Dry Bay.

PLACES TO STAY IN THE NORTHWEST

ATLIN
Atlin Inn & Kirkwood Cottages, Box 377, Atlin, V0W 1A0; (800) 68-ATLIN; atlin-inn@atlin.net. On Lake Street. New fully licensed restaurant also.

Quilts & Comforts Bed & Breakfast, Box 59, Atlin, V0W 1A0; (250) 651-0007; (800) 836-1818. Great breakfasts, beautiful gardens and views.

BURNS LAKE
Darter's Misty Willows Ranch Bed and Breakfast, Colleymount Highway, Box 455, Burns Lake, V0J 1E0; phone/fax: (250) 695-6573; mdarter@futurenet.bc.ca.

FORT ST. JAMES
Big Bay Bed and Breakfast, Box 1849, V0J 1P0; (250) 996-8857.

KISPIOX
Sportsman's Kispiox Lodge, Kispiox Valley Road, Box 252, New Hazelton, V0J 2J0; (250) 842-6455. Open year-round; lodge, cabins, fishing. Licensed dining room and lounge.

ISKUT
Bear Paw Ranch, Box 69, Iskut, V0J 1K0; (250) 234-3005; www.room42.com/wilderness.

Red Goat Lodge, Box 101, Iskut, V0J 1K0; (888) RED-GOAT (733-4628) for reservations; phone/fax: (250) 234-3261.

NEW AIYANSH
Miles Inn on the T'Seax, Nass Road, Box 230, New Aiyansh, V0J 1A0; (800) 553-1199; (250) 633-2636. Superb food and surroundings.

PRINCE RUPERT
Eagle Bluff Bed and Breakfast, 201 Cow Bay Road, Prince Rupert, V8J 1A2; (250) 627-4955 or (800) 833-1550; www.citytel.net/eaglebluff.

SMITHERS
Berg's Bed and Breakfast, 3924 Thirteenth Avenue, Box 3235, Smithers, V0J 2N0; (888) 847-5925 or (250) 847-5925; www.bbcanada.com/2125.html.

TELKWA
The Old Schoolhouse B&B, 1617 Riverside Street, Telkwa, V0J 2X0; (250) 846-5939. Self-catering. On river.

TERRACE
Mount Layton Hotsprings Resort, Box 550, Terrace, V8G 4B5; (250) 798-2214 or, in Canada, (800) 663-3862; www.kermode.net/mountlayton.

PLACES TO EAT IN THE NORTHWEST

ATLIN
Kershaws, (250) 651-0018. Coffee, soups, and sandwiches.

BURNS LAKE
China Moon, (250) 692-7411. In the Lakeview Mall.

FORT ST. JAMES
Whisky Jack Restaurant; (250) 996-8828. Licensed dining 5 miles north of town; closed Monday; reservations in the evening.

KITIMAT
Chalet Restaurant, 852 Tsimshian Boulevard, V8C 1T5; (250) 632-2662. Moderately priced meals. Motel accommodation also.

PRINCE RUPERT
Cowpuccino's Coffee House, 25 Cow Bay Road, V8J 1A4; (250) 627-1395. Light and healthful.

Cow Bay Café,
205 Cow Bay Road,
Prince Rupert, V8J 1A2;
(250) 627–1212.
Fresh halibut on the
waterfront.

TELKWA

The Crocodile,
Highway 16, Telkwa, V0J
2X0; (250) 846–9268.

VANDERHOOF

OK Café,
(250) 567–2594. Located
in Vanderhoof's Heritage
Village Museum.

The Queen Charlotte Islands/ Haida Gwaii

ell any Canadian that you're trekking around British Columbia, and the first question is inevitably: "Have you been to the Charlottes?" Canadians think of them much as a new mother does her baby. They're precious. When a drifter took a chain saw to a beloved golden spruce tree near Port Clements, not only were residents horrified at the destruction, the whole country was in an uproar.

I had dreamed for years of visiting these misty, mysterious islands, known for 10,000 years to their outspoken native inhabitants as *Haida Gwaii* ("Islands of the People"). Their appeal lies in the mythology and artistry surrounding the Haida culture, combined with their isolation and stormy, rugged loveliness.

Consisting of two main islands, the more populated Graham in the north and Moresby in the south, four smaller islands, and about 150 teeny specks of islands, Haida Gwaii stretches like an elongated, curved triangle for 166 miles (251 km) from Langara Island in the northwest to Kunghit in the southeast. The remote southern part of Moresby is entirely Gwaii Haanas National Park Reserve, an area cherished by wilderness adventurers and the Haida people, who make up about one-sixth of the population of 5,000.

We begin our journey with a six-hour sailing across a sometimes boisterous Hecate Strait on a BC ferry trip from Prince Rupert to Skidegate, a few minutes from Queen Charlotte on Graham Island. Vehicle reservations (888–223–3779 or 250–386–3431) are required, as there are only four to six sailings per week from each port in summer and three in winter. BC Ferries' Web site (www.bcferries.bc.ca) lists fares and schedules and allows on-line reservations. (As a general guide, in summer expect to pay about $25 one-way per person—$16.75 for seniors (residents of BC only) and teens, $12.50 for children five to eleven—and $93.00 per regular-height vehicle, with an extra $40.00–$46.00 if you

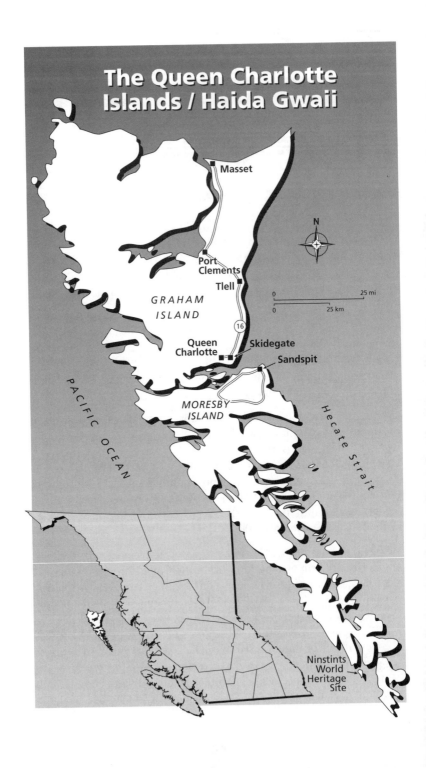

AUTHOR'S TOP TEN PICKS ON
THE QUEEN CHARLOTTE ISLANDS

*Haida Gwaii Museum
at Skidegate, with its
ancient totems*

*More ancient totems at
Ninstints—a spiritual
odyssey*

*Bird-watching at Delkatla
Wildlife Sanctuary,
north of Masset*

*Kayaking at Hot
Springs Island*

*Hiking to the blowhole
near Tow Hill*

*Golfing at Dixon Entrance
Golf and Country Club*

*Crystal Cabin Gallery
Rock and Gem Gift Shop*

*Hiking to the Pesuta
shipwreck in Naikoon
Provincial Park*

*Camping at Rennell Sound
on the wild west coast*

*Joining in the fun at Logger
Sports Day in Sandspit*

want an overnight cabin.) From Sandspit, 3 miles (5 km) from Skidegate, a paved road (Highway 16 and still the Yellowhead) leads to Masset and clam-filled northern beaches, or alternatively, a twenty-five-minute ferry ride runs south to Alliford Bay, 8 miles (13 km) from the village of Sandspit on Moresby Island. The whole of the southern part of Moresby Island is taken up by the Gwaii Haanas National Park Reserve and UNESCO World Heritage Site, Ninstints. We'll visit this mystical landscape after we've explored Graham Island.

Queen Charlotte City

Queen Charlotte City is the administrative center for the islands. Don't be fooled by the word *city*, though. It's about as laid-back as a city can be and some locals tell me the word *city* should be dropped as it is *not* official. You'll see what I mean if you start with a 6:30 A.M. coffee at *Lam's Café* on Wharf Street (250–559–4204). Previously called Margaret's, this little gem of a restaurant has been around for about fifty years and has that homey, help-yourself-to-the-coffee friendly feel about it. Don't come after 2:45 P.M., though, as the owners, Melissa and Lam, close up early. I tried the hamburger and seafood chowder lunch special, which was excellent. There's also a variety of delicious-sounding crab items on the menu and some newly added Chinese specials. Takeout is available on weekends.

Across the road, in the *Sea Raven Motel and Restaurant* (Box 519, Queen Charlotte City, V0T 1S0; 250–559–4423; 800–665–9606 toll free in BC or Alberta; fax: 250–559–8617; info@searaven.com; www.searaven. com), *Joy's Island Jewellers* (Box 337, Queen Charlotte, V0T 1S0; 250–559–8890; fax: 250–559–8896; joys@qcislands.net; www.qcislands. net/joys) sells Haida-carved argillite, gold, and silver, woven cedar baskets, button blankets, trade beads, and other souvenirs such as T-shirts, local books, and jewelry. Farther along the main street at *Rainbows Gallery* (3201 Third Avenue, Box 489, Queen Charlotte, V0T 1S0; 250–559–8420; fax: 250–559–8430; rainbows@qcislands.net; www.qcislands. net/rainbows), there's a large selection of Haida art, including antique

Native heritage crafts and collectibles, books, carved gold, and the famous black argillite, a soft slate found only on Slatechuck Mountain, west of Queen Charlotte City, and reserved exclusively for the Haida.

A quick look in at *Hanging by a Fibre* (1–3207 Wharf Street; 250–559– 4463), a clothing store/cappuccino bar with unusual Queen Charlotte– theme T-shirts and more, then on to *Meegans Store* (*The Best Little Lure House in the Charlottes;* 250–559–4428), where they have tide tables and hand out "lurist" information (if you're here for the wild steelhead or trophy halibut), and I was ready to explore this Canadian Galápagos.

One place that will turn your exploration into a one-stop shop is *Gwaii Eco Tours and Lodging* (604 First Avenue, Box 249, Queen Charlotte, Haida Gwaii, V0T 1S0; 877–559–8333 or 250–559–8333; gwaiieco@haida gwaii.net; www.gwaiiecotours.com). They have reservations-only accommodation, where you'll enjoy a garden-and-forest setting with an ocean view and outdoor hot tub. The owners, Joy and Louie Waters, will arrange land and sea day trips and multiday interpretative spiritual tours.

Some Facts on the Gray Whale: *Eschrichtius Robustus*

*L*ook out to Hecate Strait during late spring and keep your eyes peeled for the blotchy back of a gray whale. Besides their gray color, sometimes mottled orange and white with barnacles and whale lice, grays are distinguished by the lack of a dorsal fin. They can be quite active and are often seen spyhopping and breaching.

Unlike the killer whale, which has teeth, the gray whale mainly feeds by straining its food through baleen, which is made of about 150 fringed, overlapping keratin plates hanging like fine hairs from the roof of the mouth on each side of the upper jaw. When feeding, the whale rolls on its side on the ocean bottom and draws sediment into its mouth. (You can tell if it's a left or right feeder by checking the barnacles and scratches!) It closes its mouth, then water and sediment get pushed through the baleen, which traps the food near the huge tongue and is then swallowed. While migrating, the gray will feed at the surface on small fish and shrimplike mysids. Once it reaches the Arctic, it will consume its main prey, gammarid amphipods. The adult gray whale can grow to a length of 50 feet (15 m) and weigh up to 36 tons (33,000 kg). Calves are born approximately 16 feet (5 m) long and weigh about 0.8 tons (700 kg), but after suckling 200 liters of milk (53 percent fat!) daily, by the time they are ready for the 12,000-mile (19,500-km) round-trip between the northern feeding grounds in the Beaufort, Bering, and Chukchi Seas and the southern breeding grounds in Baja California and off the Korean coast, they'll have doubled in weight.

THE QUEEN CHARLOTTE ISLANDS/HAIDA GWAII

Before heading off to explore farther, though, get up-to-date information at the **Queen Charlotte Visitor Info Centre** (3220 Wharf Street, Box 819, Queen Charlotte City, V0T 1S0; 250–559–8316; fax: 250–559–8952; info@qcinfo.com; www.qcinfo.com), open May 1 to September 30, 10:00 A.M. to 7:00 P.M., or at the airport in Sandspit (250–637–5362) from 9:00 A.M. to 5:00 P.M.

Less than a mile north of the ferry landing, at the blue museum sign on Highway 16 at Second Beach, is the Haida Gwaii Watchmen Office (Box 1413, Skidegate, Haida Gwaii, V0T 1S1; 250–559–8225; fax: 250–559–8693) where you'll find information on the ancient villages in South Moresby. Next door stand six totems carved by master carvers and their apprentices, and the canoe shed containing **Loo Taa** ("Wave Eater"), a 50-foot (15-m) cedar dugout canoe, whose carving was overseen by the famous Haida artist Bill Reid. Traditional techniques were used in this Expo 1986 commission, which was paddled home from Vancouver when the fair ended. In true Haida style a great potlatch celebration greeted its arrival.

Next door **The Haida Gwaii Museum** at Qay'llnagaay (Box 1373, Skidegate, V0T 1S1; 250–559–4643; fax: 250–559–4662; muse@qcislands.net) houses a collection of Haida art and historical objects of the Queen Charlottes. Magnificently displayed totem poles, two from Tanu and two from Skedans, the ancestral home of many of Skidegate's residents, are some of the museum's most distinctive features. Other displays include fossils, hands-on discovery boxes (island nature themes), endemic birds and mammals, and one of the world's finest argillite collections. An outdoor viewing deck extending to the tip of Qaykun Point offers an excellent observation area for birds, seals, sea lions, killer whales, and the gray whales that migrate in spring. You'll also find historic photos of Mexico Tom (the area's first rancher) and a seismometer, a reminder that the strongest earthquake (8.1) ever recorded in Canada occurred on Aug 22, 1949, off the west coast of Graham Island. The shaking was so severe along the Queen Charlotte Fault (Canada's equivalent of the San Andreas Fault)—the boundary between the Pacific and North American plates, which runs underwater along the west coast of the Queen Charlotte Islands—that cows were knocked off their feet! The museum is open daily in summer. Off-season hours vary, so phone for information. The museum gift shop has an excellent selection of Haida art, crafts, and books. But there's expansion in the air.

The Qay'llnagaay Heritage Centre Society (250–559–7709) recently commissioned the carving of six poles on Second Beach; they were raised in June 2001. This event heralded the beginning of the construction of a 68,000-square-foot (6,317-sq-m) facility that will incorporate the existing museum. Aimed at preserving and celebrating Haida culture, the facility will include an expanded museum, an interpretive center, the Bill Reid Teaching Centre, a performing arts theater, and a canoe center, plus a hotel and restaurant. The new center will open to the public in the spring of 2005.

Before heading north make sure to stop at the former Skidegate Band office (now a teaching facility) to see the tall **Dogfish Pole,** also created by Bill Reid. Just north of Skidegate look for **Balance Rock,** a strange phenomenon left on the beach thousands of years ago by moving glaciers. From late April to June, a plume of rainbowed mist rising out of the water may enhance the scene, as a gray whale pauses to feed on its Mexico-to-Alaska migration.

Graham Island Central

Tlell is becoming noted for its community of artists. The first studio you pass driving north on Highway 16 (peacefully hidden on the beach, but there's a sign) is **Bottle and Jug Works** (250–559–4756).

The Dawn Watch

I had just driven off the ferry from Prince Rupert and was now between Skidegate and Tlell. A delicate first blush of sunrise added sheen to views across Hecate Strait. I quietly unlocked my Pentax, eager to capture the magic. I looked up. A lone bald eagle eyed me inquisitively from a stark conifer. Exhilarated, I clicked, hoping I wouldn't destroy the dawn's serenity. As I drove off, huge wings spread out above me. A few hundred yards on,

another rose-tinted seascape had me reaching for my camera. As if reading my mind, the brown-black body and radiant white head swooped, sharp talons finding a tall gray snag above me. Again, the golden-brown eyes pierced me intensely. I felt like an intruder, but furtively stole another image. Mysteriously, the eagle followed my journey, continuing to sear my soul with its glare, as together, we kept this lonely vigil.

John and Jennifer Davis, teachers who arrived on these isolated islands in 1965, named the studio for their two previous dogs. They create bowls and other interesting, functional pottery.

North of the post office on Highway 16 in Tlell, follow the "A" signs left onto Wiggins Road and right onto Richardson. Tucked away, just a minute from the highway, are a few little treasures. At one, the **Crystal Cabin Gallery Rock and Gem Gift Shop** (778A Richardson Road, Box 88, Tlell, V0T 1Y0; phone/fax: 250–557–4383; 866–557–4383; goldngem@island.net), Dutes Dutheil creates fabulous gold and silver gemstone jewelry. His wife, Laura, makes fiber-art-sculpture spirit dolls, intricately embroidered and beaded amulets, and incredible talking sticks—6 feet long and hand-beaded with crystals. Her spirit dolls have spellbinding stories associated with them. From Copper Woman to Medicine Woman and Jade Woman, they're all unique, all beautiful. Hidden inside there may be a stick of sage, a crystal—something special to the

Recommended Reading—The Queen Charlotte Islands

FOR ADULTS:

A Guide to the Queen Charlotte Islands, by Neil G. Carey. Grasshopper Books, March 1998. A must for travelers to the Queen Charlottes.

Puffin Cove: Escape to the Wilderness of the Queen Charlotte Islands, by Neil G. Carey. Hancock House Publishers, 1989.

Haida Gwaii: The Queen Charlotte Islands, by Dennis Horwood and Tom Parkin. Heritage House, May 2000.

The Beloved Island, by Kathleen Dalzell. Harbour Publishing, October 1998.

The Queen Charlotte Islands 1774–1966 Volume 1, by Kathleen Dalzell. Harbour Publishing, 1968.

The Queen Charlotte Islands–Volume 2, **Places and Names,** by Kathleen Dalzell. Harbour Publishing, 1973.

Ninstints: Haida World Heritage Site, by George F. MacDonald. Vancouver: UBC Press, 1984.

FOR KIDS:

The Raven Steals the Light, by Robert Bringhurst and Bill Reid (Illustrator). University of Washington Press, 1996. Ages four to eight. Adults will enjoy this book too—anyone with an interest in native legends will.

Myths and Legends of Haida Indians of the Northwest: The Children of the Raven, by Martine Reid. Bellerophon Books, June 1988. Ages nine to twelve.

doll. You'll also find here one of the island's largest Haida argillite collections, both small and large pieces. Talented native artists work with Laura, designing and creating blankets and clothing sold exclusively in the store. The gift shop also sells fossils, crystals, and Island Scenic Stone, a local stone surreally embedded with natural scenes. A new addition to the gallery is Dutes's sculpture **Tlell Stone Circle,** showing mineral and fossil specimens from the islands. It's designed in the concept of an ancient medicine wheel and depicts the geological history of Haida Gwaii. Opening hours are 9:00 A.M. to 6:00 P.M. year-round and 9:00 A.M. to 8:00 P.M. July and August; all major credit cards are accepted.

Across the road is *Sitka Studio* (Box 33, Tlell, V0T 1Y0; 800–557–4241; phone/fax: 250–557–4281; barbara@sitkastudio.com; www.sitkastudio.com). Barbara Small and artist Noel Wotten sell exceptional artwork and crafts featuring local artists. Look for batiks, bird's-eye yellow cedar boxes, and Haida art, plus quality chocolate, teas, and organic coffee beans. Upstairs there's a large selection of books and artists' supplies.

They also rent out a fully equipped two-story cottage. *Sitka Lodging* (250–557–4241; 800–557–4241) overlooks geese, ducks, and wild swans by the Tlell River. Don't leave without asking Noel to show you his unique tree house, which is the butt of an enormous burled spruce tree, roofed with cedar shakes and a droopy copper peak, looking a little like a giant guard-cockatoo. Some people might say it's more like the butt of an enormous joke. It's furnished with chain-saw-hewn chairs, and the story goes that the famous Canadian author/artist/filmmaker James Houston had a hand in it. If you're lucky, as I was, you'll find some of Houston's original work in Sitka Studio.

Trivia

The famous golden spruce that drew tourists to the Port Clements area before it was destroyed in 1997 was 165 feet (50 m) tall, was more than 300 years old, and had uniquely golden-colored needles.

Tlell has been the site of fish camps, farms, and artists' hideouts. The spread-out community, 22 miles (36 km) north of Skidegate, also has some intriguing places to stay.

Austrian-born Cacilia Honisch runs *Cacilia's B&B* (Box 3, Tlell, V0T 1Y0; phone/fax: 250–557–4664; ceebysea@qcislands.net; www.qcislands.net/ceebysea). There's loads of space to spread out in and elegant double bedrooms. *Rustic* (the toilet-roll holders are driftwood and the shower-stall floor is pebbled) and *beachy* (the dunes are right outside) are key words. You never know who you might meet sitting on the driftwood/macramé barstools. There's also a funky

Sitka Lodging burled tree house

stackwall cabin, complete with in-built glass bottles. It has no electricity or running water, but the view to the beach makes up for this. The B&B is easy to find—heading north on Highway 16, turn right after the 2 KM TO NAIKOON PARK sign, 25 miles (40 km) north of the Skidegate ferry dock.

Just north of Tlell, near the **Misty Meadows Campsite** at the southern tip of **Naikoon Provincial Park** (phone locally 250–557–4390 or visit www. bcparks.ca, search "Naikoon"), a 3-mile (5-km) trail beginning at the Tlell River Bridge leads along the north shore of the river and through the forest to Hecate Strait and the 1928 **Pesuta** shipwreck. Do the hike on an outgoing tide, as the river comes up to the dune cliffs on high tides.

If you keep walking, it's another 52 miles (84 km) to **Rose Point** (or "Naikoon," meaning "long nose," as it was called by the Haida), the most northerly spot in the Charlottes. As one local commented: *Why would anyone want to do that?* It's total wilderness hiking, with no drinking water, nothing but rugged beach scenery, Sitka blacktail deer, tufted puffins, possibly even a few wild cows (although it's a while since they've been seen), and a few streams to ford. Tide tables and a lot of common sense are necessary items, especially considering how the surf can pound against the 400-foot (120-m) cliffs just north of Cape Ball. There's some respite, though, with three rustic wilderness shelters en route, off the beach, but open one end for the wind to whistle through! You must register and have permission from the park office to hike this dramatic East Beach Trail, in this unspoiled 179,490-acre (72,640-ha), boggy, wild tract.

From Tlell the highway crosses the island for 13 miles (21 km) northwest to **Port Clements,** home to loggers and purse seiner fishers on Masset Inlet. The famous **Golden Spruce,** a feature of Haida mythology that was sadly destroyed in an act of madness in 1997, was its claim to fame. There's still a piece of history left in the area, though—the beginnings of a 300-year-old 50-foot (15-m) **Haida dugout canoe.** Follow the signs into Port Clements, staying on Bayview Drive heading toward **Juskatla.** The road quickly deteriorates and becomes a private, industrial logging road, so you must first get permission from Weyerhaeuser at their office in Juskatla (250–557–6810), open Monday to Friday 8:00 A.M. to 4:30 P.M., drive with headlights on, expect a logging truck on every corner, pull over and stop when you do see one, and obey all speed limits and posted signs. The canoe is in its original site on the east side of the road. Look for the trail sign 8 miles (13 km) south of Port Clements. The Ministry of Forests in Queen Charlotte City (250–559–6200) can also help with logging road usage.

<table>
<tr><td>

Trivia

The islands that make up the Queen Charlotte archipelago have developed in isolation from the rest of the province. They were spared the effects of the ice age that covered the rest of British Columbia up to 15,000 years ago.

</td></tr>
</table>

This gravel road from Port Clements makes for an exciting circle tour. It follows the Mamin and Yakoun Rivers south across a couple of bridges to the **Marie Lake Fish Hatchery,** 25 miles (40 km) south of Port Clements. The program is run by the Old Massett Village Council (Box 189, Masset, V0T 1M0; 250–626–5655) and is designed to enhance chinook stocks in the Yakoun River. A short walk from the 40Q bridge on the Yakoun River (renowned for its steelhead fishing), there's a campsite called **Papa John's** (picnic tables, but no toilets or water), popular with fishing fanatics.

When you see sign 23S, you're at the turnoff to Rennell Sound. Other than by boat, it's the only way to get to the rugged west coast. The road passes the turnoff to Yakoun Lake, and near the end there's a very steep hill (24 percent grade for 1 km!), with an appropriate STEEP HILL sign. Picnic

WORTH SEEING/DOING ON THE QUEEN CHARLOTTE ISLANDS

Go bird-watching north of Masset at Delkatla Wildlife Sanctuary.

Do an artisan tour of Haida and non-Haida studios.

Sail or kayak around the islands.

Take a helicopter sightseeing trip from the Sandspit airport.

tables, pit toilets, and fire pits, plus a pounding surf and miles of empty beaches, add to the appeal of these rustic wilderness campsites.

Back at the junction the main logging road continues south from the Yakoun River Bridge for 14 miles (22 km) to Queen Charlotte, ending on dust-free (yes!) paved roads. You may wish to do the circle clockwise, starting in Queen Charlotte at *Hooterville,* a squatter community of weather-beaten float homes at the west end of town.

It's but 26 miles (42 km) from Queen Charlotte to Rennell Sound. Consider doing a twenty-minute hike to *Yakoun Lake.* You'll pass old-growth, absolutely enormous Sitka spruce (Haida Giants!) en route to this pristine lake, enhanced by views of Mount Stapleton, Mount Needham, and Delta Dome. Watch for the YAKOUN LAKE TRAIL sign, after turning south off Rennell Sound Road. There's a pebbly beach to be enjoyed when you get there.

Graham Island North

Masset, 25 miles (40 km) due north of Port Clements on Highway 16, has until recently been a Canadian Forces Base. Here you're at Western "Mile Zero" for the Yellowhead Highway (Highway 16), and here I discovered a superb place for a meal. The *Sandpiper Restaurant,* at 2062 Collison Avenue (Box 669, Masset, V0T 1M0; phone/fax: 250–626–3672; engelhar@island.net), run by Thi Hai and Fritz Engelhard, is one of those unexpected treats you sometimes stumble on in the most out-of-the-way places. With Haida prints gracing the walls to add local flavor, I enjoyed an evening special: a delicate lemon-chicken vegetable soup followed by Potatoes William, Fillo Purse (stuffed with peppers and onion) and Steak and Prawns Marsellaise, and completed by sinfully rich chocolate mousse cake, the equal of any big-city haute cuisine. The poached halibut with shrimp sauce is a winner with seafood lovers. The restaurant is near the Royal Canadian Mounted Police station and is open every day except Sunday.

A newer restaurant in Masset is the now famous *HaidaBucks* (1675 Main Street, Masset, V0T 1M0; 250–626–5548). It's famous not only for the enticing aroma of fresh-roasted coffee and the taste of its delectable foods but also because coffee giant Starbucks has threatened to take legal action to stop the "confusing variation" of their name (four years after it had been operating). The name "buck" in the Haida Gwaii language is a term of endearment for a young man, and as the owners are all young Haida men, the name is appropriate. A little international fame can't go astray, but the coffee and food speak for themselves. This longhouse-style sixty-seat restaurant offers everything from coffee to quesadillas to seafood specials.

An absolutely delightful place to stay in Masset is *Copper Beech House* (1590 Delkatla, Box 97, Masset, V0T 1M0; 250–626–5441; www.copper beechhouse.com). David Phillips runs an offbeat, laid-back bed-and-breakfast establishment year-round and serves gourmet dinners by arrangement (bring your own bottle), using produce from his own lovely garden. He opened Copper Beech House in 1986 after extensive renovations to a 1914 seaside saltbox, which had been moved from Naden Harbour, 50 miles (80 km) to the west, to this delightful spot overlooking the harbor. David is renowned for his warm hospitality and gourmet cooking, having served both ambassadors and Prime Ministers alike.

Old Massett (different spelling, and sometimes called Haida) stands on the site of three ancient Haida town sites. To get there from Masset, travel west on Collison Avenue and turn right at the beach. The village is about a mile along and is spread out parallel to the beach on two main streets, Raven and Eagle.

The first thing you'll notice is the number of totems in the village. Some are erected outside homes, one outside St. John's Anglican Church (carved in 1969 by talented Haida artist Robert Davidson), and in the ball field there are replicas of two that stood in the old village of Yan. Two Reg Davidson poles stand in front of *Haida Arts and Jewellery* (387 Eagle Road, Old Massett; 250–626–5560). Behind a frontal house painting of Raven and Eagle, Sarah Hillis sells Haida art and souvenirs, including large argillite carvings, painted cedar-bark woven hats and baskets, and painted drums and paddles.

Before leaving Masset, visit the *Delkatla Wildlife Sanctuary* (Box 246, Masset, V0T 1M0; admin@birdsanctuary.org; www.birdsanctuary.org), where trails and three viewing platforms make it easy to spot some of the rust-colored sandhill cranes and white trumpeter swans that stop over during the spring and fall migration in this diverse marsh ecosystem. More than 140 species have been identified, including great blue herons, pied-billed grebes, peregrine falcons, hairy woodpeckers, and sandpipers. Trails start from points along Trumpeter Drive on the west

Haida Arts and Jewellery, Old Massett

side of the bridge, where the streets are named, delightfully, Brant, Widgeon, Pintail, Swan, and Teal. For many generations of Haida the area was a favorite waterfowl hunting area. A military settlement in the sixties brought about change, and in 1964 a causeway was built across the mouth of the Delkatla Sanctuary, thus blocking the tidal flow. In 1995, after years of lobbying and fund-raising by the Delkatla Wildlife Sanctuary Society, a $1 million restoration plan began, culminating in the construction of a 108-foot (33-m) bridge. Once again, tidal waters returned to Delkatla.

For more information on the northern section of the Queen Charlotte Islands, contact **Masset Visitor Info Centre** (Box 68, Masset, V0T 1M0; 250–626–3982 or 888–352–9292; 250–626–3955 in winter; fax: 250–626–3956; visitorinfo@massetbc.com; www.massetbc.com). When visiting the village office, check out the world's largest blue heron sculpture, carved with a chain saw out of yellow cedar by Haida carver Dick Bellis and Austrian-born Wilfred Penker.

On a cool fall day, I drove northeast from the Delkatla Wildlife Sanctuary past "The Elephant Pen," as some locals refer to the Canadian Forces Base signal station, and past one of the world's most remote (and Canada's most northwesterly) golf courses. The **Dixon Entrance Golf and Country Club** (Box 990, Masset, V0T 1M0; 250–626–3500 or 250–626–3735) works on an honor system. It's 2.5 miles (4 km) past Masset—just follow the signs. Set in the dunes, it has grass greens, great views, and lots of deer. I was soon at Graham Island's northern coastline looking across 37 miles (60 km) of Dixon Entrance waters at soft pinkish-gray shapes. I was looking at Alaska.

It seemed fitting then that I should stay at the **Alaska View Lodge Bed and Breakfast** (12291 Tow Hill Road, Box 227, Masset, Queen Charlotte Island, V0T 1M0; 250–626–3333 or 800–661–0019; fax: 250–626–3303; info@alaskaviewlodge.com; www.alaskaviewlodge.com). It's directly on South Beach on Tow Hill Road, 7.6 miles (12.291 km—hence the property numbers) from the Masset Causeway. Eliane and Charly Feller's hospitality is unparalleled. Fabulous Swiss antique furniture, views of Prince of Wales Island, and scrumptious breakfasts make this a memorable retreat. Some of Eliane's unique, esoteric collages are displayed on the walls. There's great beachcombing—you may even pick up agates or those elusive, delicious razor clams. Whales, eagles, and, occasionally,

Your Personal Birder's Checklist

*M*any rare birds have been seen at Delkatla—during the Christmas Bird Count of 1985 the only Canadian sightings of the cattle egret and the least sandpiper were made. Use this checklist of birds seen annually at Delkatla for your personal sightings:

American Coot ❏ American Pipit ❏ American Robin ❏ American Widgeon ❏ Bald Eagle ❏ Barn Swallow ❏ Belted Kingfisher ❏ Black Oystercatcher ❏ Black-bellied Plover ❏ Bufflehead ❏ Canada Goose ❏ Cedar Waxwing ❏ Chestnut-backed Chickadee ❏ Common Goldeneye ❏ Common Merganser ❏ Common Raven ❏ Common Snipe ❏ Dark-eyed Junco ❏ Dunlin ❏ Fox Sparrow ❏ Glaucous-winged Gull ❏ Golden-crowned Kinglet ❏ Great Blue Heron ❏ Greater Scaup ❏ Greater Yellowlegs ❏ Green-winged Teal ❏ Hairy Woodpecker ❏

Hermit Thrush ❏ Herring Gull ❏ Killdeer ❏ Least Sandpiper ❏ Long-billed Dowitcher ❏ Mallard ❏ Mew Gull ❏ Northern Saw-whet Owl ❏ Northwestern Crow ❏ Orange-crowned Warbler ❏ Pacific Golden Plover ❏ Pacific-slope Flycatcher ❏ Peregrine Falcon ❏ Pine Grosbeak ❏ Pine Siskin ❏ Pintail ❏ Red Crossbill ❏ Red-Tailed Hawk ❏ Red-breasted Sapsucker ❏ Rufous Hummingbird ❏ Sandhill Crane ❏ Semipalmated Plover ❏ Sharp-shinned Hawk ❏ Short-billed Dowitcher ❏ Song Sparrow ❏ Starling ❏ Steller's Jay ❏ Swainson's Thrush ❏ Thayer's Gull ❏ Townsend's Warbler ❏ Tree Swallow ❏ Trumpeter Swan ❏ Varied Thrush ❏ Western Sandpiper ❏ Winter Wren ❏

Rare Bird Sightings: Bar-tailed Godwit ❏ Brambling ❏ Cattle Egret ❏ Smith's Longspur ❏ Tufted Duck ❏ Wood Sandpiper ❏

northern lights add to this special experience. The lodge is open year-round, with rates ranging from $70 (single) to $90 (double), including breakfast. Rooms have en suite bathrooms and large showers, with decks overlooking South Beach.

From Alaska View Lodge it's just a short drive on gravel road east to **Tow Hill.** Park just before the Hiellen River bridge and follow the map directions (on a bulletin board) to the boardwalks leading to the top of this 358-foot (109-m) basalt cliff. From here enjoy the great view of the Coast Mountains (on a clear day) and North Beach, which seems to run forever. Nearby is a trail to a **blowhole,** all that remains of a whale that was turned to stone in a famous Haida legend.

Moresby Island

There are only 62 miles (100 km) of paved roads separating Masset in the north from Skidegate in the south, from where the MV *Kwuna* (250–559–4485), a small car and passenger ferry, travels to Moresby Island and the magic of Gwaii Haanas. The crossing time to Alliford Bay is about twenty minutes; the round-trip fare (approximately $22 for a car and two adults in peak season) is paid on the Skidegate side. From Alliford Bay the road hugs the ocean for 8 miles (13 km) to the little village of Sandspit and the island's main airport. If you intend to drive farther afield along any of Moresby's back roads, phone *J. S. Jones Sandspit Ltd.* (250–637–5323), or drop in to their office on the road into Sandspit (just before the baseball field and the Lions Community Hall) to find out about road traffic and conditions. This is strongly recommended.

To explore Moresby by road, do a *circle tour* (allow approximately three hours) heading southwest from Alliford Bay. Those traveling on foot should keep in mind that there is no phone at the southern ferry terminal, so if you intend to go into Sandspit, arrange a taxi (*Bruce's Taxi,* 250–637–5655) beforehand to meet you on the other side. Another choice is to rent a vehicle from Budget Car and Truck Rental (Box 133, Sandspit, V0T 1T0; 250–637–2330; 800–577–3228; fax: 250–637–2355; budgetqc@island.net). From the ferry turn right, sticking to the coast road for 6 miles (10 km) to South Bay. You're onto active logging roads now, so abide by the rules stressed in the Port Clements section. At South Bay, the road heads south for 4.5 miles (7 km) to the

Trivia

You might be forgiven for believing that Mosquito Lake, a popular trout-fishing spot on Moresby Island, was named for those maddening biters—the ones not associated with finding your hook. The truth is that the light-weight Sitka spruce trees found in abundance near the lake were used to build Mosquito bomber planes during World War II.

Moresby Road turnoff, which leads to a well-maintained campsite at Mosquito Lake (eleven units, boat launch, picnic site, and excellent trout fishing) and a major chum and coho enhancement facility on Pallant Creek; it then follows the creek (where there's good salmon fishing in fall) to Cumshewa Inlet. This is as close as you can drive to Gwaii Haanas—from here to the southern tip of the national park, transportation is possible only by air or water.

So unless you are here to kayak, head back to the South Bay Main, passing young western hemlock and Sitka spruce forests near the shores of **Skidegate Lake.** If you're visiting in fall, this area is great for edible mushrooms—notably chanterelles and boletus—or to the hard-core fungi fanatics out there, the place is loaded with *Cantharellus, Hydnellum, Lactarius, Russula, Polyozellus,* and *Sparassis,* to name a few genera. The road follows the Copper River to Copper Bay, dotted with small fishing cabins used by the Haida when the sockeye salmon are running in May and September. It then leads north to Sandspit, and west back to the ferry at Alliford Bay. If you have the time, take another side trip—14 miles (23 km) from South Bay Main—to the campsites at **Gray Bay** on Moresby's east coast. The road is not recommended for low-clearance vehicles, but phone the Moresby Island Management Commission (250–637–2466) or the Sandspit/North Moresby Chamber of Commerce/Visitor Info Centre (Box 148, Sandspit, V0T 1T0; 250–637–5362; fax: 250–637–2326; office@sandspitqci.com; www.sandspitqci.com) to get more up-to-the-minute information on these delightful areas on Moresby Island. You'll find the Info Center at the Sandspit Airport.

Golfers don't have to go far from the airport to enjoy a round of golf at **Willows Golf Course** (250–637–2388; fax: 250–637–2288), a 6,154-yarder complete with bar and grill. It's open from 11:00 A.M. to 11:00 P.M.

While at the airport take a look inside the terminal at the 14-foot dugout canoe **BiJaBoJi**, used by Sandspit's Betty Carey in a gutsy west coast trip with her son Gene in 1962. Since the mid-fifties, Betty and Neil Carey have had a love affair with the Charlottes, which can be shared in Neil's

Trivia

• *Hikers on the Queen Charlotte Islands' beache are sometimes spotted carrying one of those coveted greenish glass balls, at one time used o Japanese fishing vessels.*

• *The Queen Charlotte Islands have the highest density of Peale's peregrine falcons in the worl* famous *Guide to the Queen Charlotte Islands.* For thirty years they lived and explored from Puffin Cove on Moresby's remote west coast; today home is on the seafront in Sandspit. They're avid collectors of anything nautical or recyclable and are recipients of the prestigous CleanWorld Award.

If there's one fair not to miss in Sandspit, it's the annual *Logger Sports Day* held at the baseball field in June. You'll see record-setting ax throws, speed sawing, and birling at its best when hulking loggers dance like cats on fire trying to spin a log and dump their opponent into the freezing water. King and Queen Logger Trophies go to the male and female loggers with the highest aggregate scores. You'll need a hearty home-cooked meal after all that fun. Right in the heart of Sandspit on Shingle Bay, Monty Cobbs at the licensed *Eagle's View—Orange Roof Restaurant* (250–637–2217; fax: 250–637–5619) on Shingle Bay can come up with the goods and more. You're more likely to find *Dick's Wok Inn* (250–637–2275) open; it's across from the school yard on Copper Bay Road. Dick's is renowned for both Cantonese and Canadian cuisine. Try his famous "hot plate" specials or a tasty combo. The restaurant is licensed and does takeout, too.

Close to the Eagle's View and still on the seafront in Sandspit, there are a couple of cozy bed-and-breakfasts. The *Seaport Bed and Breakfast* (371 Alliford Bay Road, Box 206, Sandspit, V0T 1T0; 250–637–5698; fax: 250–637–5697) is different in that it has separate private accommodations from its hosts, with a self-serve hot breakfast. A complete kitchen and laundry—and plenty of lawn on which to clean out your kayak—make it an ideal base for Gwaii Haanas explorers.

But if it's the ghosts of SGang Gwaay 'llnagaay (Nan Sdins/Ninstints), Ḵ'uuna 'llnagaay (Skedans), and T'anuu 'llnagaay (Tanu), and the magic of Gwaii Haanas that you've been patiently waiting for, you need water or air transport. Too many tourists come to the islands expecting to immediately see ancient totems and wilderness, only to be disappointed that so much of it is inaccessible by road. For environmental concerns, limits are set on the number of tourists allowed to experience the beauty of Gwaii Haanas each year. You should first talk to staff at Gwaii Haanas National Park Reserve (Box 37, Queen Charlotte, V0T 1S0; 250–559–8818; fax: 250–559–8366; gwaii.haanas@pc.gc.ca; parkscanada.gc.ca) for permits and general park information. Independent travelers must abide by a reservation system (800– HELLO BC [435–5622] or from outside North America,

250–387–1642, to register) and participate in a mandatory ninety-minute orientation held seasonally at either the Sandspit Visitor Info Centre at the airport daily (to coincide with the Air Canada Jazz flight arrival times) or at the Queen Charlotte City Visitor Info Centre at 8:00 A.M. and 7:30 P.M. weekdays (but only at 8:00 A.M. from mid-May to the end of June). Appointments are not necessary. During the off-season, phone the Gwaii Haanas office (250–559–8818) to make an appointment for orientation.

Commercial tour operators authorized to take you there can help cut the red tape. *Moresby Explorers* (Box 109, Sandspit, V0T 1T0; 250–637–2215 or 800–806–7633; doug@moresbyexplorers.com; www.moresbyexplorers.com) is a Sandspit-based business owned and operated by a lifetime local. Doug Gould and his crew will take you on day trips to nearby Louise and Hot Springs Islands or on three- and four-day excursions to the hallowed, abandoned village of Ninstints in Anthony Island Provincial Park, a World Heritage Site on the remote and rugged southern part of the island. If you're experienced, try a kayak rental, which can include transportation to the Moresby Explorers Float Camp in Crescent Inlet. Check the Web page for tour and rental information and start planning for a wilderness experience unique in its combination of beauty, solitude, Haida Culture, and spirituality.

Flights from Queen Charlotte to Gwaii Haanas Tribal and National Park Reserve are available from South Moresby Air (Box 969, Queen Charlotte, V0T 1S0; 250–559–4222; toll free: 888–551–4222; fax: 250–559–4223; info@smair.com; www.smair.com). The flights land at nearby Rose Harbour. You'll be welcomed at *Gwaii Haanas Guest House and Kayaks* (Box 578, Rose Harbour, Queen Charlotte Islands, V0T 1S0; 250–559–8638; Radiophone (April to October): ask operator for a BC Telus operator, then a Campbell River Marine Radiophone Operator, Number: N-159009, Channel: Cape St-James 24; mailbox2003@gwaii haanas.com; www.gwaiihaanas.com). The guest house is open May 1 to September 30. Rates, including three meals, are $95 per person per day. Weekly, group, and children's discounts are available also. This family-owned extreme wilderness business is located on the north shore of Kunghit Island, close to Ninstints, UNESCO World Heritage site. Kayak rentals, rigid-hull, inflatable boat excursions, guided tours, and bird-watching are offered. It's accessible only by boat or float plane (ranging from $125 to $300 one way from Queen Charlotte City, depending on group size and the day traveled). It's not all "roughing it," though. Hot showers, electricity (solar energy), and a large organic garden will add a little decadence to a wilderness holiday never to be forgotten.

PLACES TO STAY ON THE QUEEN CHARLOTTE ISLANDS

MASSET

Alaska View Lodge
Bed and Breakfast, Tow Hill
Road, 8 miles (12 km)
from the Masset Causeway;
Box 227, QCI, V0T 1M0;
(250) 626–3333 or
(800) 661–0019;
info@alaskaviewlodge.com.
Double.

Copper Beech House,
1590 Delkatla, Box 97, V0T
IM0; (250) 626–5441;
www.copperbeechhouse.
com. Open year-round;
gourmet dinners by
arrangement.

QUEEN CHARLOTTE CITY

Gwaii Eco Tours and
Lodging, 604 First Avenue,
Box 249, Queen Charlotte,
Haida Gwaii, V0T 1S0;
877–559–8333
or 250–559–8333;
gwaiieco@haidagwaii.net;
www.gwaiiecotours.com.

Sea Raven Motel,
3301 Third Avenue,
Box 519, QCC, V0T 1S0;
(250) 559–4423 or
(800) 665–9606;
fax: (250) 559–8617.
Overlooks Bearskin Bay.

ROSE HARBOUR

Gwaii Haanas Guest House
and Kayaks, Box 578,
Rose Harbour, QCI
V0T 1S0; (250) 559–8638;
(see text for radiophone
directions April to October);
www.gwaiihaanas.com.

SANDSPIT

Seaport Bed and Breakfast,
371 Alliford Bay Road,
Box 206, V0T 1T0;
(250) 637–5698.
Home-baked goodies
placed in your fridge.

Sandspit Inn, 469 Airport
Road, V0T 1T0; (800)
666–1107; (250)
637–5334. Next to airport.

TLELL

Cacilia's Bed & Breakfast,
Box 3, V0T 1Y0;
phone/fax:
(250) 557–4664.
Rustic, beachy.

Sitka Lodging,
Box 33, V0T 1Y0; (800)
557–4241.
Very private cottage on
Tlell River.

PLACES TO EAT ON THE QUEEN CHARLOTTE ISLANDS

MASSET

Daddy Cool's Pub and Grill,
Collison Avenue, V0T 1M0;
(250) 626–3210.

Sandpiper Restaurant,
2062 Collison Avenue, V0T
1M0; (250) 626–3672.
Haute cuisine!

HaidaBucks, 1675 Main
Street, Masset, V0T 1M0;
(250) 626–5548. Good
food, great coffee.

QUEEN CHARLOTTE CITY

Lam's Café,
Wharf Street; (250)
559–4204. Opens 6:30 A.M.
Delicious crab and Chinese
specialties.

Keenanii's Kitchen,
237 Highway 33;
(250) 559–8347.
Authentic Haida cuisine.

Oceana Chinese and
Continental Restaurant,
3119 Third Avenue, V0T
1S0; (250) 559–8683. Great
ice creams, yogurt, and
sherbet.

SANDSPIT

Sandspit Inn Restaurant,
(250) 637–5334. At the
airport; accommodation
also (800–666–1107).

Eagle's View–Orange Roof
Restaurant, (250)
637–2217.

Dick's Wok Inn. On Copper
Bay Road, (250) 637–2275.
Cantonese and Canadian
cuisine; popular local spot;
takeout too.

TLELL

Tlell River House, Beitush
Road; (250) 557–4211.
Accommodation also.

Index

A

A. C. Christensen General
   Merchants, 216
Abbotsford, 59
Abbotsford International Airshow, 59
Acacia Leaf Cafe, 69
Ace High Resort, 207
Adams River, 181
Agassiz, 61
Agassiz-Harrison Historical Society, 61
Agri-tourism, 108
Ainsworth Hot Springs Resort, 128
Air-Hart Aviation, 106
Airport Inn Restaurant, 46
Alaska Café, 233
Alaska Highway, 232, 234
Alaska Hotel, 233
Alaska Husky Adventures, 188
Alaska View Lodge Bed
   and Breakfast, 292
Alcan Smelter, 259
Alert Bay, 40
Alexander Mackenzie Trail, 254
Alkali Lake, 205
All Fun Recreation, 29
All Seasons Cafe, 126
Alley-Way Garden Café, 27
Alpine Rafting, 164
Amarcord, 53
Amphitrite Lighthouse, 26
Amphora Tapas Bar, 104
Anahim Lake, 216
Ancient Cedar Grove, 72
Ancient Cedars Spa, 28
Angela's Bed and Breakfast, 123
Anne's Oceanfront Hideaway, 15
Annual Fall Okanagan Wine
   Festival, 105
Annual Icewine Festival, 105
Antimony Mine hiking trail, 248

Arctic Divide Bed & Breakfast, 272
Ardendale Bed and Breakfast, 238
Armstrong, 109
Arras, 229
Ashcroft, 201–2
Ashcroft Fire Hall, 201
Ashcroft Manor Teahouse, 202
Ashcroft Museum and Archives, 202
Ashcroft River Inn, 202
Aston House B&B, 15
Atlin Art Centre, 274
Atlin Historical Museum, 273
Atlin Inn & Kirkwood Cottages, 274
Atlin Lake Houseboat Tours, 274
Atlin Inn Lakeshore Restaurant, 274
Atlin Quest, 274
Atlin's Happy Trails, 275
Avely Ranch, 189

B

Bacchus Bistro, The, 58
Bahari, 24
Bailey's Chute, 188
Bakery, The, 270
Balance Rock, 284
Bamfield, 17
Bamfield Marine Station, 19
Banff National Park, 162
Barbara Lynn's Country Inn B&B, 149
Barb's Pottery, 218
BareFoot Handweaving Studio &
   Gallery, 137
Barkerville Historic Town, 214
Barn, The, 137
Barriere, 185
Bavarian City Mining Railway, 153
BC Copper Company Smelter, 113
BC Cowboy Hall of Fame, 211
BC Ferries, 45
BC Firefighter's Museum, 122

INDEX

BC Museum of Mining, 75
BC Orchard Industry Museum, 107
Beachcomber Marine Spa B&B, 79
Beach Gables Accommodation, 130
Beach Hut, The, 82
Beachside Bed and Breakfast, 102
Beacon Bed and Breakfast, 82
Beacon Hill Children's Farm, 29
Beacon Hill Park, 9
Beanstalk Coffee Company, 212
Bearfoot Outdoors, 186
Bear Glacier, 269
Bear Paw Ranch, 271
Beardale Castle Miniatureland, 176
Beaverdell Hotel, 110
Becker's Lodge, 214
Belaire Restaurant, 89
Bell Shop, The, 73
Bell II, 271
Bella Coola Valley, 216
Bennett Dam, 229
Bentley's Seaside Grill, 8
Berg Lake Trail, 191
Berg's Bed and Breakfast, 257
Bergeron Cliffs, 232
Bergeron Falls, 232
Bergeron Mountain, 232
Bernt Ronning Garden, 46
Big Bar, 205
Big Bay Bed and Breakfast, 248
Big Cedar Tree Forest Recreational
    Site, 219
Big Peach on the Beach, 100
Big White Ski Resort, 110
BiJaBoJi, 294
Bill Gruff, 24
Billings Spit Beach House, 10
Billy Barker Days, 213
Binta Lake Outfitters, 252
Birch Island, 188
Black Forest Restaurant, 174
Black Jack Cross-Country Ski Trails, 120

Blackcomb, 72
Blethering Place Tea Room, 7
Blighty's Bistro, 8
Blown Away Glass, 137
Bluebell Inn, 238
Blue Heron, 35
Blue Heron, The, 79
Blue Peter's Pub and Restaurant, 11
Blue Peter Yacht Charters, 12
Blue River Campground and
    RV Park, 190
Bluewater Houseboat Rentals, 177
Boer Mountain Road, 252
Bonanza Pass, 119
Bonfire Bistro, 107
Boston Bar, 68
Boswell, 138
Botanical Beach, 10
Bottle and Jug Works, 284
Boundary Country, 113
Bouzouki Greek Café, 15
Bowen Island, 74
Boundary Mining and Power
    Interpretive Centre, 113
Bountiful Gardens, 198
Bracewell's Alpine Wilderness
    Adventures, 216
Brackendale Art Gallery Theatre
    & Teahouse, 73
Brackendale Winter Eagle Festival, 73
Brandywine Falls, 73
Breathless Glass, 137
Brewery Bay Chalet, 274
Bridge Creek Falls, 208
Bridge of 23 Camels, 199
Bridges Restaurant, 55
Brisco General Store, 162
British Columbia Aviation Museum, 12
British Columbia Firefighter's
    Museum, 122
Broken Group Islands, 25
Bucket of Blood, 254

Buckinghorse River Lodge, 236
Bungy Zone Adrenalin
    Centre, 20
Bunkers Licensed Bar &
    Restaurant, 13
Burgess Shale, 163
Burgess Shale Earth & Life Science
    Learning Centre, 163
Burnaby Village Museum, 67
Burns Lake, 254
Butterfly World, 24
Buttle Lake, 36

C

Cache Creek, 201
Cacilia's Bed and Breakfast, 286
Caddy Marine Tours, 6
Café Deli, 7
Caffe Suzanne, 35
Campbell River, 32–34
Campbell River Museum
    and Archives, 33
Campbell River Optical Maritime
    Museum, 33
Canadian Avalanche Centre, 171
Canadian Museum of Rail Travel, 145
Canadian Rockies River
    Expeditions, 152
Canal Flats, 154–56
Canyon Hot Springs Resort, 171
Cape Ball, 288
Cape Mudge Lighthouse, 34
Cape Scott Lighthouse, 47
Cape Scott sand neck, 47
Capilano Park, 53
Capilano Suspension Bridge, 53
Cariboo-Chilcotin, 195–220
Cariboo Jade and Gift Shoppe, 201
Cariboo Lodge Resort, 204
Cariboo Ski Marathon, 208
Cariboo Waggon Road, 195
Carmanah Giant, 18

Carriage House Wines, 97
Carr's Landing, 108
Casa Blanca By The Sea, 22
Casino of the Rockies, 146
Cassiar Mountain Jade Store and
    Mine, 273
Castlegar, 124–25
Castlegar Golf Course, 125
Castlegar Museum, 125
Cat Powder Skiing, 173
Cathedral Grove, 25
Cathedral Lakes Lodge, 91
Cathedral Rim Trail, 91
Cayford's Orchard, 109
Cayoosh Creek Campground, 198
Cedar Heights Bed & Breakfast, 146
Cedar Lodge, 82
Cellar Fibre Studio, The, 122
Centre Art Gallery, 107
Chalet Restaurant, 260
Chase, 182
Chase Country Inn, 182
Chase Visitor Info Centre, 182
Chatham Village Longhouse, 266
Chatterbox Falls, 81
Chef Bernard's Platzl Inn and
    Restaurant, 151
Chef's Garden Restaurant, 117
Chemainus, 15
Chemainus Theatre, 16
Chetwynd, 229
Chetwynd Chainsaw Sculptures, 229
Chetwynd Visitor Info Centre, 229
Chickadee Ridge Miniatures, 108
Chilko Lake, 217
Chilko Lake Resort, 218
Chilko River Expeditions, 217
Chimney Rock, 200
China Moon, 254
Chinatown, 5, 55
Chinatown Millennium Gate, 55
Chinese Cultural Center, 55

INDEX

Chinese Mountain, 34
Chopaka Rodeo, 92
Choyces, 42
Christ Church, 42, 58, 63
Christina Lake, 118
Christina Lake Golf Course, 119
Christmas Island Bed &
  Breakfast, 174
Chrysalis Retreat, 66
City Bakery, 155
Civic Center Plaza, 226
Clearwater, 186
Cliff Gilker Regional Park, 77
Clinton, 204
Clinton Grill, 204
Clover Point, 9
CN IMAX, 70
Coal River Lodge, 242
Coastal Connections Nature
  Adventures, 4
Cola Diner, 23
Colander Restaurant, 123
Columbia, 39
Columbia Brewing Company, 140
Cominco Gardens, 153
Comox, 30
Comox Glacier, 31
Connaught Hill Park, 226
Conversations Coffee House, 174
Coombs Old Country Market, 24
Copper Beech House, 290
Copper Eagle Cappuccino and
  Bakery, 115
Copper Island, 177
Cornwall Mountain, 202
Cortes Island, 34–35
Costa Azul, 27
Cottonwood House, 205
Cougar Mountain Wilderness
  Adventures, 72
Country Cafe, 201
Country Elegance Bed and

Breakfast, 116
Country Pedlar Too, 208
Courtenay, 30
Courtenay & District Museum &
  Paleontology Centre, 31
Cow Bay Café, 266
Cowichan Bay, 17
Cowpuccino's Coffee House, 265
Craft Connection Cooperative, 127
Crafts with Class, 204
Craig Heritage Park and Museum, 22
Craigellachie, 174
Cranberry Junction, 269
Cranbrook, 143–47
Cranbrook Visitor Info Centre, 145, 146
Crawford Bay, 136–38
Creekside Flower Gardens, 157
Creston, 139–41
Creston Blossom Festival, 139
Creston & District Museum &
  Archives, 140
Creston Golf Course, 139
Creston Osprey Festival, 141
Creston Valley Wildlife
  Management Area, 140
Creston Visitor Info Centre, 140
Cristoforo Colombo Lodge, 124
Crocodile Restaurant, 256
Crystal Cabin Gallery Rock &
  Gem Gift Shop, 285
Crystal Springs (Historical)
  Resort, 209
Culp's Farm, 221
Cumberland, 30
Cumberland Museum & Archives, 31
Cutting Board Restaurant, 69
Cycle BC Rentals, 9

D

Darter's Misty Willows Ranch
  Bed & Breakfast, 252
Dawson Creek, 232–33

Dawson Creek Art Gallery, 233
Dawson Creek Visitor Info Centre, 232
Dease Lake, 272
Deep Bay, 23
Delkatla Wildlife Sanctuary, 290
Della Falls, 25, 36
Delta St. Eugene Mission Resort, 146
Denman Craft Shop, 29
Denman Island, 28–30
Denman Island Chocolate, 29
Denman Island General Store, 29
Desert Ecological Reserve, 96
Desolation Resort, 82
Dew Drop Inn, 233
Dick's Wok Inn, 295
Dina's Place, 197
Dinghy Dock Pub, 20
Discovery Coast Passage, 45
Discovery Fishing Pier, 32
District of Tumbler Ridge, 232
Dixon Entrance Golf and
  Country Club, 291
Dog Creek, 205
Dogfish Pole, 284
Domaine de Chaberton Estates, 58
Dominion Radio Astrophysical
  Observatory, 99
Don's Dive Shop, 81
Dora's Cafe, 242
Douglas Channel Trail, 260
Douglas Lake Ranch, 185
Doukhobor houses, 116
Doukhobor Village Museum, 124
Dr. Sun Yat-Sen Garden, 55
Drahanchuk Studios, 34
Dream Catcher Inn, 191
Duffey Lake Road, 69
Duncan, 17
Dunroven Bed & Breakfast Sea Cottage
  Oxen Farm & Forge, 42
Dunster, 221
Dunster Farmers' Market, 223

Dunster General Store, 223
Dunster Train Station, 224

E

Eagle Aerie Gallery, 26
Eagle Bluff Bed and Breakfast, 266
Eagle River Nature Park, 176
Eagle's Eye, The, 166
Eagle's View—Orange Roof
  Restaurant, 295
Eco Treks Adventures, 266
Ecological Park, 43
Edgewater Open Market, 162
Elasmosaur, 31
Eleven 22 Grill & Liquids, 165
Elizabeth Lake Wildlife Sanctuary, 145
Elk River, 152
Elk Valley, 147
Elkford, 148, 150
Elkford Info Centre, 150
Elks Rodeo, 92
Elphinstone Pioneer Museum, 77
Enchanted Forest, 176
Endako, 250
Endako Mine, 251
English Bay, 54
Escape to the Point B&B, 54
Eveneshen Nature Trail, 254
Evergreen Bed and Breakfast, 64
Evergreens Bed and Breakfast, 180
Exploration Place, 227

F

4 Pines Motel, 198
Fairmont Creekside Par 3, 157
Fairmont Empress Hotel, 5
Fairmont Hot Springs Resort, 156
Fairview Jail, 99
Fallen Giant, 18
Falls Restaurant, 100
Fat Phege's Fudge Factory, 5
Father's Country Inn B&B, 185

INDEX

Fauquier, 133

Fence Post Lane Bed and Breakfast, 59

Fernie, 147

Fernie Alpine Resort, 148

Fernie Golf and Country Club, 148

Fern's Place Bed and
  Breakfast Suite, 37

Festival of the Written Arts, 78

Field, 163

Filberg Festival, 31

Filberg Heritage Lodge, 31

Filomi Days, 45

Finnish Museum, 41

Fire Museum, 267

Fireside Car/Truck Stop, 242

Fireworks Enamelled
  Copper and Glass, 137

Fish Creek Wildlife Observation
  Site, 270

Fisherville, 154

Fishing Highway, 207

Flour Meadow Bakery & Cafe, 187

Flower Springs Lake Trail, 239

Flying U, 206

Folded Mountain, 241

Forge & Furnace Gallery, 137

Fort Fraser, 250

Fort George Park, 226

Fort Langley National Historic
  Site, 57

Fort Nelson Flight Centre, 237

Fort Nelson Heritage Museum, 238

Fort Nelson Visitor Info Centre, 237

Fort St. James, 247–52

Fort St. James National Historic
  Site, 249

Fort St. John, 234

Fort St. John–North Peace
  Museum, 235

Fort Steele, 155

Fort Steele blacksmith, 155

Fort Steele Heritage Town, 155

François Lake, 252

Fran's Place, 237

Fraser Canyon, 65–69

Fraser Lake, 250

Fraser Lake–Stuart Lake Pack Trail,
  252

Fraser River Heritage Park, 59

Fraser River Jet Boat Adventures, 198

Fraser River Rafting, 66

Fraser River Valley, 59–62

Fraser-Fort George Regional
  Museum, 227

Free Store, 30

Freedom Highway, 215–19

Frontier Family Restaurant, 174

Fructova Doukhobor Heritage
  Centre, 117

Fudge Factory, 68

Fulton River Salmon Project, 254

Fusilli Grill, 33

G

Gabriola Island, 21–22

Galena Bay, 130

Galloping Goose Trail, 10

Gang Ranch, 205

Ganges, 14

Garden Treasures Restaurant
  and Gift Shop, 153

Gate of Harmonious Interest, 5

Gehringer Brothers Estate Winery, 98

George Hicks Park, 191

Gibsons, 76

Gibsons Visitor Info Centre, 76

Giscome Portage Trail, 228

Gitanyow, 268

Gitxsan, 258

Glacier Bay National Park, 275

Glacier Inn, 271

Glacier National Park, 166, 169

Glacier Raft Company, 164

Glass House, 139

Gnome's Home, The, 218
Goat River Lodge Bed and
    Breakfast, 140
Gold River, 36
Golden, 163
Golden City Barber Shop, 122
Golden Festival of Birds and Bears, 165
Golden Golf and Country Club, 164
Golden Historical Society
    Museum, 165
Golden Mountain Adventures, 164
Golden Spruce, 288
Gold House Bed and Breakfast, The, 91
Gold River, 36
Gold Rush Books and Espresso, 122
Gold Rush Trail Sled Dog
    Mail Run, 213
Goose Spit Regional Park, 31
Graham Island Central, 284–89
Graham Island North, 289–93
Granby Mining and Smelter
    Company, 118
Grand Canyon of the Stikine, 271–72
Grand Forks, 116–19
Grand Forks Boundary Museum, 117
Grand Forks Station Pub, 118
Granite Mountain, 120
Granville Island, 55
Gray Creek Store, 138
Gray Jay Lake Trail, 219
Great International World
    Championship Bathtub Race
    and Marine Festival, 20
Great Walk, 37
Green Cuisine Vegetarian
    Restaurant, 5
Green Lake, 206
Greenpeace, 54
Green River, 72
Greenwood, 113–16
Greenwood Inn Saloon/
    Restaurant, 115

Greenwood Museum, 115
Grinrod, 178
Grist Mill, 93
Grizzly Plaza, 172
Grouse Grind, 51
Grouse Mountain, 51
Grouse Mountain Skyride, 53
Gulf of Georgia Cannery National
    Historic Site, 67
Gumboot Garden Café, 77
Gwaii Eco Tours and Lodging, 282
Gwaii Haanas Guest House &
    Kayaks, 296

H

Hagensborg, 218
Hagwilget Bridge, 258
Haida Arts and Jewellery, 290
Haidabucks, 289
Haida dugout canoe, 288
Haida Gwaii, 279–97
Haida Gwaii Museum, 283
Hainle Vineyards Estate Winery, 103
Halcyon Hot Springs Resort, 133
Halfmoon Bay, 75
Hanging by a Fibre, 282
Happy Hans Riverside RV
    Resort, 153
Harbour Air, 267
Harker's Fruit Ranch, 93
Harrison/Chehalis Bald Eagle
    Festival, 61
Harrison Heritage House and
    Kottage Bed and Breakfast, 62
Harrison Hot Springs, 62
Harrison Mills, 61
Harry's Diner, 53
Hat Creek Ranch, 200
Hatzic Rock Site, 60
Haynes Point Lakeside Guest
    House, 95
Haynes Ranch House, 97

INDEX

He-Tin-Kis Park, 26
Hedley, 91
Hell's Gate, 67
Hell's Gate Airtram, 67
Helmcken Falls Lodge, 188
Helna's Stube Restaurant, 160
Henshel Fine Arts Gallery and
    Studio, 40
Heriot Bay Inn and Marina, 34
Heritage Highway, 229
Heritage Village Museum, 245
H. G. Parson House Bed and
    Breakfast, 164
Hickory Daiquiri Doc's, 204
High Bar, 205
High Country, 169–93
Highland Glen Lodge, 241
Hill, The, 216
Hills Health Ranch, 208
Hillside Lodge & Chalets, 166
Historic Hat Creek Ranch, 200
Historic Pemberton Museum
    and Gift Shop, 71
Híwus Feasthouse, 53
H. Kershaw and Son, 155
HMCS Chaudière, 79
Holberg, 46
Hollyhock, 35
Holton House, 174
Home Restaurant, 64
Hooterville, 289
Hope, 62–65
Hope Museum, 64
Hope Station House, 64
Horizon Adventures Ltd., 109
Hornby Island, 28–30
Hornby Island Diving, 30
Hornby Island Off Road Bike Shop, 29
Hornby Ocean Kayaks, 29
Horne Lake Store and Café, 24
Horne Lake Teepee Adventure
    Camp, 24
Hornsby Steam Tractor, 45

Horsefly, 209
Horseshoe Bay, 75
Horseshoe Lake Bird Viewing
    Station, 225
Horsting's Farm Market, 200
Hosmer Mountain, 148
House of Hewhiwus, 79
House of Sim–oi-Ghets, 263
Houston, 254–55
Howe Sound Inn and Brewing
    Company, 74
Huble Homestead, 227
Hudson Bay Lodge, 257
Hudson's Hope Museum, 230
Hummingbird Bridge, 118
Hyder, 270

I

Idaho Peak Forestry Lookout
    Tower, 132
Indian Grove Riding Stable, 97
Inland Air Charters, 267
Inland Passage, 45
Innchanter, 28
Inner Harbor, 3
Institute of Ocean Studies, 12
Interlakes District, 207
International Hotel, 155
Invermere, 158
Iskut, 272
Islands, The, 1–49
I.V.'s Quarterdeck Pub, 46

J

Jack Lynn Memorial Museum, 210
Jack's Lane Bistro, 77
Jade City Store, 272
Jamie's Whaling Station, 27
Janet's Guest House Bed and
    Breakfast, 44
Jerry the moose, 186
Jill's Cafe, 80

Joe's Bar and Grill, 46
John Tod House, 7
John's Place, 6
Joy's Island Jewellers, 281
J.S. Jones Sandspit Ltd., 293
Juan de Fuca Trail, 19
Juskatla, 288

K

K&S Historic Railway Trail, 131
Kamloops, 182–83
Kamloops Farmers Market, 183
Kamloops R.V. Park &
    Dolphin Waterslides, 183
Kamloops Wildlife Park, 183
Kaslo, 128–35
Kaslo Jazz Etc. Festival, 130
Kaslo Visitor Info Centre, 130
Kawesas Lodge, 261
Keenanii's Kitchen, 297
kekuli sites, 186
Kelowna, 105
Kelowna Art Gallery, 107
Keremeos, 93
Kettle River Valley, 110
Kettle Valley Steam Railway, 102, 106
Khutzeymateen River Valley, 267
Kicking Horse Grill, The, 165
Kicking Horse Mountain Resort, 166
Kickinninnee Beach, 100
Kilby Historic Store and Farm, 61
Kimberley, 150–54
Kimberley Alpine Resort, 151
Kimberley Golf Course, 150
Kimberley Nature Park, 153
Kimberley Visitor Info Centre, 154
Kinbasket Adventures, 165
Kingfisher Campground and
    Store, 109
Kingfisher Environmental
    Interpretive Centre, 109
Kinuseo Falls, 231

Kiskatinaw River Bridge, 234
Kispiox, 258
Kitimaat Village, 260
Kitimat, 259
Kitimat Centennial Museum, 260
Kitlope Valley, 261
Kitselano Pool, 54
Kitselas Canyon, 262
Kitwancool, 269
Kitwanga Fort National
    Historic Site, 268
Kluane National Park, 275
Kokanee Springs Golf Resort, 136
Kootenay Bay, 135
Kootenay Candle Factory, 140
Kootenay Country, 113–42
Kootenay Forge, 136
Kootenay Gallery of Art, History
    and Science, 124
Kootenay Lake East, 135–39
Kootenay Lake Ferry, 135
Kootenay Lake West, 127–28
Kootenay National Park, 159, 161
Kootenay River Runners, 158
Kootenay South, 119
Kootenay Trout Hatchery, 155
Kootenay Valley Viewpoint, 162
'Ksan Historical Village, 258
Kumsheen Rafting Resort, 69
Kuskanax River, 132
Kwinitsa Station Museum, 267
Kyuquot Sound, 38

L

Lac Des Roches Canadian Resort, 207
Lac La Hache, 209
Lady Rose Marine Services, 25
Lake Cowichan Village, 17
Lake Country, 108
Lakes District, 252–54
Lakes District Museum, 254
Lakeside Park, 127

INDEX

Lam's Café, 281
Landsea Tours, 53
Langham Cultural Centre, 129
Lardeau Creek, 131
Last Spike, 176
Last Spike Pub, 251
Laughing Oyster Restaurant, The, 82
Lefty's, 23
Legacy Park, 201
Leisure Pool, 229
Lemon Creek Lodge, 134
Lennard Light, 27
Leroi Mine, 121
Liard River Hot Springs, 241
Liard River Hotsprings P/Park
    Campground, 242
Liard River Lodge, 242
Likely, 210
Likkel's Lakeside Store and
    Resort, 253
Lilac Walk and Tea Party, 221
Lillooet, 69, 195
Lillooet Bakery, 198
Lillooet Museum and Visitor Info
    Centre, 195
Lind Valley Guest Ranch, 116
Little Bavaria Restaurant, 25
Little Britches Restaurant, 90
Little Duffer Ice Cream Parlor and
    Mini Golf, 97
Little Fort, 207
Little Horse Lodge, 206
Little Mountain Peruvians, 108
Little Prairie Heritage Museum, 229
Llama Farm, 108
Log Bog Friendship Farm B&B, 192
Log House, B&B, 71
Logger Sports Day, 295
Log House B&B Inn, 71
Login Bed and Breakfast, 92
Lone Butte, 207
Long Beach, 25, 29

Loo Taa, 283
Lookout, The, 67
Loon Bay Resort, 207
Loon Creek Hatchery, 204
Lori's Lookout, 199
Lost Creek Angling, 148
Lotus Land Tours, 56
Lotzkar Memorial Park, 113
Lower Joffre Lake, 70
Lum 'n' Abner's, 237
Lunch Box Deli, 252
Lund, 82
Lund Hotel, 83
Lund Water Taxi, 83
Lundborn Lakes, 184
Lussier River Hotsprings, 156
Lytton, 68

M

Ma Murray Collection, 197
Macdonald Campground, 240
MacDonald's Pure Beeswax, 109
Macgregor Studio, 264
Mackenzie, 228
Mad Trapper Neighborhood Pub, 165
Mae's Kitchen, 235
Malaspina Galleries, 22
Malone, 91
Malone's Oceanside Bistro, 46
Manning Park Resort, 64
Maples Bed & Breakfast, The, 118
Marble Canyon, 162
Margaret Falls, 178
Market Square, 5
Marie Lake Fish Hatchery, 288
Marina House Bed & Breakfast, 76
Marina Restaurant, 7
Marmot Ridge Golf Course, 209
Marquart Lake, 184
Marsh Wildlife Sanctuary, 208
Marysville, 150
Marysville Falls, 150

Mason's Motor Lodge, 38
Matler Glacier, 70
Max and Irma's Restaurant, 126
Mazatlan Mexican Restaurant, 126
McBride, 225
McBride Info Centre, 225
McIntyre Bluff, 99
McLeod Lake, 228
McNal Placer Gold, 198
McMillan Chalet Bed and
    Breakfast, 157
McQueen Slough, 233
Meares Island, 27
Meegans Store, 282
Melvins on Main, 198
Merritt, 184
Merritt Travel Info Centre, 185
Methanex/Pacific Ammonia, 259
Meziadin Fish Ladder, 269
Meziadin Junction, 269
Mike Wiegele Helicopter Skiing, 190
Miles Inn on the T'Seax B&B, 263
Mile Zero Alaska Highway, 232
Mile Zero Rotary Park, 233
Mile Zero Trans-Canada Highway, 9
Mining Artifact Tour, 149
Minter Gardens, 67
Mission, 59–61
Mission Hill Winery, 105
Mission Museum, 60
Mission Raceway Park, 60
Mistahaya Wayatinaw Ecotourism
    Cooperative, 232
Misty Meadows Campsite, 287
Moby's Marina Pub, 15
Moha Placer Mines, 198
Molly's Lane, 77
Molly's Reach, 76
Moly Hills Golf Course, 252
Mom's Café, 10
Monashee Adventure Tours, 106
Moose Ridge Woodland Chalet, 187

Moresby Explorers, 296
Moresby Island, 293–96
Morfee Mountain, 228
Moricetown Canyon, 257
Morte Lake, 34
Mosquito Lake, 294
Moss Cottage, 10
Mothership Adventures, Inc., 39
Motherland Inn, The, 221
Mount Currie, 69
Mount Golden Hinde, 36
Mount Layton Hotsprings Resort, 261
Mount H'Kusam, 39
Mount Norman Regional Park, 13
Mount Pope, 248
Mount Revelstoke National
    Park, 169, 171
Mount Robson, 169
Mount Seven, 164
Mount Terry Fox, 191
Mount Terry Fox Viewpoint, 191
Mount Washington Alpine Resort, 32
Mountain High River
    Adventures, Inc., 149
Mountain Pottery, 224
Mountain Shadow Hostel, 123
Mountainside Golf Course, 157
Mountain View Doukhobor
    Museum, 117
Mrs. Sprague's Confectionery, 155
Mud Mamas, 137
Muncho Lake, 240
Murray Canyon, 232
Murray Ridge Ski Area, 248
Murtle Lake, 190
Museum of Anthropology, 54
Museum of Northern British
    Columbia, 266
Museum of the Cariboo Chilcotin, 211
MV *Frances Barkley*, 25
MV *Lady Rose*, 25
MV *Osprey 2000*, 135

MV *Tarahne,* 273
MV *Uchuck III,* 38
Myra Canyon, 106
Myra Creek, 36

N

19 Greens Fun & Sports Centre, 105
Nadina River Project, 255
Na Na Kila Institute, 261
Naikai Gallery, 14
Nak'azdli Handicraft Shop, 249
Nakusp Hot Springs, 132
'Namgis Burial Ground, 43
Nanaimo, 19, 20–22
National Geographic Theatre, 3
Nanoose Bay, 23
Native Sons Hall, 31
Natural Bridge, 163
Nature House, The, 211
Needles, 133
Nelson, 125–27
Nelson Guest House, 126
Neskonlith Meadows, 182
New Denver, 132
New Hazelton, 257
New Westminster, 53
Nicola Valley, 184
Nicola Valley Golf Course
    and R.V. Park, 185
Nikkei Internment Memorial
    Centre, 132
Nimpkish Lake, 38
Nimpkish Valley, 37
Ninstints, 295
Nitinat General Store, 17
Nitinat Lake, 19
Nitinat Lake Motel, 17
Nk'mip Cellars, 97
Nk 'mip Resort, 96
Nootka Island, 38
Nootka Sound, 36, 38
Nootka Sound Services, 38

North Islands, The, 39–47
North Okanagan, 108–10
North Pacific Historic
    Fishing Village, 263
North Thompson Fall Fair and
    Rodeo, 186
North Thompson River, 185–90
North Woven Broom Company, 136
Northeast, The, 221–43
Northern Cariboo, 209–10
Northern Rockies Lodge, 241
Northway Motor Inn
    and Restaurant, 272
Northwest, The, 245–77
Northwood Explorations Gallery, 227
Nuchatlite, 38
Nusatum River, 218

O

100 Mile House, 208
100 Mile Village Campground, 208
100 Mile Marsh Wildlife
    Sanctuary, 208
108 Heritage Site, 209
108 Mile House, 208
108 Resort Golf Club, 209
153 Mile Store, 209
Oak Bay, 6, 7
Oak Bay Beach Hotel, 8
Oak Bay Guest House, 8
Oak Bay Marina, 6
Oak Bay Recreation Center, 9, 29
"O Canada" House B&B, 56
Ocean River Sports, 3
Oceanside Inn, 13
Oceanside Tourism Association, 23
Odegaard Falls Recreation
    Area, 218
Odegaard Glacier, 218
Ogden Point Cafe, 9
Ogden Point Dive Center, 9
Ogopogo, 102–3

Okanagan, 87, 89–111
Okanagan Centre, 108
Okanagan Falls, 100
Okanagan Pottery Studio, 103
Okanagan Spring Wine Festival, 105
Okanagan Valley, 94–108
Okanagan Valley Wine Train, 108
O.K. Hotel & Café, 247
Ol' Keg Pub, 260
Old Cariboo Gold Rush Trail, 208
Old Courthouse Inn, 81
Old Farm Bed & Breakfast, 17
Old Fort, 238
Old Massett, 290
Old Schoolhouse, The, 256
Old Settler Pub, 62
Olde Mill House, 16
Oliver, 97–99
Oliver and District Museum, 99
One Mile Lake, 72
On-the-Rocks Lounge, 28
Onion Lake, 262
Opa Sushi, 266
Opitsaht, 27
Orchard Bed and Breakfast, 117
Orchard Blossom Honey House, 93
Original Cable Cookhouse, 39
Oso Negro, 126
Osoyoos Lake, 95
Othello–Quintette Tunnels, 63
Othello Tunnels Campground and
     R.V. Park, 63
Our Lady of Good Hope Church, 249
Our Place Cafe, 110
Outback Emuzing Ranch, 31
Oyama, 108
Oyster Shell Beach House, 83

P

Pacific Rim National Park Reserve, 25
Paint Pots, 162
Painted Chasm, 205

Panorama Mountain Village, 159
Papa John's, 288
Par 3 Sports in Motion Store, 251
Paradise Found Adventure
     Tour Company, 32
Parksville, 22–25
Paulson Cross Country Ski Trail, 119
Pavilion General Store, 199
Peace Canyon Dam, 229
Peace River, 230
Peace River Bridge, 234
Peace River Country, 227–32
Peaks Lodge, 174
Pemberton Soaring Center, 71
Pemberton Trail Steakhouse, 71
Pender Harbour, 80
Pender Harbour Tourist/Visitor
     Info Booth, 80
Pender Island, 13
Pender Island Golf and Country
     Club, 13
Penny Farthing Olde English Pub, 8
Penticton, 100
Peppercorn Trail, 36
Pesuta shipwreck, 287
Pheasant Heaven, 179
Phoenix Cemetery, 116
Phoenix Forest and History Tour, 116
Phoenix Ski Hill, 116
Pinewood Expeditions, 90
Pink Mountain, 235
Pink Mountain Campsite, 235
Pioneer Cemetery, 65
Pioneer Tinshop, 155
Platzl, 150
Pointe Restaurant, 28
The Poplars Campground &
     Motel, 240
Pony Espresso, 71
Port Alberni, 25
Port Alice, 45
Port Alice Golf and Country Club, 45

INDEX

Port Clements, 288
Port Hardy, 45
Port Hardy Visitor Info Centre, 46
Port McNeill, 40–44
Port McNeill Visitor Info Centre, 44
Potlach Collection, 42
Pouce Coupe Regional Park, 233
Pouce Coupe Visitor Centre, 234
Powder Springs Inn, 173
Powder Springs Resort, 173
Powell River, 81–84
Powell River Heritage Townsite, 81
Prince George, 226–27
Prince George Native Art Gallery, 226
Prince George Railway &
    Forestry Ind. Museum, 227
Prince George Visitor Info
    Centre, 227
Prince Rupert and the Coast, 263–68
Princeton, 87, 89–91
Princton Agricultural Fall Fair, 90
Princeton Castle and R.V. Park, 90
Princeton Golf Club, 90
Princeton Museum and Archives, 89
Process 4 Gallery, 253
Protection Island, 21
Provincial Parks
    Alexandra Bridge, 66
    Beaumont, 13, 251
    Bowron Lake, 214
    Boya Lake, 273
    Boyle Point, 28
    Buckinghorse River, 236
    Bugaboo Glacier, 162
    Canal Flats, 156
    Cape Scott, 46
    Carmanah Walbran, 18
    Cathedral, 91
    Champion Lakes, 124
    Charlie Lake, 235
    Chasm, 205
    Christina Lake, 119

Cody Caves, 128
Coquihalla Canyon, 63
Driftwood Canyon, 257
East Pine, 231
Elk Lakes, 150
Englishman River Falls, 23
Fillongley, 28
Garibaldi, 73
Gladstone, 118
Goat Range, 130
Goldstream, 29
Green Lake, 206
Grohman Narrows, 125
Gwillim Lake, 231
Haynes Point, 95
Helliwell, 28
Herald, 178
Horne Lake Caves, 24
Jimsmith Lake, 145
Joffre Lakes, 70
Kiskatinaw, 234
Kleanza Creek, 259
Lac La Hache, 209
Lakelse Lake, 261
Little Qualicum Falls, 24
Loon Lake, 204
MacMillan, 25
Macquinna Marine, 27
Manning, 64
Marble Canyon, 200
Meziadin Lake, 269
Moberly Lake, 229
Monkman, 231
Mount Edziza, 271
Mount Fernie, 148
Mount Maxwell, 14
Mount Revelstoke, 171
Mount Terry Fox, 192
Moyie Lake, 145
Muncho Lake, 240
Naikoon, 287
Nairn Falls, 72

Nancy Greene, 119
Nisga'a Memorial Lava Bed, 263
North Thompson River, 186
Okeover, 83
Paarens Beach, 247
Princess Louisa Inlet Marine, 81
Princess Margaret Marine, 11
Prophet River Wayside, 237
Roderick Haig-Brown, 181
Ruckle, 14
Saltery Bay, 81
Sasquatch, 62
Sidney Spit Marine, 12
Shannon Falls, 75
Skookumchuk Narrows, 80
Smelt Bay, 35
Spahats Creek, 187
Spatsizi Plateau Wilderness, 271
Stawamus Chief, 75
Stein Valley Nlaka'pamux, 68
Stone Mountain, 239, 240
Strathcona, 32
Sun-Oka, 102
Sukunka Falls, 231
Syringa, 125
Tatshenshini-Alsek Wilderness, 275
Telegraph Cove, 39
Tetsa River, 239
Tribune Bay, 28
Ts'ylos, 217
Tweedsmuir, 216
Tweedsmuir (North), 254
Tweedsmuir (South), 254
Tyhee Lake, 255
Valhalla, 132
Wasa Lake, 154
Wells Gray, 186, 188, 189
Whiskers Point, 228
Whiteswan Lake, 156
Purcell Heli-Skiing, 165
Purcell Mountains, 163
Purcell River Odysseys, 158

Purple Door Unique Crafts and
    Curios, 136

Q

Quaaout Resort and Conference
    Center, 181
Qay'llnagaay Heritage
    Centre Society, 284
Quadra Island, 34–35
Qualicum Beach, 22–25
Quatse River Hatchery, 29
Queen Charlotte City, 281–84
Queen Charlotte Islands, 279–97
Quesnel, 212–15
Quesnel and District Museum and
    Archives, 213
Quesnel Forks, 210
Quesnel Lake, 210
Quesnel Museum, 213
Quilchena Hotel, 184
Quilts & Comforts Bed &
    Breakfast, 274
Quw'utsun' Cultural and
    Conference Center, 16

R

R. J. Haney Heritage Park and
    Museum, 178
Radium Hot Springs, 159
Radium Hot Springs Visitor
    Info Centre, 160
Radley Park Campground, 260
Railway Station Museum, 232
Rain Store, 266
Rainbows Gallery, 281
Rainey Creek Campground, 270
Rat River Enterprises, 38
Red Goat Lodge, 271
Red Mountain, 120
Red Rock Trail Rides, 198
Rennell Sound, 288–89
Revelstoke, 171–76

INDEX

Revelstoke Courthouse, 174
Revelstoke Dam, 175
Revelstoke Golf Course, 173
Revelstoke Museum, 173
Revelstoke Railway Museum, 172
Revelstoke Visitor Info Center, 172
Rhododendron Flats, 64
Rickaby's, 126
Rip'n Richard's Eatery, 148
Ripple Rock, 33
Riverbend Cave, 24
River–Front Trail, 214
Riverside Golf Course, 157
Robert W. Starratt Wildlife
    Sanctuary, 190
Roberts Creek, 77
Robertson Square, 204
Robson Bight (Michael Bigg)
    Ecological Reserve, 39
Rockies, The, 143–67
Rockwood Centre, 78
Rocky Mountain Beadworks, 127
Rocky Mountain Rafting
    Company, 164
Rocky Mountain Trench, 143
Rogers Pass Information Centre, 169
Rose Garden, 100
Rose Point, 287
Roseberry Manor Bed &
    Breakfast, 40
Rosewood Café, 129
Rossland, 119–23
Rossland Bank of Montreal, 122
Rossland Courthouse, 122
Rossland Historical Museum, 120
Rossland Post Office, 122
Rossland Thriftlodge, 120
Rotary Centre for the Arts, 107
Rowat's Waterside Bed and
    Breakfast, 210
Royal Alexandra Hall, 146
Royal British Columbia Museum, 3

Royal LePage Comox Valley Snow to
    Surf Adventure, 30
Royal Holographic Art Gallery, 5
Rubber Rainbow Condom
    Company, 6
Ruphi Fabrics and Ceramics, 14

S

60th Parallel, 273
70 Mile House, 205
Saddle Bar Lodge, 247
St. Eugene Mission and Church, 146
St. Eugene Mission Golf Course, 147
St. John the Divine Anglican
    Church, 65
St. Mary's Anglican Church, 195
St. Mary's River, 152
St. Paul's Anglican Church, 268
St. Peter's Shared Ministry Church, 230
Salmon Arm, 177–82
Salmon Arm Bay Nature
    Enhancement Centre, 177
Salmon Arm Grebe Festival, 178
Salmon Glacier, 270
Salmon House Restaurant, 68, 264
Salmon River, 39
Salt Spring Island, 13–15
Salt Spring Island Saturday
    Market, 14
Salt Spring Island Visitor Info
    Centre, 15
Saltery Bay, 75
Sam Kee Building, 55
Sam's Deli, 5
San Josef Bay Trail, 47
Sandon, 131
Sandpiper Restaurant, 289
Sandspit, 293
Sandtrap Restaurant, 90
Sasquatch, 61
Savary Island, 83
Savary Island Lodge, 83

Sayward, 39

Science World, 70

Scout Island Nature Centre, 210

Sea Breeze Lodge, 29

Sea Raven Motel and Restaurant, 281

Sea to Sky Highway, 69–75

Sea to Sky Stables, 74

Seal Cove, 267

Seaport Bed and Breakfast, 295

Seaport Limousine, 270

Seasmoke Whale Watching, 44

Seawalk, 77

Sechart Whaling Station, 25

Sechelt, 78

Secwepemc Museum and
Heritage Park, 183

Seton Dam Campground, 198

Seton Reservoir Recreation
Area, 198

Seven Hills Golf and
Country Club, 44

Shadow, The, 81

Sheep Pasture Golf Course, 199

Shere Lake, 224

Sheridan Lake, 207

Shoe Tree, 46

Show and Shine Columbia Valley
Classic Car Show, 160

Shuswap, The, 176–82

Shuswap Lakes Vacation Inc., 177

Sicamous, 177

Sidka Tours, 274

Sidney by the Sea, 11

Sidney Harbour Cruise, 11

Sidney Historical Museum, 12

Sidney Island, 11–12

Sidney Marine Museum, 12

Sidney Spit Ferry, 12

Siegel's Bagels, 55

Sikanni Chief Falls, 236

Sikanni River RV Park, 236

Silver Ledge Hotel, 127

Silver Star Mountain Resort, 105

Silversmith Hydroelectric Station, 131

Silverton, 133

Silverton Outdoor Mining
Museum, 133

Silverton Resort, 133

Similkameen Backpack Shack, 93

Similkameen Valley, 91–94

Siska Art Gallery, 68

Sitka Lodging, 286

Sitka Studio, 286

Skaha Bluffs, 100

"Skeena, The," 268

Skeena-Eco Expeditions, 258

Skeena Valley Farmers' Market, 262

Skidegate Lake, 294

Skookumchuck, 156

Skookumchuck Narrows, 80

Sky Blue Water Resort, 200

Slocan Mercantile Building, 131

Slocan Valley, 133

Smiles Seafood Café, 266

Smithers, 256

Smuggler Cove Marine Park, 79

Snowdrift Café, 151

Snug, The, 8

Snug Harbour Inn, 26

Sointula, 40

Soo-Spokane Train Deluxe, 145

Soo Valley, 72

Sooke, 10

Sooke Fine Arts Show, 10

Sooke Region Museum, 10

Sorrento, 179

Sorrento Centre, 180

South Cariboo, 195–209

South Cariboo Historical
Museum, 204

South Cariboo Visitor Info Centre, 208

South Central Vancouver Island, 15–17

South Cowichan Lawn Tennis Club, 17

Southwest Mainland, 51–85

INDEX

Sowchea Bay Provincial
  Recreation Area, 247
Sparky's Lakefront Sports Centre, 106
Sparwood, 148, 149
Sparwood Visitor Info Centre, 149
Spinnakers Brew Pub and
  Guest House, 9
Spirit Caves Trail, 65
Spirit of the West Adventures, 34
Splash Zone Water Slides, 145
Sportsman's Kispiox Lodge, 259
Spotted Lake, 94
Springs Golf Course, 160
Spuzzum, 66
Squamish, 73
Squamish Visitor Info Centre, 75
Squilax General Store and
  Caboose Hostel, 181
Squilax International Powwow, 181
SS *Moyie*, 129
SS *Sicamous*, 100
Stanley Park, 54
Stawamus Chief, 74
Steamboat Mountain Lodge, 239
Stellako Lodge, 252
Stewart, 269–71
Stewart Historical Society
  Museum, 270
Stewart–Cassiar Highway, 268–69
Stikine RiverSong Cafe, Lodge &
  General Store, 272
Stolen Church, 157
Stonehouse Pub, 11
Stork Nest Inn, 257
Strait Coffee Traders, 77
Strands Old House Restaurant, 158
Strathcona Park, 36–39
Strathcona Park Lodge/Outdoor
  Education Centre, 36
Strawberry Flats Campground, 240
Streetcar 23, 127
Strider Adventures, 226

Sturdy's North Arm Farm, 70
Sturgeon Bay Bed and Breakfast, 198
Summerland, 101
Summerland Museum, 102
Summerland Ornamental Gardens,
  102
Sun Peaks Resort, 185
Sundance Guest Ranch, 203
Sunmore Ginseng Factory, 184
Sun–Oka Beach, 100
Sunshine Coast, 75–81
Sunshine Coast Arts Centre, 79
Sunshine Coast Golf and
  Country Club, 77
Sunshine Coast Tours, 80
Sunshine Coast Trail, 83
Sushi Bar Wabi Sabi, 54
Sweet Apple Bed and Breakfast, 139

T

Tachick Lake Fishing Resort, 247
Tahsis, 36
Takakkaw Falls, 163
Tak Restaurant, The, 35
Takysie Lake, 253
Tall Timbers Resort, 207
Tanglewood Lodge, 187
Tantalus Range Lookout, 75
Tara Shanti Lodge, 135
Tatlayoko Lake, 216
Tatshenshini Expediting, 275
Taylor, 229, 234
Tea Room, The, 94
Tea Room Restaurant, The, 121
Teague House Bed and
  Breakfast, 65
Teck Cominco Interpretive
  Centre, 123
Teck Cominco lead zinc smelter, 123
Telegraph Cove, 39
Telegraph Creek, 272
Telkwa, 255

Telkwa Museum, 256
Ten Mile Lake Provincial
    Campground, 214
Ten Ren Tea and Ginseng, 55
Terex Titan, 150
Terracana Resort and Chalets, 224
Terrace, 259–63
Terrace Heritage Park, 262
Terri's Attempts, 224
Tête Jaune Cache, 192
Tetsa River Services Gas &
    Lodging, 239
Theatre in the Sky, 53
Thompson River, 68
Three Sisters, 18
Three Valley Gap Heritage Ghost Town,
    175
Three Valley Lake Chateau, Ltd., 175
Tin Cup Café, 132
Tinhorn Creek Estate Winery, 98
Tlell, 286
Toad River Lodge, 240
Toby's, 179
Tofino, 28
Toonie Tuesdays, 72
Tow Hill, 293
Trail, 123–24
Trail Aquatic and Leisure
    Centre, 123
Trail Interpretive Centre, 123
Trail of 42, 241
Trans Canada Trail, 90
Trans-Canada Waterslides, 70
Trapper Ray's Hotsprings
    Lodge, 242
Tribune Bay Campsite, 29
Trophy Mountain, 187
Trout Lake, 130, 131
Tumbler Ridge, 231
Tutt Street Gallery, 107
Tutt Street Square, 107

Two Rivers Art Gallery, 226
Tzoonie Outdoor Adventures, 79

U

U-Pick Old Airport Gardens, 198
Ucluelet, 25
U'mista Cultural Centre, 42
Umbrella Shop, 55
UNESCO Mt. Arrowsmith
    Biosphere Reserve, 22
Upana Caves, 36
Upper Arrow Lake, 131
Upstairs Gallery, 64
Uptown Market, 53

V

Valemount, 190–91
Valemount Museum, 191
Valemount Pines Golf Club, 191
Valhalla Mountain Range, 124
Vancouver, 51–57
Vancouver Aquarium Marine
    Science Centre, 70
Vancouver Museum, 67
VanDusen Botanical Garden, 67
Vanderhoof, 245, 247
Vanderhoof Bird Sanctuary, 245
Vaseux Lake, 99
Vavenby Trail Rides, 189
Vermilion Pass, 162
Vernon, 108
Vernon Visitor Info Centre, 109
Victoria, 1–11
Victoria Golf Course, 9
Victoria Visitor Info Centre, 5, 10
Victorian Hotel, 56
View to Remember Bed and
    Breakfast, A, 106
Village Country Inn and Tearoom, 159
Vindsdalur, 250

INDEX

W

W.A.C. Bennett Dam, 230
Waldie Island Trail, 125
Walls' Fish Camp, 219
Walter Moberly Theater, 175
Walter Wright Pioneer Village, 233
Wanda–Sue Sternwheeler, 184
Wasa Lake, 154
Wasa Lakeside Bed
    and Breakfast Resort, 154
Watch Lake Lodge, 207
Waterfront Inn, The, 264
Wedgwood Manor, 137
Welcome Home Tea Room &
    Gift Shop, 115
Wells Gray Chalets & Wilderness
    Adventures, 188
Wells Winter Carnival, 213
West Coast Trail, 19, 25
West Coast Trail Express, 18
West End Campground, 238
Western Canada Ski Hall of Fame, 120
Westminster Abbey Benedictine
    Monastery, 59
Wet 'n Wild Adventures, 164
Whisky Jack Restaurant, 248
Whispering Pines Tent and
    R.V. Park, 177
Whistle Stop Gallery, 225
Whistler-Blackcomb, 72–73
White Crystal Inn, 110
White Swan Park, 252
Wickaninnish Inn, 28
Wickaninnish Interpretive
    Center, 25
Wickaninnish Restaurant, 26
Wild Blueberry Bakery, 77
Wildflour Coffee Shop, The, 271
Wild Horse, 154
Wild Horse Theatre, 155
Wild Pacific Trail, 26

Williams Lake, 210–12
Williams Lake Golf &
    Tennis Club, 212
Williams Lake River Valley Trail, 211
Williams Lake Stampede, 211
Willingdon Beach Municipal
    Campground, 82
Willingdon Beach Trail, 82
Williston Lake, 228
Willow Creek B&B, 149
Willow Tree Cafe, 7
Willows Galley, 7
Willows Golf Course, 294
Windermere Valley, 156–61
Windermere Creek B&B Cabins, 158
Windermere Valley Golf Course, 158
Window, The, 40
Windsor Hotel, 131
Windsor House Tea Room and
    Restaurant, 8
Windsor Park Place, 8
Windwalker Ranch, 138
Wine Museum, 107
Winfield, 108
Win's Place, 274
Winter Harbor, 46
Wonowon, 235
Woodbury Mining Museum, 129
Woods End Landing, 19
World Championship Sand
    Sculpture Competition, 62
World's Largest Burl, 44
World's Largest Cross Country
    Skis, 208
World's Largest Cuckoo Clock, 150
World's Largest Gold Pan, 213
World's Largest Hockey Stick, 16
World's Largest Teepee, 74
World's Largest Totem Pole, 43
Woss, 37
Woss Lake, 37

X

XÁ:YTEM Longhouse Interpretive
   Centre, 60
Xats'ull Heritage Village, 212

Y

Yakoun Lake, 289
Yale Museum, 65
Yasodhara Ashram, 135
Yodeling Woodcarver Arts and
   Crafts Shop, 151
Yoho National Park, 159, 163

Z

Zeballos, 38
Zeballos Expeditions and
   Kayaks, 38
Zip and Dip, 233
Zuckerberg Island Heritage
   Park, 125

About the Author

As an enthusiastic traveler to many of the world's lesser known places, and with a sailing circumnavigation under her belt, Tricia Timmermans is well qualified to uncover British Columbia's unique destinations. Australian by birth, she is a qualified teacher and photojournalist. She has lived in some of Canada's more remote areas, from Baffin Island to the Yukon, and currently resides in Victoria, BC, where she is a photographer and travel writer.